Renaissance
Debates
on
Rhetoric

OTHER BOOKS BY WAYNE A. REBHORN

Courtly Performances: Masking and Festivity in Castiglione's "Book of the Courtier"

Foxes and Lions: Machiavelli's Confidence Men

Creative Imitation: New Essays on Renaissance Literature in Honor of Thomas M. Greene (co-editor with David Quint, Margaret Ferguson, and G. W. Pigman, III)

The Emperor of Men's Minds: Literature and the Renaissance Discourse of Rhetoric

Renaissance Debates on Rhetoric

EDITED AND TRANSLATED BY

WAYNE A. REBHORN

Cornell University Press

ITHACA AND LONDON

First published 2000 by Cornell University Press
First printing, Cornell Paperbacks, 2000

Printed in the United States of America

Library of Congress Cataloging-in-Publication Data
Renaissance debates on rhetoric / edited and translated by Wayne A. Rebhorn.
    p.   cm.
  Includes bibliographical references and index.
  ISBN 0-8014-3008-9 (cloth)
  ISBN 0-8014-8206-2 (pbk.)
  1. Rhetoric, Renaissance.   2. European literature—Rennaissance, 1450–1600
—History and criticism—Theory, etc.   I. Rebhorn, Wayne A., 1943–
  PN721 .R445   1999
  808′.0094′09024—dc21

                                                              99-34446

Cloth printing   10   9   8   7   6   5   4   3   2   1

Paperback printing   10   9   8   7   6   5   4   3   2   1

Contents

Acknowledgments

I have incurred numerous debts in writing this book. First, I thank the Casa Editrice Le Lettere in Florence for permission to translate Francis Petrarch's letter to Tommaso da Messina that was originally published in Francesco Petrarca, *Le famigliari,* edited by Vittorio Rossi; the publishing house E. J. Brill in Leiden for permission to translate George of Trebizond's *Oratio de laudibus eloquentie,* which was published as Appendix 11 in John Monfasani, *George of Trebizond: A Biography and a Study of His Rhetoric and Logic;* and the Casa Editrice Giuseppe Laterza Edizioni in Bari for permission to translate Anton Maria de' Conti's *De eloquentia dialogus,* which was published in *Trattati di poetica e retorica del Cinquecento,* edited by Bernard Weinberg. I also thank the Harry Ransom Humanities Research Center of the University of Texas at Austin for permission to use as a cover illustration the figure of Hercules Gallicus from Andrea Alciati, *Emblemata.* Finally, I am grateful to the University Research Institute of the University of Texas at Austin for sabbatical support in the spring of 1998 that enabled me to bring this project to completion.

I am not sure how I could have completed this project at all if I had not had the generous assistance of numerous colleagues both at the University of Texas and elsewhere who helped me fine-tune my translations and track down the often quite obscure references that abound in the texts I have presented here. For his help with the works originally in Latin I owe a large debt of gratitude to Paul Allen Miller; for help with the Italian, French, and Spanish texts, I owe similar debts, respectively, to Douglas Biow, Robert Hill, and Rolando Hinojosa-Smith. For their much appreciated aid with the annotations of this book, I thank Paul Allen Miller, Edward George, Thomas Palaima, Michael Gagarin, Paul Woodruff, and Douglass Parker. John Mulvihill has done a splendid job of editing my manuscript, and I am grateful to Lois Rankin and Candace Akins for their conscientious work in seeing this project through. I owe much to Bernhard Kendler, my editor at Cornell University Press, whose consistent support in this and other projects over the years is deeply appreciated. Last, but not least, I thank my wife Marlette who went well beyond the call of duty by reading through all my translations at least twice and who made too many suggestions for stylistic improvements for me to begin to enumerate.

Renaissance
Debates
on
Rhetoric

Introduction

It is well known that rhetoric enjoyed a position of great importance in the culture of the Renaissance. Throughout Europe, students who went to grammar school encountered it as an essential part of the curriculum, and university professors taught it as well, lecturing on it and presenting commentaries on key rhetorical texts from the ancient world, such as Aristotle's *Rhetoric* and Cicero's *De oratore* (*On the Orator*). Displacing dialectic, which had reigned supreme during the late Middle Ages, rhetoric became the queen of the liberal arts. Towns appointed scholars to give public lectures on it, and many of them employed public orators to make speeches on special occasions, especially for visiting dignitaries. Perhaps the most revealing indication of just how important rhetoric was in the period is the vast outpouring not just of editions of ancient rhetoricians, but of contemporary works concerned with the subject. There were manuals and handbooks by the dozens, some of which grew to prodigious length: the *Retorica* published by the Florentine Bartolomeo Cavalcanti in 1559 is over 550 pages long, while the *De eloquentia sacra et humana* (*On Sacred and Profane Eloquence*) published by the French Jesuit Nicholas Caussin in 1619 tops out at over a thousand. Renaissance writers also churned out books dealing with different kinds and aspects of rhetoric, books on preaching and letter writing, on the topics to be used in the invention of arguments, on delivery and memory,

[1]

and especially on style. There were countless commentaries on classical rhetoric texts and on rhetoric texts written by contemporaries; books of exercises and collections of model speeches; and letters, orations, essays, and dialogues about the subject. Finally, starting in the early sixteenth century, treatises and manuals began appearing even in the vernacular languages, although the vast majority of books about rhetoric continued to be written in Latin right down to the end of the period. James J. Murphy has calculated that more than a thousand books on rhetoric were produced throughout Europe between the mid–fourteenth and mid–seventeenth centuries.[1] As a result, considering the central place rhetoric had in education during the Renaissance as well as the enormous volume of material that was published about it, perhaps it would be best to speak of the Renaissance not in traditional terms as the rebirth of antiquity or the age of exploration, but as the age of rhetoric.[2]

If the importance of rhetoric in the Renaissance is well known, what is less well known is what Renaissance writers actually thought about the subject, how they evaluated it, and what roles they saw it playing in their lives and their cultures. This is especially true of works from the continent, most of which have not been translated into English and are available in the original only in the collections of major research libraries. This anthology thus attempts to make up for this deficit by providing modern readers with editions and translations of a selected number of important Renaissance works concerned with rhetoric. Since only a relatively small number of texts could be included here, this anthology cannot help but be partial, both in the sense that it omits far more than it includes, and in the sense that the choices involved have been made by a single individual with particular interests in the subject. Nevertheless, I have tried to select texts that present the widest possible range of views about rhetoric. Arranged in chronological order according to the birth dates of their authors, they cover the full length of the Renaissance, starting with a letter written by Petrarch in the mid–fourteenth century and ending with Jean-François Le Grand's *Discours*, published with René Bary's *Rhetorique Françoise* in 1658. Taken together, the authors of these texts lived all over western Europe and wrote in Latin, Italian, Spanish, French, and English. Finally, if some of them are relatively familiar figures to modern readers, others are quite obscure, although most were considerably less so in their own age; nor does their obscurity prevent them from saying important things about the art. In general, by editing and translating these texts, I am pursuing a decidedly historical goal: I am giving a

---

1. "One Thousand Neglected Authors," in *Renaissance Eloquence: Studies in the Theory and Practice of Renaissance Rhetoric,* ed. James J. Murphy (Berkeley: University of California Press, 1983), 20–36. Murphy has amply documented this claim with his bibliography, *Renaissance Rhetoric,* ed. James J. Murphy with Kevin P. Roddy (New York: Garland, 1981).

2. Marc Fumaroli has dubbed it the *aetas ciceroniana,* the Age of Cicero; see *L'âge de l'éloquence: Rhétorique et "res literaria" au seuil de l'époque classique* (Geneva: Droz, 1980), 40.

host of Renaissance writers on rhetoric, including both its defenders and its critics, the opportunity to speak for themselves and to show us why rhetoric mattered so much for them and their culture.

One thing these writers certainly show us is how deeply conflicted the Renaissance was about rhetoric. Even though they often share the same vocabulary, recount the same anecdotes, and appeal to the same authorities, they simply do not speak with one voice about the subject. As the title of this book indicates, they are everywhere engaged in debates concerning the nature, goals, and value of rhetoric. To put it differently: even though only a few of these texts are actual dialogues, they are all nevertheless dialogic in character, constantly summoning up contrary views and imaginary opponents even when they seem most determined merely to present their own positions. Since rhetoric is a contested subject in virtually every period of its history, it should not be surprising to find writers in the Renaissance rehearsing arguments, sometimes even repeating the exact words, used by their predecessors—and thereby providing material that writers in subsequent periods would appropriate from them in turn. Although sometimes they are indebted to medieval culture, they most frequently echo the writers of Greek and Roman antiquity, reviving the debates about rhetoric that appeared not only in the works of the major writers—Plato, Aristotle, Cicero, Quintilian, and Tacitus—but also in those of myriad other figures, many of whom are less well known nowadays. Nevertheless, although all of these Renaissance writers take a great deal from their ancient forebears, participating in the *renaissance,* the rebirth, of classical antiquity in this way, they inevitably define the material they appropriate in their own terms. As they give that material the characteristic inflection of their culture, they reveal that Renaissance debates about rhetoric are also, more profoundly, debates about the Renaissance itself.

One of the most striking of those debates focuses on the notion that rhetoric is an instrument of politics.[3] Accordingly, some writers praise it as the power responsible for creating and maintaining the peace and order of the state, while others condemn it as a dangerous source of social and political instability, as the cause of riots, rebellion, and civil war. A version of this debate was, to be sure, also staged in antiquity. Cicero and Quintilian especially stressed the politically constructive nature of oratory, and at the start of his *De inventione,* Cicero presents a mythic view of the orator that was repeatedly reworked by Renaissance writers, a story that credits him with having established the first civil society by persuading his savage fellow humans to give up their lives in the fields and to come together and settle in cities. However, the Renaissance could also find ancient works that manifest a real fear of the politically destabilizing potential of rhetoric. Tacitus, for

3. For fuller versions of the arguments I review in the following pages, see my *Emperor of Men's Minds: Literature and the Renaissance Discourse of Rhetoric* (Ithaca, N.Y.: Cornell University Press, 1995).

instance, associates oratory with the disorder of republican rule, saying, not without some irony perhaps, that it has become irrelevant in the Empire whose one-man rule ensures peace and harmony; and Cicero worries about the civil strife that can be caused by the misuse of rhetoric, as does Quintilian, who famously defines the orator as a "vir bonus dicendi peritus" ("good man skilled in speaking").[4] Nevertheless, if the Renaissance revived classical debates like these about the political function of rhetoric, it did so using its own distinctive terms.

What separates the Renaissance from antiquity is its reliance on a very different political model. Classical writers, especially Roman ones, associated rhetoric with an essential republican vision of the political process: they presented the art as combat and imagined the orator as a soldier, gladiator, or athlete struggling with other orators in verbal battles that were staged in the forum or the Senate house. Perhaps they feared the politically destabilizing effect of rhetoric because they saw it essentially as a simulation of war that always threatened to get out of control. By contrast, Renaissance writers about rhetoric characterize the orator as a ruler, label him a prince or king or emperor, and identify the audience he controls in a complementary manner as being his subjects. Even writers such as George of Trebizond and Sperone Speroni talk about the orator as a ruler, not as a participant in the give-and-take of parliamentary debate, although both men were associated with the Venetian republic when they produced their major works on rhetoric. The proponents of rhetoric in the Renaissance praise it as the chief means by which the ruler controls his audience of subjects and thus establishes peace and order in the realm. In fact, some of them actually tell this to the ruler himself, as Jacques Amyot does in the rhetoric manual he composed for Henry III of France. But, if Renaissance writers see oratory as essential for social and political order, they also worry that it will do precisely the opposite and create disorder, violence, and war. Although proponents of rhetoric in the Renaissance repeatedly insist that its aim is the conservative one of enabling the legitimate ruler to maintain the stability of the established order, they can never prevent people *in addition to* the ruler from becoming effective orators. The problem here is that the equation Renaissance writers make between rhetor and ruler is just not reversible: although all rulers could conceivably be effective orators, all effective orators will not necessarily be rulers—or rather, they will not necessarily be *legitimate* ones. Writers of rhetoric books simply cannot prevent the art from being used by those who might oppose the supposedly legitimate ruler and threaten the peace and harmony of the realm. Indeed, they are actually writing their

4. See Tacitus, *Dialogus*, xxxvi.2–4, Cicero, *De inventione*, I.iii.4–5, and Quintilian, *Institutio oratoria*, II.xvi.1–6 (the quotation comes from XII.i.1 and is attributed to Cato). Note that both Cicero and Quintilian concede that rhetoric may be harmful, but only owing to a misuse of the art; when rhetoric is used correctly, it will invariably be beneficial to the state.

books for a broad readership that may well include such potentially sub-versive people.

The threat of subversion posed by rhetoric reflects real historical devel-opments in the Renaissance. On the minds of many people in the period was the seemingly endless supply of insurrections and rebellions that were led by both noblemen and commoners and directed against those who suppos-edly had a legitimate right to rule over them. From the triumph in 1378 of the lower-class Ciompi ("wool-carders"), who created a short-lived, demo-cratic government in Florence, through the Dutch uprising against Philip II of Spain in the 1570s, down to Essex's ill-considered attempt at some sort of coup d'état against Elizabeth in 1599, and the revolt of the Fronde against Louis XIV in 1648—European history in the Renaissance is filled with ex-amples of rebellions and wars that in one way or another can be seen as at-tempts to resist the centralization of political power in the hands of increas-ingly absolutist contemporary rulers. Moreover, for Renaissance writers, rhetoric's political and religious powers were never far apart, just as politics and religion were deeply intertwined through the period. Thus, it should not be surprising that Heinrich Cornelius Agrippa and Francis Bacon, both of whom see rhetoric as politically dangerous, relate its flowering in their age directly to the Reformation. For the Reformation profoundly disturbed the order of Europe and led to violence, destruction, and death, from the Peasants' War in Germany in 1525, through the Saint Bartholomew's Day Massacre in France in 1572, down to the Thirty Years' War (1618–1648) that resulted in the death of 40 percent of Germany's population. In short, when Renaissance writers are debating the political value of rhetoric, they are clearly engaging some of the most fundamental historical developments in their culture: the increasing centralization of the state, the growth of abso-lutism, and all the upheavals caused by the Reformation.

Renaissance writers on rhetoric also debate the question of the orator's so-cial mobility. Proponents of the art celebrate it for enabling people to climb up the social ladder, to become, if not literally kings or emperors, at least members of the elite. Not unexpectedly, critics of rhetoric are horrified by such social climbing and condemn overly ambitious orators for violating the proper boundaries between social classes or groups and thus threatening to undermine the entire social order. Ironically, although Renaissance writers often look back to figures from the ancient world, such as Pericles, Cicero, and Julius Caesar, as examples of the orator's social mobility, ancient rhetor-ical theorists largely ignore the issue. Cicero and Quintilian may both ideal-ize the orator, for instance, but they do not talk about his achieving social prominence by means of his eloquence. Tacitus is particularly revealing on this score. In his *Dialogus de oratoribus* (*Dialogue on the Orators*), one of the characters, reflecting on how important eloquence once was in the Roman republic, declares: "The more power a man had in speaking, the more easily did he achieve high office [*honores*], the more did he, when in office [*in ipsis honoribus*], surpass his colleagues, the more favor did he have with the great, the more authority with the Senate, the more fame and repute among the plebeians."[5] What is at issue in this passage is not the changing of one's social class, but what the Romans called the *cursus honorum*, literally the "race for honors or offices," a phrase that refers to the sequence of offices a young aristocrat might go through as he climbed up the *political* ladder of success.

By contrast, Renaissance writers on rhetoric see the orator moving from one *social* class to another simply by means of his skill with words. George Puttenham goes even further, claiming that eloquence can take a man "first from the cart to the school, and from thence to the court" and will eventually earn him the favor of the monarch, Queen Elizabeth, herself.[6] Here stands revealed the deep fantasy that motivates so many Renaissance rhetoricians: the dream that through a mastery of the art, a presumably baseborn orator can achieve a glorious ascent, going from the lowly position of peasant (the cart) to the heights of power and prestige (the court and the queen). That the proponents of rhetoric in the Renaissance embrace the idea of social mobility should not really be surprising. After all, virtually all of them were men on the make, men who came from the lower and middling orders of society and sought advancement through their mastery of the word, an advancement that many of them, in fact, achieved. Although they seldom soared to the heights reached by the orator they fantasized about, a fair number did become educators and secretaries, some were given positions as administrators in the state bureaucracies that were gradually expanding during the course of the Renaissance, and a few even made it all the way up to the courts of the king or prince, which were increasing in size as a result of the centralization of political power. By contrast, when Renaissance critics of rhetoric denounce this fantasy of upward social mobility, they stigmatize the social and political pretensions of the orator as both ludicrous and dangerous, pronouncing him a mountebank, a charlatan, a juggler, or a rope dancer. The critics see rhetoric as the art of lying and insistently identify it as makeup and masquerade. Mockingly, they remind rhetoric's defenders that Mercury, who was often claimed as the patron of eloquence, was also the god of thieves. In short, they condemn the socially mobile orator as a lower-class trickster who deceives himself and others with delusions of grandeur, achieves status and identity in profoundly illegitimate ways, and should be sent back to the place reserved for such mountebanks and charlatans: the very bottom of the social order.

The issue of social mobility, which vexes these writers on rhetoric, also vexed their culture as a whole. Historians have shown that in comparison with the Middle Ages, the Renaissance saw a substantial increase in the

5. *Dialogus*, xxxvi.4.
6. See the selection from Puttenham in this anthology, chapter 18.

movement of people from one social class to another. Throughout Europe, capitalist entrepreneurs made fortunes in banking and cloth manufacturing, mining and trade; and many became rich through the exploitation of the recently discovered lands and peoples of the New World. They then used that money to built grand houses and palaces and to buy country estates, thus establishing themselves as members of the elite of their cultures. Some even acquired noble titles, as did the Medici, who had the rank of grand duke of Tuscany created for them; and countless Englishmen became baronets, a new title James I invented for them in order to fatten his coffers with their "gifts." In general, however, more people lost status during the Renaissance than gained it: peasants were driven from the land they farmed in order to make room for sheep, whose wool offered landowners greater profits; investors in trading expeditions and other ventures lost fortunes as often as they made them; young prodigals wasted their inheritances by trying to keep up with the latest fashions at court; and rising inflation throughout the period, caused by an increase in the supply of money thanks to the gold and silver of the New World, impoverished thousands who lived on fixed incomes. Moreover, Renaissance people were well aware of all these changes; they knew how labile one's social position could be, despite their culture's ideological conviction of the supposed permanence and stability, the unchanging nature, of the social order. It is striking that even those who embraced the idea of social mobility in one form or another often did so with reservations, worried that it threatened the secure, hierarchical order of their universe. Although Shakespeare, for instance, bought land and the right to call himself "gentleman" with the money he made through writing plays, and clearly sympathized with the upwardly mobile Helena in *All's Well That Ends Well*, he more typically portrayed the socially and politically ambitious in negative terms, ranging from the comic mockery of Malvolio in *Twelfth Night* to the savage indictment of Iago as diabolically evil in *Othello*. Thus, when Renaissance writers on rhetoric debate the issue of the orator's social mobility, they are clearly debating something that mattered deeply to their culture; nor should it be surprising that many proponents of rhetoric would feel obliged to defend the orator explicitly against charges of social climbing.

The accusations against rhetoric as the art of lying, which were noted earlier, point to yet another debate about rhetoric in the Renaissance, a debate that arises because rhetoric, by its nature, operates in the realm of opinion and contingency, assumes a skeptical epistemology, and can thus promise only probable, not absolute truths. Its partisans in the Renaissance may assert that it provides access to some sort of truth, but they can never really guarantee that that truth will be unconditional, universal, and unquestionable—which is precisely what makes the art vulnerable to attack by its critics. This quarrel dates back to Plato and the Sophists, and pitted Plato's belief in the realm of Ideas as constituting an absolute reality that offered sure knowledge, against the Sophists' more skeptical view that accepts the world as a place where we can argue for ideas that are only more or less true than others and where words cannot have a secure, one-to-one relationship to things. Plato's disagreement with the Sophists in such dialogues as the *Phaedrus* and the *Gorgias* became available to western Europeans toward the end of the fifteenth century, when Marsilio Ficino and Giovanni Pico della Mirandola published Latin translations of all of Plato's works as well as of those written by many of the Neoplatonists who followed him. As a result, critics of rhetoric in the Renaissance such as Francesco Patrizi and Pico could—and did—rehearse Platonic arguments against rhetoric as flattery and lies, as cookery and makeup rather than medicine and gymnastics. By contrast, while Renaissance defenders of the art may be troubled by the criticism that Plato inspired, most of them respond to it by repeating versions of the moves Cicero and Quintilian made in antiquity: they simply assert that the true orator will, of course, be a good man who deals in truth, not falsehood, and they generally do not bother to specify, let alone argue about, the nature of that "truth."

What distinguishes the Renaissance from antiquity in this debate is that it does not exactly share Plato's notion of what constitutes truth. Revealingly, when Pico rejects rhetoric, he does not turn instead to some sort of Platonic realm of Ideas, despite his being saturated with Platonic and Neoplatonic notions, but rather, he defends the Scholastic philosophers of the late Middle Ages because of their theological commitment to the truths of Christianity. Equally revealing of the gap between antiquity and the Renaissance are the works of two writers who may pay lip service to the value of rhetoric, but are actually quite hostile to it precisely because it can only offer knowledge that is relative and contingent, and because they are convinced that they have discovered other, better ways to reach the truth. The first writer, Peter Ramus, privileges his notion of dialectic or logic over rhetoric, although he does not see dialectic in Platonic terms as a rigorously deductive method leading ultimately to truth in the realm of Ideas. Instead, it is a mode of arguing that starts with true propositions and then, working by means of definitions, dichotomies, and syllogisms, concludes with knowledge about specifics that is true, universal, and timeless. Ramus calls this procedure "method," and he is convinced that if human beings were perfectly rational creatures, they would use it and be persuaded by it and would thus have no need of rhetoric. Since he concedes that we are not perfectly rational, however, he grudgingly accepts the rhetorical use of tropes and figures in order to move people through their emotions and to get them to believe what dialectic should have been able to convince them of all by itself. Like Ramus, the second writer, Francis Bacon, feels he has found a sure method that will enable him to reach the truth. However, his method works by induction and relies on empirical observations in order to make generalizations that constitute true knowledge about the world. Like Ramus, Bacon sees rhetoric as a concession to human insufficiency; its role is to take the truths that have been grasped by reason and to present them in so vivid a manner to the imagination that people's wills and appetites are moved to accept them. As Ramus and Bacon privilege their two different methods for arriving at different notions of absolute truth, they wind up giving rhetoric only a subordinate role to play; they reduce it essentially to a question of style, thereby turning it into *mere rhetoric,* an art concerned with words rather than matter.

This philosophical debate about the truth value of rhetoric resonated powerfully in Renaissance culture, which was shaken by profound challenges of various sorts to many of its basic institutions and ideological assumptions. A few people responded to those challenges by embracing some form of skepticism and some degree of tolerance and cultural relativism, but most did so by clinging fiercely to what they saw as the absolute truth, demonizing and destroying those who dared to disagree with them. Galileo, for instance, was forced by the Inquisition to recant his heliocentric theory of the universe. Giordano Bruno, by contrast, was not so lucky: he was burned at the stake in 1600 because of his unorthodox philosophy. Moreover, the traditional notion of the political order as a hierarchy composed of king, nobles, and commoners was attacked in the period by a variety of theorists, including apologists for absolutism, such as Jean Bodin, at one extreme, who wanted all power in the hands of the monarch, and, at the other extreme, by exponents of republicanism, such as Machiavelli, who wanted to enfranchise the people. Such theoretical positions then became articles of faith for many people and were played out in the real world of history in the form of insurrections, brutal acts of repression, and the horrific civil wars that raged throughout the period. Similarly, people's confidence in the absolute character, the rightness, of their social order was undermined by the humanists' theoretical arguments about the historical contingency of all societies as well as by the discovery of other viable cultures in the New World; for every Montaigne who responded to this situation with a skeptic's embrace of something akin to cultural relativism, there were many more who tortured dissenters, killed witches, and perpetrated genocide in the Americas, relying on violence to confirm what they wanted to believe was the correct order of things. Perhaps most important, the Renaissance saw repeated challenges hurled at the supposedly unimpeachable authority of the church, that ultimate guarantor of some sort of absolute truth and knowledge. Protestant reformers thus presented Catholics essentially as diabolic rhetoricians who used their eloquence to persuade people to damn themselves, and Catholics characterized the Protestants in exactly the same way. Although the proliferation of religious authorities would eventually lead to toleration in the Enlightenment, during the Renaissance it produced executions, massacres, and hideously destructive wars as each faith attempted to impose its truth on everyone else. The price people paid for being on the "wrong" side was clearly enormous. No wonder the defenders of rhetoric were so nervous about attacks on the art because of its potential for fraud, its commitment to a world of appearances, and its inability to supply anything more than probable truths. And no wonder its critics—and even some of its grudging supporters—thought of it as *mere rhetoric* as they turned elsewhere in their quest for some sort of absolute certainty and real knowledge.

There are, to be sure, other debates that can be followed in the texts that make up this anthology. There is a debate, for instance, about gender. For the Renaissance, as for classical antiquity, the orator was a potentially problematic figure because men were supposed to be warriors and knights, models of the active life, doers rather than talkers; by contrast, words—and hence rhetoric—were associated with women.[7] As a result, the man who played the orator ran the risk of appearing effeminate so that the defenders of rhetoric were led to emphasize his masculine power in order to protect him. Needless to say, this debate can be related to the problematic status and complicated redefining of gender roles that many scholars have argued was going on in the period. Finally, there is a debate among some of these writers on rhetoric concerning the value of Scholastic philosophy, the work of late medieval thinkers such as Thomas Aquinas and Duns Scotus that was studied under the rubric of dialectic. Petrarch and many of his humanist followers denigrated Scholasticism for its abstruseness and seemingly barbarous Latin style, and sought to replace dialectic with rhetoric as the queen of the liberal arts. In a profound sense, this debate is not just one between competing disciplines, but between the Renaissance and the Middle Ages— or perhaps it would be better to say it was a debate the Renaissance staged in order to define itself into existence by distinguishing itself from the historically "other" culture it saw as its predecessor.

It should be clear that works concerned with rhetoric in the Renaissance are always special sites where some sort of important cultural work is going on, where the writers are attempting to grapple with the reality of their historical situation. It should also be clear that this activity is most intense and appears most dramatic when writers are engaging in debates about the nature, goals, and value of the art. Renaissance writers on rhetoric do not, of course, invent the concerns about political stability, social mobility, and the like, that vexed people in the period. They do, however, give voice to those concerns. As they do so, they reveal aspects of issues that might not otherwise have been articulated, or might not have been articulated with such clarity and force. Thus, by listening to what these Renaissance people are saying in their debates about rhetoric, we can do something of great im-

7. On this point see Patricia Parker, *Literary Fat Ladies: Rhetoric, Gender, Property* (London: Methuen, 1987), and "On the Tongue: Cross Gendering, Effeminacy, and the Art of Words," *Style* 23 (1989): 445–65.

portance: we can eavesdrop on them and learn not only what they think about rhetoric, but also, most profoundly, what they are saying about themselves.

I have been responsible for selecting, editing, translating, and annotating all of the texts included in this volume. Although the principles that guided me in the selection process here have been explained, I should add that almost every text in this anthology is really an excerpt. Since I wanted to include as many different authors as possible, I decided sometimes to cut out material even from quite short selections when that material had little to do with the author's view of rhetoric. Such omissions within a sentence or a paragraph or between paragraphs have been indicated by the conventional three periods. Sometimes, in order to make an excerpt fully comprehensible, I have provided a brief summary of what has been omitted, placing it either in the headnote that precedes each selection or within parentheses in the body of the selection itself.

For each selection I have tried to utilize original editions whenever possible, comparing them with other early editions when that seemed necessary and with modern ones in the few cases whenever one could be found. Fortunately, there are relatively few problems of an editorial sort with these texts, so there has been no need to supply a textual apparatus. In the case of the selections originally written in English, I have modernized them according to the principles used by scholars for most modern editions of Shakespeare and other Renaissance English authors. Thus, I have used modern spellings for everything except words no longer currently in use, and I have modernized even those older words whenever possible. I have also modernized punctuation, taking care not to remove intended ambiguities. Finally, I have eliminated stylistic eccentricities, such as Puttenham's italicizing foreign words and placing them inside square brackets. These editorial practices should make the English-language selections more readily comprehensible to modern readers, although they will not, of course, eliminate the sense of strangeness or foreignness that those texts will inevitably retain.

In the translations, I have tried to be as accurate as possible. However, being accurate is a problem, in that it involves two contradictory, or at least competing, principles: on the one hand, it means attempting to preserve as much of an author's characteristic mode of speech as possible; on the other, it means writing clear, idiomatic English. Setting aside the fact that the vocabulary, grammar, and syntax of English are not the same as those of Latin, Italian, French, and Spanish, the two principles collide with each other whenever the idiosyncratic structure of an author's sentence or his idiosyncratic use of a particular word simply cannot be reproduced in English, even though those things may "work" in the original language. This has meant some rather free translating at moments: an explanatory phrase may have been added to clarify connections among ideas that are left implicit in the original; connectives have been changed to suit the sentence logic of English rather than that of the original language; and the same word has required different translations in different contexts. For many words, of course, there is really no modern English equivalent. For instance, "bonae literae," which can be translated literally, though awkwardly, as "good letters," is the phrase that humanists used to designate everything in writing that had been preserved from the cultures of ancient Greece and Rome. However, since no short phrase in English can express what was said in the last clause in the preceding sentence, I have chosen sometimes to say simply "good letters," sometimes to use a circumlocution. Equally troublesome has been the word "civilis" in Latin, "civile" in French and Italian, for it can mean "civic," "civil," "political" in the sense of being involved with the "polis" or city-state, even "polite." Although Shakespeare puns on all these meanings of "civil" in the sonnet that opens *Romeo and Juliet*, the word no longer allows quite that range, so that I have been forced to translate it differently from one passage to the next. In the final analysis, however, I have always opted to write idiomatic English rather than produce a stilted or opaque sentence, although occasionally I have been willing to allow a little strangeness to remain in the translation, if only because it gives the reader some small sense of what is in the original text.

I have tried to annotate all the selections fully in order to make this book as "user-friendly" as possible. Each selection is preceded by a headnote providing biographical information on the author, a brief overview of his works, an introduction to the selection, and an identification of the text from which the selection has been taken or on which my translation has been based. Within the selections, whenever the author uses a name for someone that is different from the one we now employ, I have added the modern name in square brackets, as in "Tully [Cicero]." Each selection also has footnotes explaining unfamiliar ideas, clarifying occasional obscurities, and providing sources for anecdotes, allusions, and quotations (in a few cases I have been unable to locate those sources). Some selections have required quite a few footnotes, for these writers on rhetoric, like many others in the Renaissance, defend their positions less by producing logical arguments and citing empirical evidence than by appealing to authorities and relating anecdotes; they were obviously counting on such moves to enhance their ethos and thus persuade their readers. A great deal of the material they cite or allude to comes from the works of the most familiar and important ancient writers on rhetoric: Plato, Aristotle, Cicero, Quintilian, and Tacitus. A very large portion of it, however, also comes from those who are considerably less well known, including many late antique encyclopedists, historians, and compilers, writers such as Diogenes Laertius, Macrobius, Plutarch, Athenaeus, and Eunapius. In the English-language selections I have also annotated words no longer current in the language or whose Renaissance meanings differ from their modern ones. In the footnote, the word to be glossed appears in boldface; the gloss follows it in normal typescript. At the end of the book I have supplied a biographical glossary that briefly identifies the more important historical figures—and a few mythological characters as well—whose names are mentioned within the selections. Finally, I have included a bibliography of selected works dealing with Renaissance rhetoric.

[1]

Francis Petrarch

Francis Petrarch (1304–1374), or Francesco Petrarca, to use the Italian version of his name, is generally thought of as the "father of the Renaissance" because of his passion for classical antiquity, his attempt to unite classical learning with Christian piety, and his invention in his works of a particularly modern "self" that is uncertain, changing, and acutely self-conscious. Although born in Arezzo, Petrarch grew up in Avignon, the seat of the papal court in the fourteenth century. He studied law in Montpellier and Bologna between 1316 and 1326, but disliked it and returned to Avignon in 1326 intent on pursuing literary scholarship and writing. That year he took minor orders in the Church, and that partly enabled him to support himself, although he was also aided by a series of important patrons, including Giovanni Cardinal Colonna (1330–1347), the Visconti in Milan (1353–1361), the Venetian oligarchy (1362–1367), and Francesco da Carrara (1367–1374). By the 1330s, Petrarch was the leading figure in Italy associated with what is seen as the rebirth of classical culture. He actively worked to recover ancient texts and produced scholarly compendia such as his *De viris illustribus* (*Of Famous Men*), a collection of biographies of famous Romans, which he wrote between 1343 and 1353. He also published his letters, as Cicero, Pliny, and other Latin writers had, and he composed Latin literary works, including the incomplete epic *Africa*, begun in 1338, and the *Epistolae metricae* (*Metrical Letters*). Petrarch wrote a number of treatises in Latin that are largely biographical in character and helped to make him and his personality widely known throughout Europe. These include the *Secretum meum* (*My Secret*, 1342), an inconclusive, self-chastising dialogue between himself and Saint Augustine, *De vita solitaria* (*On the Solitary Life*), *De remediis utriusque fortunae* (*On the Remedies of Both Kinds of Fortune*), and *De sui ipsius et multorum ignorantia* (*On His Own Ignorance and That of Many Others*). Petrarch was most widely known in the Renaissance, as he is today, for his *Canzoniere* (*Songbook*), also known as the *Rime sparse*, his collection of lyric poems in Italian that record his relationship with his beloved Laura. Although Petrarch never produced a treatise on rhetoric, he did discuss the subject in one of his *Familiar Letters*. The translation of that letter is based on the text in Francesco Petrarca, *Le familiari*, edited by Vittorio Rossi (Florence: Sansoni, 1933), I: 45–48.

LETTER TO TOMMASO DA MESSINA, CONCERNING THE STUDY OF ELOQUENCE[1]

The care of the mind requires a philosopher; the education of the tongue belongs to the orator. Neither one should be neglected by us if, as they say, we are to rise up from the earth and soar on the lips of men.[2] But I will speak of the former elsewhere, for it is an important subject which, though involving immense labor, promises a very rich harvest. Here, lest I go off on some matter other than the one that led me to write, I will encourage and admonish that we correct not just our life and conduct, although that is the first thing necessary for virtue, but also our habit of speaking, something we can accomplish through the study of the art of eloquence. For speech is no small index of the mind, and the mind, no small guide for speech. Each depends on the other, but while the one is hidden away in our breasts, the other emerges into the outside world. The mind adorns what is about to appear and forms it as it wishes to, while speech, as it comes out, declares what the mind is like. People obey the judgment of the mind, which gains their credence through the testimony of speech. Therefore, both are to be cultivated in such a way that the mind may learn to be reasonably severe in managing speech, and speech may learn to be truthfully magnificent in expressing the mind. However, we cannot really be neglecting speech when we are caring for the mind, just as, on the other hand, dignity cannot be present in speech unless its majesty is also present in the mind.

Now, what difference does it make if you have immersed yourself completely in the Ciceronian springs, and if nothing written by the Greeks or by our Latins escapes you? You will indeed be able to speak ornately, charmingly, sweetly, and loftily, but you will certainly not be able to do so gravely, seriously and wisely, and, what is most important, consistently. For unless our desires are first made to harmonize with one another—and you realize this cannot be accomplished by anyone except a wise man—it will

---

1. Tommaso da Messina is Tommaso Caloria, or Caloiro (ca. 1302–1341), a student Petrarch met when he was studying law at Bologna and with whom he developed a close friendship. There is a scholarly debate about whether Petrarch wrote this letter in 1333 or 1350–1351. If the latter date is correct, then it cannot have been sent to Tommaso da Messina (as several other letters addressed to him clearly were not). However, knowing the date of the letter, while important for Petrarch's biography, is not particularly relevant for this anthology.

2. Petrarch is citing Vergil, *Georgics*, III.9. To soar on the lips of men means to acquire fame.

necessarily be the case that since our feelings are in disarray, both our conduct and our words will be so as well. By contrast, the well-ordered mind, like unshaken serenity itself, is always placid and tranquil; it knows what it wants, and it never stops wanting what it has once desired. Thus, even if it did not have the ornaments of the art of oratory to hand, it would still be able to draw out of itself the most magnificent and gravest words, words that would be entirely consonant with itself. And indeed, it is undeniable that something quite wonderful will emerge whenever the emotions have first been composed. By contrast, when they are boiling, we cannot hope that anything felicitous will result. Much time is needed for the study of eloquence. If eloquence were not necessary for us, and if our mind, relying on its own powers and exhibiting its goods silently, did not need the support of words, we should still labor, in any case, to be useful to the other people with whom we live, whose minds would no doubt be aided greatly through our conversations with them.

You, however, approach and say: "Ah, how much safer for ourselves, and more effective for others, would it be to urge them on by means of erecting examples of our virtue before their eyes, so that, delighted by the beauty of those examples, they would be seized by an impulse to imitate them! For naturally we are much more effectively and easily moved by the stimulus of deeds than by that of words, and we can ascend more expeditiously along this path towards the heights of virtue." But I do not disagree: you can see what I thought about the matter when I admonished that among the first things we should do is to order our minds. Nor, for my part, do I think the satirist said without good reason that "first of all you owe me the goods of the mind"—and I do not think they would come first if anything preceded them.[3] Nevertheless, how much eloquence can also do to advance human life can be ascertained through the works of many authors as well as through what we find in our daily experience. How many people have we seen in our time who have not been affected at all by received models of correct speech, but who, as if awakened, have been suddenly converted from the most wicked course of life to the greatest modesty merely by the words spoken by others! I will not repeat to you now what Cicero says about this subject at great length in his *De inventione*—for the passage is extremely well known[4]—nor will I bring up the fables of Orpheus and of Amphion, the first of whom is said to have moved monstrous beasts by his songs, and the latter, trees and rocks, which he was able to lead wherever he wished, except to say that, by relying on their superior eloquence, the first is believed

3. See Juvenal, *Saturae*, VIII.24. In this satire, Juvenal denounces those who take pride in possessions and family name, insisting that the only true virtue is nobility of character (the "goods of the mind"). The "you" in the quotation is Juvenal's addressee Ponticus.

4. Petrarch is alluding to the myth of the orator as civilizer that was widespread in antiquity; see, for example, Cicero, *De inventione*, I.ii.2–3; Quintilian, *Institutio oratoria*, II.xvi.9; and Horace, *Ars poetica*, 391–401.

to have induced gentleness and patient endurance in lustful, savage beings whose behavior resembled that of brute animals, while the second did the same thing for beings who were rustic, intractable, and hard as rocks.[5] Add to this that by means of this art we are permitted to be useful to many people who live far away, for our speech reaches those with whom we will perhaps never share the riches of our social intercourse. Finally, just how much we will be able to bestow on our posterity through speech can best be judged by remembering how much the words of our forefathers have bestowed on us.

But here you object once more: "Why is it necessary for us to take so many pains, if all the things that are supposed to benefit people have already been written down in an absolutely marvelous style by divine geniuses during the past thousand years and preserved in countless volumes?" Put this concern aside, I beg you, and never let it induce you to be lazy, for certain ancestors of ours have already removed this worry, and I myself will now remove it for those who come after me: for although ten thousand years may pass and centuries pile upon centuries, never will virtue be praised enough; never will there be enough lessons about how to love God and to hate sinful pleasures; never will the road to the discovery of new ideas be closed to eager minds. Therefore, let us be of good spirit: we do not labor in vain, nor will those do so who will be born many ages in the future right up to the end of this aging world. Rather, it is to be feared that men will cease to exist before their efforts in humanistic studies will have enabled them to penetrate the most secret mysteries of truth. Finally, even if love of other men should not compel us to it, still, I should think that the study of eloquence is the best and most beneficial thing for us ourselves, not something to be held in the lowest esteem. Others may decide for themselves, but I cannot possibly tell you what value certain familiar and famous words have had for me in my solitude, words which I not only conceived in my mind, but spoke aloud, and which I have been accustomed to use to rouse my sleeping spirit. How delightful is it at times to repeat the writings of others or my own, and to feel through such reading how I am actually freed from the burden of the weightiest and most bitter troubles! In this I am sometimes aided more by my own words, in that they are more suited to my languishing sickness, for they are words which have been applied by the knowledgeable hand of a doctor who was languishing himself and could feel where the pain was. I could never really achieve this relief if these salutary words did not caress my ears and gradually flow into me, stimulating me through the force of their innate sweetness to reread them repeatedly, and with their hidden barbs transfiguring me deep within. Farewell.

5. In various ancient texts, Orpheus is said to have been able to tame wild animals by means of his songs, and Amphion is credited with having built the walls of Thebes by the same means; see, for example, Horace, *Ars poetica*, 391–401. Petrarch allegorizes both stories in this passage, treating Orpheus's wild animals and Amphion's trees and rocks as figures for savage human beings.

[2]

Coluccio Salutati

Coluccio Salutati (1331–1406) was an influential Florentine humanist and politician. He studied law in Bologna, and although he did not find it to his liking, he nevertheless apprenticed himself to a notary after the death of his father in 1351. He then began a successful political as well as scholarly career, winning appointment as the chancellor of Todi in 1367, of Lucca in 1371, and of the papal Curia in Viterbo shortly afterward. From 1375 to his death thirty-one years later, Salutati served the Florentine signoria as chancellor of the city, being especially active in diplomatic affairs and defending the city through his writings against its archenemy Milan. While a youth, Salutati was attracted to Petrarch, and the latter became both his teacher and a close personal friend. Like Petrarch, Salutati encouraged the revival of classical culture, attacked the Latin style and the logic taught by Scholastics, joined the hunt for long-lost pagan texts (he discovered a copy of Cicero's *Familiar Letters* in 1392) and produced learned treatises and collections of personal letters. Salutati brought the important Greek scholar Manuel Chrysoloras to Florence in 1396 to occupy the public chair of Greek, and he had a decisive influence on a number of important humanists, including Niccolò Niccoli, Poggio Bracciolini, and Leonardo Bruni, the last of whom succeeded Salutati as chancellor in Florence. His main works include *De saeculo et religione* (*Of the Secular World and of Religion*), *De fato, fortuna et casu* (*Of Fate, Fortune, and Chance*), *De tyranno* (*On the Tyrant*)—a work defending republican Florence against despotic Milan—and *De laboribus Herculis* (*On the Labors of Hercules*), which celebrates the ancient hero and extols poetry for its power of persuasion. Although Salutati never wrote a rhetoric treatise, he did discuss the subject in two letters, both involving praise for Petrarch and his eloquence. The first excerpt below is taken from a letter written to Roberto Guidi, count of Battifolle, on the occasion of Petrarch's death; it is dated 16 August 1374. The second comes from one written 17 December 1405 to the humanist Poggio Bracciolini, in which Salutati defends his praise of Petrarch's superiority to the ancients. The texts of the letters are taken from his *Epistolario*, edited by Francesco Novati (Rome, 1891), I: 179–83 (Book III, Letter xv), and IV: 136–42 (Book XIV, Letter xix).

ON PETRARCH'S ELOQUENCE

(The first letter opens with a lament over the death of Petrarch, who is praised for his learning, judgment, and religious faith.)

Go ahead and compare him to any person living or dead. Whom can you offer who is his superior, or even his equal, in every high office of virtue? What shall I say of literary studies? In them, by universal consent, our Francis has shone so brightly that he easily surpasses anyone you could find among the great men of antiquity—a time that produced them in greater numbers than does this age of ours and that glittered with them as if it were adorned with stars. I will pass over the liberal arts in silence, but just think about his writings to see how much natural ability he had in those arts. Moreover, good lord, how greatly did he excel in philosophy, which is recognized as a divine gift, the guide of all the virtues, and, to make use of a phrase from Cicero, "she who drives out vice," as well as being the empress and teacher of all the arts and sciences![1] I do not mean that kind of philosophy that our modern sophists, with their empty, windy boasting and shameless chattering, make a fuss about in their schools, but that other kind that refines souls, plants virtues, washes away the filth of vice, and, having removed the obscurities in disputations, causes the truth in all things to shine.[2] Let those who delight in finding out what they call unresolvable arguments, the products of enormous labor, and those who are moved by the glory of their scholastic academies, rejoice in that first kind of philosophy, but let us revere the second kind in our minds and embrace it with all the might of our souls. As for this second kind of philosophy, I say, read over the poems, consider the letters, and think about the books which Petrarch, that great man of truly divine genius, brought forth while he was alive, and you will see how fully he succeeded with it. But as for that high priestess of all the sciences and, if I may express it thus, that philosophy of philosophies, the one that examines the sacred mysteries of divinity, something that seems to rise above the summit of all that can be known—I cannot easily express how he absorbed it with his capacious mind and mastered it thanks to his clear understanding, as you may conjecture from his works once you have pondered them.

1. See *Tusculan Disputations*, II.v.2.
2. The "modern sophists" are the Scholastics.

But let us pass over all this, and, if you like, contemplate his eloquence, for by its means he clearly demonstrated the preeminence it has among all other humanistic studies. I have reserved praise for it until the end since, in my judgment, it seems the greatest thing there is. For what can be better than to be the master of the emotions, to bend your auditor to go wherever you might want, and to bring him back from that place, filled with gratitude and love?[3] Unless I am deceived, this is the strength of eloquence, this is its work; rhetors strive with all their power to reach this end. It is certainly a great thing to embellish one's writings with words and ideas, but the greatest accomplishment, and indeed the most difficult, is to bend the souls of one's listeners as one wishes by means of a polished and weighty oration. Eloquence accomplishes all these things at one and the same time. In this connection, I want you to consider how man has been created for the sake of others and how God has placed reason above all the human appetites, letting it, as leader and guide, regulate our turbulent emotions from its seat in the lofty citadel of the mind. Consider also how eloquence has in addition been bestowed on the same creature, something which man shares with no other animal, so that through it, he might be able to awaken by means of the fires of mutual love the reason of his fellows, when that reason has been lulled to sleep by perverted moral behavior or by the heaviness of our gross bodies, and so that, whatever one man might lack by nature or have ruined through his wicked habits, the eloquence of his fellow man could build up and restore. Although it is clear that our marvelous Petrarch, whose fame will be eternal, enjoyed enormous success with this faculty, still, I will extend the discussion in order to express his praiseworthy qualities more richly. For your part, do not let yourself be frightened by the length of my letter.

Wherever you may turn, although this faculty of eloquence we are speaking about is always the same, I think it can be treated under two heads, for either it flows forth free and relaxed in melodious prose, or it is confined continually within the narrow straits of meter. The former, which goes forward in a freer manner, is divided into debate and discussion, for either it is employed in the contentious arguing of controversies, or, once the possibility of refutation has been removed, it is managed by means of a certain quiet kind of talk. The difference between the two is so great that, according to Cicero, even among the Greeks, who achieved glory in all fields of study, only Demetrius Phalereus appeared to have achieved fame in both, although that orator is granted sweetness, but little power.[4] How much majesty and elegance and power Petrarch achieved in these two parts of eloquence is revealed by the thousands of letters he wrote in which he used both styles as the occasion dictated. His many treatises also demonstrate

---

3. Cf. Cicero, *De oratore*, I.viii.30.
4. See *De officiis*, I.i.4.

this. Let me review several of them, starting with his *Invective Against the Doctors* (*Invectivarum in medicum*), a work which, I submit, if anyone looks it over carefully, would easily be granted, with respect to our Cicero, to exceed the latter's *Verrine Orations* and his *Philippics* and even his *Orations Against Catiline*. Next, there is Petrarch's *Of the Solitary Life* (*De vita solitaria*) and his sacred work *On the Remedies for Both Kinds of Fortune* (*De remediis utriusque fortunae*), his treatise *On His Own Ignorance and That of Many Others* (*De sui ipsius et multorum ignorantia*), his treatise *Of Fragments* (*Fragmentorum*), which he completed and published, and his work *Of Famous Men* (*De viris illustribus*), which I know has been composed by him, but am uncertain whether it has been published.[5] O magnanimous Count, if we were permitted to hold all these books together in our hands and to feed ourselves by reading them, believe me, although someone might maintain that Petrarch is Cicero's equal in vehement oratory, nevertheless he would say that, without a doubt, that great parent of Roman eloquence has been surpassed by our Petrarch in both stylistic grace and weightiness of content, whether he is making the forum resound with his voice or is speaking and writing in his room.

However, in that other form of eloquence which proceeds by measured feet and through the restrictions of poetic forms, Petrarch's divine *Pastoral Poems* (*Bucolica*) teach us, the fame of his *Africa* shows, and many other works produced by him in verse bear witness to how much he was worth. I should add this one thing, that among the ancients, whose works we marvel at and adore, very few at all have had success in both prose and poetry. Cicero, the very fountain of eloquence, fell short in verse, although he was worthy of great admiration for his prose. Read his book *Of Divination* (*De divinatione*) and see how many verses Cicero has repeated from Aratus in it.[6] I think that unless you simply bow to the authority of Cicero himself, you would entirely deny that that verse proceeded from some lofty pole of eloquence, as one may describe him. By contrast, we understand that Vergil once pled a case before the judges with the most unfortunate results, so that, frightened away from rhetoric, he retreated to poetry, in which he surpassed all the Greeks and Latins, although it is still amazing that nothing remains extant in prose from such a great man.[7] But believe me: to the same degree that he succeeded in poetry, he failed in prose. Therefore, we may rightly and boldly prefer our Francesco to both of them whom he surpassed so gloriously in both kinds of eloquence.

5. In this passage Salutati refers to many of Petrarch's most important prose works, but it is not clear to which work he is referring with the title *Fragments*. Petrarch did identify his Italian love poetry, the *Canzoniere*, as his *Liber fragmentorum*, but that volume cannot be the one in question here.

6. Since Cicero does not, in fact, cite much verse in *De divinatione*, Salutati may be confusing this work with Cicero's *De natura deorum* (*Of the Nature of the Gods*), which does contain a great deal. Cicero translated Aratus's work, although only fragments of the translation survive.

7. Salutati's anecdote about Vergil's failure as an orator is taken from Donatus's *Life of Vergil*.

(This letter ends by lamenting once again Petrarch's demise, but then praising him for having achieved both earthly and heavenly immortality. The second and later letter to Poggio Bracciolini opens by reproving him for his overly mordant wit and sarcasm. Salutati then defends his praise of Petrarch by arguing that if writing is to be valued for both content and style, then the Christian content of works produced by even mediocre stylists makes those works superior to those of their most eloquent pagan rivals.)

But you say I should come to the subject of eloquence: even if we excel them, that is, the pagans, in knowledge and the truth of things about which they knew nothing, at least we should not be compared to them in the same way with regard to eloquence and weightiness of style. It is surprising that although you and that ally of yours think Christians surpass the ancient pagans in truth and knowledge—something you ought to think, since it cannot be denied—you prefer the latter in regard to eloquence.[8] After all, whatever we say involves content and style, and the value of the content is so great that a weighty and learned speech lacking verbal polish must be given precedence over one whose style is most eloquent and ornate. As Horace says, "The principle and source of correct writing is knowledge."[9] And as our Cicero says, no one can be an orator perfect in every praiseworthy quality unless he has acquired knowledge of all the important arts and sciences.[10] For speech to flourish and be copious, one must have a knowledge of things, so that if the orator has not understood and mastered a great deal, his oration will be empty and almost childish. It must thus be acknowledged that all those who excel others in wisdom will similarly surpass them in eloquence. But you will say, "Are you trying to drive me crazy? Will you force me to say that the theologians of our time as well as those who have achieved fame during the last three centuries are eloquent, although they might be numbered among those who, according to the divine Augustine, recounted the truth in such a way that it was irritating to hear, could not be understood, and, finally, might not be believed?"[11] I know, my dear Poggio, that just as our theologians excel the pagans in the knowledge of the truth, so the pagans surpass the moderns not in skillful and majestic speech, which is childish if it does not contain the truth, but in that sort of speech to which Horace was referring when he spoke of "verses without substance and melodious trifles."[12] Moreover, I believe the pagans knew they were speaking lies, for they knew they had not yet penetrated the most secret recesses of truth. Just as all of us are naturally inclined to be industrious about things we value and desire, so the pagans eagerly studied not just what they could understand by nature, but also eloquence, an art which, as Cicero puts

8. The other critic, Poggio's "ally," to whom Salutati addresses his remarks, has not been identified.
9. See *Ars poetica*, 309.
10. Salutati is citing *De oratore*, I.vi.20, both here and in the next sentence.
11. See *De doctrina christiana*, IV.1–3.
12. *Ars poetica*, 322.

it, is not hidden away, but is placed in the midst of things, that is, before the eyes and in the common grasp of everyone.[13] Thus, with absolutely marvelous completeness they investigated arithmetic, geometry, and music, grammar, logic, and this rhetoric, of which we are speaking, mastering them as much as they could by means of conjecture. However, they could in no way understand, in fact could scarcely touch, physics and metaphysics and that which transcends everything else, theology, so that the Philosopher was right when he wrote that just as the eyes of nightravens are not adapted to the light of day, so our minds are not constituted so that we may grasp the aspects of nature which are most familiar to us.[14] Moreover, because of the difficulty involved in understanding natural, not to speak of supernatural, matters, many believe that Socrates, that most wise man, heeding the oracle of Apollo, put aside his investigations of nature and turned all his studies to ethics because he felt confident, or so it seemed to him, that with that subject he would certainly be able to accomplish his goal and reach a conclusion.[15] But since God alone is the goal of all things, and the pagans knew nothing at all about Him, how could they know what would lead to that goal? Thus, since they realized they had not yet understood the nature of things, they strove in every way to master the method and art of speaking. I believe they judged things incorrectly, for Socrates, who was almost their god, was accustomed to say that everyone is sufficiently eloquent about a subject he knows; Cicero may say this idea is plausible, while denying that it is true.[16] I, by contrast, think it is absolutely true and certain, for, although a person who knows what he must say may not be called eloquent in any simple and absolute sense, he must be considered sufficiently eloquent with regard to what he knows—unless he is completely foolish and ignorant.

To return to the men of our times: the learned make use of two or three modes of speech which pertain to eloquence, to wit, disputation, preaching, and teaching. Now tell me: don't we see many in our days who, through the sweetness of their marvelous preaching, are able to hold the people in their spell not in front of the rostrum in the forum, but in church? What part of eloquence was lacking in my venerable father, our elder and teacher Luigi Marsili? For thus he is called in the vernacular, although his name should be Ludovico. What, I say, did that man lack in erudition, eloquence, or virtue? What orator ever moved people more forcefully or persuaded them more effectively to do what he wanted? Who remembered or knew more, whether you are asking after human or divine matters? Who was better supplied with a knowledge of history, even among the pagans, and who was readier to use it and more tenacious in retaining it? Who was more enlightened about theology, subtler in understanding the arts and philosophy, more

13. See *De oratore*, I.iii.12.
14. "The Philosopher" is Aristotle; see *Metaphysics*, I.i.12–14 (981b5–981b18).
15. On Socrates' change of heart, see Cicero, *De amicitia*, ii.6, and *Academica*, I.iv.15–16.
16. See *De oratore*, I.xiv.63.

knowledgeable about antiquity or more expert in those things that this modern age thinks it understands? Who was more learned among the orators and poets, cleverer in untangling the knots in texts and books, and clarifying the obscurities in any work whatsoever? But Ludovico left nothing in writing. Neither did Pythagoras of Samos, who was famous for his teaching and gained fame through his many disciples in Italy and Magna Graecia. Nor did Socrates write anything, except for certain fables of Aesop he is said to have compiled in verse during the time he was in prison in order to satisfy his familiar daemon, whom Apuleius called Socrates' god, and who used to suggest things to him in dreams that he would unfold in poetry.[17] And Christ wrote nothing, although many people said that he had written down many things which he said and did, even beyond those recorded by the four evangelists. And the fountain of eloquence himself, Cicero, declared that none of the Greeks had mastered the legal and forensic kind of oratory or this quiet one which we are working at writing here.[18] Moreover, since the lords and princes of peoples throughout the earth and the senates of republics have been, and are, drawn from among the uneducated, it should not be surprising that the modern age shines less brightly through its eloquence. Nevertheless, I do not believe that you could judge us to lack eloquence in preaching the word of God, teaching dogmas, or disputing with subtlety. On the contrary, I think you could not reasonably reproach the eloquence that the modern age has retained or recovered in these areas, and therefore, you must confess that what Socrates said is true: everyone is sufficiently eloquent about that which he knows. Nor is the modern world so destitute of eloquence, as you write, that no comparison, not even a tiny one, can really be made between it and antiquity on that score. But why do I defend our age so obstinately? Let us come to our Petrarch.

I know that you judge him preferable to almost all the moderns, but since eloquence is a varied and complicated matter, please stop being shamelessly contentious, and tell me: does Petrarch seem to dip so far below the ancients in history, which I think is the most difficult rhetorical genre, that he may be compared to none of them at all in it? Read his book *Of Famous Men* (*De viris illustribus*), and tell me, if you can, what it lacks in majesty, beauty, and elegance.[19] Doesn't he preserve the dignity of the characters' speech, the greatness of the events, the propriety of the words, the refinement of the actions, and a solidity, sobriety, and beauty of style? Do you insist that he must surpass Livy and Sallust? So do I, but it is just too difficult to snatch poetry away from Homer, his club from Hercules, the glory of history from Livy,

17. Socrates imagines an Aesopian fable in Plato's *Phaedo*, 60c–61b. Apuleius wrote a short work entitled *De deo Socratis* (*On Socrates' God*) about the daemon, or spirit, that Socrates said used to inspire him.

18. See *De officiis*, I.i.3. The "quiet" kind of rhetoric is that of the letter.

19. Petrarch's *De viris illustribus* is a collection of biographies of famous Romans he began in 1338, but then expanded in 1351–1352 to include men of all nationalities from Adam on. It remained incomplete at his death in 1374.

or a praiseworthy brevity and reputation for truth from Sallust.[20] These heights are either too difficult or impossible to transcend. Such an achievement was not even conceded to antiquity itself: in those two writers, Livy and Sallust, it conquered itself. And yet, does no glory remain for anyone else? As I have been accustomed to remark so very often, I acknowledge the fact that Cicero has so occupied the heights in prose that no one else may attain them; Vergil has done the same thing in poetry, as have both Dante, with his long work in rhyming verse in the vernacular, and Petrarch, with his short works in the same medium. Nor perchance will anyone be able to scale those heights in the future. Who could ever equal John the Evangelist or Paul the Apostle in theology? Does that mean that no praise is to be given to Dionysius the Areopagite, Origen, Didymus [Thomas Aquinas], Ignatius, Cyprian, Basil, [John] Chrysostom, John of Damascus, or Gregory Nazianzus? And, to skip over an infinite number of Greeks, is there no glory for the divine Augustine, Jerome, father Ambrose or our Gregory, Hilarius of Poitiers or Bede, or, to make an end, Anselm or Bernard and many others, who have shone with distinction among the greatest theologians?

Once, when Hannibal was asked by Scipio Africanus about the excellence of generals, it is said that he responded, not going back much before his own time, that Pyrrhus, the king of Epirus, held the first place, since he is said to have been the first person to have taught correct methods and measures for pitching camps, and that Alexander of Macedonia had the second place, since he, with a small army, subjugated an enormous portion of the world and was a great expert in besieging cities. When Hannibal was asked about the third, he did not hesitate to name himself, although he had been conquered by Scipio, and when the latter replied, "And what if you had conquered me?" Hannibal retorted, "I would have proclaimed myself the general of generals over all the others."[21] Thus, neither you, nor anyone else, should be too hasty in putting the ancients in first place and the moderns in second, because you might not be giving precedence to those who by reason ought to have it.

Tell me, please: you reprehend me for having preferred our Petrarch to the ancients, but since he has examined both pagan and Christian wisdom, has digested the first sufficiently well while doing a great deal with the second, and has studied and understood both, as is apparent in his works, why do you accuse me of ignorance if I place him above pagans who knew nothing of Christian truth? Doesn't someone who knows both grammar and rhetoric seem greater and worthier than someone who knows grammar alone, even if the latter knows more about grammar than does the former who is both grammarian and rhetorician? I cannot believe you are so foolish that you will deny a matter that is so clear and practically right in front

20. Cf. Macrobius, *Saturnalia*, V.iii.16.
21. See Plutarch, *Life of Titus Flamininus*, xxi.3–4.

of your eyes. Therefore, you should bear it patiently when I assign this just precedence to our Petrarch, nor should you strive any further in a matter so clear, indeed, so absolutely clear: you should confess that learned Christians excel pagans in the knowledge of nature and that true eloquence, which must shine with learning and knowledge, as Cicero insists, is surely not to be found among the pagans, but among the Christians. The learning of the former is, according to Cicero, empty and childish, and, as Horace puts it, they have produced that which is "without substance and melodious trifles."[22] And those who study only eloquence, as Cicero himself says, are never going to be of use; indeed, without wisdom, they will generally be very harmful. However, since the method of correct speaking, that is, the joining together of eloquence and true teaching, is available to Christians, then they will produce something marvelous that we will not be able to praise sufficiently.

(After this point, Salutati again defends his claim that Petrarch has surpassed Cicero as a poet and Vergil as an orator and writer of prose, and concludes that Poggio must abandon his opposition to the notion that Petrarch was superior to the ancients.)

22. Salutati repeats his earlier references to Cicero, *De oratore*, I.vi.20, and Horace, *Ars poetica*, 322.

[3]

George of Trebizond (Trapezuntius)

George of Trebizond (1395–1472 or 1473), often referred to by the latinized version of his name, Trapezuntius, was born in Crete, which was held by Venice in the late fourteenth and early fifteenth centuries. In order to pursue a career as a teacher of Greek and rhetoric and as a translator, he transferred himself to Venice in 1416 and studied Latin with Vittorino da Feltre, one of the leading humanists in northern Italy. George sought and obtained the patronage of various Venetian patricians, was made a citizen of Venice by 1420, and was awarded the chair of Latin in Vicenza by the mid-1420s. He finished his monumental *Rhetoricorum Libri V* (*Five Books on Rhetoric*) in 1433 or 1434. This was the first complete rhetoric produced in the Renaissance, and it was particularly important for making the thought of various ancient Greek rhetoricians, such as Hermogenes of Tarsus, available to the Latin West. The first three books of the work deal with invention, the fourth with arrangement, and the fifth with ornamentation, or style, delivery, and memory. A brief excerpt from the beginning of the fifth book is translated here. At about the same time, George composed and delivered in Venice an oration entitled *Oratio de laudibus eloquentie* ("An Oration in Praise of Eloquence"). His defense of rhetoric in this work, which is also translated here, is consistent with the anti-Platonic character of much of his other writing. After the mid-1430s, George spent the remainder of his life moving every few years from city to city throughout northern and central Italy in quest of patronage, especially from the Vatican. He produced a large number of translations of important Greek texts, including many of the works of Aristotle, and wrote a number of religious commentaries and theological treatises that have a markedly apocalyptic character. The translation of the excerpt from his *Rhetoricorum Libri V* is based on the Venice edition of 1523; that of his *Oratio* is based on the version of it in John Monfasani's *George of Trebizond: A Biography and a Study of his Rhetoric and Logic* (Leiden: E. S. Brill, 1976), Appendix 11, 365–372.

George of Trebizond (Trapezuntius)

From *Five Books on Rhetoric*

Book V

I think I should present ornamentation more carefully than the other parts of rhetoric, not only because it has been entirely neglected by writers on the art, but because it seems to be the most useful among them.[1] Although I easily conceded the first place to the invention of one's arguments, it is not something for people of all ages, nor can it be completely managed through formal instruction in rhetoric, for it requires both broad experience and an almost divine recollection of a great deal of material.[2] Moreover, that skill must be reinforced by challenges involving both favorable and adverse events, and assisted by a knowledge of the laws and the institutions of society and by precision in the use of dialectic. It is impossible for the art of rhetoric to include all these things, because they are so numerous, indeed, almost infinite. For unless someone has seen, heard, and experienced a very great deal, he will have nothing to say about many subjects proposed to him. In fact, scarcely even in old age will we have enough material for invention to work with, material that can be suited to the subjects, persons, topics, times, and cases involved, in a way that will be in accord with the orator's dignity. By contrast, ornamentation is a subject for people of all ages and can be completely contained within the formal teachings of the rhetorician. Indeed, adolescents and young people, perhaps even more than men who are mature or older, are attracted by the artful arrangement of words, by rhetorical periods, rhythms, and other things of this sort. Whereas the old are delighted by weighty subject matter, youth is delighted by the sweetness of words.

It is certainly proper for the rhetorician to discuss ornamentation, insofar as there have been many who have thought—wrongly, to be sure, although their opinion could conceivably be defended—that memory and delivery are not connected to rhetoric, but are entirely a matter of nature, while invention and arrangement belong to different arts that sharpen one's prudential judgment and natural talent. By contrast, no one has ever dared to take ornamentation away from the rhetorician, for thanks to it, you can speak ornately, clearly, and aptly, and for that reason you truly seem to be eloquent. Thus, I think that ornamentation should be placed ahead of all the other parts of rhetoric, for even if what you have found out by means of invention is excellent, it will seem low and base unless it has been polished by means of ornamentation. Moreover, it is surely the case that of all the most beautiful things, the one that excels all the others is the one by means of which man naturally surpasses all the other animals. Hence, if speech is proper to man and because of it he is especially differentiated from the other

---

1. I have translated "elocutio" as "ornamentation," although it also means "style."
2. George devoted the first three books of this work to this subject.

[28]

animals, then I think no one will doubt that ornamentation is the finest thing that nature has bestowed on the human race.[3] Indeed, unless reason itself, which has been hidden away in the inner recesses of the mind, is drawn forth by means of speech, it will have only as much brilliance as fire does that is hidden in flint, something no one will call fire until it is called forth by steel. Therefore, if we want our speeches to produce as much lightning as possible, the rules of ornamentation must be mastered through methodical study, reinforced by exercise, and made so easy for us by practice that we seem to have been born using them.

Nature itself, which does not allow adolescents to comprehend the more substantial methods of invention and the subtler theories of the liberal arts, allures us to this part of rhetoric. Indeed, nothing is grasped more easily during adolescence, nothing is retained longer, nothing delights and allures people of that age more than speech that is rhythmical and properly arranged. What could be more barbaric, then, than to despise that which perfects human beings? What more annoying than to discard that which renders one man more eminent than the rest? What baser than not to pursue that without which it is contrary to human nature to lead one's life, since nature itself has granted you the time for it? Has it not occurred to you that since you make dogs, cattle, donkeys, parrots, and other monsters of this sort either understand or utter human words against nature, you really ought to blush if you neglect those capacities that nature has implanted in you? But why are more words needed? All admit that this is the case and affirm that we should work hard on this subject. Still, I do not understand how some people, who have been corrupted and ruined by pleasures and delights, have wasted their adolescence, and have already lost their chance at eloquence, can, when they have reached a mature age—if even then— begin to grieve because they cannot accomplish anything worthwhile now that they want to do so. For since they completely lack the basics, either they are repelled by the work involved or are carried away by disdain for their task. However, it would perhaps be excessive to say more about those who are averse to learning. By contrast, those who study philosophy and all the other good arts seem to me much more worthy of reprehension, since all knowledge and learning, unless they shine with the brilliance of eloquence, will lie in darkness, rough and dirty, entirely without distinction, elevated by no authority, adorned by no narration, raised up by no dignity. This point has not escaped the whole tribe of the Socratics, nor been hidden from the Stoics and the Academics in their teaching.

You will not easily find anyone among our ancestors, whether Latin or Greek, who lacks an elegant style. I will skip over Carneades, Critolaus, Aristippus, Theophrastus, and Diogenes, who as eloquent men were thought to excel all others just as uncivilized men themselves stand apart from the

---

3. Cf. Cicero, *De inventione*, I.iv.5.

animals. And I will omit innumerable others, including Plato himself, the fountainhead of eloquence, and all those who followed diligently in his foot-steps, to come to Aristotle, really the greatest teacher of philosophy, the one philosophers desire as their chief, the one they follow with all their might, the one they esteem, admire, and embrace. Let us look at Aristotle, I say. Does he, the head and eye of philosophy, disdain the teachings of eloquence? On the contrary, no one, in my judgment, has spoken more ornately, more lu-cidly, more rhythmically, and at the same time with greater dignity, so that if someone were to imagine a god using human language, I would dare to as-sert that that deity would not use a more excellent or elegant form of speech. Not only do I dare to assert these things, but also this, that Aristotle, desiring to speak of this art, left behind more ornaments of speech than did those who professed to be rhetoricians. As a result, people would sooner deny that he was a philosopher than refuse to grant him eloquence, for it is said that he used to walk around the Lyceum before lunch explaining the secrets of na-ture,[4] something he himself called his entertainment, whereas after lunch, by Heaven, during the greater part of the day, he would teach the arts of oratory and the rules of eloquence. He thought that a philosopher who is not elo-quent differs little, if at all, from one who professes himself a rich man, yet suffers from a serious lack of all the necessities of nature. And he is surely right: it is just like someone boasting he is rich when he has neither great es-tates nor magnificent houses. In fact, if his toes stick out of his shoes and his entire body is covered with a dirty, ragged garment, he will be derided not only as poor, but as completely destitute and wretched. Thus, if a person claims to know about the revolution of the earth, the causes of things, the na-ture of the heavens, and whence things come into being and where they will fall into ruin, he will appear destitute of all knowledge unless he also adorns and illuminates what he teaches with a rich abundance of words as if with gold and gems. But of these things I will speak at greater length elsewhere.

Now, since it should be clear that eloquence is the prince of human affairs, we will consider more diligently what can be taught about it, with this one proviso, that we do not approve of ornamentation that is not connected to real content or knowledge. For what is so foolish, so worthless, so mad, as words arranged rhythmically that seem to contain nothing, or to be un-suited to the matter being discussed, or to possess only some slight signifi-cance? If the choice were given to me either to have ornate, rhythmical speech or knowledge of things, I would select the latter as something divine and reject the former as madness. But when both are produced at the same moment—something that was common in the ancient world, but seems hardly capable of happening in these degenerate times—then a certain something that is perfect and truly divine will be created. Therefore, if someone, because of his age, has no hope of possessing both things, and if

4. The Lyceum was a gymnasium near Athens in which Aristotle taught. For his teaching oratory during the afternoon, see Quintilian, *Institutio oratoria*, III.i.14, and Diogenes Laertius, *Aristotle*, in *Lives of the Eminent Philosophers*, V.2–3.

he seeks nothing other than knowledge, it seems right to us that he should strive to find the causes of things and to acquire lofty kinds of knowledge. But if he wants to attain the glory of governing the state, then he must apply himself to rhetoric. Both things, however, can be accomplished splendidly if he devotes his adolescence to the latter and his more mature age to all the rest.

An Oration in Praise of Eloquence

Most noble men, since I see how rhetoric, the most distinguished of the liberal arts, lies in ruin, covered up by darkness nowadays, I have decided to rush to its aid and to defend it both privately and publicly. For I could not bear that this art, so honorable and useful to the human race and especially to this city, should have been insidiously slighted and scorned for so long—indeed, with the greatest inconvenience to everyone—either by those who practice it ignorantly or by those who are its detractors. Nevertheless, I have no confidence that I can expound all its remarkable intricacies to you by means of my precepts and instruction: I am not so insane not to see that I lack more than I have. However, I am happy to devote all of whatever knowledge I have—which I recognize is very slight—to the common good, so that even if nothing else is accomplished, at least we see how much honor and utility, how much worth, what distinction, and what glory the orator possesses.

Although the essence of humanity is reason, this reason seems to be of absolutely no use to men unless it is brought into common use by means of speech. For what benefit can derive from a subtle mind, what advantage from sharp thinking, what utility from the best invention, unless the power of speech reveals one's subject, having dragged it out of the obscure places where all such things lie hidden? Thus we must confess that nothing was ever given to us by God that is better than speech.

But speech, according to the nature of things, has been divided into two parts. Just as some things are extremely removed from our ordinary civil life and are considered merely for the sake of knowledge, while others are established directly in the social intercourse of men, so that part of speech by means of which we pry into the secrets of nature is called dialectic, whereas that other part, which is necessary for civic affairs and without which no one ever carried on his business with distinction, especially in the state, was called rhetoric by our ancestors, both the Latins and the Greeks. Indeed, rhetoric excels the other arts inasmuch as it alone embraces almost every aspect of human life. For some arts investigate the revolution of the earth, others the motions of the stars and magnitudes in astronomy, still others the force of sounds and their relationships, and yet others strive to explain the nature of individual entities—all of these things are both difficult and honorable, but neither are they capable of being adequately understood nor, if

[31]

we actually held them in our hands, would they prove all that useful to civic life. Meanwhile, rhetoric alone has undertaken the managing of private as well as public matters. For what could be thought up or said in the conduct of our affairs that does not require the power of oratory? In court, it defends what is right. In the Senate, it shows you both the useful and the useless. In public meetings, it has always protected the state as a whole. It teaches us to be provident and to avoid adverse things before they happen. If they should happen through chance or ignorance, rhetoric alone will come to our aid and will support us with hope or consolation. It adorns our successes and mitigates our disasters. It intimidates our enemies and strengthens our friends. It founds, preserves, and enlarges cities. It both promulgates and abrogates laws. But it is really foolish to want to enumerate all this, for the number of things that men have drawn from rhetoric, as from a divine fountain, is almost infinite.

Thus, our ancestors seem to me to have been most correct in calling this the art of humanity. Indeed, Aristotle, whom Cicero follows in his rhetorical teaching, thought that this was the greatest and noblest part of political science, which is the teacher and mistress of all human affairs.[5] But if I may be permitted to say openly what I feel, I do not think that eloquence in all its richness is contained as a part within political science; rather, I maintain that the entirety of that science is contained and guarded within eloquence. For, although things placed under some general category often merely overlap, nothing will ever be found in political science that eloquence does not order, arrange, and complete. "What about the military?" you'll say. But this art urges soldiers on into battle; it excites them to destroy the enemy; it drives forward those who hold back, and calls back those who are running away. "What about economics?" You will never be able to engage in business transactions with another unless you persuade him. "And legal science?" By means of this art, laws are passed and preserved for a long time, and although they are mute in themselves, they are given a voice by the orator's flowing eloquence. Moreover, he confirms the moral behavior of men by means of praise, reinforces it through examples, establishes it by appealing to custom, and corroborates it through appeals to equity and the good—or by means of vituperation and every other technique at his disposal he reproves, refutes, weakens, and destroys it. Nor is he less used to exhorting and inflaming people to embrace virtue than he is accustomed to deterring them from vice. Therefore, if rhetoric embraces, guards, and discharges all the parts of politics, one should not think that it is contained in political science rather than the reverse. Nevertheless, the longer I think about the matter, this oratorical faculty seems to me neither to be the genus to which politics belongs, nor to be entirely identical to it. Rather, it is such a unique, singular, and most noble instrument of politics that it seems less to serve all

---

5. I have translated George's "civilis scientia" as "political science," though it means something like "the knowledge necessary to manage civil and political affairs."

the individual parts of politics than to be their master. For the orator, I say, declares war, makes peace, honors brave men, punishes deserters, celebrates marriages, disparages divorces, warns freemen, consoles slaves, entertains the speaker's followers, and terrifies his opponents. Indeed, that singular part of rhetoric we call invention seems to me identical with politics itself, for it is the function of rhetoric alone to investigate methodically whatever is to be said or done in any given affair. Indeed, we judge that person to be a politician who by his actions can easily maintain the name of rhetor for himself. Therefore, if things are this way—just as you all surely know they are—it seems one must concede that through this single one of its parts, invention, the orator's office includes politics within it, on which when it lavishes its other parts as instruments, it shows that nothing nobler, better, or more divine can be found in human affairs than aptness of speech.

But since we did not propose to review all the merits of rhetoric, but just to touch on a few of them, and since we are urging noble men to pursue this art—and it is of the greatest importance that they exert themselves in doing so with real diligence—now, lest there be any impediment to anyone who might want to undertake this study, let us refute the arguments of those who, because of their wickedness and their depravity, dare to remove it from the liberal arts. What, then, do they say? "This art, which you praise to the stars, has sometimes harmed states. The power of speech is great. Eloquence can do a great deal. It forces the minds of men to go wherever it wants. Therefore, it ought to be removed and exterminated from well-ordered states as if it were a pest." Oh, by all that's holy, do you think that men would be capable of living together if they were mute? Would you prefer them to be inarticulate? What ingratitude toward God and nature! Although He created us men, you want to turn us into wild animals and savage beasts, for unless reason, which makes us human, is transformed into action by means of speech, it is worth as much in a man as fire is when it is hidden away in flint.

"But I don't want mute men," you say. "I concede that they may speak, for otherwise they cannot live together. I just deny them eloquence." It's not possible that someone who grants us that we may have a man who is knowledgeable would give him to us in such a way that he thought we were obliged to shape him as badly as possible! Most distinguished listeners: if speech is good for man, it should certainly be best for the human race to speak in the best manner. "But it has sometimes caused harm."[6] What if speech has generally caused harm? Should we cut off all men's tongues? If a lawyer perverts justice by too clever an interpretation of the laws, should the laws be thrown away? If a doctor takes away a man's health through ignorance or viciousness, is medicine to be banished? Finally, if a pilot overturns a ship, are pilots to be thrown overboard? Just as no ship has ever sailed correctly without a pilot, so no state, once eloquence has been

6. Cf. Quintilian, *Institutio oratoria*, II.xvi.5–6.

expelled, has ever been well piloted. Don't you see—if I may omit older examples—how this most flourishing republic is steered by eloquence alone? If you find that anything was done by the people or the Senate before they were persuaded to do it, I will give up and go away, nor will I trouble you any more once I have been thus defeated. "But few orators have any real mastery of the art." But they do have experience and practice with it. Besides, nature itself, just as it is accustomed to produce in abundance all those other ordinary things necessary for human life, so, since eloquence contains all of civil life within it, nature has implanted in us more of the most familiar principles of that art than of any other. If, then, by the practice of speaking we acquire the greatest verbal ornaments, and if art is indeed added to practice, what a remarkable, unparalleled, divine specimen of eloquence will be produced. Therefore, just as we drive out not medicine, but bad doctors, not lawyers, but crafty and wicked ones, not the steersman's art, but vicious steersmen, so we should cast out headfirst and tear away from the tiller of the state not eloquence, which is the safeguard of commonwealths, but those men who, although eloquent, are wicked. For what is more foolish, what more senseless, than to grant swords, spears, axes, shields, and other arms to the state, but to reject the sharp sword of eloquence with which nature equipped us, the shield bestowed on man by the heavens, just because some people have used it badly? Eloquence, therefore, eloquence with all its resources, must be preserved. If the eloquent are indeed wicked, then let them be punished for having abandoned all virtue. We don't think we ought to do anything different in this matter than we do with gladiators and assassins: when they have used their arms wickedly against the state or against some citizen, they themselves, rather than their arms, are removed.

Therefore, most distinguished men, unless we want to be mute, let us embrace eloquence. With it we will govern best both the state and our private affairs, for political science has no other instrument. Accordingly, apply yourselves to eloquence so that we may bestow Ciceronian ornaments on it, since nothing is worthier of a free state and a free people, nothing more pleasant to know and hear, nothing so regal, so liberal, so magnificent.[7] This alone from among the liberal arts knows how to succor the afflicted, is able to encourage those who are cast down, does not hesitate to offer safety to the despairing, is not ignorant of ways to free people from dangers and preserve men in their city and their very own homes. Cowards are spurred on by its dignity, men are inflamed by its vehemence, and finally, the hot-tempered are calmed by its gravity. Apply yourselves to it and take pains with it, for, believe me, it will adorn, embellish, and amplify you and all of yours in a marvelous manner.

---

7. Here George is loosely paraphrasing Cicero, *De oratore*, I.viii.32, and Tacitus, *Dialogus*, v.4–6.

[4]

Lorenzo Valla

Lorenzo Valla (ca. 1407–1457), one of the most important Italian humanists, had an enormous impact on legal and religious reforms, the development of Latin literary style, and the application of critical methods to philosophy and to Biblical, classical, and historical scholarship. Educated at Rome, he taught in Florence and in various cities throughout Italy. King Alfonso V of Aragon, who ruled the Kingdom of the Two Sicilies in Naples, made Valla his secretary in 1435 and also employed him frequently on diplomatic missions. Despite his attacks on the temporal power of the Papacy and his pursuit by the Inquisition, Valla was made apostolic secretary by Pope Nicholas V in 1448. Valla served Nicholas and his successor, remaining in Rome until his death nine years later. In 1431 he published his first work, *De voluptate* (*On Pleasure*), a dialogue presenting Stoic, Epicurean, and Christian philosophies; although Christianity emerges victorious, Valla reveals a considerable sympathy for Epicureanism. In later works, he attacked the Aristotelian logic of the Middle Ages and wrote a series of groundbreaking, historically informed critical notes on the New Testament, which were not published until 1505 by Erasmus. In a short treatise of 1440, Valla demonstrated that the so-called Donation of Constantine, by which the emperor Constantine supposedly granted temporal power to the Papacy in Italy, was a forgery. In addition to translating portions of Homer, Herodotus, and Thucydides, Valla edited Livy and expounded on Quintilian. His *Elegantiae linguae latinae* (*The Refinements of the Latin Language*) was completed in 1440 and quickly became the leading textbook for Latin style throughout Europe. The six books of this work have six prefaces treating different topics, including one in which Valla identifies the spread of the Latin language as the most durable conquest made by imperial Rome. Much of the preface to Book IV, which is translated here, deals with eloquence in the course of Valla's defense of himself from the charge that he has been irreligious in advocating the study of the secular works of the pagans. The translation is based on the Venetian edition of the *Elegantiae* of 1476.

Lorenzo Valla

From *The Refinements of the Latin Language*

Preface to Book IV

I know that some people, and especially those who seem to themselves to be holier and more religious, will dare to criticize my enterprise in this work as unworthy of a Christian, since I am urging people to read secular books. Jerome confesses that because he was too eager to read those books, he was whipped before the tribunal of God and accused of being a Ciceronian, not a Christian, as though one could not be both a believer and a disciple of Cicero at the same time.[1] In response, he made a solemn promise, and that amidst dire execrations, that he was not going to read secular books after that time. Actually, this charge of producing something unworthy of a Christian does not apply just to the present work, but to me and all the other writers whose study and teaching of secular literature is being condemned. Let us respond to that accusation, and let us accuse our attackers in turn for both present and past actions, since they are in no small way guilty of having caused the ruin and shipwreck of Latin culture.

Do you say, citing Jerome as your authority, that secular books are not to be read? What are those books, I ask you? Are they all the orators, all the historians, all the poets, all the philosophers, all the jurists, all the rest of the writers—or just Cicero alone? If you say the former, as you should, why don't you reprehend those interested in the other kinds of writing, and either condemn me or acquit me together with them? But if you don't think that way and consider Cicero alone a criminal, look out that you don't make Jerome seem a fool, since he promised he was not going to read secular writers when he should have promised that only about Cicero. But you say it's not what he promised that one must pay attention to, but what he was accused of, for he was accused of being a Ciceronian. Is that so? Then let's let Cicero go, let's abandon him, let's throw him away. What do you think of the other authors, and of so many disciplines? Surely they are all secular, indeed pagan; that is, the works involved were not written by Christians, nor are they concerned with the Christian religion. If you say they are to be read, then you contradict yourself when you object to my reading them. If you deny that they are to be read, then you should think long and hard about whether the followers of the secular disciplines might attack you and tear you to pieces all by themselves.

But it's not like that, you say. When Jerome is reprehended for being a Ciceronian, he is reprehended for being a student of eloquence. This means that people who read and study for the sake of acquiring eloquence are being condemned and rejected. I see: what you fear is the hostile condemna-

---

1. Valla is alluding to the famous account of a dream Jerome put in a letter of 384 to Eustochium, the daughter of one of his Roman disciples; see Epistola 22, in his *Selected Letters*, trans. F. A. Wright (Cambridge: Harvard University Press, 1933), 126.

[36]

tion of others. But you are doing so too late, and you will be stuck in the mud just as you were before if you condemn only the eloquent. Why, as you are often accustomed to do, did you first forbid me to read the books of secular writers in general, but afterward moderate your accusation and mean it to apply only to the eloquent? Well, let it be thus: you are really in error, but, although provoked, I pardon your ignorance and forgive your desire to injure. But why do you dissent from Jerome who promised he would not touch secular writers, rather than just the eloquent? Why don't you, like that great judge, think that Cicero alone is to be condemned, or like Jerome, condemn all secular writers?[2] What does your ambiguous and changing opinion mean? But good lord, there is nothing in those books except eloquence; nothing except the record of times past and the histories of peoples, without which one would remain a child; nothing but a host of things that pertain to morality; nothing but a review of all the disciplines. Should I neglect all these things because, while I am seeking to learn them, I might also be learning eloquence and drinking the poison that has diluted the wine of knowledge? Should I drink water, indeed muddy water, rather than that marvelously sweet Falernian wine because I worry about the danger of poison?[3] And just what are those books in which the poison of eloquence lies hidden? Certainly, I know of none that lack eloquence except for yours and those of people like you, books that have neither strength nor brilliance. By contrast, the works written by all the others display, each in its own way, a certain marvelous elegance and refinement of speech. Thus, one must read either eloquent books—or none at all.

As for those two, whom Jerome mentioned: was that Greek [Plato] ineloquent, or was our Latin [Cicero] second to anyone among the Latins in philosophy? You do not know which of the two is more excellent, the philosopher or the orator. Now, since all the books of the ancients are eloquent in such a way as to contain the greatest wisdom, and teach wisdom in such a way as to contain the greatest eloquence, which of them do we think should be condemned on account of eloquence? But when Jerome confessed that he read those two authors repeatedly, take care and don't think he was speaking so much about Cicero's oratorical works as about his philosophical ones. I certainly believe he was talking about the latter because he mentions only philosophers. Moreover, he did not face criticism for being a Platonist— and that was not because he was behaving in a saintly manner by reading Plato—but only that he was a Ciceronian, because, as a Latin, he sought to express himself more in Cicero's style, in the style I say that Cicero employed in philosophical discussions rather than in legal cases or public speeches or in the Senate. For Jerome did not seek to prove himself an orator concerned with civil cases, but a writer of pious disputations.

2. "That great judge" to whom Valla refers in this sentence is most likely the universal judge, Christ, before whom Jerome appeared in his dream and who condemned him as a Ciceronian.
3. Falernian wine was proverbial for its excellence in Roman antiquity.

Then why don't we believe that Plato was as harmful to him as Cicero? Why aren't philosophers as bad as orators? Is it that the ornamentation of speech is what was being criticized, not its content? If that is so, then we all stand condemned for this one thing. For who is free of ornamentation? Here, however, you are making use of an intolerable misrepresentation, since no mention of ornamentation was made in the accusation against Jerome, only that he was a Ciceronian. Is ornamentation only to be found in Cicero, and not in philosophy and the rest of the arts? Is there no eloquence, as I said, in Plato? Or in the others? Why are we not all equally cast aside? Why should Cicero's philosophy be thought to have been more harmful to Jerome than his rhetoric was? I don't want to make a comparison here between philosophy and eloquence as to which one can be more harmful, for many have spoken of this subject, showing how philosophy is scarcely consistent with the Christian religion and how all heresies have flowed from its fountains. By contrast, they have argued that rhetoric has only laudable qualities: it enables you to invent and arrange arguments as if you were inserting bones and muscles into your speech; to adorn it, that is, to clothe it in flesh and give it color; and finally, to commit it to memory and to deliver it in a decorous manner, that is, to endow it with breath and movement. Would I believe that these things can injure anyone, except one who neglects everything else for them, and especially neglects true wisdom and virtue, as Jerome was doing? For my part, do I think this art harmful? Certainly no more so than painting, sculpture, engraving, and, to speak of the liberal arts, music. And if from those who sing well, paint well, and sculpt well, as from all the rest of the arts, religion derives many practical benefits and adornments, so that those arts practically seem to have been created for that purpose, surely it derives much more from the eloquent. The accusation was not that Jerome was a Ciceronian, but that he was not a Christian, such as he falsely proclaimed himself to be even while he was scorning Sacred Scripture. Thus, it was not the study of this art that was being criticized, but excessive study, whether of this art or any other, such that no space was left for better things. And no one else, just Jerome, was accused; otherwise, the rest would also have been attacked with a similar accusation. After all, one particular medicine is not appropriate for everyone, just as one thing is suited to one person, another to another, nor is the same thing permitted or forbidden at all times and in all places. In fact, Jerome did not dare to forbid others to speak well; on the contrary, he praised a great many eloquent people from previous ages as well as from his own time.

But why are we going on at such length? Who was more eloquent than Jerome himself? Who greater among the orators? Who, although he often wished to dissimulate it, was more solicitous, more eager, or more respectful with regard to fine speech? But he did not dissimulate it, for when Rufinus reproaches him by mentioning his dream, the latter mocks him and confesses plainly that he read the pagans continually and that he had to do so, and while he says this in many other places—something that is evident even without such a confession—he does so as well in his letter to this great orator.[4] Go ahead and worry that harm is being done to you by the accusations of others, although the accusation against Jerome did not harm him; and don't dare to do what he had no fear of breaking his promise in order to do. There are some, however, who believe that Jerome learned those things when he was young and simply retained them in his memory ever after. O ridiculous and ignorant men, who think that he could acquire so quickly such a great abundance of information and knowledge, in which he yields pride of place to no other Christian, or that he would not forget it after so much time! For those individuals are rare who can achieve the hundredth part of his knowledge, and, as they said in antiquity, no less effort is required to retain such resources than to acquire them. Moreover, consider this: how little difference is there between stealing and not returning what was stolen, for what good does it do to forbid others to steal when you openly take possession of what has been taken? In other words, if we are not supposed to learn eloquence, then we certainly should not make use of it after having learned it. Yet note how often Jerome calls up the books of the pagans to testify in his own writing. If it is not permitted to read them, even less is it permitted to display what one has read. So, even if we were being discouraged from reading the pagans—something Jerome does *not* do—I should think we would still pay more attention to what he does himself than to what he says others should do.

In truth, however, Jerome himself always says and does the same thing. After his younger years, he nourished himself on the most salubrious food of Sacred Scripture, and having reinforced himself with the knowledge he formerly despised, he returned to the reading of the pagans, so that, having gotten out of danger, either he might acquire eloquence from them, or he might confirm the things they said well and correct what they said badly. This is what all those Latins and Greeks, including Hilarius, Ambrose, Augustine, Lactantius, Basil, Gregory, Chrysostom, and all the rest, did, for in every age they decked themselves with the precious gems of divine speech, using the gold and silver of eloquence, and never abandoned one kind of knowledge for another. In my opinion, if anyone should undertake to write theology, it makes little difference whether he has any other resources of any sort, for they contribute almost nothing to it, but I think a person who is ignorant of eloquence is entirely unworthy of speaking about the subject. It is certainly the case that only the eloquent, only men such as those I have just enumerated, have been the pillars of the Church, even if you go back as far as the Apostles, among whom Paul seems to me to excel for no other reason than his eloquence. You see, therefore, that this argument has resulted in the

---

4. For Jerome's letter to Rufinus, see his *Apologia adversus libros Rufini*, in *Patrologia Latina*, ed. Jacques-Paul Migne (Paris: Garnier, 1883), 23: 457a–490 and esp. 481a–482a.

contrary conclusion: not only is the study of eloquence not to be criticized, but the failure to study it must be.

Now, I have been behaving as if I were undertaking the defense of eloquence against its false accusers, something that is really beyond what I proposed. For I am not writing about this subject, but about the elegance of the Latin language, from which there is nevertheless just a short step to eloquence itself. If someone does not achieve eloquence, however, he should not finally be blamed for not having turned out that way, as long as he has not shirked the work involved. But a person who does not know how to speak elegantly and yet puts down his thoughts in writing, especially on theology, is really impudent, and if he says he did so on purpose, then he is extraordinarily foolish—although there is no one who does not want to speak elegantly and eloquently. And when people like these bad theologians do not achieve the goal of elegant speech, they try to make it seem as if they did not pursue it—they are really being perverse here—or they maintain that one should not speak thus. And so they say that since the pagans spoke eloquently, it is not fitting for Christians to speak in the same way—as if the men I named above were speaking like Christians and not like Cicero and the other pagans! But then, our critics have neither knowledge nor experience of how the pagans speak.

One should not condemn the language of the pagans, nor grammar, nor rhetoric, nor dialectic, nor any of the other arts—note that the Apostles wrote in the Greek language—but rather, only dogmas, religions, and false opinions concerning the performance of virtuous actions by means of which we are supposed to ascend to heaven. All the other arts and sciences are matters indifferent in that you can use them for good or for ill. Therefore, we should strive, I beseech you, to reach the goal—or to come as close to it as possible—that the luminaries of our religion have reached. You see what marvelous ornaments distinguish Aaron's clothing, the Ark of the Covenant, and the Temple of Solomon: these things seem to me to signify eloquence, which, as the noble tragic poet says, is the queen over everything and the perfection of wisdom itself.[5] And so, let others adorn their private houses—those are the people who study civil and canon law, medicine, and philosophy, giving nothing to holy religion—but let us adorn the house of God, so that when we enter it, we are not roused to feelings of contempt by the neglect of the place, but to religious faith by its majesty. I cannot restrain myself from saying what I think: those ancient theologians seem to me like bees flying about distant meadows who have produced the sweetest honey and wax through marvelous art, whereas the recent ones resemble ants who

5. Valla is citing a passage in Quintilian, *Institutio oratoria*, I.xii.18, in which eloquence is identified as a queen by a "not ignoble tragic poet." In the Renaissance this was thought to be a reference to Euripides' *Hecuba*, 816, but it is more likely that it refers to a fragment from Pacuvius's *Hermione* which is also cited in Cicero, *De oratore*, II.xliv.187.

have taken grain stolen from places near by and hidden it away in their lairs. As far as I'm concerned, I would not only prefer to be a bee rather than an ant, but even to be a mere foot soldier under the queen of the bees than to be a general in the army of the ants. And I am confident that this view will be approved by young people of good understanding, for I despair of the old.

[5]

Rudolph Agricola

Rudolph Agricola (1443/1444–1485) played a most significant role in bringing the humanist program of revived classical studies from Italy to northern Europe. He was also one of the most widely influential writers on dialectic and rhetoric in the Renaissance and laid the groundwork for Peter Ramus's comprehensive redefinition of those arts. Born Roelof Huisman, the son of a priest and a woman named Huisman, Agricola initially studied Latin in Germany, but went to Pavia to pursue law in 1468, then to Ferrara to study Greek in 1475. He came back to Groningen, The Netherlands, in 1479 to serve as secretary to the city, completing his *De inventione dialectica libri tres* (*Three Books Concerning Dialectical Invention*) during the course of his journey. He went to Heidelberg to study Hebrew in 1484 and died there the next year, after having just returned from a brief trip to Rome. In addition to the *De inventione*, he left behind him a number of other works in Latin, including studies of dialectic and rhetoric, orations, poems, translations, and commentaries. His real influence began in 1515 with the first printing of the *De inventione*, which then saw forty more editions appear by 1579. Erasmus, Melanchthon, and the Protestant reformer and educator Johann Sturm all spread the influence of Agricola's ideas, as did Peter Ramus even more decisively. In his *De inventione*, Agricola says he is seeking to renew dialectic, claiming that rhetoric has usurped many of its traditional materials, and especially the *loci*, the places in which classes or categories of arguments are to be found in the process of invention, the "finding out," of one's arguments. He also claims that *dispositio*, or the arrangement of those arguments, belongs to dialectic. Thus essentially only *elocutio*—that is, style or ornamentation—delivery, and memory are left for rhetoric. However, it is important to note that the dialectic Agricola defines is really a kind of rhetoricized dialectic. That is, he sees arguments in rhetorical, rather than traditionally dialectical, terms in that he is concerned with probable, not absolute, truths. Moreover, he defines the goals of dialectic in terms of the traditional rhetorical triad of teaching, delighting, and, most important, moving the auditor. This translation of the text is based on the edition of Johann Knobloch published in Strasbourg, 1521.

FROM *Three Books Concerning Dialectical Invention*

Book I

Chapter 1. Concerning the Reasons for Finding Out Places, and Their Usefulness

Every speech on whatever subject, indeed, every conversation by means of which we bring forth our thoughts has as its function and its first and essential duty to teach something to the listener. Of this what more certain and intimate proof can one have than the fact that God, the parent and author of all things, granted to man alone of all animals, a being capable of reason and learning, the gift of language and speech? For if speech is a sign of the things that are contained within the speaker's mind, then it follows that its proper function is to display and unfold that which is its task to express. Nor has it escaped my notice that the greatest authors believed that a perfect oration should accomplish three things: teaching, moving, and delighting. Teaching is indeed an easy matter, and something each person can accomplish in some measure, unless he is a complete mental incompetent. However, stirring up the emotions of the auditor and transforming his mental condition in whatever way you want, alluring him and holding him enraptured by the pleasure of listening—these things cannot be done unless our minds are touched by the highest kind of inspiration and are overwhelmed and possessed by the Muses. I am certainly not going to deny that these things are the special rewards of eloquence and the results of speech, but they are more truly its consequences than its intended effects, its by-product rather than its proper result. But of these matters I will speak in more detail elsewhere. For the present let it suffice to say that a speech can teach without moving or delighting, but cannot move or delight without teaching. Thus, although those who entreat and complain, and even those who question, too, all seem to aim at these specific ends in speaking, they always accomplish this one first: they teach their listeners to understand what desire moves them [to entreat], what grief presses down on them, and what it is that they wish to know.

Often we teach only so that the hearer gains knowledge, but sometimes also that he should believe in what he hears. Either we awaken faith in one who already believes in us and we get him to follow us as if of his own free will, or we completely overcome one who does not believe and we drag him along although he fights against us. In the first instance, this is done through exposition; in the others, it results from argument. I call an exposition a speech that merely unfolds the thinking of the speaker, nothing having been added to it to gain the faith of the listener, whereas an argument is a speech in which someone strives to awaken belief in the matter about which he is speaking. However, since in the case of a doubtful subject, faith cannot be established on the basis of the subject itself, we must necessarily arrive at certainty in each instance by way of certain other things that are more familiar and better understood. Now, some people, relying on their mental acumen, can readily think up quite an ample argument, that is (as Cicero says), a plausible invention, in order to produce belief.[1] Others, on the contrary, whose mental power is blunter, see things only darkly and either can find nothing to say about the matter at hand or can do so only too late. Therefore, those who have identified certain places (*sedes*) of discovery for arguments, which are called places (*loci*), appear to have done something very useful indeed. Instructed by these places, as if by certain kinds of signs, we think about the issues themselves, and we can see what in each case is available as plausible and fitting proofs for our speech.

This method of employing places seems useful in the first instance because it contributes something to many of the liberal arts, for most subjects in them are stuck in ambiguities and have been abandoned to the strife of discordant opinions. Indeed, only a tiny portion of what we teach is sure and unshaken, to such a degree that, if we believe the Academy, we know only this, namely, that we know nothing.[2] Unquestionably, most things are borne hither and thither by each person's ingenuity in an effort to think up the most suitable argument. In the second instance, this method [of using places] is also especially beneficial for those who handle matters for which no art has been handed down to us, I mean, for those who govern the state with their prudence and who must often produce belief in the Senate or the people about some present matter involving peace or war or other civic business. It is also useful for those who must do the same thing in the law courts, whether they prosecute or defend, petition for something or oppose it, and for those whose profession is to instruct the people in justice, religion, and piety. For although some elements of these activities have been included in the arts, nevertheless the more subtle points derived from instruction at school, because they are just too abstruse, either do not gain entry into the rather gross understanding of the people or do not stick there. The latter are influenced more by cruder things and by those things, more popular and robust, that are derived from ordinary life. Thus, just as the lyre or the cithara delights more delicate ears, so you could not excite a soldier except with a bugle; as the proverb has it, dull things suit the dull.

Nor does this method [of using the places] seem only to instruct the tongue just by supplying a copious amount of material for speaking; it also

---

1. For the reference to "plausible invention," see Cicero, *De partitione oratoria*, ii.5.

2. This saying is attributed to Socrates by Plato (*Apology*, 21c). The Academy in question is the so-called Middle Academy, which succeeded the Academy of Plato and embraced a thoroughgoing skepticism; its most famous representative was Carneades.

enables the mind to exercise foresight and provides a method for correct de-liberation. For prudence, it appears, consists in nothing other than perceiv-ing what is involved in a given case, arranging the arguments that support and oppose it, and concluding by showing where each one is leading or what might result from it. As evidence for this, one should consider those two men who were most eloquent in both languages [i.e., Greek and Latin], Demosthenes and Cicero. Their speech was most prudent, and even though their rivals asserted that there were some things worthy of reprehension in their lives, praise for their powers of judgment and their prudence was granted them even by the consent of the envious. For, indeed, one cannot speak prudently unless one has thought prudently. It may happen that a person does not *do* what he thought about in advance, yet surely no one *says* what he has not thought about in advance. But let what has been said so far about the origins and usefulness of the places suffice.

(In the second chapter of this book, Agricola defines what he means by a place. He says that although human reason cannot comprehend individually all the things and events in the world, it can still arrange them according to the similarities involved in their substances, causes, effects, and so on: "These commonalities are therefore called places, since they con-tain in themselves both whatever can be said about a particular matter and every possible argument, so that in those places, as in a receptacle or a treasure house, have been stored all the instruments needed to produce belief. A place is therefore nothing other than a certain common sign for a thing that teaches us how to find out whatever is plausible in any sub-ject." The remainder of Book I is devoted to sorting out and describing the twenty-four places Agricola distinguishes.)

Book II

Chapter 1. How Preposterous the Dialecticians of Our Age Are, and Then of the Use of the Places and How One Goes About Obtaining Copious Amounts of Material from Them

It is well known that when Demosthenes, the leading figure of Greek elo-quence, was urging the Athenian people to make great preparations and ef-forts in order to wage war against Philip, King of Macedonia, he explained that whatever progress and increase in strength Philip enjoyed were not achieved so much by his own power as through the idleness of the Atheni-ans and the uselessness of their public speeches. Then, he made the follow-ing pronouncement, among others: all the rest of the world is accustomed to act after having taken counsel, whereas the Athenians, when they have already accepted a fait accompli, then they finally take counsel about it.[3] "What is the point of all this?" you ask. I answer that it does not seem to me possible to present the dialecticians of our time by means of an image that is apter and resembles them better than that one. For the only proper func-tion of dialectic is to enable one to construct plausible arguments about any

3. Agricola is referring to statements made by Demosthenes in his first and seventh *Philippics*.

subject whatsoever, insofar as the nature of the subject permits, and as I said before, this art comprises two parts. The first one teaches us how to find out arguments and is called invention; to it belongs all the discussion of places. The other part, called judgment, teaches us the particular form to give the argument we have found, that is, a sure rule for examining arguments by means of which, as with coins, one can distinguish whether they are either good, or bad and counterfeit. And while the first part has the function of giving counsel and helping us decide what to say about any particular subject, the second takes what one has decided to use as proof and turns it into an argument that produces belief in the auditor—just as if one were waging a military campaign. By contrast, when a contemporary dialectician has produced a complete argument in its proper form, an argument he has conducted in a rash and disorganized manner, if his adversary should then perhaps express doubt and say that the argument is either incoherent or invalid, our dialectician returns to the planning stage again, even though he has completed his task. Now he confuses invention and judgment, striving to show that he has argued well just because his argument was derived from a greater or similar genus or species. Nor do these wisest of men—for thus modesty on my part makes me denominate them—understand that no argument is necessarily valid just because it is derived from the species or the genus or from any of the other places, since one can make arguments that are absurd and totally invalid from all the places. Rather, an argument is valid only when the arrangement of its parts is such that they can be put into a syllogism or proved by some other form of argumentation by means of which one can show that its subjects are consistent and necessarily connected to one another.

I know, however, what some might respond to me—that one should feel less indignation over the decline of dialectic, considering the immense, filthy confusion that afflicts all studies, since all of them, like wild beasts who have burst out of their cages, have forced their way across the lawful boundaries of their neighbors, so that there is almost nothing that is learned nowadays in its proper place. Thus lawyers stammer out confused and convoluted rules for disputation. Thus the study of medicine has been reduced for the most part to questions of natural science that are irrelevant to its purpose. Thus natural philosophy has snatched mathematics for itself, whence it has become a verbose blustering about the "maximum" and the "minimum" and what they call the "method of doing calculations." And mathematics itself, which has little to do with the empty disputing of groups of people and has little capacity to produce clamor, and which, instead, content with some sand and a stick to draw in it, seeks a mute proof for the eyes rather than a chattering one for the ears—mathematics itself has been deserted, though for that reason, just like the mysteries, which are inaccessible to the profane, it has been the least contaminated. But what should one say about theology? If today you were to take away from it metaphysics, natural philosophy, and dialectic, you would leave it naked in the future, forsaken and incapable of defending its own name. Thus, when the people are to be taught and admonished to be religious, just, and continent, then from all of those arts some completely tangled disputation is produced that just wastes time and wounds the ears of the listeners with empty noise. These theologians, like boys who are accustomed to propounding riddles, teach in such a way that when they have finished, they do not know what they have taught any more than those who are listening know what they have learned. I myself have heard these complaints from the most serious and learned men, whom either their advanced age or the great sharpness of their intelligence has urged to a better course, and who take it most ill that the order of all these most beautiful arts has been upset and their individual elements confused with one another—something which, as I would not dare to affirm it to be true, so I would most fervently wish it to be false.

(The remainder of chapter 1 is taken up with Agricola's complaint that dialecticians ignore the study of the places or treat them in a confused manner.)

Chapter 2. In What Order the Subjects to Be Explicated in This Book Are to Be Treated, and What Dialectic Is

Our purpose in this book is to teach the use of the places, that is—to say the same thing more plainly—to explain how to develop that verbal skill called dialectic. It seems to us that we can do this most agreeably if we show what its material is, what tools it uses, and how it goes about handling things. By material, I mean the subject matter of which we speak; by tool, the language we use to explain what we want to say about that subject; and by handling, how these things are prepared and what is suitable for each subject.

To see all this more easily, it would be best to define at the start what dialectic is and for what use it is destined, since how it is used will constitute its end. . . . Some have thought that dialectic is one of the arts, while others have called it a certain faculty, but to call it one or the other should really not trouble us at the present moment. Common opinion accepts it as an art, and in our common speech we call it the art of discourse, and books written about it use that phrase as a title. Now, it would certainly be improper to exclude from the number of the arts the one that is the steadfast leader of the rest and without whose defense the others could not protect their boundaries very easily. If an art is, as some have defined it, a gathering together of many observations about a single subject for the sake of some useful purpose, or, as others say, the correct method of doing things, then no one will hesitate to call dialectic an art, for it gathers together many observations about how an argument is to be found and then judged once you have found it, and it teaches the correct method of making those arguments, to the extent that the word "making" is appropriate here. And surely dialectic is useful, if we think that being mistaken, being deceived, and taking true things for false and false for true are the opposite of useful. Still, sometimes the dialectician errs and teaches false things for true ones. That happens indeed, but sometimes a steersman overturns his boat and a doctor kills his patient: these are faults of the men, not the arts. And it is all the more readily to be admitted that dialectic is useful, since those who mislead by means of speech frequently do so through cunning and without any knowledge of the art, so that the one who is deceived, if he had understood the art, would not have allowed that to happen at all, or at least only infrequently. Truly, just as all the other arts, which were invented as remedies for human needs, could not provide help in troubles unless they were first fully understood, so dialectic, since for the most part it is concerned with the means by which we may avoid logical snares and deception in speech, must necessarily reveal those traps and show in how many varied ways a person can be caught in them. Then, if anyone decided to use the tricks that he learned from this art, that is not the fault of the art, which shows us how to avoid things that we ought to flee, but of wickedness, which desires things that ought to be avoided. For evils are to be exposed so that we may beware of them, even if no artist has knowledge of all the cures. Therefore, let it be granted to us that dialectic is an art.

(Agricola goes on to argue that the function of dialectic is to enable us to speak with plausibility on any conceivable subject.)

Chapter 3. What the Goal of Dialectic Is

From this vantage point it is hardly going to be difficult to see what the goal of dialectic is to which all its parts are to be directed. For if the goals of the arts are the ends for which they are learned—for instance, the goal of those arts studied for the sake of contemplation is contemplation, the goal of those studied in order to form character is probity, and the goal of those studied for any particular practical activity is the activity itself at which they are aimed—then it will not be surprising that the goal of dialectic is to speak in a plausible manner about the subject proposed, since the art has been established for this one purpose alone, to wit, as I said at the start, to teach the listener something. Nevertheless, this notion is not to be taken to mean that any person who teaches, using any sort of method, performs the function of the dialectician. For although the grammarian who explicates the story of a poet, reviews history, or interprets words also teaches, and even the individual who responds "yes" or "no" when someone asks him a question is teaching, nothing done by either one of these persons pertains to dialectic. Indeed, since such persons are satisfied if the listener understands them—something which, as we said before, depends on following the precepts of clear and correct speech—then they will rest content within the bounds of grammar, which teaches such things. But if a person teaches with the intention of awakening belief by means of his speech and in order to draw the mind of the auditor to him through his words, then insofar as he does this, he is carrying on the business of the dialectician.

(In the remainder of this chapter, Agricola distinguishes between clarity of language, which he says concerns the grammarian and the rhetorician, and clarity of concepts as well as their arrangement, which he assigns to the dialectician. In chapter 4 he initially argues that teaching is not distinct from moving and delighting the auditor. He then discusses how dramatists, historians, and orators arouse the emotions, and offers specific examples of how Cicero produces the feeling of pity in his orations. Next, he turns to the issue of the delight that speech produces, claiming that it is a matter of making appeals to the idiosyncratic responses of each individual listener's appetites. Delight, he says, is thus not the end or goal of speech, for it does not depend on speech but on the mind of the listener. Finally, in the remainder of Book II, Agricola analyzes the various classes of general questions to which all arguments can be referred and which constitute the actual subject matter of dialectic.)

Book III

Chapter 1. What an Emotion Is, Whence It Arises, and by What Means It Moves Us, Then How the Emotions Are Divided, and from What Source Orators Have Earned the Greatest Praise

Since this is the place to speak of the emotions and I promised in my earlier considerations that I was going to do so, I will indicate briefly their nature and function, so that when a person who desires to practice invention has mastered them, he will have them as the little targets, so to speak, at which his arguments, like darts, are to be aimed. An emotion seems to me nothing other than a certain impulse of the mind by which we are impelled either to desire or reject something more vehemently than we do when our minds are quiet. Thus every emotion arises from our desire either to seek out or to avoid things. And we seek whatever is good in reality or appears to be good, and by contrast, we avoid those things that are harmful or believed to be so. Not only are we affected by things that we deem good or evil for ourselves, but we also grieve, rejoice, grow angry, and feel pity about the condition of another person.

In every emotion there are two factors that especially move us: the thing that happens or is expected, and the person to whom it happens. Therefore, when something happens, whether good or ill, to a person who deserves it, we rejoice, whereas we are annoyed if it happens to someone who does not deserve it. And if the latter indeed gets something good, then we feel envy or anger, but if it is bad, then we feel pity and enter into a comradeship of sorrow. However, with those emotions that concern one's own person, what has happened generally suffices by itself to arouse feeling, and only a very brief consideration is given to the person involved. For there is hardly anyone who does not favor himself and persuade himself, if anything turns out well for him, that he deserves it, and if otherwise, that he does not.

Sometimes a person is part of an event—not the one to whom it happened, but the one who caused it—so that frequently we judge something good or bad, not so much on the basis of what happened, as on that of the disposition and intention of the person who did it. Hence, the saying of the comic writer: "You should know this one thing, that I did not do it for the sake of insult, but out of love." And from the same writer, in another place: "When it is needed, you should rejoice to receive a benefit from any man whatsoever. But it is especially pleasing only if the benefit fits the person who gives it."[4] When one treats the event, the person is to be considered under the place of the agent, although sometimes the person pertains to the place of the subject, as, for instance, when someone loves another on account of his virtues or beauty, and likewise hates vices and ugliness in him. Virtue and vice and the rest are things that, once seen, especially move the mind, and the person becomes merely a kind of passage to them, since we are moved by them even without the person, and would think that the person did not matter at all to us without those things. And since the person is the subject of those things, when we are considering them, he is to be put in that place [i.e., the place of the subject]. However, because the emotions associated with them seem to include the persons, and the name of the emotion is attributed to the person, and despite the fact that our primary concern should be for virtue or beauty, without which we would neglect the person, it is nevertheless the person himself who is said to be loved, hated, envied. Therefore, in these matters we often put the person in place of the thing, and situate the thing among the places of the person.

It makes no difference to the emotions whether something actually is the case, or just seems so. For every emotion is rash and inconsiderate; it seizes the mind, and frequently one emotion grows directly out of another. Thus it happens that the mind reaches decisions in all matters not on the basis of truth, but judges them good or bad on the basis of opinion, which has been implanted in it erroneously because of some other emotion, or which it has arrived at by way of some trivial and worthless persuasive argument. Some of the emotions are more enduring, since they have been reinforced by long use, such as love, hate, envy, grief, fear, and especially all those that have taken possession of the mind through the persuasion of some weighty cause. Others are more short-lived and sudden, and are stirred up both by other causes and by the wind of speech, as fire is in straw. And just as these also burst out unexpectedly, so they then often settle down again swiftly and for ever so slight a cause.

Although speech is capable of arousing all the emotions, and there is no one of them that does not claim a place somewhere for itself in speech,

4. Terence, *Eunuchus*, 877–78, and *Adelphoe*, 254–55.

nevertheless two of them have won the greatest praise among orators: hate and pity. To be sure, in the books he composed about rhetoric, Aristotle enumerates many of the emotions, and describes in most copious detail what each one is, and how it arises and is extinguished in turn, for that great man was most ingenious and extremely knowledgeable about everything.[5] Whoever wishes to learn such things will find them waiting to be searched out in his works. It seems to me that for a person who is not entirely devoid of common sense, once he has measured the subject of which he is to speak against the mind of his auditor, and considered the effect he wishes to achieve in speaking, there will be no mystery about what sort of emotion to use in order to take possession of the auditor. Then, when he has united the things to the persons, as we just mentioned above, he will easily deduce from the thing whether it is good or bad, and from the person, whether he has deserved it or not.

Chapter 2. Of the Three Ways to Handle the Emotions

The emotions are treated in three ways. First, we may express an emotion by means of speech, that is, employ the words of someone who is angry, fearful, in love, or grieving, as one sees in almost every utterance in comedy and tragedy. The latter genre, however, involves more fiery feelings, since it includes more prominent characters and loftier subjects, whereas the former involves feelings that are quieter and closer to tranquillity, since it takes its characters from the middling part of society. In this method of treating the emotions, it is necessary for language to express thoughts, vows, complaints, desires, prayers, and disputes, in each case according to the nature of the emotion involved. But what must principally be achieved by this form of speaking is that language itself should imitate the tumult and disturbance of an excited mind. And indeed, in this imitating of emotion has been placed that power that we sometimes call the coloring of a speech. Thus, although many people may say the same thing whether they are engaged in exposition or argument, still one of them will take on the coloring of someone who is merely advising, another that of an angry man, another that of a complainer, and yet another that of someone displaying pity. We see in satire that this same technique has been practiced by the three writers still extant, Horace, Persius, and Juvenal, and that the same subject is treated by them, to wit, the improving of life and manners and the reprehending of vice, although each has sought out his own coloring. Horace affected the image of someone laughing and, as he himself says, aiming at "hitting off faults with playful frankness."[6] Persius put on a persona that was more severe and close to that of the philosopher: thus he scolds while teaching and teaches while scolding. Juvenal generally presents the appearance of someone

---

5. See the *Rhetoric*, II.i–xi.
6. Horace asks who would forbid a laughing man to speak the truth; see his *Sermones*, I.i.24–25. The quotation Agricola attributes to him actually comes from Persius, *Saturae*, V.16.

indignant and angry. As a result, a loftier and more fluent mode of poetical composition was more suitable for him, as were generally a sharper wit and a more unbridled freedom of speech. Nor would I think that that decorum of speech, which Cicero praised in his *Orator* so greatly and followed everywhere with such great care, consists of anything other than the coloring derived from this imitation [of emotion], which has aptly and carefully been fitted to the persona of the speaker and is based on the appraisal he has made of the listener and of the facts.[7] However, to say more about these things pertains rather to the realm of style than to that of invention.

The second method of handling the emotions is to describe someone who is aroused by some emotion, explaining what he did and what he said in such a way that from all these details the emotion involved can be grasped. Although authors supply many examples of this method in many places, a special one can be found in our tragedian's *Oedipus:* "After he grasped what the fates predicted and his unspeakable breeding . . . ," and so on—the citation is well known.[8] This method also includes our showing how we or someone else is or has been moved by some emotion that can be explained in either way you please, that is, by means of either argument or exposition. However, there is a great difference between this method and the preceding one, since from the preceding one we merely take on a coloring that we can display even though doing something else. For although someone who scolds generally acts as if he were angry, still we can scold and wax indignant, complain and reprehend, all while playing the role of lover. For instance, Vergil's Dido first complains, "Did you really hope to be able to hide so much wickedness, you wretch?" and then blazes out in anger, "Your parent was no goddess, nor was Dardanus the founder of your tribe."[9] Everything here has the coloring of a woman mad with love. However, in this second method [of handling the emotions] it is not the coloring of the speech, but the subject matter itself—in other words, that which we are striving to teach—that provides the content. For in this case our speech is employed to show, in one way or another, that someone has been moved.

The third way of handling the emotions involves our attempt to affect the mind of the auditor: our speech does not strive to make our own emotion evident, but seeks to elicit and excite that of another person. And this is what those people place second who feel that the orator has three offices—teaching, moving, and delighting. For, as we said, every emotion, if it is actually concerned with another person, arises out of the nature of the event that has happened or is expected to happen, according to whether, in the first place, the event is judged good or evil, and then, whether the person is judged to be deserving or undeserving of what happened. In the third place,

7. *Orator*, xxi.70–xxii.74.

8. This is the beginning of the Messenger's speech about Oedipus's final judgment on himself and his self-blinding; see Seneca, *Oedipus*, 915–16.

9. *Aeneid*, IV.305–6, 356.

there is often the issue of the person who has brought the event about either through action or advice. Although as far as the emotions that affect our own being are concerned, the event itself suffices to move us; frequently the person who caused it is also added into the equation. With these same emotions, where questions of desert or the lack of it are involved, often we also bring our own person into play, in case it can offer something noteworthy in one respect or another. From these things, then, whether taken singly or all together, we derive our arguments according to the condition of the case and the nature of the emotion we seek to arouse. . . .

Arguments are not to be conducted, however, as if we were striving to prove that something should be pitied or envied, or should be the source of anger or sympathy. It suffices to show, with regard to the matter and the person, merely what the nature of the emotion requires: that the matter is good or evil, and that the person is deserving or not deserving of what happened. Because if this is done correctly and scrupulously, and the mind of the auditor is shaped so that it can be conquered by speech, then the emotion will follow of its own accord. For emotion is impetuous, and it is merely necessary to have given it an initial impulse. For the rest, when once it has been given that impetus, it rushes down the slope making a headlong flight like a torrent descending from a mountaintop.

(In chapter 3, Agricola explains how speech may be amplified and diminished. Beginning with amplification, he notes how the emotions can be manipulated through such things as references to persons' good qualities and the piling up of descriptive terms. He also speaks of what the Greeks call enargeia, *that is, of making something vivid for an audience. The technique of diminishing things is simply the inverse of amplifying them.)*

Chapter 4. The Things That Delight Us Are Twofold, to Wit: Partly What We Perceive through the Senses and Partly What We Perceive through the Mind; and the Pleasure That We Derive from Speech Is Generally Twofold, in That It Arises Either from the Subject or from the Nature of the Speech Itself. Then, Which Subjects Delight the Senses and Which Ones, the Mind, and How the Auditor Is to Be Given Delight by the Nature of the Speech

I must now complete this portion of my work, and since we have added instructions about moving people to our theory of speaking, it seems right to include the things that make a speech pleasing, even if we taught elsewhere that no definite method of invention could be adapted for producing delight and that explaining this subject was more the property of the rhetorician than the dialectician. Nevertheless, since delight in a speech also arises from things, and things are chiefly assigned to invention, let us therefore also say a few words about this subject.

Since delight, as we have said, is an excitation of the cognitive power, and since there are two cognitive powers, namely the senses and the mind, then the things that cause delight are of two sorts: those perceived by the senses, and those perceived by the mind. Now, those people who live more for their senses, being possessed by corporal pleasures and having spirits enslaved to their bodies, tend to pursue the form of delight that offers itself to the senses. By contrast, those who have loftier and more erect spirits and have devoted all their care to the mind will despise the pleasures of the body as hostile and dangerous to their purpose, and pursue only what gives delight to the mind. Those who are in the middle between these two think that each ought to be given its proper portion, and they are thus taken by both sorts of pleasure. Every man is also delighted by the memory of those things that he enjoyed when he experienced and perceived them, so that with him one may certainly achieve grace in speech simply by referring to the things involved.

On the whole, the pleasure that one takes in speech is twofold: one part of it derives from the things that are the subject of the discourse, and the other from the kind of speech involved. That which gives pleasure to the senses is known, for each sense is delighted by what is proper to its nature, as the eyes are by the brightest colors, the ears by rather mild sounds, and each of the remaining senses by its particular object. There are certain things, however, that also reach as far as the mind, although they are also counted among the pleasures of the senses because they are closer to them by nature. These include: feast days, spectacles, games, choral dances, banquets, gardens sown with flowers, the grace of springtime, rivers flowing through verdant meadows, the first beauty of youth, bodies conspicuous for their loveliness, love relationships, jokes, harmonious songs, dances, and all the pursuits of happier years and minds. Still, of these things, those are really noble that hold the interest of the eyes and ears; others are more crass; and a great number are even quite vulgar, so that some cannot even be mentioned without our making some excuse to protect our honor.

Since the pursuit of the true and the good is necessarily proper to the mind, it is delighted by everything that teaches and is great, marvelous, surprising, unexpected, and unheard of; by the investigation of recondite matters, knowledge of antiquity, and acquaintance with things that are far away; by the exceptional deeds and words of great men; and by the most excellent acts of virtue of every sort. To speak about these things, each in its own way, unfailingly makes an oration pleasant. If the subject of which one speaks is somewhat harsh and sad, then the ears are accustomed to seek out the [pleasant] things I have just mentioned. Either comparisons are taken from those things as the means by which we explain our subject; or arguments are sought out so that, as one unfolds them, one must necessarily employ something like those [pleasant] things; or we slip quite freely toward them in a digression, which is done most conveniently when, by means of a deceptive transition, we arrive at those things in such a way that we do not seem to have pursued them, but to have been forced to go to them. In fact, a transition is effected most aptly when we find some general topic to which there is a ready way leading out from our subject, and from which there is at the same time an easy access to the topic about which we wish to digress. For instance, if someone who speaks in praise of music wants to digress into a description of the charms of spring, he might say that the muses, who rejoice in the carefree freedom of the spirit, seek out forests and rivers. Here, since the speaker has already got forests and rivers as well as the music that rejoices in them, he can easily digress into a description of spring, since the greatest beauty of such things appears in that season, and the most extraordinary pleasure can be taken from them then. And so, he will explain how great the beauty is of all green and growing things and what charm there is in them, how harmonious the chattering of birds among the leaves, how pleasing the murmur of streams gliding through the meadows, and other things of this sort. If, in connection with this theme, he wants to speak of the great labor involved in running the state, he will be well prepared to talk about how music lightens cares and refreshes the mind and to connect such things with the administration of the state, since they are especially necessary for one who is involved in politics, who is burdened by such great labors and sustains so many cares—which the speaker will then enumerate. There are examples of this procedure in many writers, and especially in the dialogues of Plato and Lucian: we see how, having begun with an introduction quite removed from the subject proposed, they creep little by little and with stealthy steps to that which they are aiming at.

(Agricola goes on to analyze an example of the use of digression in one of Cicero's orations.)

We said that the second thing by means of which speech delights us is its style. In this case, the first requirement is that a speech should contain passionate feelings, colloquies among people, wise counsels, and events with unexpected outcomes.[10] Although these things might seem to pertain to the subject matter, nevertheless it is from the language of the speech itself that people derive what delights them. A proof of this is that if we see these same things, for the most part they not only fail to delight, but actually offend us. Therefore, in a speech the source of pleasure is not so much the subject itself as the mutations of language by means of which it is expressed. And just as in a picture a great many things are most pleasing because of imitation alone, and we do not marvel so much at the thing that has been portrayed in it as at the genius of the imitator, so the same thing happens in a speech. There, when words have been attributed to persons in accordance with their nature and condition, when an image of all the thoughts and passions involved has been created so that the speech makes things seem not to be

10. The edition I am translating reads: a speech should contain "the feelings of love" ("motus amoris"). However, other editions refer to "passionate feelings" ("motus animorum"), and since the rest of the sentence does not deal with *specific* conversations, counsels, or events, I have opted for the more general phrase.

spoken, but done, and when the mind of the auditor, by means of a certain stark image, has been transported into the midst of the crush and stir of events, then all the credit must be given to language since everything has been done by its power rather than by the nature of the things themselves.

(In the remaining chapters of his work, Agricola discusses the uses of copia, *or abundance of speech, and of conciseness, and then turns to the topic of arrangement. He goes on to argue that other genres, including historical, pedagogical, and scientific writing, also belong to dialectic and rhetoric. He concludes by discussing how arguments are to be arranged and changed from one part of a speech to the next, provides certain cautions about what he has taught, and finally makes a case for the importance of practice and exercise.)*

[6]

Giovanni Pico della Mirandola

Giovanni Pico, count of Mirandola (1463–1494), an Italian philosopher and scholar, was, with Marsilio Ficino, the most important spokesman for Neoplatonism in the Renaissance. After being educated in Mirandola, a town near Ferrara, he studied canon law at Bologna and Aristotelian philosophy at Padua, whose university was a bastion of Scholasticism. Pico also studied in Florence and Paris, learning Hebrew, Arabic, and Aramaic as well as Latin and Greek. He investigated the Cabala with his Hebrew teachers and later attempted to use it to support Christian teachings. In 1486 he went to Rome where he proposed to defend in a public disputation 900 theses he drew from Latin, Greek, Hebrew, and Arabic thinkers. As a prelude to this disputation, he composed an oration, usually referred to as the "Oration on the Dignity of Man," which has since become his most famous work. Thirteen of his theses were declared heretical, however, and the disputation was halted. Pico attempted to defend his ideas in an *Apologia*, but was unsuccessful and fled to France. At the request of Lorenzo de' Medici, he was allowed to return to Florence, where he worked with Ficino in the Platonic Academy the former had founded in order to study and translate the works of Plato and his ancient followers. Pico was finally absolved of any suspicion of heresy in 1493. His works include the *Heptaplus*, an exposition of Genesis; *De ente et uno* (*On Being and the One*), part of a project attempting to reconcile Plato and Aristotle; and a treatise attacking astrologers, which was part of a larger work directed against the enemies of the Church. His letter to the Venetian humanist Ermolao Barbaro, translated here, is dated 3 June 1485, and reflects Pico's study of the Scholastics as well as his deep involvement with Plato from whom he derives a number of his arguments against rhetoric. The letter is something of a showpiece and may well be partly tongue in cheek; in a letter replying to it, Barbaro says as much. Philip Melanchthon, whose *Praise of Eloquence* is included in this volume, also composed a letter in reply to Pico. The text of the letter comes from Giovanni Pico della Mirandola and Gian Francesco Pico, *Opera omnia* (Basel, 1557; reprint, Hildesheim: Georg Olms, 1969), 351–58.

FROM GIOVANNI PICO DELLA MIRANDOLA TO HIS FRIEND ERMOLAO BARBARO, GREETINGS

I cannot be silent, my dear Ermolao, concerning what I feel about you, nor can I fail to feel what one should about a person in whom almost every single excellence could be found. But I wish I had the mental capacity to conceive you according to your merits, or that I had the power of speech so that I could express at some time what I think at all times. I know that what I have thought about you remains infinitely beneath the heights of your learning. You especially should know that whatever we say is by far inferior to what we think, that words are not adequate to the mind just as the mind falls short of things, and still, you think that I could ever hope to be able to describe your capacities although I cannot estimate their greatness. Everyone marvels at you, few match you, no one finds fault with you. Would that I had such felicity that what I write might produce some sort of image of my Ermolao. To pass over everything else in silence, it is marvelous how much that very style of yours, to which you are devoted even to a fault, affects me, how much it delights me. It is so learned, substantial, well arranged, erudite, hammered into shape, full of wit; in it there is nothing common, nothing vulgar, nothing trivial, whether one considers words or matter. I and our friend Poliziano often read whatever letters we have from you, whether written to us or to others, and the more recent ones always compete with the earlier ones, and new delights bloom luxuriantly while we read, so that we scarcely have room to catch our breath in the midst of our almost perpetual acclamations. It's marvelous how you persuade and how you force the mind of your reader to go wherever you wish.

As I have always been impressed by your other letters, so have I been by your most recent one to me, in which you now attack those barbarian philosophers who you say are considered filthy, rude, and uncultured by the general populace; they were people who did not really live during their lives, and are not to live on now that they are dead—or who, if they were living now, would be doing so in suffering and shame. Like Hercules I am enraged; I am so ashamed about my studies and regret them so much—for I have been involved with them now for a six-year period—that I wish I had done anything else, rather than to have striven so laboriously in a matter that will come to nothing. I have lost, I say, my better years and so many sleepless nights on Thomas [Aquinas], John Scotus, Albertus [Magnus], and Averroës, time I could have used to achieve something in good literature. I have been thinking, in order to console myself, that if any of those men were to come back to life now, they might produce a speech in which, since they are skilled in argumentation, they would defend their own cause with some sort of reason. Finally, perhaps to defend his barbarousness in a way as little barbarous as possible, it might occur to one of them, who is slightly more eloquent, to speak thus:

"We have been famous in our lives, Ermolao, and afterwards we will live on not in the schools of the grammarians and the pedagogues, but in the circles of the philosophers and the gatherings of the wise, where one considers and disputes not about Andromache's mother, Niobe's children, and light trifles of that sort, but about the meaning of human and divine matters. We have been so subtle, acute, and sharp-witted in thinking about, inquiring into, and resolving these things, that we seem perhaps sometimes to have been too solicitous and overly scrupulous—as if anyone can be too scrupulous or solicitous in hunting down the truth! And if in these matters anyone should accuse us of being dull and slow, I would really like that person, whoever he may be, to come to us and learn for himself that the barbarians have had Mercury not on their tongue, but in their breast, and that, even though they lacked eloquence, they have not been lacking in wisdom.[1] He will find out that we should not be blamed for not having yoked eloquence to wisdom, since it is wicked to have joined them at all. For who would not condemn as detestable curly hair and makeup in an upright virgin?[2] Who would not detest it in a Vestal? There is such a great opposition between the functions of the orator and the philosopher that they could not contradict one another more. For what is the office of the rhetor other than to lie, deceive, circumvent, practice sleight-of-hand tricks. It's your business, as you say, to turn black into white and white into black as you will; by means of speech to raise up, cast down, amplify, and diminish whatever you wish; and finally, to transform things themselves, as if by the magical force of eloquence, which you boast about, so that they assume whatever face and dress you wish, not appearing what they are in actuality, but what your will wants them to be—and even though they are not really transformed, they nevertheless appear that way to your auditors. All this is nothing other than sheer lying, sheer imposture, sheer trickery, since by its nature it enlarges things through amplification or reduces them through diminishment, and by producing the deceptive harmony of words, like so many masks and simulacra, it dupes the minds of your auditors while it flatters them. Can there be any affinity between this and the philosopher whose entire activity is consumed in discovering the truth and demonstrating it to others?

"Add to this that no one would have any faith in us were we to affect verbal elegances and beauties as if we had little confidence in the things we spoke about, and, lacking that solid support, we sought to drag people to

---

1. Mercury is the god of eloquence.
2. I have consistently translated as "makeup" the Latin *fucus*, which refers to a white pigment used by the Romans to color their faces.

our opinion by means of allurements of this sort. It's for this reason you read the Scriptures, written in a rustic rather than an elegant manner: because nothing is more indecorous and offensive in any matter where knowing the truth is involved than all that overly elaborate kind of speech. That is fitting for law cases, not for studying nature and the heavens. It is not for those who are occupied with such matters in the academy, but in the state where what is said and done is weighed in the people's judgment, for whom flowers are far heavier than fruit. You know this, don't you? Is not everything here connected together by a common thread?

"We confess that eloquence is an elegant thing, full of enticements and pleasure, but it is neither fitting nor pleasing in a philosopher. Who would not approve a delicate walk, clever hands, and playful eyes in an actor or a dancer? In a citizen, in a philosopher, who would not disapprove, blame, and abominate them? If we see a girl who is polished in her manners and loquacious, we will praise her, will kiss her tenderly. These things in a matron we will condemn and prosecute. Hence, it is not we who are tactless, but they, who put on bacchanalias at the feet of a Vestal, who dishonor the gravity and chastity of philosophical matters as if with games and curling irons. Actually, what Sinesius said about adolescence can be said quite fittingly of oratory: a long-haired speech is always sodomitical.[3] That's why we prefer ours to be shaggy, stuck together, and tangled rather than beautifully kempt, and either known to be or suspected of being filthy. Besides, the robe of Athena was not revealed, but its profane use was kept separate from her sacred rites.

"Everything else may be of no consequence, but this one thing is really true: nothing can be further from the profession of philosopher, in whatever respect, than that which smells of pomp and arrogance. Socrates used to say that Sicyonian shoes were easy and well-suited to one's feet, but not at all fitting for Socrates.[4] The conditions of the civilian and the philosopher are not the same, whether one is talking, as it were, about the table or about speech. The philosopher makes use of these things as far as necessity dictates; the civilian uses them also for the pleasantness they entail. If the latter neglects this consideration, he will not be a civilian, and if the former affects it, he will not be a philosopher. If Pythagoras could have lived without food, he would have abstained from vegetables, too; if he could have unfolded his ideas by his looks, or at least by some effort less than the labor of speaking, he would not have spoken at all, so far was he from polishing and adorning his language. Let us especially beware of the person who, allured by a colored complexion, makes the reader tarry at the level of the skin, never penetrating to the marrow and the blood, which we have often seen hidden beneath a face dyed white with makeup. We have seen such things, I say, in all

3. *Praise of Baldness*, 23. I have translated as "sodomitical" the Latin *cinaedus*, which refers to the passive partner, typically a youth, in a homosexual relationship.
4. See *De oratore*, I.liv.231.

those who have taken to detaining the reader on the surface of things by means of varied rhythms and harmonies, since there is nothing inside that is not empty and vain. If a philosopher did this, Musonius would exclaim that it was not a philosopher speaking, but a flutist playing.[5] Therefore, it should not be counted a vice in us not to have done such things, for it would have been a vice in us to have done them.

"We seek *what* to write, not *how;* or rather, we seek how to do so without the pomp and flowers of speech. We do not want it to be delightful, beautiful, and eloquent, but useful, grave, and venerable; it should achieve majesty by inspiring dread, rather than charm because of its delicacy. We do not expect the applause of the theater because a balanced or rhythmical clause has caressed the ear, because this is witty, that is charming. But we do expect instead the silence that comes from the wonder of those few who look more deeply into something, whether that something is extracted from the inner temple of nature or brought down to men from the palace of Jove, or indeed something so well argued that it cannot be defended against, so well defended against that it cannot be attacked. Let them marvel at us as wise in inquiring into things, as careful in exploring them, subtle in contemplating them, grave in judging, fully engaged in making syntheses, handy at analysis. Let them marvel at the brevity of our style, pregnant with matters many and great; at our most abstruse opinions, expressed in accessible words, that are full of questions as well as solutions; at how fit we are, how well trained, to remove ambiguities, to dissolve difficulties, to smooth out the convoluted, to weaken false matters with mind-bending syllogisms, and to confirm the true with them.

"By these means, Ermolao, we have preserved our memory from oblivion thus far and do not doubt to preserve it in the future. If, as you say, the common crowd holds us to be vulgar, wild, uncivilized, this is to be counted as our glory, not a matter of reproach: we do not write for the common crowd, but for you and those like you. We do not behave differently than the ancients who kept uneducated people away from the mysteries by means of enigmas and the disguising of fables, and we have become accustomed to scaring them away from our ceremonial feasts, which they cannot avoid polluting by means of the rather irritating skin of words they use. Those who want to hide treasures, if they cannot put them out of the way, cover them up with junk or rubbish so that passersby, unless considered worthy of such gifts, will not take them. Philosophers make the same effort to hide their subject from the people, by whom it would not be fitting for it to be approved, let alone understood. It can hardly be decorous for their writings to have something theatrical, applause-provoking, or popular about them, because they would seem, finally, to be accommodating themselves to the judgment of the multitude.

5. For Musonius's remark, see Aulus Gellius, *Noctes atticae*, V.i.1.

"But you want me to give you an idea of what our sort of speech is like. It is the very same thing as that of the Silenuses of our Alcibiades: there were images of those figures with a shaggy face, ugly and despicable, but inside they were full of gems and of rare and precious furnishings.[6] Thus, if you looked at them from outside, you would see a wild beast; if you looked deeply within, you would recognize something divine. But, you will say, our ears cannot bear a speech whose texture is now harsh, now disconnected, always inharmonious; they cannot tolerate barbarous words whose sound alone almost fills us with fear. Oh, you delicate one, when you approach flute-players and singers, be all ears, but when you approach philosophers, call yourself away from the senses and return into yourself, into the inner sanctuary of the spirit and the retreat of the mind; assume the famous ears of the philosopher [Apollonius] of Tyana, with which, when he had transcended his body, he used to listen not to the terrestrial Marsyas, but to the celestial Apollo who was composing on his divine zither a cosmic melody in ineffable modes.[7] If, with such ears, you would nibble at the words of philosophers, they would seem to you honey-sweet, the envy of Nestor.[8]

"But let us put aside these overly lofty thoughts. To be disgusted by the less polished eloquence of a most subtly disputing philosopher is not so much a matter of a delicate stomach as of one that is unaccustomed to such food. It is no different than if someone were offended at Socrates because he taught ethics when his shoe was untied or his toga on crooked, or if someone were to get upset because of a badly cut fingernail. Cicero does not call for eloquence in a philosopher, but that he have sufficient knowledge and be adequate in his teaching.[9] Since he was a prudent and erudite man, he knew that our chief business was to compose our minds, not our words; that we should take pains lest reason, not speech, err; that we should seek the word as thought, not the word as expression. It is praiseworthy for us to have the Muses in our minds, not on our lips, for we wouldn't want what is in our minds to sound harsh because of anger, or feeble because of lust. Finally, there should be no discord in that innate harmony by which our minds are regulated melodiously. When Plato understood that that harmony was often destroyed by the theatricality of the poets, he eliminated all of them from his Republic and left it to be governed by philosophers, who would certainly soon be condemned to exile themselves if they had imitated the poets' luxuriance of speech.[10]

6. See Plato, *Symposium*, 216d–217a.
7. Marsyas was a skillful flute player who challenged Apollo to a music contest and, when he lost, was flayed alive; see Ovid, *Metamorphoses*, VI.382–400. In his *Apollonius of Tyana*, Philostratus speaks of how the philosopher had social intercourse with the gods, including Apollo (I.1), and of how he was able to appear to people outside his body.
8. Nestor is an old man in the *Iliad* famed for his eloquence.
9. See, perhaps, *De finibus*, I.v.15.
10. See the *Republic*, X.i.595a–viii.608b.

"But Lucretius will insist that even if the treatises of philosophy do not need the amenity of speech on their own account, nevertheless it ought to be used in order to disguise the austerity of their arguments.[11] In the same way, wormwood repels diseases by itself, but it is covered with honey in order to trick unsuspecting children. Perhaps you would have to do it this way, Lucretius, if you were writing for children; if for the crowd, you would have to do it thus since you would be offering a cup not merely of wormwood, but of the purest poison. But we must use a far different method, since, as we said before, we do not seek to allure the crowd, but to frighten it off; nor do we offer them wormwood to drink, but nectar.

"Lactantius will maintain that the truth is sufficiently well established to influence more strongly the minds of even rather older auditors if it comes equipped with its own force and is adorned with the light of eloquence.[12] O Lactantius, if you had busied yourself more with Sacred Scripture and less with imaginary disputes, you would not have said this, and you might have supported our views no less well, perhaps, than you have destroyed those of others. For tell me, I ask you, what moves people more strongly and is more persuasive than the reading of Sacred Scripture. No, the crude and rustic words of the Law do not move, do not persuade—they compel, stir up, convey force; they are alive, animated, flaming, sharp, penetrating to the depths of the spirit, transforming the entire man through their marvelous power. Alcibiades said that he was not moved at all by the elaborate, brilliant orations of Pericles, but the naked, simple words of Socrates filled him with rapture, placed beyond himself, and willy-nilly made him do what Socrates prescribed.[13] But why do I waste words in a matter already granted? If an auditor is not a fool, what can he hope for but treachery from a speech wearing makeup? He is persuaded principally by three things: the life of the speaker, the truth of the case, and the sobriety of the oration. These are the things, Lactantius, that bring others to put their faith in a philosopher; that is, if he has been good and truthful and has sought that sort of discourse that does not flow from the pleasant woods of the Muses, but from the horrendous cave in which Heraclitus said truth lies hidden.[14]

"But someone will say, 'Come on, friend; let's examine these matters without contentiousness. Wisdom is something to be reverenced as divine in itself, nor does it need any adornment beyond itself. Yet why grudge adding things to it? Who can deny that what is decorous in itself becomes more decorous if it is adorned?' I deny this, friend, in many, many ways. There are lots of things whose splendor you would indeed eliminate, not make more

---

11. Lucretius says that writers must give pleasure in order to make their teaching palatable just as doctors put honey on the rim of glasses containing bitter medicine; see *De rerum natura*, IV.11–25.

12. See *Divine Institutes*, III.i.

13. See Plato, *Symposium*, 215c.

14. There is no such statement among the remaining fragments of Heraclitus.

brilliant, if you added anything to them. That is, they are things that are in their optimal state by their own nature so that they cannot be changed from that state except to become worse. A marble house cannot be painted, unless you cover it first with plaster, but you would lessen its dignity and beauty in doing so. It's no different with wisdom and the things philosophers discuss: they are not clarified, but obscured, by a covering of plaster. What more need I say? Isn't it widely known that beautiful appearances are disfigured by white face-paint? In general, whenever we put any beautiful covering over something else, it hides what it covers and shows only itself. Therefore, if that which was extraneous before should now be on display, then that thing, no matter what it is, will have produced loss, not gain. For that reason philosophy displays herself naked, open to view, entirely exposed to everyone's eyes; she is delighted to be subjected to judgment and knows she has the wherewithal to be pleasing when seen from every direction. Should you wish just a part of her, you would diminish her beauty and merit by just that much; she wants to keep herself clean and pure; whatever you would add to her would taint her, adulterate her, and change her character; she stands firm like a point that is whole and indivisible. Therefore, we shouldn't play with tropes or words, run riot, play the wanton with metaphors, or carry artifice to daring lengths in a matter so serious and of such moment, in which it would be a scandal to remove, add, or change anything.

"'But,' you will say, 'come on, we grant that it is not your place to speak ornately, but it is certainly your place—though you do not boast about the matter—at least to explain things in Latin, and if you do not use flowery words, you nevertheless do use those that are appropriate. I don't demand an elegant oration from you, but I don't want one that is filthy or perfumed or that smells like a goat. If it need not be polished, it shouldn't be neglected either. We don't need something that aims to delight, but we do complain about what is offensive.'

"It's good: you're already weakening toward us. Still, I would like us to determine what that good Latinity is that you say is the one thing philosophers ought to employ, but fail to do so. For example, if it should happen that one must speak of how man is "brought forth" (*produci*) by the sun, our colleagues will say that he is "caused" (*causari*) by it. You will shout that that is not Latin, and that's true up to a point; it is even truer when you say that that is not the Roman mode of speech. But your argument fails when you conclude that it is not correct. An Arab and an Egyptian will say the same thing, although not in Latin, and yet they will speak correctly. For the names of things are established by convention or by nature. If it is a matter of convention, in the sense that a society of men all share the opinion that one particular thing is to be called by a particular word, then they are certainly naming that thing correctly among themselves. So, what prevents those philosophers, whom you proclaim barbarians, from having agreed upon a single norm for speech, which is as sacred among them as the Roman language is among you? There is no reason why you should call their speech incorrect and yours correct, if the determining of names is entirely arbitrary. What if you do not wish to dignify their speech with the appellation 'Roman'? You could call it Gallic, British, Spanish, or even what is commonly denominated Parisian. When they speak to you, it will happen that you will laugh at them in many instances and will not understand them in many others. But the same thing will happen when you speak to them: 'If Anacharsis commits a solecism in Athens, the Athenians do so among the Scythians.'[15] But what if the correctness of names depends upon the nature of things; should we consult rhetors about this matter, or philosophers, who alone have examined and explored the nature of all things? Perhaps the ear rejects those names as somewhat harsh-sounding, yet reason accepts them as more cognate with the things themselves. But why did they have to invent a language, and despite being born among the Latins, not speak Latin? They could not do it, Ermolao; for while they were reading in the heavens the laws of the fates, the signs of events, and the order of the universe, while they were reading in the elements the vicissitudes of birth and death, the forces of simple substances and the composition of mixed ones, they could not, I say, note down at the same time the properties, laws, and particular features of the Roman language in Cicero, Pliny [the Younger], and Apuleius. They were seeking knowledge of what was in conformity with and what was repugnant to nature; they did not care in the meanwhile what the Romans thought about it.

"But for the time being let's say that you have the stronger position and grant that eloquence and wisdom may be bound tightly one to the other. The philosophers have separated wisdom from eloquence, while the historians, orators, and poets have separated eloquence from wisdom—something that caused Philostratus to grieve.[16] You have little doubt that the latter are going to live on in glorious fame, while the former will suffer punishment and abuse. But just look at what you are doing: Cicero himself prefers a wisdom without eloquence to a foolish loquacity.[17] In the case of money, we do not ask how a coin was minted, but of what material it is made. Nor is there anyone who does not prefer to have pure gold with a German stamp on it to a counterfeit one with a Roman symbol. People err who create discord between the heart and the tongue, but, as Cato says, aren't those foolish individuals, who are totally devoted to the tongue,

15. See Anacharsis, *Epistulae*, 1. No antique writer, including compilers such as Diogenes Laertius and Athenaeus, quotes this saying; so Pico's source for it is something of a mystery. However, Anacharsis's letter was published by Aldus Manutius in the edition of the *Epistulae graecae* he brought out in 1499; and since Manutius was also the publisher of the editions of Plato and the Neoplatonic philosophers produced by members of the Florentine Platonic Academy, it is possible that Pico had access to a manuscript of the letter.
16. See, perhaps, Philostratus, *Lives of the Sophists*, I.481 and 484.
17. See *De oratore*, III.xxxv.142.

nothing but dead glossaries?[18] We can live without a tongue, perhaps not comfortably, but in no way can we live without a heart. He is not humane who is unacquainted with polite learning, but he is not human who is unaware of philosophy. The most inarticulate wisdom can be of use; witless eloquence, like a sword in the hand of a madman, cannot help but threaten the greatest harm.[19]

"Therefore, you will respond, statues are to be commended not for their form, but for the material they are made of, and that if Choerilus had sung of the same subject as Homer, Maevius the same as Vergil, then they would enjoy an equal place among the poets. But don't you see the insufficiency of this comparison? We too assert that a thing should be judged by its appearance, not by its material, for a thing is what it is by virtue of its appearance. However, one is placed among the philosophers because of one kind of appearance and among the poets because of a different kind. Let Lucretius write of nature, of God, of providence; let anyone of us write of the same things—let Duns Scotus do so, and in a poem to boot, that he may be the more inept. Lucretius will speak of the principles of things, that is, of atoms and the void and of God who is corporeal and ignorant of our affairs; he will boldly declare that all things were made by chance through the coming together of tiny particles; but he will say these things in Latin, elegantly. Scotus will say that what constitutes nature is determined by its matter and its form, that God is a mind separate from nature, that He knows all things, judges all things. Nor does the fact that He sees all things, down to the most insignificant, constrain Him to depart from His peace, but, as the saying has it, 'He descends without descending.' But Scotus will say these things in an insipid, crude manner, and not use proper Latin words to do so. I ask whether there is anyone who would doubt that Scotus philosophizes better while the other one speaks more ornately. Just see how they differ: the words of the former are insipid, whereas in the latter it's the mind; the former does not know the decrees of the grammarians, let alone those of the poets, whereas the latter does not know the decrees of God and Nature; the former, most inarticulate in speech, senses those things that cannot be praised enough in speech, whereas the latter, most eloquent, says the most abominable things."

This is what those philosophers might assert, my dearest Ermolao, in defense of their barbarity—or perhaps they would even say much better things if they employed their skill at subtle argument. I do not completely agree with their opinion, nor do I think that a noble and liberal person will do so. But I have engaged myself freely in this subject, as in something disreputable, so that, like those who praise the quartan fever, I might try out my judgment. My aim has been like that of Plato's Glaucon who praises in-

18. For Cato's statement, see Aulus Gellius, *Noctes atticae*, XVIII.vii.3.
19. Cf. Cicero, *De oratore*, III.xiv.55.

justice, not out of conviction, but to goad Socrates into praising justice.[20] Similarly, so that I might hear you plead the cause of eloquence, I have inveighed against it rather boldly for a little while, though my feelings and nature fought against doing so. If I thought it right for eloquence to be neglected by the barbarians, I would not have almost totally deserted them for it—something I did recently—or for Greek letters and for your never sufficiently praised *Themistius*.[21] However, I will say freely what I feel: certain grammarians turn my stomach who, when they have established the origins of a couple of words, so parade themselves about, so advertise themselves, and go about so boastfully that in comparison with themselves, they would have philosophers held to be of no account. We do not want, they say, these philosophies of yours—and no wonder, since dogs don't like Falernian wine.[22]

But let us close this letter with this final remark: if those barbarians have deserved any honor and glory simply for their knowledge of things, it is not easy to say what place, what praises you may claim for yourself, you who are the most eloquent among the philosophers, and among the eloquent, if I may say it in Greek, the most philosophical.

20. Glaucon's praise of injustice occurs in the *Republic*, II.iv.360e–v.362c. The quartan fever was praised by the Roman philosopher Favorinus, and his work was frequently cited in the Renaissance as an example of a mock-encomium.
21. Barbaro had produced an edition of the works of the Greek philosopher Themistius in 1479–1480.
22. Falernian wine was proverbial in Roman antiquity for its excellence.

[7]

Desiderius Erasmus

The leading humanist of the Northern Renaissance, Desiderius Erasmus (1466–1536) was a prolific writer and editor, producing a vast series of educational treatises and handbooks, moral and religious works, as well as satires such as the *Encomium Moriae* (*The Praise of Folly*) of 1509, the book for which he is best known today. Born the illegitimate son of a cleric and a widow, Erasmus was sent to a school in Deventer that was run by the Brethren of the Common Life, a pietistic lay order that stressed morality and good works and that deeply influenced Erasmus's Christianity. He was ordained a priest in 1492, but disliked the clerical life and pursued instead a career as a scholar, teacher, and writer. In the last years of the fifteenth century, he established his reputation as one of the foremost classical scholars of his age by publishing a number of important, widely read texts, including *De conscribendis epistolis* (*On Letter Writing*), *De copia verborum ac rerum* (*On Copiousness in Style and Matter*), *Colloquia familiaria* (*The Colloquies*), and *Adagiorum collectanea* (*The Adages*). After his encounter with prominent English humanists such as John Colet and Thomas More in 1499, he turned his attention to Biblical and theological matters, studied Greek intensively, and in 1516 brought out what proved to be his most controversial work, an edition of the New Testament in Greek, with his own Latin translation and commentary. Sympathetic to the idea of reform, but unwilling to break with the Church, Erasmus wanted to serve as a mediator between Catholics and Protestants during the first few years of the Reformation. In 1524, however, he was finally persuaded to take a public stand against Luther, and did so by attacking the latter's theology in *De libero arbitrio* (*On the Freedom of the Will*). Erasmus spent the last years of his life expanding earlier works and producing a constant stream of new ones as well as editing many of the church fathers. In 1528 he entered the Renaissance debate on imitation with his dialogue *Ciceronianus* (*The Ciceronian*). Ironically, although its subtitle, *De optimo dicendi genere* (*Of the Best Kind of Speech*), echoes the title of one of Cicero's works, *De optimo genere dicendi* (otherwise known as *Brutus*), Erasmus rejects the strict imitation of Cicero urged by many Italian and French humanists. The excerpts included here have been translated from the text in the *Opera omnia*, edited by J. LeClerc (Leiden, 1703–6), I: 973–1026.

FROM *Ciceronianus*

(As the dialogue opens, Erasmus's spokesman Bulephorus ["giver of counsel"] is talking with his friend Hypologus ["backup"] about Nosoponus ["mad for work"] whom he characterizes as suffering from the "disease" of Ciceronianism. Nosoponus then enters, complaining about the seven long years he has labored in vain to master Cicero's style. Bulephorus condemns such a pursuit as a waste of time and mocks contemporary writers for thinking themselves good imitators of Cicero when they merely include a few of his phrases in their works. Bulephorus then produces his main argument: in writing about the present world, one cannot actually imitate Cicero at all, for times have changed, and the modern world is filled with things—and words for those things—that Cicero never dreamed of. Thus, the true Ciceronian will do what Cicero himself did by suiting his style to his subject and speaking the language of his own time. All three speakers agree that words, like clothing, should suit the people wearing them and that it would be inappropriate for artists to represent contemporary subjects in ancient garb.)

Bulephorus. And what if someone represented the Virgin Mother today the way Apelles once depicted Diana, or the virgin Agnes the way he painted that Aphrodite Anadyomene who is celebrated by all the writers, or Saint Thecla the way he painted Lais, would you say that that painter was just like Apelles?[1]

Nosoponus. I don't think so.

Bulephorus. And if someone decorated our churches with statues like the ones with which Lysippus once adorned the temples of the gods, would you say that he resembled Lysippus?

Nosoponus. I would not say so.

Bulephorus. Why not?

Nosoponus. Because the signs would not fit the things they represented. I would say the same thing if someone painted an ass that looked like an ox or a falcon in the shape of a cuckoo, even though he otherwise did the painting with the greatest care and skill.

Hypologus. I wouldn't call a man a virtuous painter who represented an ugly man as handsome in a painting.

---

1. One of Apelles' most admired paintings was that of Diana in the midst of a group of maidens. "Anadyomene" means "rising from the sea." Lais is the name of two courtesans of Corinth celebrated for their beauty.

Bulephorus. Even if he otherwise displayed the greatest skill in doing so?

Hypologus. I wouldn't say the painting displayed a lack of skill; I'd call it a lie. For he could have painted it differently if he had wanted to, but he preferred to flatter—to deceive—the person he portrayed. But do you really think such a man a virtuous artist?

Nosoponus. If he were, he has certainly not shown himself to be one in this instance.

Bulephorus. But do you judge him a good man?

Nosoponus. Neither a good artist nor a good man, since the chief rule of art is to represent something to the eyes exactly as it is.

Bulephorus. For that sort of thing one does not need Ciceronian eloquence, since your rhetoricians permit the orator to lie sometimes, to elevate low things by means of his words and to cast down lofty ones, using some sleight-of-hand trick to creep by deceit into the spirit of the auditor, and finally to overwhelm his intelligence by moving his emotions, which is a kind of witchcraft.

Nosoponus. True—when the auditor deserves to be deceived.

Bulephorus. But our discussion is getting off the point; let's set these things aside for now. It's enough for me that you don't approve of a cloak that doesn't fit the body it's on and you condemn a picture that isn't suited to the thing it's supposed to represent.

Nosoponus. But what is all this Socratic questioning of yours leading to?

Bulephorus. I was just coming to this point, my dear Nosoponus: you and I agree Cicero was the best speaker of all.

Nosoponus. That's agreed.

Bulephorus. And no one would deserve the most fair name of Ciceronian unless he could speak like Cicero.

Nosoponus. Certainly.

Bulephorus. Furthermore, if a person does not speak appropriately, he does not speak well.

Nosoponus. I agree with this point, too.

Bulephorus. And we speak appropriately only if our speech is suited to the persons and things present before us.

Nosoponus. To be sure.

Bulephorus. Well then, does the present condition of our world seem to resemble that of the age when Cicero lived and spoke? Since that time, everything has changed completely: religion, empire, government, the state, laws, customs, pursuits, the very appearance of men—indeed, what is there that hasn't changed?

Nosoponus. Yes, nothing has remained the same.

Bulephorus. Then, what cheek does that person have who demands that we speak in every situation in the manner of Cicero? . . . In fact, since the entire scene of human affairs has been turned upside down everywhere, who can speak in a fitting manner nowadays unless he is most *unlike* Cicero? Really, it seems to me that our discussion has led to a conclusion quite different from yours. You deny that a person is speaking well unless he reproduces Cicero, but the very nature of the matter cries out that no one can speak well unless he prudently stays away from Cicero's example. Wherever I turn, I stand on a different stage on which all things have been changed; I see a different theater, indeed, a different world. What shall I do? As a Christian, I must speak of the Christian religion among Christians. In order to speak in an appropriate manner in this case, shall I imagine that I am living in the age of Cicero and am speaking in the crowded Senate before the *patres conscripti* on the Tarpeian height, and in order to do this, shall I scrounge a few words, figures, and rhythms from speeches that Cicero delivered in the Senate?[2] My speech has to be made to a mixed crowd in which there are maidens and wives and widows. I have to speak in praise of fasting and penitence, the benefits of prayer, the usefulness of almsgiving, the sanctity of marriage, contempt for transitory things, and zeal for Sacred Scripture. How is the eloquence of Cicero going to help me here, since the things of which I am to speak were unknown to him, just as he could not have used the new words that came into being, together with the new things themselves, after his death? So, won't that orator be a bore who sews the rags he stripped from Cicero onto such material?

(Bulephorus says he actually prefers the otherwise despised Scholastics because at least they used Christian words for Christian subjects, and he finally identifies what he sees as the real motive behind the interest in being a Ciceronian—an unacknowledged paganism that makes sacred mysteries of Cicero's writings. He insists that, like Cicero himself, people should study many different authors, assimilating what they can, but speaking with their own voices.)

Bulephorus. Nothing prevents a person from speaking as both a Christian and a Ciceronian, if only you confess that a Ciceronian is one who speaks clearly, copiously, vehemently, and aptly in keeping with the nature of the subject and with the circumstances of the times and the people involved. Certain individuals have argued that the ability to speak well is not a matter of skill, but of prudent judgment, and Cicero himself in his *On the Classification of Oratory* elegantly defines eloquence as "wisdom speaking

2. *Patres conscripti* ("elected fathers") was a phrase used for the Roman senators. The Tarpeian height is the Capitoline hill on which the Temple of Jupiter was located; the Senate occasionally met there.

copiously"—nor is it to be doubted that he himself practiced this type of eloquence.³ Good lord, how distant from this formulation are those who want to speak in Cicero's manner about matters that are entirely alien to him and that they neither understand nor care about! The notion that whatever diverges from Cicero should seem to us a base fault in language is a pernicious, lying dream, which we must banish from our minds if we want to be praised among Christians the way Cicero was among his own people. "Understanding is both the principle and the source of correct writing," said that most acute of critics.⁴ What then is the source of Ciceronian eloquence? A mind richly supplied with a wide knowledge of all sorts of things, especially those things that you have undertaken to speak about; a mind prepared by the precepts of art, and then by much practice in writing and speaking as well as lengthy thought on the matter; and, what is the most important part of this business, a mind that loves what it proclaims and pursues with hatred what it attacks. Together with all these things, this person must have by nature judgment, prudence, and discretion, qualities that cannot be taught. Where, I ask you, will he get these things when he reads nothing except Cicero and wants to be turning the pages of this author alone day and night?

Nosoponus. But yet, it has been said, and not unwisely, that those who have spent a lot of time in the sun take away a tan from it, and those who have been sitting for a while in a spice shop bear away with them the odor of the place when they leave.⁵

Bulephorus. This comparison really pleases me very much, for all they bear away with them is a mere coloring of the skin and a scent that will soon pass away. Let those who are content with such glories sit idly as long as they like by the perfume boxes and the rose gardens of Cicero; let them bask in his sun. If there are any things around giving off a good aroma, I prefer to eat them and digest them, so that I do not merely sprinkle a faint odor on those around me, but get thoroughly warmed and invigorated, with the result that, as often as necessary, I can produce a speech that seems to come from a healthy, well-nourished individual. For an oration that holds the attention of the listener, that moves him and forces upon him any state of feeling you like, will arise from the depths of your heart, not from your skin.

I'm not saying that I think the knowledge of things one gets from Cicero's books is merely mediocre or without advantages, but it alone does not suffice to produce richness of speech about whatever argument you may be making. What remains, therefore, for us to do except to learn from Cicero himself the very way to imitate him? We must imitate him just as

3. See *De partitione oratoria*, xxiii.79.
4. Horace, *Ars poetica*, 309.
5. Cf. Seneca, *Epistulae morales*, cviii.4, and Cicero, *De oratore*, II.xiv.60.

he himself imitated others. If he settled down to reading a single author, if he delivered himself up to the teaching of just one man, if he took greater care of words than of things, if he never wrote except at bedtime, if he tormented himself for an entire month for the sake of writing one letter, if he thought something was eloquent although it did not fit the subject at hand, then we should do the like in order to be good Ciceronians. But since all these things are very different from what Cicero did, let's take him as our model: let us equip our minds to the full with all necessary knowledge; let our first concern be for ideas, our second for words; and let us fit words to things, not the other way around, so that when we speak we never take our eyes off the principle of decorum.[6] A speech will really come alive if it is born in our hearts, not if it floats on our lips. Let's not ignore the teaching of rhetoric, for it helps us greatly in finding out, arranging, and managing arguments, and in avoiding things that are irrelevant to or hinder our case. However, when a serious case is to be undertaken, judgment should have the first place, although even in fictitious cases, which one engages in for the sake of exercise, it is advantageous if the things one says are very close to the truth.[7] Cicero wrote that the mind of Laelius breathed in what he wrote.[8] By contrast, it is stupid for you to try to write in another's humor, to strive to have Cicero's spirit breathing through your words. What you have devoured through long and varied reading is to be digested, transferred through meditation into the veins of the mind rather than placed in your memory or on a list of words. Thus, fattened on every kind of food, your genius will give birth to a speech out of itself, a speech that is not redolent of this or that flower or leaf or grass, but of your natural character and the passions of your heart. The result will be that the reader will not recognize in it bits and pieces torn out of Cicero, but will see the image of a mind filled with every kind of knowledge. Cicero had read all of his predecessors and had considered diligently in what way each one was to be approved or criticized. However, you will not recognize any one of them specifically in Cicero himself, only the force of a mind alive with the ideas of all of them. . . .

But now, my dear friend, let's consider first whether it's proper for us to purchase the honor of the name "Ciceronian" by means of so much work, and then whether it's worth the price.

Nosoponus. There is nothing more honorable, and what is honorable cannot help but be proper.

Bulephorus. As we are talking about what is proper, you will confess, I think, that the diction of Cicero would not have been pleasing in the time of Cato the Censor, since its elegance and luxuriance were not suited to

6. Cf. Cicero, *De oratore*, I.xxix.132, and Quintilian, *Institutio oratoria*, XI.iii.177.
7. Cf. Quintilian, *Institutio oratoria*, II.xii.2ff.
8. See Cicero *Brutus*, xxiv.94.

the standards of that age. Life was sober then, and so was speech. Indeed, in the age when Cicero lived, there were men who still breathed that old-fashioned severity, men such as Cato of Utica, Brutus, and Asinius Pollio, who would have wished for greater severity, less theatricality, and more masculinity in Cicero's eloquence. And yet at that time eloquence flourished everywhere, in popular assemblies as well as meetings of the Senate and the law courts, and to such an extent that jurymen expected, indeed demanded, of advocates an ornamented and pleasant style. Now, do you really think that what was considered insufficiently masculine in Cicero would seem decorous for Christians, whose way of life is focused on good living rather than on speaking ornately and elegantly, and whose behavior has to remain distant from anything even vaguely connected with the artificiality of cosmetics and theatrical pleasure?

But even suppose it were decorous to speak like Cicero, what benefits can you hope for that would make up for so much sweat? The goal of the entire art of rhetoric is to persuade, but how much more powerful was Phocion than Demosthenes and Aristides than Themistocles, how much more effective Cato than Cicero, who sometimes burdened the accused when he defended them and helped the people he was supposed to be prosecuting. I have nothing to say against that truly wonderful aphorism, "it's a finer thing to be Phidias than a record-keeper or a cook," although their activities are more necessary for the state than are the statues of Phidias.[9] The arts of painting and sculpture have been invented for the sake of delighting the eyes; when they have achieved this end, they have fulfilled their function. Eloquence that does nothing other than delight is not eloquence, for surely it was invented for some other end, and if it does not reach that end, then it should not seem decorous to a good man.

But even granted that Cicero's eloquence was useful once, what utility does it have nowadays? In the law courts? There matters are handled by means of articles and formulas, by procurators and advocates who are anything but Ciceronians, and in front of judges before whom Cicero would seem a barbarian. Nor is that eloquence used much more in council meetings where individuals reveal what they think to very few, and if they do, do so in French or German. The greatest matters today are decided in what they call the privy council, to which scarcely three men are invited, and those almost illiterate; others are merely asked to give their advice. But even if today affairs were conducted in Latin, who would put up with Cicero delivering the perorations he made against Verres, or Catiline, or Clodius, or the witness Vatinius? What senate would be so free from official duties and so patient that it would put up with the orations he made against Antony, although in these his eloquence is that of an older man and hence less excessive, less exuberant. So, for what purpose have we labored so much to acquire this Ciceronian eloquence? To make

9. See Cicero, *Brutus*, lxxiii.257.

popular harangues? The common people don't understand the language of Cicero, nor are political matters discussed before them. Moreover, this kind of eloquent discourse is little suited to sacred oratory. So, what use remains for it, except perhaps in diplomatic missions that are conducted in Latin, especially at Rome, although that is done more because of tradition than out of conviction, and more for the sake of the magnificent spectacle involved than for reasons of utility? For in these missions almost nothing serious is ever discussed; your entire speech is taken up with praise for the person to whom you were sent, with testimonies to the benevolence of the person from whom you were sent, and with lots of vulgar commonplaces. In short, the whole affair is of such a sort that you will have accomplished a great thing if you merely avoid the appearance of flattery in a situation where you are not permitted to avoid flattery itself. Moreover, what is customarily said in response to such a speech is insipid: sometimes its prolixity produces heavy boredom; sometimes it embarrasses the person who is praised excessively; often the speaker is exposed not merely to embarrassment himself, but to danger, for he'll break into a sweat while reciting what he has learned by heart, or he'll get stuck, or he'll lose his place either because of forgetfulness or because he's emotionally upset. What is there to admire in such a speech, when the person who recites it has simply learned by heart what some rhetor has worked out for him, with the result that no praise can redound to the credit of our orator except for fortitude in recitation? Thus, nothing is accomplished here beyond official greetings, while serious business is transacted privately through letters and conversations in French.

So what theater can our Ciceronian discover for his performance? He will write Ciceronian letters. To whom? To the erudite. But there are very few of them, and they care nothing for Ciceronian phrasing; they just want the words to be sensible, prudent, well chosen, and learned. To whom, then? To four Italians who have begun recently to boast of being Ciceronians, although, as I have shown, one cannot really be just like Cicero—and, in fact, they scarcely have the slightest hint of Cicero about them.[10] Now, if this achievement, such as it is, cost very little, if it were available of its own accord, and if it did not get in the way of things offering us greater advantages, perhaps it should not be rejected. But just consider in your own mind whether it is all worthwhile: to pay the price of so many long hours of labor and so much sweat, to risk your health, just so you can be included in the catalogue of Ciceronians by four dull Italian adolescents?

(In the final section of the dialogue, the three speakers pass in review a long list of Latin authors from the classical world to the contemporary one, and in all cases Nosoponus pronounces them insufficiently Ciceronian. The work ends with Bulephorus summarizing his arguments against Ciceronianism, after which Nosoponus pronounces himself cured of the disease.)

10. It is uncertain who the "four Italians" are.

[8]

Heinrich Cornelius Agrippa

Heinrich Cornelius Agrippa von Nettesheim (1486–1535) was a German writer, soldier, and physician, who also gained a reputation as a magician because of his works on the occult sciences. He served as a captain in the army of the German emperor Maximilian I from 1501 to 1507. When he went to France in 1509 to lecture on theology, he ran afoul of ecclesiastical authorities and had to flee to London where he stayed with the English humanist John Colet. Traveling and lecturing in Italy after 1515, he was appointed public orator and advocate in the German town of Metz in 1518. However, that same year he undertook the defense of a witch, once again offending ecclesiastical authorities, so that he had to remove himself to Cologne. During the remainder of his life he continued to move around, serving as physician to Louise of Savoy from 1524 to 1527, working as historiographer to the emperor Charles V in Antwerp in 1529, and dying in the French town of Grenoble six years later. Agrippa's principal work was *De occulta philosophia* (*On Occult Philosophy*), which he wrote around 1510, but was first published, in revised form, in 1531. This work mixes Christianity, the doctrines of Neoplatonism, and the teachings of the Cabala, defending magic as the most perfect science because of its ability to supply knowledge of nature and God. Agrippa wrote *De incertitudine et vanitate scientiarum et artium* (*On the Uncertainty and Vanity of the Arts and Sciences*) between 1527 and 1528, and published it in Antwerp in 1531. It satirizes the pretensions of the learned disciplines, belief in witches, and various superstitions that had attached themselves to Christianity during its history. Because of its highly ironic nature, the seriousness of its attacks on specific professions, doctrines, and practices has been questioned by some scholars. The following extract is taken from the version of that work contained in Agrippa's *Opera* (Lyons, 1600[?]; reprint, Hildesheim: Georg Olms Verlag, 1970), 2: 27–33.

FROM *On the Uncertainty and Vanity of the Arts and Sciences*

Chapter VI. On Rhetoric

Very serious men debate whether rhetoric, which comes next after these [i.e., poetry and history, the subjects of preceding chapters], is an art or not, and the decision is still before the judge. In fact, Socrates himself in Plato's works argues that it is neither an art nor a science, but a certain shrewdness that is neither noble nor honorable, but rather, base, illiberal, slavish flattery.[1] Lysias, Cleanthes, and Menedemus thought eloquence did not derive from art, but merely from nature, which, whenever necessary, could teach anyone to flatter, to unfold his case, and to support it with arguments. Indeed, correct delivery, memory, and a rich means of inventing arguments can come only from nature. This very thing is seen in [Marc] Antony, the prince of Roman orators.

Even though no one had written down or taught the art of rhetoric before Tisias, Corax, and Gorgias, there were nevertheless many men who were most eloquent, thanks to the excellence of their natural talent. Moreover, although the art may be defined as a collection of precepts all aiming at one end, rhetoricians still debate what that end is, whether to persuade or to speak well. Moreover, not content with true matters, they think up new and feigned ones. They have found out so many theses, hypotheses, figures, tropes, periods, characters, persuasive speeches, disputes, declamations, introductions, insinuations, means to render the audience benevolent, and artificial ways to state arguments that one can scarcely count them—and still they deny that the end of rhetoric has been achieved. The Spartans entirely rejected this discipline, judging that the speech of good men should not come from art, but from the heart, and only very late in their history did the ancient Romans admit rhetors into their city. Cicero argued elaborately in order to show that the ability to speak did not derive from art as much as it did from prudence, and for this reason he wrote his work about the perfect orator.[2] Nevertheless, that orator, who is fabricated there as a model, has not been approved by everyone, and in fact, seemed quite suspect to Brutus himself, a man of singular integrity who, in the opinion of the rhetoricians, always prevailed in debate, and thought that the precepts of oratory were more of a hindrance than a help in human life.[3]

To confess the truth, it is generally granted that the entire discipline of rhetoric from start to finish is nothing other than an art of flattery, adulation, and, as some say more audaciously, lying, in that, if it cannot persuade others through the truth of the case, it does so by means of deceitful speech.

1. See Plato, *Gorgias*, 463a–463c.
2. Cicero's *De oratore* is meant.
3. For Brutus's views on oratory, see Tacitus, *Dialogus*, xviii.5.

Hence, according to Eunapius, when Archidamus was speaking of the sophist Pericles and was asked who was the stronger of the two, he replied, "Even if Pericles were beaten by me in war, he is nevertheless equipped with such eloquence that if he spoke of what had happened, he would not appear the conquered, but the conqueror."[4] And Pliny says of Carneades that when he was arguing, it was scarcely possible to distinguish the truth in what he was saying.[5] Of this same man it is said that if one day he spoke at length in public both elegantly and wisely on behalf of justice, on the next day he would deliver a peroration no less learned and copious against it.

In Syracuse there once lived the rhetor Corax, a man sharp of mind and quite ready with his tongue, who used to teach this art for money. To him came Tisias, and since he did not have any ready cash, he promised Corax twice his usual fee once the training process was complete. Corax accepted him on those terms and taught him. After Tisias had learned the art, he wanted to cheat his master of his fee, and so asked him what constituted rhetoric. When Corax replied that it was the source of persuasion, Tisias argued thus with his teacher: "As far as the fee is concerned, if I persuade you that I owe you nothing, then I will give you nothing since I have persuaded you that I do not owe you anything. If I fail to persuade you, I will also owe you nothing, since you have not taught me how to persuade." Then Corax strove to turn the argument against Tisias and said, "As far as the fee is concerned, if I persuade you that I should get it, then I should get it, since I have persuaded you. If I do not persuade you, I still ought to get it, since I have turned out a student who is so wonderful that he is able to beat his teacher." When the Syracusans heard them fighting with one another and making these arguments back and forth, they exclaimed, "Bad crows have bad eggs," meaning that the pupil of a bad teacher will be worse than his master. [Aulus] Gellius recounts a similar story about the sophist Protagoras and his pupil Evathlus.[6]

To know how to speak precisely, ornately, gravely, and copiously is certainly beautiful, delightful, and always useful, but it is sometimes base and inconsiderate, more often dangerous, and always suspect. That is why Socrates himself thinks orators are unworthy of admiration and should never obtain power in a well-ordered state. Plato thought they should be excluded

4. See Eunapius, *Lives of the Philosophers and Sophists*, 498. War is not mentioned in that passage, in which Archidamas is asking an unnamed third party whether he or Pericles is the stronger. Eunapius takes this anecdote from Plutarch, *Life of Pericles*, viii.3–4, in which Archidamas asks Thucydides, not the historian, but the son of Melesias and Pericles' chief opponent, which of the two is the better wrestler.
5. See Pliny, *Naturalis historia*, VII.xxx.112.
6. This story about Corax and Tisias goes back to antiquity, but was not recorded when the two men were alive. The earliest version seems to be that of the Sophist Sopater, in his *Commentary on the Rhetoric of Hermogenes*; see *Rhetores graeci*, ed. Christian Walz (Leipzig, 1833), 5: 6–7. Sopater's work was published in Aldus Manutius's edition of the *Rhetores graeci* (Venice, 1509), but the story owes its European diffusion to Erasmus, who recounted it in one of his adages, "Mali corvi malum ovum" ("Bad crows have bad eggs"); see *Adages*, II.x.12. For the story about Protagoras and Evathlus, see Aulus Gellius, *Noctes atticae*, V.x.3–16.

from his republic together with tragic actors and poets, and surely he is right, for nothing is more dangerous to civic functions than this art, since it produces prevaricators, shifty tricksters, perverters of the law, sycophants, and all kinds of men with wicked tongues.[7] Equipped with it, many people plot against the state and foment sedition, while by means of their artful loquacity, they betray others, attack them, satirize them, flatter yet others, and obtain something like a tyranny over the innocent. Thus Euripides rightly said that to know how to speak volubly is the mark of a tyrant, and Aeschylus declared, "I say that the basest evil of all is to have composed speeches."[8] Raphael Volaterranus, a very great student of history and collector of exempla, confesses that, having reviewed all the examples he had heard and read from the ancients and the moderns, he found the fewest good men among the eloquent. By means of this craft, haven't mighty states often been sorely vexed and often completely destroyed? As examples of this, there are all those like Brutus, Crassus, the Gracchi, Cato, Cicero, and Demosthenes, who, as they were considered most eloquent of all, so they were always most seditious of all. Cato the Censor, accused of crimes forty times, himself accused others seventy times and more, disturbing the tranquillity of the state with his insane speeches throughout his life.[9] The other Cato, the one from Utica, having provoked Caesar, entirely subverted Roman freedom. Moreover, Cicero provoked Antony into the destruction of the Republic, and Demosthenes did the same with Philip [of Macedonia] to the harm of Athens. Finally, there is no state that has not been at some time overturned by this art; none has remained uninjured by the vice of eloquence once it lent its ears to it.

Eloquence can do a great deal in the law courts: with it as counsel, bad causes are defended, and the guilty criminal is snatched from the punishment of the law; with it as prosecutor, the innocent is often condemned; and, by contrast, there has never been any guilty party who has come to harm if he was defended by this art. Marcus Cato [the Censor], the most prudent of the Romans, forbade that those three famous Athenian orators, Carneades, Critolaus, and Diogenes, should be allowed to be heard publicly in the city of Rome, since they were equipped with such keen intelligence, fluency of speech, and powerful eloquence that they could easily persuade people to believe both just and unjust matters.[10] It is well known that Demosthenes used to boast to his friends that he could bend the opinions of the judges to his own will whenever he wished by means of the art of speech. Thus,

7. See Plato, *Republic*, X.i.595a–viii.608b, and *Gorgias*, 466d.

8. For the passage in Euripides, see *Hecuba*, 816. Agrippa is probably referring to a passage in Quintilian, *Institutio oratoria*, I.xii.18, in which eloquence is called a queen by a "not ignoble tragic poet" who was thought to be Euripides. However, the passage in question is more likely a fragment from Pacuvius's *Hermione*, which is also cited in Cicero, *De oratore*, II.xliv.187. For the quotation from Aeschylus, see *Prometheus Bound*, 686.

9. On Cato the Censor's many lawsuits, see Pliny, *Naturalis historia*, VII.xxvii.100, and Plutarch, *Life of Cato the Elder*, xv.4.

10. See note 5.

simply as his will dictated, there was often war, and often peace, between the Athenians and Philip. The force of eloquence in that man was so great in rousing up and settling down the feelings and wills of men that by means of speech alone he could turn them in whatever direction he wished just as if he held supreme military command over them. For a similar reason, Cicero was called by many the king of Rome, since he turned the Senate in whatever direction he wished by means of his words, ruling all things through his eloquence. In short, it appears that rhetoric is nothing other than the art of persuading and moving the emotions, seizing the spirits of the thoughtless by subtle eloquence, exquisite deception, and the cunning appearance of probability, leading them into the prison of error while perverting the sense of the truth.

If, thanks to nature, each thing is expressed by means of an appropriate word, what pursuit is more pernicious than that of false words? The speech of truth is simple, but alive and penetrating, and it is able to distinguish the intentions of the heart. Like a double-edged ax or sword, it easily cuts through and tears away the artful enthymemes of orators. Hence, Demosthenes, although he despised all other speakers because they rely on art, used to fear Phocion alone because he spoke simply and briefly, saying true and pertinent things, and for this reason Demosthenes used to say publicly that his own orations suffered an ax-blow at Phocion's hands.[11] The ancient Romans knew these things, so that, according to Suetonius, they threw the orators out of Rome twice by public edict, once during the consulships of Gaius Fannius Strabo and Marcus Valerius Messala, and a second time when Gnaeus Domitius Ahenobarbus and Lucius Licinius Crassus were censors. A third time, when Domitian was emperor, they expelled them by a general decree of the Senate not only from the city of Rome, but from all of Italy as well.[12] The Athenians prohibited them as perverters of justice from entering the court in the forum, and they punished Timagoras with death because in greeting ceremonies for King Darius, he had flattered him in the manner of the Persians.[13] The Spartans expelled Ctesiphon because he boasted that he could speak all day about any subject, for nothing was more hateful to them than the affected verbal skill of a man who has no concern for the discovery of the truth, but who, when propounding a straightforward matter, dresses it up with bawdy verbal disguises and bombastic words in order to deceive the spirits of his auditors with the sweetness of speech and to lead them away tied to his tongue by their ears.[14]

11. For Demosthenes' remark, see Plutarch, *Life of Phocion*, v.4, and *Life of Demosthenes*, x.2.
12. The first attempt to throw out the rhetors occurred in 161 B.C.; the second, in 92 B.C.; see Suetonius, *De rhetoribus*, i. I have not been able to locate a source for Agrippa's statement about Domitian.
13. For the Athenians prohibiting orators from entering the court, see Aristotle, *Rhetoric*, I.i.5, and Quintilian, *Institutio oratoria*, II.xvi.4. For their putting Timagoras to death, see Valerius Maximus, *Ditorum et factorum memorabilium libri novem*, VI.3.ext.2.
14. I have not been able to locate the source for Ctesiphon's expulsion by the Spartans. In the last part of the final sentence in this paragraph, Agrippa is alluding to the figure of the Hercules

It is well known that no one is made better by this craft, and that many are actually made worse by it. Even if they can speak quite neatly of the virtues, nevertheless we see that they are more elegant and eloquent by far in defending errors, sowing disputes, exciting factions, and heaping up abuses, curses, and false accusations, than they are in bringing people together in peace, concord, and tranquillity, and preaching charity, faith, and religion. What is more, many of them, relying on this art, have deviated from their orthodox faith, and sects, schisms, superstitions, and heresies have grown up as a result. Some so disdain Sacred Scripture because it lacks eloquence and Ciceronian charm that, relying on the deceiving persuasion of pagan arguments, they have sometimes taken positions against Catholic truth. This is chiefly manifest in connection with the Tatian heretics and with those whom the sophist Libanius and the orator Symmachus, both defenders of idolatry, as well as Celsus Africanus and Julian the Apostate seduced, scoffing at Christ with their great rhetorical antics. From their pernicious and blasphemous speech the heretics took away many persuasive arguments, which they injected into the ears of simple people and seduced them completely from the word of truth. But why do we dwell on the examples of ancient heretics? Let us look to our own time. Who are the leaders of the German heresies, which, although they all started from Luther alone, are so numerous today that almost every single city has its own peculiar brand? Aren't the authors of these heresies the most articulate men, who possess both verbal eloquence and an elegant writing style? These are men who were so renowned a few years ago for their knowledge of languages, the adornments of their speech, and their readiness in talking and writing, that nothing could have been added to their praise; today they are the heads and princes of the heretics. Besides, there are many who, having devoted themselves to eloquence and sought to become Ciceronians, have turned into pagans. Similarly, there are those who thoughtlessly apply themselves to Aristotle and to Plato: the former are certainly superstitious; the latter, impious. But no matter who these men are, as they pour their idle speeches into the ears of others and go beyond the simple words of truth, all of them will stand in judgment and will have to face an accounting for the things that they have vainly conjectured and fabricated against God.

Gallicus whom Lucian described in his *Herakles* as being identified with Hermes, the god of eloquence, and who, as a symbol of the power of eloquence, had chains of gold and amber stretching from his tongue to the ears of his followers.

[9]

Juan Luis Vives

The Spanish humanist Juan Luis Vives (1492–1540), widely known in the Renaissance for his works on educational theory and psychology, was one of the most original thinkers of the age. He studied in Paris between 1509 and 1512, and was appointed Professor of Humanities at the University of Louvain in 1519. In the following years, he produced a commentary on Saint Augustine and dedicated it to Henry VIII of England, who appointed him tutor to his daughter Mary in 1523. During his stay in England, Vives lectured on philosophy at Oxford. Because of his opposition to Henry's plans for a divorce, however, he was imprisoned briefly in 1527 and then returned to the Spanish Netherlands, where he remained until his death. Among his most important writings on education are *De ratione studiis puerilis* (*On the Method of Children's Studies*) of 1523, *Introductio ad sapientiam* (*Introduction to Wisdom*) of 1524, and *De ratione dicendi* (*On Rhetoric*) of 1532. He also published *De institutione feminae Christianae* (*On the Education of the Christian Woman*) in 1524, which he dedicated to Catherine of Aragon and in which he advocates a limited humanistic education for women. His *De disciplinis libri XX* (*Twenty Books on Education*), published in 1531, contains *De causis corruptarum artium* (*On the Causes of the Corruption of the Arts*) as well as *De tradendis disciplinis* (*On Teaching the Disciplines*), and portions of those works are translated here. They reveal Vives's strikingly republican sentiments as well as his keen understanding of the historical development of rhetoric between the ancient world and his own day. Finally, his claim to fame in the field of psychology rests on his *De anima et vita libri tres* (*Three Books on the Soul and on Life*), which he brought out in 1538 and which anticipates the inductive method championed by Francis Bacon. The translations are based on the versions of the texts in Juan Luis Vives, *Opera omnia*, edited by Francisco Fabian y Fuero (Valencia, 1745; reprint, London, Gregg Press, 1964).

From *On the Causes of the Corruption of the Arts*

Book IV: The Corruption of Rhetoric

1. Society Itself Cannot Continue at All Without Justice and Speech. Why the Latter Flourishes More in a Democratic State, and How it Was First Cultivated by the Sicilians. Rhetoric Has Exceeded its Bounds, from which One May Conclude that Quintilian's Complaint Was False.

All human societies are linked together and kept within their bounds by two things in particular, justice and speech, and if either one is missing, it would be difficult for any group or any society, whether public or private, to endure for very long. Since no one, whether he is the best of men or the worst, can live and carry on the business of life with another person who is wicked, and since he will not want to live with someone whom he does not understand, these two things, justice and speech, are the rudders by means of which societies of men are steered. Justice has a power that is quiet and leisurely, whereas that of speech is more immediate and swift, for the first displays the force of reason and counsel, while the second excites the emotions. As a result, although men easily allow themselves to be ruled by someone they think just, if a person has a real command of language and is well trained in speaking, then they will want him to be their leader and guide, and will give themselves up to him completely, for they believe that the force residing in the spirit of the speaker is identical to the one they experience in that river called speech that flows out from his mind. However, not all human societies can determine their own goals, for in some of them everything is controlled by one person, or by just a few who are bound together by a certain agreement and conspiracy, and who have great forces and powers to support them if anyone refuses their rule. Here the masses do not have the power to decide matters and to carry out what has been decided, or even to frequent meetings and assemblies where there is nothing more to fear than the power of just a few men. There are other societies that are called free; in themselves they possess the supreme right of governing and the power to carry out whatever they have ordered done.

If anyone in those first two kinds of societies is really capable of speaking, either no one listens to him because he is not allowed to speak in public, or if he does speak in order to persuade the crowd, he will be shackled by fear and have his hands tied when he does so. In a democratic state, however, whatever appears good to the crowd gets their approval right away, so that the power of speech has enormous influence in everything. In these societies, therefore, where men are led by their natural inclination to pursue honor, wealth, property, dignity, and power, a great number of them have studied how to speak as well as one can before popular assemblies. Those who did this were called *orators* and their art *oratory*, in Greek *rhetors* and *rhetoric*. This is the origin of speaking in public, although the art of speaking more ornately and of inventing things to say in a more subtle manner arose out of a specific need. Aristotle attributed its origin to the Sicilians, a clever breed of men, eloquent by nature and well equipped to speak.[1] There, where tyrants succeeded one another frequently—and there is no kind of government more savage—the people would have their possessions and property taken away from them and given to others. Then, however, when the tyrant had been either killed or expelled, those who were in exile and had been deprived of their patrimonies, would seek to get their things back by means of the laws and the courts and appeals to justice. They introduced into the forum a certain style of speech that was not only more refined and polished, but also more clever and argumentative, capable of persuading and moving the minds of the judges and all the people in attendance.

From that country have come the most ancient teachers of the art: the Pythagorean Empedocles, who, according to Quintilian, is said to have taken a few steps in the direction of rhetoric; then Corax and Tisias, who passed on certain precepts based on their own practice and on their observation of others' customary way of speaking.[2] They were succeeded by Gorgias Leontinus from the same island who was even more refined and polished and by whom many Athenians were taught. From the necessity of recovering one's own property, this instrument was directed to other aims, so that just as speakers once used to move judges, they now also moved the minds of the people in public meetings, of the Senate in the Senate house, and of all those who had the greatest political power and in whose hands and will was placed the entire fortune of the city. And that instrument was more effective to the same extent that the speaker was graced with an audience composed of intelligent, quick-witted, unrestrained, and excitable people who were easily moved by his oration, shaken by it as if by the wind. In well-regulated cities and in a people, who, albeit free, are quiet and orderly, though also a bit dull, eloquence has not been left a lot of room to throw its weight around, as was the case, for example, in Crete and Lacedemonia. However, in Athens, that hot-blooded and excitable city-state, in the Greek colonies of Asia, whose people were practically transplanted there from Athens, in Rhodes and Sicily and finally Rome—in places where eloquence came upon crowds of people endowed with a shrewd intelligence and who were unsettled, ambitious, and puffed up by the air of liberty—there the orator was lord.

Thus, Zeno the Stoic, who declared that rhetoric was like the open palm of the hand and dialectic like a fist, said even more aptly that the dialectician put together arguments for the subtle examination of the learned, whereas the rhetor applied them to the feelings of the people.[3] For often the orator

1. Cicero attributes this explanation to Aristotle; see *Brutus*, xi.46.
2. See *Institutio oratoria*, III.iv.8.
3. Zeno's saying that dialectic is a closed fist and rhetoric an open palm can be found in a number of texts; see, for example, Quintilian, *Institutio oratoria*, II.xx.7.

puts things together in a more condensed form than does the dialectician, as when he puts a single proposition in place of an entire, sometimes rather lengthy argument, as has been shown by us in our *Instrument of Probable Proofs.*[4] Therefore, as this training was a step up to immense power, men who were desirous of honor, rich, and engaged in public affairs sought out this art. And once they had put into action and turned to its destined use whatever they had learned from their preceptors, or discovered through experience, or found out through cogitation and thanks to their own mental alacrity, they did not care about making inquiries into the nature of this art, what its materials and limits were, how wide a field it covered, or what its scope was. In other words, they did not cultivate it as an intellectual discipline, but in order to obtain a position of distinction in an important city, to heap up wealth and honors, and, as it were, to exercise a kind of tyranny, surrounded by the forces of eloquence as by a troop of guards, that would allow them to help their friends and vex their enemies.

(In the remainder of chapter 1, Vives rejects the notion that he says is shared by many ancient and modern writers, namely that rhetoric includes within its purview detailed and specific knowledge of all sorts of other subjects. Specifically, he speaks of how Quintilian was wrong to lament that rhetoric had been stripped of all that connected it to the study of nature and of ethics, for such things do not really belong to the discipline. Finally, he grants that rhetoric manuals often contain a certain amount of moral philosophy, but argues that that is not their primary concern.)

2. On the Definition of Rhetoric, its Parts, the Genres of Oratory, and Style, Including Many Things Argued against the Ancients.

Now, what is rhetoric? Is it an art, or a kind of knowledge, or a virtue, or a power, or a tool, or, as the Greeks say, an organon?[5] Some people have raised it up by means of such lofty names in order to oppose the ill will of others who said it was a depraved art, calling it by the Greek word a *cacotechnia*, a bad or evil art. Socrates, in Plato's *Gorgias*, says it is a flattering simulator of just a tiny part of political science, while others have spoken of it as a practice, still others as an art divorced from knowledge and virtue, and a few have allowed it to be some kind of knowledge.[6] The Stoics say that eloquence is virtue and wisdom and that rhetoric is so, too, just as Quintilian concludes that no one can indeed be an orator unless he is a good man, because Cato proclaimed, speaking like an oracle, that the orator is a "good man skilled in speaking."[7] In this case Quintilian works up such a sweat striving to convince everyone that Cicero and Demosthenes, who are held

4. Vives's *Instrumentum probabilitatis* is concerned with various kinds of proofs, both logical and rhetorical.
5. The Greek word *organon* means "tool," that is, an instrument for acquiring knowledge, and hence, a body of scientific or philosophical principles to be used for that purpose.
6. See *Gorgias*, 463c–463e.
7. See Quintilian, *Institutio oratoria*, XII.i.1.

to be among the greatest orators, were good men, that I really feel sorry for this most grave man because he has sought to join together things that are so different by their natures, trying to make a whole out of two entities that oppose and resist the process.

In the third book of his *De oratore,* Cicero, speaking of oratory, says with some obscurity, but still with somewhat greater truth: "Where its force is greater, there it is all the more to be united with probity and the greatest prudence; if we hand over the means of speaking eloquently to people who lack such virtues, we will not really make them orators, but will put arms in the hands of madmen."[8] Thus speaks Cicero, although he returns to his former partiality a little later and makes oratory the same thing as wisdom, that is, when he speaks of "the method involved in thinking and expressing one's thoughts, the faculty of eloquence." He is confusing things here that are quite discrete, imagining that the arts of thinking well and of speaking well are identical. This is a profitable idea—and one might hope that it would persuade people—but it is not true, for the two arts are separated by their ends, their materials, and the entire way in which they are practiced. Cato defined the orator as a good man skilled in speaking, and I marvel how this common and familiar definition of eloquence has been twisted in all sorts of directions by learned men, for according to ordinary usage in all languages, good men are simply called good and considered to be good if they escape the notoriety of having committed some wicked deed. . . .

Now, benefits have been sought through the practice of this art, whether that meant prosecuting guilty citizens in the forum or defending the innocent, giving one's opinion about some matter under consideration at court, or doing so in a public assembly, and as a result, two kinds of cases have been established: judicial ones and *suasoria,* or exhortations. However, people in Greece frequently delivered panegyrics at assemblies, and they also pronounced funeral eulogies, which were called "epitaphs" in Rome, it being the custom for men initially, and then for women as well, to be praised at public funeral rites after their deaths. As a consequence, a third genre was added to the first two and labeled laudatory or demonstrative, that is, epideictic, oratory. Thus, the number seemed sufficiently full in that there were three genres of cases, as I have just explained. Aristotle formulated this division in his writings, and everyone else, totally agreeing, followed their great leader.[9] In this matter, however, as in almost all other aspects of this art, Aristotle has not so much seen into its nature as he has explicated a customary practice or taken it as his guide. For rhetoric, like a kind of universal tool, is actually diffused through all verbal acts, just as grammar and dialectic are. Moreover, neither Cicero nor Quintilian was silent about the fact that there are more than three genres of speech, Quintilian himself having

8. III.xiv.55; in his next sentence, the passage Vives cites is the next sentence in Cicero's work: III.xv.56.
9. See *Rhetoric,* I.iii.1–3.

explicated many of them.[10] Still, they thought that from the precepts given
for those three one could derive what was necessary for the others, even
though they all have the most diverse methods of invention, organization,
and ornamentation. Who does not see that the forms of invention and ornamentation for giving thanks, congratulations, and consolations, composing
histories and descriptions, and teaching disciplines, are necessarily very
different from the ones for making judicial, deliberative, and epideictic
speeches? And all of that first set of things mentioned do frequently supply
material for speaking. That is why Dionysius of Halicarnassus undertook
the task of teaching something about a certain number of those genres individually. To Quintilian the argument seemed convincing that a large number of genres should be defined, but he thought that the most secure method
was to follow a host of authors, especially since he placed his beloved Cicero
among them. Add to all this the fact that people in the city made huge
profits from practicing the three genres, and they thus scorned the others as
if they were sterile. Moreover, men who were experienced in those first
three, if anything had to be said of other matters, easily adapted from their
own practice what they needed in order to gain the favor and applause of
the public, so that in the case of this faculty, experience counted for more
than art.

*(In the remainder of chapter 2, Vives reviews the parts of oratory, asking whether there are
just the traditional five of them—invention, arrangement, ornamentation, delivery, and
memory—and questioning whether each of them really belongs exclusively to the art. He
ends by rejecting the notion that there are just three levels of style: the high, the middle, and
the low.)*

*3. Refutation of the Very Old, Common Opinion that Verse Should Be
Removed from Prose as if it Were a Filthy Stain on it. The Great Change
Eloquence Once Went Through, and Why.*

*(Vives opens chapter 3 by attacking the idea that one should never use verse in prose com-
positions. He then returns to the topic he left in the first chapter, namely, the decline of
rhetoric in the ancient world after the transformation of Rome into an imperial state.)*

Whenever they engaged in disputes or established certain positions concerning matters of this sort [i.e., the use of verse in oratory], those early orators brought together all the enormous resources of language, drawing on
their immense intelligence, zeal, experience, and practice, all of which were
whetted and stimulated by the huge prize proposed for eloquence: dignity,
wealth, and political power. From the moment that that prize was taken
away, eloquence also collapsed, for when people saw that the orator was
granting himself too great a license, making himself a danger to the innocent

10. See Cicero, *De oratore*, II.x.40–48, and Quintilian, *Institutio oratoria*, III.iv.

and a protector of the guilty, and boasting arrogantly in public that he could make weaker causes appear stronger and stronger ones weaker, then they concluded that he needed to be restrained as if locked behind bars. In Athens orators were forbidden to make appeals to the emotions, a decision that seemed extremely just to philosophers, who feared that the minds of the jurors—surely the norm by which things are to be judged—might be bent away from what is right in one direction or another.[11] In Rome during his third consulate, Pompey the Great proposed a bill *that a plaintiff be allowed two hours for speaking, a defendant three, and the case be concluded on the same day.* Cicero complained about this in his *Brutus,* saying: "This activity of ours, frightened by the threat of arms, suddenly fell silent and ceased because of the three hours allotted for speaking by the law of Pompey."[12] And Tacitus speaks of how a bridle was put on eloquence.[13] When everything was reduced to the authority and power of a single man, that man did not allow the people to gather together very often or in very great numbers, nor did he let anyone speak freely in public because it was thought—and it was indeed the case—that that was a danger to his power as a single ruler. Thus, eloquence was excluded from public meetings, that is, from the theater, its nurse, as Cicero explains in the second book of his *De oratore:* "It is the case, moreover, that since a public meeting seems the greatest stage to the orator, he is naturally excited to a more ornate kind of speaking there, for the multitude possesses such a great power that just as a flutist cannot make music without his flute, an orator cannot be eloquent unless he has a crowd listening to him."[14]

Princes would rarely speak to the people themselves and would then say very little, generally preferring to issue proclamations, as one would do with slaves. In the Senate, opinions were uttered, not freely as before, but composed in order to flatter the powerful, and there were more speeches in praise of princes than deliberations about the public good. In the forum, if the prince were involved in a case, others' sense of embarrassment would keep them from detaining him, since he himself would also sometimes indicate, merely by making a gesture, that he was in a hurry. Considering that everything was focused on his pleasures and any care for the state abandoned, the judges themselves, who were ignorant and pampered, did not tolerate long orations, only short and also pleasant ones, and—something disgraceful in the person of a judge—they preferred to hear anything that was amusing rather than that which gave them information about the case. Orations were adapted to feelings of this sort, so that men brought into the forum things that would have been more suitable for the stage. Thus, the na-

11. Aristotle notes that the Areopagus, the law court in Athens, forbade using arguments that excited anger, pity, and the like; see *Rhetoric,* I.i.4–6, and Quintilian, *Institutio oratoria,* II.xvi.4.
12. See *Brutus,* lciv.324; Pompey's law was passed in 52 B.C.
13. *Dialogus,* xxxviii.2.
14. *De oratore,* II.lxxxiii.338. This passage is slightly different in modern editions of the work.

ture of public speaking was profoundly changed; from being healthy, sober, and severe, it became extravagant and voluptuous, as if, having taken off its manly clothes, it had put on a woman's. The people themselves gathered in the forum and the courts not, as before, in order to consider what was transpiring and whether it was credible or not, as if they were the lords and rulers of all, but as if they were going to be entertained in the theater, unmindful of their freedom, and apathetic and unconcerned about the condition of the state. And since that sort of speaking was pleasing to the public, it was introduced into the schools as exercises.

The declamations of that time were not invented to gain victory, but for pleasure, for orators did not fight one another, but showed off and sought poetical charms in digressions, something which the declamations of Quintilian reveal, as do those passages that are cited by Seneca [the Rhetor] from the public speakers of his time. Cicero digresses and describes things, of course, but severely, gravely, and to the point; he is indeed sometimes a bit too diffuse, particularly in speeches on general topics, but he always preserves the dignity of the speaker, the audience, and the subject matter itself. By contrast, you would say that those other orators were singing songs to the sound of the cithara for the sake of amusement, not meditating on extremely serious matters, something that Tacitus, Quintilian, and Seneca judged quite undignified. And since those declamations that are circulated under the name of Quintilian are so far from his own teaching and are the sort of thing against which it would seem he would have inveighed mightily, it is reasonable that many should deny those works are actually his. Thus, although ancient orators such as Cicero used to make declamations, they did so in real cases, cases that were then to be tried in something like a real battle, cases that they had to transfer from the dust and shade and take to the sunlit battlefield. By contrast, later speakers made declamations that were fictive and served no practical end, and none of them could ever attain the forum or the Senate, for those men wanted speeches in which one could show off as much as possible and charm a crowd of idle auditors.

Finally, when courts conducted their business according to laws laid down by princes, it seemed better to employ an expert in justice and the law than an orator to examine a case. Thus, as the power of legal interpreters grew, even in conjectural cases, the study of the art of oratory declined absolutely, a process that began near the time of the Antonines, when lawyers, who enjoyed the greatest favor with princes, determined to take charge of everything themselves. And perhaps that seemed right to the philosopher Marcus Aurelius who did not think it expedient that justice and injustice should be confused by eloquent speech.[15] Once the body was destroyed, the form perished: declaiming was abandoned, as was any study of the art,

15. See his *Meditations*, I.7; for his hostility to rhetoric, see also a letter about him by his teacher, Marcus Cornelius Fronto, *Epistulae*, II.63.

which was not going to be profitable at all without practice, for people thought it pointless to undertake any kind of work when the reward for it had been removed. Thus, little by little the study of refining the language ceased, since it was absolutely not worthwhile to do so, and eloquence, more prematurely than any of the other liberal arts, was shaken off like a delicate flower blown away by the north wind. In other words, when the popular breeze that is so very healthy for eloquence had been removed, when the cultivation of the language had been forsaken, and when the language itself had been abandoned without a defender, laid open to injury and attacks of every sort, and exposed to the arrival of the barbarians—then, eloquence perished as if it had been given a fatal wound. Once they had embraced Christian piety, rulers allowed priests to speak to the people about sacred matters because that was useful to everyone generally. Thus, sacred haranguers succeeded the great ancient orators, but with a very different effect, for just as we are superior to the ancients because of our subject matter [i.e., Christian truth], we are inferior to them in all the parts of eloquence, in persuasive force, maxims, arguments, the arrangement of a speech, language, oratorical genres, and delivery. And both speakers and listeners must share the blame for this situation.

In the past, orators used to be artists who were extremely clever in practicing their art; they possessed every sort of prudence and were really expert at manipulating people's feelings. How different are those who speak nowadays! They are inexperienced, ignorant about life, nay rather, about our common human feelings, and entirely unaware of what the affections are and how to excite them or restrain them. Nor do they know which words and which oratorical genres are to be employed with which subjects, since they have concluded that everything goes with everything else. Their sentences are leaden, frigid, lifeless, inert, quicker to cast down spirits than to arouse them. They collect ridiculous little arguments from some scholastic exercise, which they blow about them and sometimes tickle their audience with, but with which they never strike or slay. The arrangement of their speeches is diffuse and disorganized; they say nothing in its proper place; their delivery is uncontrolled; and nothing is adapted to the place or the time, whether one speaks of their voice, their eyes and face, their hands and fingers, their gestures, or the entire posture of their bodies. They consider all these things so well known that they think they are of no consequence, nor do they feel it makes any difference whether the person speaking dances about or sits down. Moreover, whereas orators once had auditors who were sharp, attentive, and, for the most part, educated, now they are stupid, slow, distracted, rude, and ignorant, so that those who are speaking have to repeat the same things over and over again, not only to impress them on the memories of their listeners so that they stick there, but even just to make sure their ideas are understood. If there is anything more subtle to be said, unless the speakers explain and clarify it—in which process the grace and force of the discourse are lost—they will have cried out in vain, their words directed to the deaf. If they have anything to say that is indirect, unless they explain it in a simple, straightforward manner, they will have wasted their words—nor is there any less of a waste when they dishonor the charm and beauty and crush the sinews of their speech.

4. Who the First Individuals Were, After the Decay of Eloquence, to Have Delighted in the Study of Oratory, and How Little they Accomplished. A Brief and Clear Presentation of the Precepts Handed Down by Professors of the Art Concerning the Imitation of Authors.

In the time of our fathers and grandfathers the study of languages was first called back to life in Italy by the disciples of Peter of Ravenna, for Latin, and Manuel Chrysoloras, for Greek.[16] Among them, the most famous were Leonardo Bruni Aretino, Francesco Filelfo, Lorenzo Valla, Guarino of Verona, and Niccolò Perotto. Following them came Giovanni Pico della Mirandola, Ermolao Barbaro, Angelo Poliziano, and others whom it is inappropriate to enumerate here. All these men, as well as all those who spoke Latin in a more learned fashion than the rest, were called orators, although people hardly understood the force of the term, since the practice of the art of oratory has still not been restored. On the contrary, the zealous efforts of all of those men were so directed at renewing and raising up languages that had been utterly cast down and ruined, that their teaching of the principles of rhetoric has been of little avail since there has been no proper exercising of it.

Up until now no one has practiced public speaking, or has done so, at any rate, using real arguments as if they were struggling in a battle or in the gymnasium. On the contrary, many men have amused themselves making insignificant little speeches where there was no real adversary involved, as when they would orate in praise of the arts, or the virtues, or members of the ruling class. Or, using a canine eloquence, they have exercised themselves with rabid invectives, by means of which they lacerated one another; that is, they have heaped together as many jeers and slanders as possible in order to slash their adversary to pieces, turning up their noses in scorn at him and making a spectacle of him to be laughed at and despised by everyone. Of the case itself, they have said nothing, or very little—if, that is, there really was a case, rather than some feud they were carrying on that had been started over some trivial matter. Nor do I see that they were ever truly careful with their phrasing or selection of oratorical genres; they were concerned only about selecting particular words. And just as those who used to read Cicero or other Latin writers a hundred years ago focused solely on the sense and did not consider the words, so these men who have been attentive to the

---

16. Peter of Ravenna seems to be a slip on Vives's part. He is probably conflating two people: Pier (Peter) Paolo Vergerio and Giovanni di Conversino da Ravenna.

individual words alone have neglected the issue of correct style. Thus, you might see them using the same style to write about matters that are both great and small, happy and sad, low and sublime, as well as for letters and orations, for agriculture and natural science, for moral and legal matters. And no wonder: accommodating one's style to the nature of the argument and to the character of one's audience, indeed, the very invention of arguments appropriate to the case and the situation—these things constitute a task that is long, varied, and intricate, about which Pliny wrote, "In my nineteenth year I started speaking in the forum, and only now do I see, albeit as if through a mist, what really makes an orator." [17] Yet most of them have expended no, or only a very tiny, effort on this matter, which is otherwise so very difficult in itself. How much more do I marvel at the—shall I call it impudence? or temerity? or both?—of those who, though untrained, do not hesitate to judge the ornamentation, coloring, and style of a speech, finally its entire composition and phrasing, and all from a brief and hurried reading of one little page or another.

(Vives goes on to attack his contemporaries for seeing the imitation of ancient authors not as a tool in education, but as its end. In particular, he attacks contemporary Ciceronians for the futility of their anachronistic enterprise and for using up so much life and energy in it.)

I myself would not pay such a high price for, I will not say the joining together of words in a Ciceronian fashion, let alone for the chance to be a complete Ciceronian in every phrase, but even for something much more noble and desirable, namely, to understand all the philosophy that has been written about the nature of things. These imitators, together with those others who have dedicated themselves to the long neglected cultivation of languages, have expended so much energy in selecting words and adorning their style that they have not even glanced at what has been written gravely and copiously about the understanding of nature and about public and private morality. This is so partly because some of them have not had the leisure, for they have been so very busy with noting words and with the nature and adornment of their style that they cannot look deeply into other matters; it is also partly because they feared that if they touched writers who were insufficiently cultured, they might catch something from them that would pollute their beautiful speech. Thus, they stopped at the mere observation of languages and used up all their efforts on words, both simple and complex.

But what can those people accomplish who have nothing except a bunch of tools? Although in speaking they may have arranged their immense crowd of words as if in battle formation and have made them indeed seem beautiful in appearance, still, their words are useless and ineffective, and

17. Pliny the Younger, *Epistulae*, V.viii.8.

they have produced nothing worthy of the subject itself or of the minds of their auditors. They thus bring great disgrace to their art, which has been judged on the basis of men who are, in their own opinion and in that of others, its first and foremost professors. How much more truly should that person be called an orator who expounds great matters in arguments equal to them, no matter what language is being used. For, if speaking is a kind of fight and aims at persuasion as if at victory, who would not prefer a soldier who is spirited, protected by leather armor, and armed with an iron sword, to one who, unwarlike and effeminate, shines with his golden arms and sword? Since, as people say, rhetoric is supposed to treat every conceivable subject, and political and civil matters in particular, what will those individuals say who have not seen such things even in a dream, who do not know in what world, let alone what city, they live, and who, since they are always meditating on that ancient Rome of theirs, have become strangers in this place and age of ours? One cannot call people eloquent who, since they strive to say everything in the language of another, wind up being mute themselves, unable to fit three words together properly in that learned and polished language of theirs. "To speak," says Quintilian, "is to bring forth all the things you have conceived in your mind and to convey them to your auditors."[18] If you do not do this, everything that comes before it is superfluous and resembles a sword hidden away and stuck in its sheath.

FROM *On Teaching the Disciplines, or Of Christian Education*

Book IV

3. On Rhetoric: Refuting the Opinion of Those Who Think That This Art of Eloquence Is Pernicious and Ought to Be Thrown Out; What Sorts of Things Should Be Taught about it; Then Who the Writers of Rhetoric Books Are; What Suasoria Are, What Their Subject Is, and How to Correct them.

After these things [grammar, literature, and moral philosophy] comes the art of speaking, which it is hardly fitting for men who are both good and wise to repudiate or neglect, seeing that it is extremely productive and powerful as well as being necessary in every aspect of life. In man, justice and supreme command lie within his will, and while reason and judgment have been bestowed upon him to serve him as counselors, his passions are torches that are kindled by the sparks of speech, by means of which reason is excited and moved. Thus, speech obtains an enormous power over the entire kingdom of man and displays its effects immediately, so that Euripides is right in calling eloquence a tyrant,[19] and it is a fact that by means of

18. See *Institutio oratoria*, VIII.Pr.15.
19. See *Hecuba*, 816. Vives is thinking of a passage in Quintilian, *Institutio oratoria*, I.xii.18, in which eloquence is called a queen by a "not ignoble tragic poet" who was thought in the

speech, many people, such as Pisistratus and Pericles, have acquired incredible wealth, power, and political authority. However, some say that since our morals have declined, men should not be entrusted with things that they can use to harm others. For my part, I explained just a short while ago just what sorts of students I thought should be entrusted with this art and how much, it seemed to me, ought to be learned about it.[20]

But surely, the more the minds of men are corrupted, the more this art should be practiced with the greatest care by prudent and upright men, for it dominates our minds to such an extent that it can lead them away from scandalous and wicked behavior to a love of virtue. That speech is an absolute necessity is revealed by the fact that no mode of living and no activity whatsoever can exist without it, whether we are in public or in private, at home or in the forum, with a friend or an opponent or an enemy, a superior, an inferior, or an equal. It is the cause of the greatest good and the greatest evil. How important, then, to use a form of speech that is proper and suited to the persons, places, and times involved, so that we let nothing slip out that is perverse, childish, or indecorous! Indeed, there is no other way for us to go about this business. We must not engage in the empty study of words that are elegant and brilliant, polished and linked together charmingly, just as we must also avoid speaking in a disagreeable, inelegant, and inappropriate manner. As a result, it should be evident that this art really is the principal part of prudence.

In my judgment, students should be taught first to consider the end of their oration, contemplating it from a certain distance, and then, to consider what instruments and what paths can be found for reaching it. If, for example, the end is to teach, to persuade, or to move, and the instruments are simple and compound words and their meanings, all of these things—and all of their attributes—must be clarified and examined. Then we must see how our tools can be used in our work: we must identify what they are, the ends they serve, and the manner in which they can be employed. Next we must consider what is involved in teaching and all its parts, in persuading, and in moving the emotions and all the different forms that that takes. We

---

Renaissance to be Euripides. However, it is more likely that the passage in question is a fragment from Pacuvius's *Hermione*, which is also cited in Cicero, *De oratore*, II.xliv.187.

20. In the preceding chapter, Vives wrote: "Both the arts of dialectic and rhetoric are quarrelsome by their nature and incline to contentiousness and stubbornness. They are therefore to be denied to students of a quarrelsome and contentious character, and to those who always suspect the worst, for they twist everything in that direction. Both arts bring with them a great deal of malice, so that it is not fitting that they should be taught to those who have a malicious character and are inclined to engage in fraud. Nor are they to be taught to a person who is wicked, seditious, venal, irascible, or vengeful; for him they would become 'a sword in the hand of a madman,' as the proverb has it. No matter what person is taught these things, he is to taste them in moderation and for just a short period of time, rather than drink them up completely, for they make people thorny, contentious, and inclined to fraud. It may well be that, as they say, this happens because the arts are badly used, but many people do slip into vice if the occasion merely presents itself to them."

will consider the nature of the speaker and the auditor, the place, the time, and the subject matter, and which instruments are suitable for which things and for which end here and now, with this speaker and this auditor. Unless I am deceived, our ancestors taught these things long ago, but in a disorderly and confused manner singularly unsuited for putting them into practice. Still, a diligent teacher can gather many things from their writings. . . .

(Vives provides a lengthy review of writers on rhetoric from both antiquity and recent history from whom the teacher can gather useful information.)

The nature of languages must also be studied: how they were invented, grew, and decayed; how one assesses their force, character, richness, elegance, gravity, refinement, and other qualities. Cicero preferred that one should not follow the rules of rhetoric too closely, for the simple reason that scarcely any teacher of the art has ever been eloquent himself. It seems to me that the same thing ought to be said about all the instruments we employ, for in using them, elegance and careful arrangement are not required so much as that we devote ourselves to employing them properly. Nor would I approve at all of exercises in rhetoric that are assiduously and frequently repeated, for fear that that two-headed instrument might stimulate a desire to harm others when the occasion presents itself and give birth to a proclivity to practice fraud and malice. However, at the beginning I do want exercises to be more frequent than when students are later composing varied and complicated arguments. At first, let them handle certain easier, simpler matters that do not particularly require style or intensity of expression or special structures: little fables, short stories, the expansion of a contracted period, and the contraction of one that is spread out and diffuse—these are things that they can find frequently in the writers they are reading. Then they will study the various ways to teach and delight, and will move on to speeches that involve controversy, questions, and adversaries. Finally, they will focus on moving and exciting the emotions. . . .

Students should never get accustomed to speaking against the truth or on behalf of something that rhetors say is disreputable, such as speaking against Socrates and for Busiris, for pleasure and against equity and piety, lest what they do in play at one moment, they do for real on another occasion because the perverse desire of their spirit drives them to do so.[21] Instead, one should put all of one's eloquence in full battle formation, as it were, ready to defend goodness and piety against wickedness and sacrilege. On the one hand, words that contain no meaning are truly empty and vain and appear all puffed up, and we laugh at and mock ignorant little sentences; however, prudence, on the other hand, when it is divorced from probity, is simply malice and pernicious fraud. Thus, a true and genuine rhetoric is nothing less than

---

21. Quintilian remarks on the perverseness of speaking in favor of Busiris; see *Institutio oratoria*, II.xvii.4.

eloquent wisdom that can in no way be separated from the character of a just and pious man.[22] Nor should we imitate what has been accepted by the nobility: cursing, reviling others, spreading wicked suspicions, perverting what is right, making a bad case out of a good one and a good one out of a bad. It is better to suffer the loss of a case than of virtue. Nor should we imitate things that are bad in themselves, not just when wicked men do them, but when anyone does, no matter how completely holy and blameless such a person may be.

(Vives says there is no need to study judicial rhetoric, "in which there is a great deal of maliciousness." He also insists that students need to practice declaiming and that each week the teacher should publicly correct one of their speeches.)

He will consider first what is being said, then who is speaking, at what time, and to whom the speaker feigns he is directing his remarks. Then the teacher will examine the simple words, the compound ones, the sentences, the arguments, and their order, considering the quality of every single one of these things in itself. Next he will consider how each one of them is appropriate to the subject of the speech, and how all are suited to the specific time, place, audience, and speaker. However, he will not worry too much about making everything exact and using arguments that are powerful and irrefutable; rather, his main concern will be to prevent those arguments from being unsuitable, for there is really nothing in this art that is worse than to lack decorum. And it has certainly been said with justice that "the chief thing is to do what you do with decorum." Now, you see what intelligence, experience, prudence, and attention are necessary for the teacher to make his critique, and why this is the most difficult task he faces, although it is also by far the most fruitful activity for both himself and his school, because the student listening to him gets more knowledge and a better training of his judgment from one correction than from many lectures and commentaries. Therefore, the students should throng to these critiques, should listen as intently as possible, and should use their notebooks to record summaries of the chief topics, which, immediately afterwards, they will explore more fully in their rooms, impressing and engraving them on their memories so that they forever avoid the dangers that have been revealed to them. For those young people should be made to realize that, because of the huge number and the great variety of evils by which we are often attacked from every direction, one must use greater judgment and make a greater effort to avoid evils than is needed to maintain what is good.

22. Cicero frequently links wisdom and eloquence; see, for example, *De oratore*, III.xxxv.142.

[10]

Philip Melanchthon

Protestant theologian, reformer, and educator, Philip Melanchthon (1497–1560) was born into a family of skilled craftsmen, but was given a humanistic education thanks to the help of his uncle, Johann Reuchlin, one of the leading humanists in Germany. Since he made excellent progress in Greek, his uncle rechristened him Melanchthon, a Greek translation of his German surname, Schwarzerd ("black earth"). By 1509, Melanchthon had obtained his B.A. at Heidelberg and by 1512 his M.A. at Tübingen, where he taught for several years until he was called to Wittenberg in 1518, at his uncle's recommendation, to teach Greek. He obtained a B.D. there in 1519 and began to collaborate with Luther on the latter's translation of the Bible, a collaboration that eventually led him to embrace Luther's reforms and to break with his Catholic uncle. After defending Luther in a treatise proclaiming Holy Scripture the supreme authority in matters of religion, Melanchthon established himself as one of the leaders of the Reformation in 1521 when he published his *Loci communes rerum theologicarum* (*Commonplaces of Theology*). In 1528, when asked to attempt to regulate the constitution of the reformed churches in Germany, he produced his *Unterricht des Visitatoren* (*Instruction for Church Inspectors*). This work also contained an educational plan for elementary education that led to the creation of the first Protestant public school system in the country and earned Melanchthon the title of "Preceptor of Germany." At the Diet of Augsburg, held in 1530 in an attempt to unify the Protestant churches, Melanchthon prepared the Augsburg Confession, which has influenced all subsequent Protestant statements of the creed. After his death, Melanchthon was buried beside Luther in the Schlosskirche in Wittenberg. The work translated here was produced in 1523 and reflects Melanchthon's humanist-inspired hostility to Scholasticism. The text is taken from his *Declamationes*, edited by Karl Hartfelder (Berlin, 1891), 27–48.

Philip Melanchthon

From *The Praise of Eloquence*[1]

Just as Hesiod grieves that mortals do not know how much profit the mallow and the asphodel can bring to human affairs, even though they are base
weeds, so we, too, complain—and this is not the first time—that adolescents do not know how much importance the arts of speech have for the acquisition of solid erudition.[2] Although by their appearance they promise
nothing that would make the rabble applaud, they easily surpass all human
things in usefulness, for there is nothing in the entire world from which
mortals derive ampler benefits than from arts of this sort. But since young
people are ignorant of their value, they often appear worthless and are
judged to be scarcely worth the effort expended to learn them. Nowadays,
to be called a philosopher is excellent, to be named a lawyer is magnificent,
and nothing is worthier of applause among the rabble than the name of theologian. The arts of speaking are held to be of no account, as though they
were worthless Megarians.[3]

Therefore, it seems right to show here what most recommends the study
of those arts to us. Now, what I should really like to have is the power of Pericles, as I strive to recall young people to the right path who scorn more
refined literature partly out of error, because they think it is useless for
learning the rest of the disciplines, and who flee the arts of speech partly out
of laziness. For the nature of literary studies, as of all other good things, is
such that no one acquires them without the greatest labor, and it is well
known that those things that are beautiful are difficult. If someone balanced
the account here by reckoning how much profit he would make from how
little labor, and if he envisioned the immensity of the benefits involved, then
nothing, no matter how hard, would deter him from the study of these
arts. Moreover, unless you have learned them, words cannot express how
unsuccessful you are going to be in handling the other disciplines. Consequently, listen impartially to the reasons that have led me to conclude that
the more elegant literary studies are truly necessary for human life.

In the first place, no one is so insane as not to see that an artful method of
speaking is necessary for us, if we are to explain our thoughts clearly concerning what should be done in public or private matters. Perhaps it would
be ridiculous to argue here about how basically necessary speech is to man,
for even those who despise literary studies do not seem on any account to

1. The full title of Melanchthon's work is "The Declamation of Philip Melanchthon That
the Arts of Speech Are Necessary for Every Kind of Intellectual Pursuit (or: The Praise of
Eloquence)."
2. See Hesiod, *Works and Days*, 41. Mallow and asphodel were edible plants and served as sta-
ples of the poor man's diet in ancient Greece.
3. In one of his *Adages*, "Megarenses neque tertii neque quarti" ("The Megarians are neither
the third nor the fourth"), Erasmus explains that to say someone is neither the third nor the
fourth is to say that that person is exceptionally worthless and that the inhabitants of the Greek
city of Megara were generally judged that way in antiquity; see *Adages*, III.i.79.

want to deprive man of speech, but merely to reject polished oratory. Therefore, we will explain briefly how much it matters that an artful method of speaking be learned. For you will not be able to expound what you think so that it can be understood, unless you acquire and then strengthen the faculty of speech through the discipline of art.

Prudent men have discovered through experience that nothing is more difficult than to speak clearly and distinctly about a given subject. For first of all, unless you observe the force and weight of words in speaking, what auditor will be able to follow your oration? Since words, like money, are approved by custom, one should make use of those that have been accepted and that, since eloquent men have handed them down to posterity as though from father to son, are free of obscurity. In the preceding century, when each person forged his own words for himself and foreign ones were mixed with Latin ones, speeches were composed in such a way that they could not be understood even by the men of that age. It is really unsuitable for us to follow our predecessors, for nowadays who understands Scotus or other writers of his ilk? Moreover, the best-trained people can scarcely keep themselves from violating somewhere the structure and diction of their speech—and if those things are corrupted, one's speech is necessarily rendered obscure. Indeed, at this time how many things do even the erudite say that are unsuitable? How often do they render their speech obscure with absurd and inept metaphors? Who can endure Apuleius and his apes? Apuleius did well, however: since he took on the role of an ass, he preferred to bray rather than speak.

Even when you have mastered words and diction sufficiently, it is still very difficult to put each thing in its proper place, to lower some things and raise up others, to abridge certain things in a brief space, to expand others more freely, to dissimulate and hide certain things, and to reveal others so that they stand out conspicuously like lights against shadows. Eloquence is something altogether grander than a confused heaping up of words. However, I see that young people, who know neither the power nor the nature of eloquence, have slipped into the error of thinking that it is not worth the effort to acquire this art with so much study and exertion, and believe that it is praised by us ridiculous little professors in the same way that quacks praise their ointments. Nor are they impressed by the authority of the best and most prudent men who, with a general trumpet call to battle, unanimously invite adolescents to pursue the study of the art. I have not spoken of human nature in general, since, like all the best things, it is really so hard to see that we scarcely recognize it, but I would not doubt that if the worth of eloquence could be discerned with our eyes, then, as that famous man said, it would excite marvelous affection.[4] However, young people live by the hazards of chance, not by reason; they are driven

---

4. "That famous man" is probably Erasmus.

by rash impulses and descend to those things that are most prized by the rabble.

Therefore, if someone is a prudent judge of things, he should consider first of all that there is nothing whose advantages extend further than do the benefits of speech. All relationships among men, the methods we use to maintain our lives in public and private and to procure all the things by means of which we protect our livelihoods, and finally, all our business dealings—all of these things are managed by speech. Furthermore, that person should also persuade himself that no one is going to speak appropriately and clearly on any subject who has not shaped his speech with great care, basing it on the language we use in public, and employing a certain artful imitation of the best speakers. When he thinks about this, he will conclude that, without a doubt, there is nothing better, nothing more venerable than learning the arts of speech. For if people are to be aided by counsel or to be taught, or a certain doctrine is to be defended, or if one has to discourse on law, justice, and equity, then you will accomplish nothing more than do mute actors on the stage unless you have produced a speech elaborated by art that brings obscure things, as it were, into the light.

I am not ignorant of the fact that there are those who separate elegance from the correct method of speaking and do not think it matters whether they use any particular kind of language, provided that they explain their subject. If they had examined this issue more closely, however, they would have concluded that professors of eloquence were by no means asking for the use of dainty and superfluous cosmetics. Elegance resides in the very purity and natural appearance of language, and unless you take care of them, not only will you speak without charm and in a filthy manner, but inappropriately, obscurely, and foolishly. For just as in fashioning bodies one finally obtains elegance when all the members harmonize with one another in just proportion, and if you do anything differently, the body becomes monstrous, so, when you deform the true shape of a speech through some unusual arrangement, you make it completely monstrous and absurd. Pico, in the letter in which he defends those barbarous philosophers—having fun I believe by making a crazy argument—both separates elegance from the correct method of speaking and supposes that things can be explained by means of any sort of speech whatsoever.[5] However, I am not going to get angry with someone who defends barbarism with no more heartfelt sincerity than Favorinus praised fever. I marvel that there are those who have been persuaded by such frivolous subtleties to believe that it does not matter how we speak. Can a painter correctly imitate a body if he has no system for manipulating his pencil, his hand is moved by chance, and his lines are drawn without art? Using such a method, you will not have placed your real opinion before the eyes of others, nor will you have made use of proper

5. For Pico della Mirandola's letter, see the selection included in this anthology.

and noble language, aptly arranged your words, or rightly ordered your thoughts. For just as we represent bodies by means of colors, so we represent our real opinions by means of speech. Therefore, it is necessary in speaking to use art in order to conceive a certain definite image that keeps the features, as it were, of your ideas distinct from one another.

It is scandalous to show a person who is ignorant of the right way a path that goes off the beaten track, but how often do those people who have no concern for correct speech lead the reader from the right way? How often, through the misuse of a single word, do they make a fool of him? They have never imposed their grammatical mistakes on me in philosophy or Sacred Scripture when I have been the interpreter. . . . What confusion misleads Augustine so that he does not grasp the main point in interpreting what is written in John: "Even the same that I said unto you from the beginning."[6] Innumerable things of this sort exist everywhere in which barbarous expressions have sometimes deceived even the erudite. Truly, you will not satisfy a reader with just any kind of speech, but you must take pains and study in order to obtain the skill by means of which you can place your thoughts clearly before the eyes of others and say everything in an appropriate manner that your subject requires—for that is what speaking elegantly means.

Therefore, we offer a toast of hellebore to those who disdain the beauties of speech, for they are really so far from the common feelings of humanity that they hardly understand what speech is.[7] Necessity is the mother of elegance, for all barbarous expressions are obscure, while those that are rendered lustrous by means of oratorical ornamentation can be perceived more clearly. Quintilian wrote that in this activity one ought to employ figures of speech, for he did not feel that true beauty could ever rightly be separated from what was useful.[8] In sacred writings, to omit profane ones for the time being, do you really long for rhetorical figures? Yes, for I do not think the prophets would have used them if they thought those figures would do nothing for the subject matter.

You see with what arguments I commend the study of eloquence to you: we cannot explain what we ourselves want, or understand correctly the extant writings of our ancestors, unless we have learned thoroughly an artful method of speaking. For my part, I do not see how people are even going to seem human to others if they cannot explain what they are thinking or follow that which is spoken correctly. In fact, even if eloquence had no dignity or grace, nevertheless it has power that is such that we do not make use of fire, air, or water, as they say, in more places. For how could human affairs

6. John 8:24. Augustine interprets Christ as responding to the question who He was by saying He was the "Principle," taking the Greek word "arche" to mean this rather than "beginning"; see *The City of God*, X.24.

7. Hellebore was a plant used as a purgative to cure various mental illnesses.

8. See *Institutio oratoria*, VIII.iii.1–11.

continue if eloquence should abandon its protection of both sacred and profane law, if oratory should not exhibit what can be understood in public and private consultations, if men's deeds could not be transmitted to posterity in writing? Would any vestige of humanity be left in such a state? In fact, how little did the preceding age differ from such a state, for then almost no one actually understood the language of the sacred books, and sacred laws were made and annulled on a daily basis because of the judgment of foolish sophists? The deeds of those times lay buried in eternal darkness, for there was no one who could shine the light of letters on them. All the disciplines were so darkened because of their mode of speech that not even the learned themselves knew with sufficient certainty what they were professing. Philosophers fought among themselves about figures of speech, like blindfolded gladiators in the dark, nor was anyone clearly understood by his servants. That famous man rightly remarked, "Anacharsis committed a solecism among the Athenians, but the Athenian committed a solecism among the Scythians."[9] But these individuals committed solecisms in their own homes, and each one individually would take remarkable freedoms in inventing his own dialect. You would swear it was a pleasure for them, not otherwise than for Heraclitus, to bury all other mortals in darkness. Now, since it is clear how much contempt toward this eloquence of ours has persisted, why do we not abominate such barbarism as the most harmful plague? Why do we not, with one accord, hiss those people out of the schools? Why have we begrudged eloquence to ourselves for so long a time even though the sun sees nothing better, nothing grander on earth?

Thus far we have shown how necessity forces us to follow and observe a definite method in speaking, and how, if anyone fails to be persuaded by this argument, then truly the gods should put ass's ears much more justly on him than on Midas. In addition, another benefit deriving from the study of eloquence that is not to be despised is that, by practicing those arts that compose eloquence, one's natural abilities are stimulated and developed, so that one comes to consider all human affairs with greater prudence, for a shadow does not follow a body more closely than prudence attends on eloquence. Thus far I am speaking of human affairs; I will treat sacred ones later. Our ancestors saw that these two things, the art of speaking well and the faculty of judgment [i.e., prudence], harmonized with each other by nature, so that certain men said, and not foolishly, that speech was the disclosure of our mental reasoning. The poet Homer attributed eloquence and prudence to the same people; omitting other authors here, I note that to Ulysses, whose speech Homer compares to winter snow, he ascribes both traits in a single little verse, when he says: "you have a beautiful form of

9. See Anacharsis, *Epistulae*, 1. The "famous man" may be Anacharsis, but it may also be Pico della Mirandola, who cited the saying in his letter to Ermolao Barbaro. The saying means that a person who is not a native speaker of a language is likely to make linguistic mistakes, that is, solecisms, in it, but the saying's relativizing implications seem to have escaped Melanchthon.

words, and you have a good mind."[10] Nor do I restrain myself from repeating what was said in Latin by a certain learned man: you have a healthy mind that has been united, by grace, to eloquent words. O divine saying, which should be carefully grafted onto the hearts of youth, and which is much more worthy than that Delphic saying known by some.[11] For what was that best of old men aiming at except the notion that prudence and eloquence should be so joined together that they could in no way be torn apart. I wish all adolescents would think that this little verse was for them, so that they would aim all their studies and understanding at this end as at a target and would think that all their effort, care, industry, thought, finally all their mental activity should be directed at acquiring these arts, which Homer mentioned doubtless because he wanted them to seem the most beautiful and useful of all the human attributes that exist.

Why do you think the ancient Latins decided to call the arts of speech the humanities? They thought that surely through the study of those disciplines not only would one's language be polished, but the wildness and barbarism of one's innate disposition would also be corrected. For by means of education, many people cast off their savage natures, and in the process their characters become mild and tame.

There are two reasons why one's prudential judgment is sharpened by the study of correct speech. The first is that those people who take pains with these arts necessarily prepare themselves through the examples of writers who, involved in handling and managing the greatest affairs, have arrived through experience at the heights of prudence. Through commerce with them, readers contract a certain capacity for judging, being tanned, as it were, by them, just as people are who walk in the sun. Normally, a certain model of correct speech and thought is proposed for young minds from which they might learn about the power of words, the structures of orations, and the figures of speech needed to explain their thoughts. For imitation helps in the teaching of speech just as it does with the other arts. It is not likely that Apelles could have added so much beauty and grace to the art of painting if, much before him, those who did monochromatic work and who painted side views, had not revealed the method of making sketches. Thus, from the best writers one should derive a certain definite method, like a Platonic Idea, of speaking and judging that you should follow no matter what subject you have to discuss.

The second reason [that the study of speech sharpens one's judgment] is that those who have eloquent writers in their hands will ponder what it is especially fitting to admire, praise, and imitate in any one of them. The first authors whom young people are invited to become acquainted with are the

---

10. *Odyssey*, XI.367. The comparison of Odysseus's speech to winter snow occurs in the *Iliad*, III.222.

11. On the temple front at Delphi was engraved the famous saying "gnôthi seautón" ("know thyself"), which Socrates took as his motto.

poets and historians who are summoned only for the sake of pleasure, as female lute players are to banquets, lest esteem for superior writers be seriously impaired. Now those authors wanted to be of use, and the best things do especially delight good minds. Thus, one should seek one's form of speech in those writers and observe what they have generally thought about our everyday life.

(Melanchthon praises Homer as a master of rhetoric and for his representation of characters, the prudence taught by his texts, and even the scientific knowledge they contain. He also emphasizes the importance of studying Vergil and the Greek historians.)

Since orators have administered states and, having been involved in trials, have discussed so many things concerning law, justice, and equity, one could certainly learn a great many useful things from them. For what topic is there in moral philosophy that Demosthenes and Cicero have not touched on? No philosopher has done better political analysis than they have in their lawsuits, where they draw their pen like a sword against wicked and seditious citizens, and with their counsel, defend their states against hostile forces. Has anyone ever thought up things to say about peace that are more apt to win popular favor and truer than what Cicero said in his oration arguing against the agrarian law?[12] What has more civic value than that praise of the laws that lawyers have transferred to their commentaries from Demosthenes' oration "Against Aristogeiton"? But why should I weave a long encomium of these writers here? Why don't you try yourselves to show how each one excels all others like him, how clearly and gracefully he explains and how prudently he assembles all those things that pertain to our habits and customs? For unless you are disposed to imitate them, you must completely despair of ever being able to speak and judge things correctly.

We still have to unfold the other reason why we declared that judgment is sharpened by the study of eloquence. The answer is that a concern to speak well in and of itself makes one's mind livelier and capable of ascertaining more accurately what is most fitting or useful in every case. For just as we see that bodily strength is reinforced by exercise, so one cannot prevent the minds of those who are not stimulated by mental labor from growing dull. No one doubts that the reading of good writers is of great value, but unless the habit of writing and speaking is joined to that of reading, you will not be able to determine with sufficient acuity just what their ideas and virtues are, or formulate intellectually a sure rule for judging and imitating them. Thus, to train the faculties of both speaking and judging, nothing is as necessary as exercising your pen. . . . In fact, Cicero attributed a great deal to the pen, writing that it was the best and most excellent source and teacher of oratory, and that he was accustomed at times of leisure sometimes to turn

12. Cicero delivered this speech, *De lege agraria contra Rutullum,* in 63 B.C., when he was elected consul. In it he opposed a law that would have led to democratic land reform.

Greek works into Latin ones, at other times to forge new ones, and to practice declamation at yet other times.[13] By means of such industry, he maintained the strength and vigor of his natural talent and enriched his eloquence. . . . By contrast, how few of our young people have learned to write
just one single little verse even in a whole decade? Many of them think that
the shortcut for acquiring erudition is just to hear or read as much as possible. And so, some of them run to and fro everyday, sneak around all the
schools, listen to teachers here and there, marveling at what they do not understand, scribbling down lessons, writing pearls of wisdom in their notebooks in tiny little letters, and underlining them in red. Interpreters are held
in high esteem if they waste time saying over and over as many things as
they can, nor is anyone entitled to remove a teacher who has departed from
this custom by even a hairsbreadth. Other young people, by contrast, never
take a step outside their homes and devote themselves to their books like
drudges in a mill, reading the pages over and over again, and thinking
themselves blessed when they have gone through a great number of them
every day. But do not both groups seem wretched since, with such labor and
such a sacrifice of health, they are only learning to play the fool? . . .

Demosthenes, about to speak before the Athenians, rejoices in the fact
that they can understand on their own accord what things are best.[14] By contrast, we praise the exercise of writing to those who have never made an attempt to do it and who have not caught a glimpse even in passing of the
power and extent of the advantages that this exercise brings with it. Thus,
we fear all the more that our speech here will have little credibility with
them since we are attributing so much to writing in it. But if there is someone who is not entirely the enemy of the Muses, he should meditate on the
method of education used by the ancients, by means of which all the disciplines were not merely adorned, but enriched. In their elementary schools,
few authors, though those were the best, were proposed for the young to imitate. And as in agriculture it is taught that a farm should not have more
acreage than can be properly cultivated—for Vergil says, "Praise great estates, farm a little one"[15]—so the ancients, when they saw that many authors could not be learned thoroughly or imitated successfully and that
young talents were confused rather than polished by exposure to a host of
writers, admitted very few of them, but had their students become as familiar with them as possible. Moreover, they practiced declamation assiduously, some writing verse, others prose. And since they strove with one another in their enthusiasm for speaking, this concern and care sharpened
their judgment. As no spectacle produced more pleasure than did that practice, so nothing could be done that would have been more beneficial for

13. See *De oratore*, I.xxxiii.150; in this passage, the speaker Crassus explains how he used to
spend his leisure doing the things Melanchthon attributes to Cicero himself.
14. See the prologue to his *First Olynthiac*, I.i.
15. *Georgics*, II.412–13.

either public or private ends. For from schools of that sort came forth the most remarkable men of previous centuries, both Greeks and Latins, and a great many Christians. If our young people strove to imitate them, good lord, how much more would the humanities now be flourishing and how much more successfully would we be interpreting Holy Scripture. Furthermore, since the ancients made so much of an effort to practice writing, since neither erudition nor a modest eloquence can be acquired without such exertion, and since the prudent things written by others cannot be understood unless we ourselves stimulate our talents by means of writing, let me procure a commitment from you that you will occasionally test your powers by doing so. I insist that this is not as difficult as it is beneficial, nor will you find a better way, using any other source, to improve your studies.

Still, you will just be limping along in light verse and prose, since I think all those who have not had any contact with poetry speak rather tediously and truly crawl along the ground, possessing neither a weighty vocabulary nor real power in their figures of speech. . . . In Roman times, incredible ignorance and the inability to speak used to go hand in hand with contempt for poetry, whereas recently, once our contemporaries had begun to compose a few poor little verses, poetry returned to favor, together with the better sorts of writing. And I do not see how the little bit of elegance that has been flourishing again in this century can be preserved unless young people practice writing poems when they exercise their pens. Cicero thought that eloquence was nourished by writing verse, and it is well known that for that reason he often wrote poems and was very enthusiastic about the poets. He left many epigrams to posterity, and today there are extant several passages from the Latin verse of famous poets that have been brilliantly explicated by him. The poems published by Pliny the orator testify to the fact that one's power in speaking is aided by this art. Accordingly, those who want to occupy their best hours in learning should imitate the example of the ancients and, as Quintilian says, using a faithful pen, they should acquire eloquence and sharpen their judgment.[16] For they are greatly deceived if they think they are going to advance in humanistic studies without this exercise. The sea will bear a grapevine sooner than a person will achieve erudition and the ability to speak who, as though dulled by mandragora, never comes to life and awakens his inborn talent through the practice of writing.

I have now explained what reasons prompt me to the study of the arts of speech, that an artful method is surely to be observed in speaking, and that a certain amount of prudence will be acquired by those students as they practice these arts. If anyone thinks they are irrelevant to him, he is without a doubt as far away from humanity as he can be. By contrast, there are good men who, having contemplated the number of benefits that come to us through speech, have realized both that it is necessary to have a definite

16. See *Institutio oratoria*, X.vii.7.

method in speaking and that one's natural abilities will be rendered more refined by means of these arts. Thus, those men hasten to pursue these studies, as they say, with might and main.

But there are quite a few, especially nowadays, who delay the progress of these good things. They deny that knowledge of the arts of speaking is conducive to the study of theology, and this error has spread widely like some sort of contagion and has infected many who, lest they appear not to be real theologians, despise all the more humanistic disciplines. But I should like them to theologize in a serious manner and to behave in a way consistent with Christianity. Nowadays I see that the name of theologian is just used as a pretext for sloth—although that is actually what they confess by their actions. Since it is irksome to learn elegance and to torment oneself by studying the most difficult authors and by practicing writing—for literary knowledge is not acquired without hard study—these people, returning home drunk on some occasion, will read some trifling little harangue, and then, when they have derived from it what their stomachs can handle, will make disorderly declamations at their banquets—for there they are really wise! And because the rabble applaud, they seem to themselves to be perfect theologians, although these obscene men dispute about the most serious matters with filthy, irreverent mouths. Indeed, even though Paul forbids people to "corrupt the word of God," no one traffics in the word of God more impudently than do these people.[17] They deem themselves good men despite their lack of morals and learning, and they fully earn the favor of the rabble through their impious treatment of sacred writing. What more shall I say? You see that they scorn our literary studies, which are concerned with all good and honest things, with piety, with public morality, in fact, with Christ himself. If we would have a well-ordered state, then I would not be criticizing them with a speech; the magistrates would be punishing them with force. For what gallows do they not merit who, though they sinned in no other way, turn young people away from literary studies by means of their example? For unless those young people acquire that learning, we are going to have future generations who are no sounder than those of previous centuries when a lack of literary knowledge impaired all studies, both human and divine.

As a matter of fact, I think that one time in the past, when God became seriously enraged at the Church, literary knowledge was lost, with the result that sacred matters were no longer understood.[18] Although God willingly chose to speak in the language of men, people who were ignorant of the arts of speech could only make foolish judgments about His divine utterances. What blindness possessed the minds of those men in the past! How few of

17. 2 Corinthians 2:17.
18. Melanchthon is referring in a general way to what the Renaissance lamented as the decline of classical languages and culture in the Middle Ages and is blaming it for what he sees as the decadence of the Church.

them were acquainted with Christ! They felt the books containing sacred matters had already been worn out. In their place, the Parisians established articles that, for the time being, the world adored as if they were divine laws; nothing was pious except what they had dreamed up.[19] And those gallant men, although they were ignorant of letters and thus had no means of acquiring knowledge, produced that well-known sophistry of theirs and began to squabble about imaginary problems of word arrangement in order to play the part of rhetorician, producing such questions as: what is the difference between "the Pope I see" and "I see the Pope"? Still extant today is the Parisian article that says: "Whoever should dissent from the opinion that to say 'I runs' is bad Latin is a heretic." Do literary studies, which have been so neglected, seem to have avenged their mistreatment here, for who would believe that the authors of such nonsense had a brain?

This calamity is to be attributed largely to an ignorance of literature. Since sacred matters, as though shut in behind thickets and branches, were not clear, a method of correctly educating the mind had to be so, and yet eloquent writers, who might have provided instruction in the humanities, were neglected. How much more tolerable would it have been for the Church to have been punished with pestilence or famine than with such folly? Truly, I am persuaded that when the world is deprived of literature, it is a sure sign of divine wrath. For the pious are frequently afflicted with all the other punishments, but public impiety is accompanied by ignorance of literature. Recently, however, when our best Father began once again to gaze upon the afflicted, and when the Gospel was about to be restored to us, through His liberality He also revived literary studies in order to assist in the interpretation of the Gospel. The gift of tongues conferred upon the Apostles should not seem more wonderful than the fact that literature, recovered from such filthy desolation, has been recalled into the light from a darkness greater than that of Tartarus.

Clearly, a knowledge of literature has helped certain good men restore theology. Thus, in the first place, we would be ungrateful to despise this heavenly gift, and in the second, since sacred things have been restored with the help of literary studies, we would be impious if we had no regard for what is essential to the maintenance of theology. Let me explain briefly what I believe the knowledge of languages contributes to the interpretation of Sacred Scripture. Note, however, that I have not fallen into the error of thinking that the sacred can be penetrated by the industrious efforts of human intelligence; there are aspects of the sacred that no one may ever understand unless shown them by God, nor can Christ be known by us except through the teaching of the Holy Spirit. For Christ Himself said that he

19. In the Renaissance, the theology faculty of the University of Paris (the Sorbonne), a bastion of Scholasticism, which had been celebrated during the Middle Ages, was criticized by humanists and Protestant reformers for its conservatism, rigidity, and oppressiveness.

was "glorified" by the spirit.[20] But leaving aside such matters of prophecy, one should certainly seek to know the meaning of the words in which the divine mysteries have been hidden as in a shrine. For if you did not understand the words you spoke, how could you even be uttering them? by means of magic? And wouldn't I be telling my tale to the deaf? No one can judge linguistic matters correctly unless he has mastered the correct method of speaking. For what is easier than to be deceived by a particular word or figure? Recently, when a certain one of our "Masters" was interpreting the words that have been recorded in Genesis about Melchisedec, "the king brought bread and wine to Salem," he did not recognize that "Salem" was the name of a place, and so he discoursed at length about the nature and virtue of the condiment salt ("salem"). Thus, the similarity of the words tricked the good man.[21] Those who have not exercised their natural talents by means of the arts of speech read all things as if they were half asleep. . . .

Finally, what other reason did those sophists have for dismissing Sacred Scripture and inventing a new kind of theology than that they could not understand the language and discursive method of those books? If their example does not deter anyone from barbarism, he should be punished by a beating, not by words. Moreover, if young people will go on continually scorning good literature, then it will surely happen that, with the best things neglected, all that is good and sacred will go to ruin once again. For he deceives himself who thinks that those petty theologians have been barbarians just in their style and not also in their thoughts. If ecclesiastical doctrine is ever to be protected, how, I ask you, will a person be able to take on this task who cannot explain what he is thinking? Or will he produce a kind of confused and Stoical oration in which he squabbles about the punctuation of words? The auditor expects a clear interpretation of sacred doctrine from him, but will go away disappointed, like a hungry raven, finally exhausted by labored distinctions. Thus, those who are possessed by a love of piety should take upon themselves the duty of learning to speak correctly for the sake of Christ and the general need of the Church. Even Paul calls for this when in Corinthians he approves of the study of languages—and his authority should rightly carry great weight with you since his name is so often on your lips.[22]

I have indicated in a few words how the knowledge of correct speech is conducive to the interpretation of sacred and profane writing. Now it is your task to reconcile yourselves with more refined literature and to embrace it eagerly. I see a great many people hastening intemperately toward what they call the more serious disciplines: the hope of gain draws certain

20. John 7:39.
21. Melanchthon's references to "Masters," by which he means the Scholastics, and to "good man" are, of course, ironic.
22. 1 Corinthians 14:5–39.

ones to study law and medicine, while others aspire to theology, and all do so before they have acquired a solid basis by studying the arts of speech. If they undertook each art in its proper order, good lord, how much more successfully would they manage the business! Now they hinder themselves, thanks to their foolish attempt at a shortcut.

Once there was a certain fool at our house who customarily carried logs into the master's kitchen, and he used to pull out those from the bottom of the pile although they could not be moved without great difficulty. Asked why he did it that way, he replied that he was going to complete the most difficult part of the task first, for then those at the top would be easier to move. He failed to see how much of a difference it would make to take up each single thing in the proper order. Those men who turn up their noses at the arts of speech and fly right up to the loftiest studies seem to me very similar to that fool. Since they have not yet reached perfection in the basics, the labor they expend in learning is increased, and everything they do is carried out with a great deal of trouble. Good lord, how unhappily did this rushing blindly forward turn out for our ancestors. Every art in previous centuries was foully defiled by those who, since they had not come into contact with the more refined sorts of writing, rushed into all the best and most serious disciplines like bulls into a china shop.[23] Theology completely fell into ruin through their foolish and impious method of inquiry. Those who taught philosophy did not understand sufficiently even what the name of their art meant. And there was no way that men, who were ignorant of the more refined sorts of literature, could have devised something sensible in the study of law, justice, and equity, because that particular discipline comes right from the heart of the humanities, and the works of the lawyers of antiquity are full of erudition that is both ancient and true. I blame those professors of the arts not only for the foulness of their language, but for their lack of prudence, from which vice men cannot free themselves if their natural talents have not been refined by the arts of speech.

Therefore, I will continue to encourage you in the study of elegance and of those arts that are essential if the other disciplines are to be mastered successfully, something that public necessity rightly requires that you do. For where barbarism has corrupted the weightier disciplines, men's morals will usually be in jeopardy, and it is much truer that morality is obtained from learning than, as Plato wrote, from the songs of musicians.[24]

23. Melanchthon's Latin phrase is "tamquam in rosas porci," literally "like pigs into rosebushes."
24. For Plato's notion that music shapes character, see the *Republic*, III.x.398d–399c.

[11]

Sperone Speroni

Sperone Speroni (1500–1588) was an Italian writer, philosopher, and critic. Born in Padua, he studied there and then later with the Aristotelian philosopher Pietro Pomponazzi at the University of Bologna. He held the chair in logic at Padua during the 1520s, but was in Venice between 1534 and 1548, where he was a member of one of the ruling councils of the city. From 1560 to 1564 he served as Guidobaldo of Urbino's ambassador in Rome, in which he lived a second time between 1573 and 1578. He spent the last ten years of his life in his native city. Speroni wrote numerous dialogues and treatises in Italian concerned with various moral and social questions as well as with poetics and rhetoric. An edition of his dialogues appeared in 1546, which included his *Dialogo sulle lingue* (*Dialogue on Languages*) and his *Dialogo della rettorica* (*Dialogue on Rhetoric*), which is translated here. His most important work, the *Dialogo sulle lingue*, played an important role in the so-called *questione della lingua*, the debate that raged in Italy throughout the sixteenth century concerning the "correct" form of the Italian language. Speroni's tragedy *Canace e Macareo* (*Canace and Macareo*) of 1546 was based on Seneca and inspired a debate about the nature of tragedy that lasted for the rest of the sixteenth century. Speroni himself defended his work on several occasions both in writing and in public lectures that he delivered in Padua in 1558. His *Discorsi sopra Virgilio* (*Discourses on Vergil*), written about 1563 and published after his death, was also controversial: it attacks Vergil and elevates Homer over him. The *Dialogo della rettorica* is set in Bologna in 1530, and its speakers are three Venetian gentlemen: Gian Francesco Valerio (d. 1542), who authored a collection of novellas and held numerous ecclesiastical benefices; Antonio Brocardo (1500?–1531), a well-regarded poet; and Marcantonio Soranzo (d. 1536), who died young and was the close friend of the poet Giovanni della Casa. The translation of the *Dialogo* is based on the text published in Speroni's *Opera*, edited by Natale dalle Laste and Marco Forcellini (Venice, 1740), 1: 202–42.

FROM *Dialogue on Rhetoric*

(The dialogue opens with Brocardo and Valerio rejecting the idea of going to visit some Venetian friends who are having a theological and philosophical debate about the nature of the soul. However, they are concerned that their young friend Soranzo might regret spending a day without intellectual profit, and so they offer to let him choose a topic for discussion.)

Soranzo. Perhaps I will be considered presumptuous in accepting your offer, but I will not do so to my own loss. We will stay here, if you like, and leaving their speculating to the philosophers, would you deign to speak to me a little about civic life, which is our secular profession. I define civic life as involving not only good manners and moral activity, but speaking well for the benefit of people's property, persons, and honor. This last activity is perhaps a virtue no less beautiful in itself or less helpful to humanity than are prudence and justice, but it is difficult for us to learn and practice it—indeed, nothing else is more so. In truth, I willingly devote as much time and wit as I have all to the study of eloquence, which I do partly through reading and partly through writing and by putting into practice those doctrines that Cicero and Quintilian sought to teach with such care. For all that, I don't know anything about the subject, nor do I know if I should hope to know anything, no matter how much I write or read, and that's because it seems to me that the precepts of this art are infinite and often—or I deceive myself—self-contradictory. For this reason, I think that Cicero was a much better orator than a rhetorician, for he speaks better than he teaches us how to speak. Besides, I doubt if the oratorical art of the Latin language would suit other languages, especially the Tuscan one we use nowadays. In this language I think one could give delight to a melancholic person by writing novellas in imitation of Boccaccio without doing anything beyond that—and that sort of writing is really different from the three kinds of cases that Latin writers denominate the only general subject matter of their art of rhetoric.[1] From these and other such doubts, then, which whirl about in my brain, up to now I have not found anyone who could disentangle me, for I have often asked many people about the subject, but they lack either the necessary knowledge or the method to teach it. However, since you know enough about it and are accustomed to discussing everything you know in a wonderfully reasonable and orderly manner, I beg you to talk to me freely about the precepts of that art, telling me as much as you think it's appropriate for me to know about them.

1. Soranzo is referring here to the traditional division of rhetoric into judicial rhetoric (concerned with legal cases), deliberative rhetoric (concerned with legislative debate), and epideictic or demonstrative rhetoric (concerned with praise and blame). On this division, see Aristotle, *Rhetoric*, I.iii.3.

From *Dialogue on Rhetoric*

Valerio. What you say is certainly true: a good part of our civic life involves rhetoric, for without it every virtue would be mute. Moreover, it is something that is infinite in all its parts, and there is just as much difficulty in finding its beginning as its end. That's why Cicero, who speaks of the subject in many of his books, never discusses it in one single way. How, then, would it be possible for us, speaking impromptu, to explain such a great art in one day?

Brocardo. That *is* impossible, but it's not what Soranzo is asking. Rather, at present, it's appropriate that you should speak informally and comply with his wishes by discussing a part of it. You can select whatever part you prefer.

Valerio. As far as I'm concerned, I'm ready to satisfy him to the extent that I can. So speak, and ask him what he would like me to talk about.

Soranzo. My desire would be to be informed about every single part of the subject, from the beginning right down to the end. But since that's impossible, tell me at least one thing, and that is this: considering the fact that the function of the orator is to persuade his audience by delighting, instructing, and moving them, by which of these three means does he put his desire into effect in a way that is most suited to his art and will win him the greatest praise for himself?

Valerio. Insofar as you're asking me to do many things with just a few words, I can conclude that you already know more about rhetoric than there remains of it for us to teach you. Your question is really good, and I'll respond to it not by furnishing solutions, but by engaging in disputation. You should prepare yourself not merely to listen, but to contradict me, and let Brocardo do the like, since his opinion about the present topic will perhaps be different from mine.

Brocardo. Without giving the matter any further thought, my opinion is that by virtue of delight oratory acquires the beauty and force needed to persuade the listener. Granted that the orator has the power to teach and to move, there is an infinite number of accidents that will prevent him from carrying out his function. These include the ugliness of his body, the lack of harmony in his voice, the bad reputation of his client, the dishonesty of the case, and finally, the fatigue of the auditors who, because they have been paying attention to the words of his opponents for a long time, are averse to listening to him—not to mention that his moving others to anger, mercy, or some such other passion must not be forced, and therefore irritating, but must be supremely pleasing to the person whom he is moving and spurring on. As a sign of the difficulty involved, we see that it does not suffice for teachers of this art to have us understand in general terms how the orator is capable of moving the emotions; instead, they describe the particular behaviors of young men and old, the noble and the base, the rich and the poor, and they employ their splendid artistry in seeking to adapt their efforts at moving the audience to the natures of their listeners. I am talking about moving the audience, not about teaching, for the world knows no greater pain than being made to learn against one's will. . . . Therefore, we will tire ourselves out vainly trying to teach and move people unless we give them delight, for it is by means of delight all by itself—so great is the power of giving pleasure—that we are able to persuade our listeners, achieving the desired victory not by force, nor as something rightfully ours by merit, but as a grace bestowed on us by our listeners because of the delight that a well-composed and delivered oration gives birth to in their minds. Now, that person is truly a good orator who, when speaking on one particular subject, does not argue the case as philosophers do, but rather, relying on the free acceptance and consent as well as the pleasure of his listeners, seeks out and obtains their agreement, alluring them by having his speech provide just as much joy when it moves and teaches them as we see it doing when he uses ornamentation simply to give them delight. Now, this is as much as I believe I should say about the present subject.

Valerio. Don't think to free yourself so quickly from the undertaking you've begun, because unless you clarify the arguments you've made, they will not suffice to make us accept your opinion. In this case, you should argue differently, and in order to satisfy Soranzo fully, you should approach the matter in greater detail and show in good order how and by what means one can proceed so that vernacular oratory may acquire that virtue of delighting the audience. For, unless I deceive myself, this is why we heard him make his request.

Brocardo. There are many arguments through which one can show clearly that the perfect orator carries out his function by delighting more than teaching or moving. I decided to pass over them in silence, desiring to be brief so that the duty of speaking should come to you. However, if you or Soranzo really desires to hear them, and if you think it's pertinent for me to speak about them, I will gladly do so in order to please you. Thus, to begin at the beginning, rhetoric is nothing other than a noble art of arranging well and attractively those words by means of which men signify to one another the concepts in their hearts. We say that words come into the world out of the mouth of the people as colors do out of the grass. However, the grammarian, the orator's cousin, is like the painter's servant-boy, and he arranges and polishes those words so that the master of rhetoric can then paint the truth as he speaks and delivers his orations in his own way. For just as the painter knows how to represent the actual faces and bodies of people with his paintbrush, imitating nature who generated them thus, so, whether he is speaking in the senate, or in the law court, or to the people, the orator uses the pen of words and has his tongue paint the truth for us. This is the very same truth that is the proper object of speculative knowledge, something we would otherwise only finally master after we had spent a lot of time frequenting the schools and conversing with philosophers and expended a great deal of effort and study as we did so. Moreover, it's true that just as it is sufficient to see me in order to paint my appearance successfully, without having to have any knowledge of my behavior or to have lived on familiar terms with me for a long time—that is, if the artist is painting nothing of me except what is right on the surface and apparent to the eyes of everyone—so, in order to speak well about every subject, it is sufficient to know a certain je ne sais quoi about the truth, which stands there continuously right in front of us, for it is a thing that God from the beginning wished to impress in our souls, which are naturally desirous of knowing it. It may well be—indeed, it often happens—that the ignorant crowd, listening to the orator, takes the painted representation he has made in exchange for the truth, which they think it to be, just as idolatrous plebeians take paintings and statues, our human creations, and make them their God and worship them like God. It may also happen that the orator will speak with the intention of deceiving people, leading them to think that his aim is the truth, rather than something merely similar to the truth. In that case, such a person, not withstanding his marvelous intelligence, would merit being banished from the world. So, the words of those who attack rhetoric ought to be understood as being about orators of this sort, that is, about orators who practice their art for some other end than the one civic zeal has fixed for it. Such a thing easily happens not merely with rhetoric, but with any of the other honorable and useful arts that exist among us.[2]

Now, to return to my argument: certainly, as far as the things already discussed are concerned, reaching a conclusion in some way about the question we were debating should not be difficult. For teaching, which is, properly speaking, the road to truth, is not the orator's business, but is the task of speculative learning, which is an art not of words, but of things that are partly divine and partly the products of nature. Thus, it will only remain for us to determine whether delighting or moving is the proper function of the orator. . . . Certainly, to speak in accordance with nature, all delighting really amounts to moving one's audience, just as, on the contrary, by contrast, to remain within the terms of this art, all moving in oratory gives delight. For surely the perfect orator does not move others through force and with violence, in the way we move heavy objects upward and light ones down; rather, he always moves people in conformity with the inclination of their emotions, something that can only be extremely pleasing and joyful for them. As I was saying before, teachers of rhetoric have gone into great detail to distinguish the different dispositions of the

2. Cf. Aristotle, *Rhetoric*, I.i.13, and Quintilian, *Institutio oratoria*, II.xvi.5–6.

audience, whose emotions normally vary with changes in fortune and over time; nor would those teachers have done so except that they want the good orator, once he learned where the passions in people's breasts are directing them, to study and strive with his vigorous words to draw them back from there. And surely, if being moved by rhetoric worked differently, every free and well-born individual would feel mortal hatred for the orator who seemed to force and tyrannize over him. Nor can I believe that any republic, whether well or badly ordered, provided that it loved liberty, would allow its citizens to practice such an art, by means of which they would be doing their best to dominate not just their peers, but the magistrates and the laws.

I still have to tell you in what way this being moved delights us and why the delight that a speech gives birth to in a man's feelings should be considered the same thing as being moved. Despite the fact that such matters appear to pertain somewhat more to philosophy than to rhetoric, still, it's good to know about them, especially since they are really pertinent to the matter we are discussing. Now let me briefly address the first subject: how being moved delights us. Just as the painter and the poet, two artists who are similar to the orator, in order to delight us make images and verses in different ways, some horrifying and some pleasant, some mournful and some gay, so the good orator will delight his listeners not only by means of witty remarks, stylistic ornaments, and verbal rhythms, but by moving them to anger, hate, and envy. Truly, I never read the tragedy of Dido in Vergil that I don't weep with him over her misfortune. Still, considering with what noble art the poet has painted her love and her death for us, and conquered as I am by pity, I cannot do otherwise than feel delight— something that should not seem a marvel to anyone who at some time has been forced to weep because of too much happiness.[3] To be sure, such reading is capable of moving me more or less depending on whether I am more or less disposed to feel compassion, but in any case, weeping with Vergil is more pleasing to me than laughing with Martial. But, to return to the subject of oratory, it seems to me that just as a person bitten by a tarantula, hearing music adapted to the bite, lifts himself up and dances until the disturbed humor dissolves in sweat and settles back into its proper place like a quiet, waveless sea, so a choleric man, moved to anger by the words of an excellent orator, gets great pleasure from releasing the heat that his natural complexion or some external occurrence has created in his soul. Since that pleasure arises from a thing that is in itself unpleasant and quite irritating, it produces delight only because it is in conformity with the emotion of the listener (this is what made Filostrato, when he was the king of his day, order his companions to talk about characters whose loves

3. Brocardo's point here is that sometimes the experiencing of an emotion that is in itself unpleasant can actually be pleasurable.

finished in misery).[4] However, it is best not to call such a pleasure delight, but, speaking more accurately, to say that we are being moved: for although that pleasure may have given us delight initially because it was in conformity with our emotions, it would eventually distress us of its own accord because it is naturally irritating (although it does not do so as long as we are not made to feel it for a long period of time—since any harmony among things that are not good should be short—and that is the reason why rhetoricians have always wanted the orator to dispatch it briefly and with just few words).[5] Truly, the delight that is involved in our being moved is like laughter that does not arise from true mirth, but from being tickled: if it continues, it will finally be converted by us into spasms of pain. However, pleasantries, witty and pithy remarks, figures and tropes, the selection, number, and placement of words, the digressions we make from our subject that sometimes involve our wandering with our minds, like a man desirous of solace, through a nearby garden filled with all sorts of different things—all of these rhetorical devices are enormously pleasing by their nature, and our minds will derive pleasure from them in a continual manner just as our bodily senses take delight in odors, sounds, and colors.

Valerio. Hold on a little, Brocardo. Let us go back to the beginning of your argument (albeit at a distance), and before the sweetness of delight and of being moved that you've been talking about transports you beyond this point, I hope it would not be a burden to hear what I think can be truly said about moving the emotions. For I am sure that the orator's principal concern is not to stir up, but to quiet the storms that anger, hate, and envy (winds contrary to the clear sky of reason) are accustomed to arouse in the lowest parts of our souls. And this is something the orator can do not only at the end, but at the start of his speech, if he imitates the oration that Caesar made to the Senate in favor of the imprisoned plotters.[6] It's true that the same orator who has the power to quiet can also disturb the emotions, but either the one who does so is a bad person who is using his knowledge wickedly, like a doctor who poisons the sick, or he is constrained to do it, since it is impossible to turn another suddenly away from extreme hatred and to bring him back into the midst of reason without making him feel something of the contrary extreme. However, although what I've

4. Brocardo is alluding to a character in Boccaccio's *Decameron* who suffers from unrequited love and commands, when he has been made the "king" of the fourth day of storytelling, that everyone should tell tales about unhappy love relationships.

5. Brocardo's point here is that it is not appropriate to identify as delight any pleasure that naturally involves unpleasantness, but rather to say it is a matter of our being moved, something that is neutral and can involve both pleasant and unpleasant emotions.

6. In 63 B.C., when Cicero and his allies had arrested and imprisoned a number of Catiline's fellow conspirators and sought to have them condemned to death by the Roman Senate, Julius Caesar delivered a powerful oration in their defense and temporarily persuaded the Senate to spare them. That oration is recorded in Sallust, *Bellum Catilinae*, li.1–43.

just argued may be true, we normally say in the language of the common people that the orator's function is to "move the emotions," and Soranzo was using that language when he asked his question. For the idea of moving the emotions is more familiar to the common people and seems a task requiring greater strength than does quieting the emotions—not to mention that most orators speak for the purpose not of calming, but of moving their listeners. And there is a third reason why I think that it is the orator's business to move the emotions more than to calm them, for it is self-evident that his art, not only when it disturbs the emotions, but also when it pacifies them, is actually moving and spurring them on. As a result, the orator must have the greatest, most violent power over our souls, for he can persuade us to do good deeds, accomplishing with words in one hour what the philosopher, living virtuously for many years, can achieve for himself only with great difficulty. Now you can finally see whether rhetoric is an art fit for civic life and public liberty and whether moving the emotions is an activity that is either more or less honorable for the orator than teaching and delighting are.

Brocardo. If the orator's moving of his listener were such as you have described it, surely the Areopagus was wrong to forbid it in Athens.[7] However, I don't see it that way. I believe that the orator, in handling the emotions, should concern himself with the times and the situation that is disturbing us rather than with reason to which alone has been assigned the task of tempering the emotions. But granted that things are as you say, I am convinced that just as we have reached the conclusion, based on the arguments made so far, that what orators teach their listeners is not the knowledge of the truth, but merely opinion and an image of the truth, so the calming of the emotions, which oratory can produce in people's souls, is not a virtue, but a simulacrum of virtue. For virtue is a good habit, something we gain for ourselves not instantly by means of words, but by thinking and acting over a long period of time.

However, lest you think that the good art of rhetoric, the queen of all the arts, is a certain ridiculous clownishness (for there are those who liken it to the art of cooking), you should know that among the arts there are some that are pleasing and some that are useful.[8] The useful ones are those we commonly call mechanical; among the pleasing ones there are those that have the virtue of delighting people's souls and those that delight the body, or, to speak more clearly, some delight the senses, others the mind. Through a pleasing sort of mastery, painting gives comfort to the eyes, music to the ears, perfumes to the nose, cooking to the taste, and a stove, with the seasonable warmth it supplies, to the entire body. However, the

7. Aristotle notes that the Areopagus, the law court in Athens, forbade using arguments that excited anger, pity, and the like; see *Rhetoric*, I.i.4–6, and also Quintilian, *Institutio oratoria*, II.xvi.4.

8. On rhetoric as cookery, see Plato, *Gorgias*, 462b–463a.

arts that delight the intellect—limiting ourselves here to those that are appropriate to our discussion—are two, namely rhetoric and poetry, and although they can reach the mind only by passing through the ears, they should nevertheless be called intellectual since they are arts that make use of the word, which is the instrument of the mind, by means of which we signify to one another what we understand intellectually. To be sure, music also involves both the voice and sounds, and by its means we blend high and low sounds as we measure them out, joining those different ones—for they are different—together to generate a harmony that moves and delights not just us, but many brute animals marvelously. But rhetoric and poetry are arts involving the utterances of human beings, utterances brought together not as high and low sounds, but properly as words— that is, those arts treat our utterances as signs of our thoughts—and they make of them a harmony that the first rhetoricians, speaking metaphorically and comparing it to rhythm in music, also called rhythm. And thanks to that rhythm, every speech, even a vernacular and unlearned one, can be called an oration.

However, in order to make this point clear—since on it alone, as on the firmest center, is founded the entire art of rhetoric—it is necessary that we go back to the beginning again by means of another road and recognize that the entire body of eloquence, no matter how large, has only five members, that is, to speak in the Latin manner, invention, disposition, elocution [style], action [delivery], and memory. Among these, without a doubt, elocution holds the chief place as if it were the heart—although if someone were to call it the soul, I wouldn't say he was lying. From elocution is derived nothing less than the very name of eloquence, just as "alive" comes from "live." To be sure, invention and disposition are the parts of rhetoric that are concerned with the things that we find out in all the branches of learning and then arrange in our oration. The third part, however, according to the meaning of the word, is properly concerned with words, which we select and arrange not randomly, but in a judicious manner.[9] Then, granted that elocution is considered the third part of eloquence and is quite different from the first two, nonetheless it is truly the principal part, for in elocution itself can be found a new oratorical invention and disposition.[10] And this is the case because not every kind of elocution can be regarded as rhetorical, for in every language there are many words that are too base or vulgar or harsh or old, so that a civil person would avoid uttering them in the senate and the law court, and even when talking with friends and familiars. (To be sure, an individual could avoid this sort of speech without having recourse to art, if only he had had the habit at one time in his life of conversing with men who were both

9. Cf. Cicero, *Orator*, xix.61.

10. Brocardo's argument here is that elocution involves the selection and arrangement of words and thus includes a kind of invention and disposition within it.

noble and discreet.) But for the orator to put together the sweet, clear, musical words he has found, and, after having initially made sure they are appropriate to the things they signify, then to arrange them so that their accents and their syllables all harmonize together—this is the stuff of art that alone and before all else makes the orator an orator. And if what I have read in the rhetoricians is true, namely that invention and disposition are the work of prudent and shrewd men rather than eloquent orators, then in the arranging of words alone consists the entire art of oratory. . . .

Although previously I told you that according to the rhetoricians, teaching and moving are the concerns of invention, in that the prologue and the epilogue move us while the narration and confirmation teach us, nevertheless, I will now change my opinion for the better and put things in their proper proportion. I feel I must say that teaching really depends on disposition, for if the order of our speech were confused, it would produce ignorance. Thus, we will always be correct if we pair invention with moving and disposition with teaching—and delight, of which we have been speaking, with elocution, its mother, the form and life of eloquence. Then, passing on to the three kinds of rhetoric handled by the orator and coming then to the three styles, that is, the three modes of speech, let's make a reasonable set of equations among them. Thus, judicial rhetoric, for which the high style is appropriate, can be justly connected to moving and invention; deliberative rhetoric, with its low and detailed style, to disposition and teaching; and finally, epideictic rhetoric, which involves the middle style, to elocution and delight.[11] Having established this much, we can proceed forward and argue the following: if among the parts of oratory elocution is the chief, and epideictic rhetoric is nobler and more open to every kind of ornamentation than are judicial and deliberative rhetoric, and among the styles of speaking the middle one is the most perfect and virtuous—neither stingy nor prodigal, proud rather than haughty or abject, valorous rather than foolhardy or cowardly, and temperate rather than lascivious or dull—then, oratorical delight is well worthy of being placed ahead of moving and teaching. And that is why we see that although the orator does not always move or teach, he really tries to delight us with elegant words in every part of his speech and in every type of oratory. Moreover, not content with the delight deriving from words, in order to redouble the pleasure they produce and to sweeten them to perfection, he has recourse to gesture and delivery as the seasoning of oratory, the sweetest honey and sugar for our ears and eyes. Indeed, on delivery, thanks to the grace contained in it, depends the efficacy of his oration, for without a good delivery, it is worthless. Just a little while

11. Cicero equates the low or plain style with proving one's case, the middle style with delight, and the vehement or high style with moving; see *Orator*, xx.69–70.

after Demosthenes had uttered this opinion, his adversary Aeschines confirmed it with a splendid proof, for when he was reading Demosthenes' oration to the people of Rhodes and his auditors marveled at it, he had to admit that the oration would have been truly marvelous if Demosthenes had been delivering it.[12] It's as if he wanted to say that the speaker's delivery could lessen or increase the force of an oration so as to transform it beyond itself and make it no longer appear to be what it was.

Valerio. Before Soranzo agrees that a speech persuades us more by delighting than by teaching or moving us, he expects to hear the arguments you would use to refute Cicero's opinion as you prove that epideictic rhetoric is nobler than the other two kinds and that the middle style is the best.[13] For clearly, if we simply accept two assertions like those, which actually seem false rather than doubtful to us, we will have difficulty deciding the question we've been discussing.

Brocardo. I've been just waiting here for you to interrupt my speech, feeling certain that you would immediately object to what I've said about epideictic rhetoric and the middle style. However, you should know, and so should Soranzo, I was presenting such matters by means of a simple narration unsupported by any sort of argument, for I merely wanted to join together the three parts of oratory with the three styles, the three kinds of rhetoric, and the three modes of persuasion, so that moving in judicial rhetoric would be seen to correspond principally to invention and the high style, teaching in deliberative rhetoric to disposition and the low style, and finally, delight in epideictic rhetoric would properly be related to elocution and the middle style. Anyone who considers the works of all the rhetoricians, the Greeks as well as the Latins, will easily discover that these correspondences were also noted by them. If this is the case—and surely it is—then you yourselves will rightly conclude by means of the same consideration that rhetorical elocution with its entire army ought to be given preference over the other two parts of oratory with all their ordinance. For it's not right to equate the good with the wicked, but the good with the good, and so, it's reasonable that the best style, the best part of rhetoric, the best rhetorical genre, and the best form of persuasion should all be matched with one another. . . .

Having considered the three kinds of rhetoric according to their ends, their functions, and their subject matters, I can only conclude that epideictic rhetoric must be the chief among them, for its end is what is honorable, its subject matter is virtue, and its function is to delight the mind and admonish us to do good. Thus arose the custom in the Athenian republic of praising those citizens each year who had been killed after having

---

12. See Cicero, *De oratore*, III.lvi.213, and Quintilian, *Institutio oratoria*, XI.iii.6.

13. Cicero usually insists on the superiority of judicial and deliberative oratory; see, for example, *De oratore*, I.vi.22. He also expected the perfect orator to use all three styles.

fought bravely for their country. If we believe Plato, this annual oration in praise of the dead and their virtue at one stroke gave gentle consolation to their mothers and fathers and wives, while marvelously inciting the brothers and children and grandchildren who remained behind them to imitate them and make themselves their equals.[14] Thus Cicero used to say —and not in vain—that no kind of rhetoric was more ornate or more useful to the Republic than this one, since its teaching has the virtue not only of making good orators, but of exhorting them by means of splendid artifice to live honorably.[15] This does not happen with the other two kinds, by means of which we often persuade people to wage unjust wars, and by seeking to avenge injuries done to us, now we harm the innocent, now we defend the guilty. . . .

To continue my argument, and considering what I said earlier about how the oration by Demosthenes was enormously dependent on delivery, I am of the firmest opinion that in deliberative and judicial rhetoric the nature of the orator and his subject matter accomplish much more than does the art of oratory. And just the contrary is true with epideictic orations, for they are no less beautiful when they are read than when they are delivered. Thus, we see that even mediocre orators who are well informed about civic matters are capable of speaking rather well, aided by their delivery and their memory, before the senate and the law court, for in such cases, the words arise in us from the matter being treated, and once they are brought into agreement with our ideas, they produce a harmony that makes the listener marvel. For this reason rhetoricians often command us, if we will speak to the crowd, to pay no attention to the charm of the words we've selected and even to choose others less beautiful instead, as long as they are appropriate and have the ability to unfold our concepts. However, in epideictic rhetoric we are required not merely to harmonize words and ideas, but to arrange what has been chosen so that equals are beautifully matched with equals, similar things with similar things. Sometimes we have to double and repeat frequently the same words, and sometimes join them to contrary ones, imitating the prospectival art of painters who frequently fit black to white with the purpose of making the whiteness appear more beautiful, loftier, and more lustrous to us. All these things are matters of pure artfulness and are difficult to such a degree that it would be a truly miraculous accomplishment to deliver impromptu an eloquent speech of praise or dispraise. . . .

It may well be the case that those two kinds of rhetoric, the senatorial and the judicial, are more necessary for men than this third one, the epideictic, and that Tisias and Corax and other ancient orators sought to de-

14. Plato has Socrates discuss this custom and deliver a sample funeral oration in the *Menexenus*.
15. Although Cicero wants the orator to master all kinds of oratory, he does treat epideictic oratory as the source and nourisher of great eloquence; see *Orator*, xi.37.

rive the art of rhetoric from them, since they were the first kinds to be used. But most often the last thing to appear is the first when judged in terms of perfection. Moreover, it's always the case in human affairs that there is greater art where there is less necessity, since it is thought that our mother Nature, all by herself and aided by no art, takes care of our basic needs. Thanks to Nature, the bear and the lion fight with claws and teeth, and the deer removes itself from harm by running swiftly away. The swallow makes its nest, and the spider by weaving obtains what it needs to feed itself. However, we men, as civilized creatures, seek the aid of words, the messengers and signs of the mind, as we take counsel with our friends about the future, and by restraining the hands that are the instruments of the wrathful, we sometimes defend ourselves from present enemies, sometimes attack them. Art can teach us little in such cases, except to arrange and order what Nature has invented. However, in epideictic rhetoric, which does not concern the necessities of life, words and things, together with their arrangement and placement, are matters of pure artifice. Initially, that artifice was planted in the nature of the first two kinds of rhetoric; then, nourished with diligent care, it grew, and in the third kind, as if in its third age, it was made whole and perfect. In fact, so whole and perfect is that art that it not only gives luster to epideictic oratory, the true nest of its splendor, but it warms and illuminates marvelously the other two inferior kinds of rhetoric through the reflection of its rays. That's why in judicial oratory justice and the laws are frequently praised while those who disturb them are blamed, and in the councils of republics, liberty, peace, and just war are exalted with the highest praise, while tyrants are attacked and insulted. . . .

If somewhere in the world a good man, possessing eloquence and intelligence, left his country and came to stay in Bologna, alone and naked, like another Bias, what would he do with his art?[16] If he accuses or defends people, he will become a base lawyer who sells his words to the crowd; if he engages in deliberation, not being a citizen of the state, his counsels will not be heard. Will he be quiet then and lead an idle life? Not at all. He will exercise his eloquence constantly with his pen and employ epideictic rhetoric to blame and praise others. And by doing this not out of hatred or for a reward, but for the sake of truth, in a short while he will be feared and esteemed not only by his peers, but by lords and kings.

Soranzo. If I don't miss the resemblance, this eloquent man of yours is the portrait of Aretino.

Brocardo. I name no names, but whoever it is, he can be nothing less than a great man. Hence, it seems to me that epideictic rhetoric is to the deliberative and judicial kinds as ecclesiastical dignities are to secular greatness:

16. Cicero praises Bias, one of the proverbial Seven Sages of Greece, for his indifference to the goods of fortune; see *Paradoxa stoicorum*, 8–9.

the latter is the result of natural succession, the former we acquire through our own industry. Thus, just as a particular gentleman who has been made pope is adored by his lords, so the great ones of the world, who would not deign to cast a glance at a lawyer or a senator, make way for the good orator because of his mastery of epideictic rhetoric. However, it is not difficult to judge how it comes about that the speeches made by orators practicing the other two kinds of rhetoric are, because of their seriousness, no less precious to an audience than epideictic orations are. For the subjects of those two kinds of rhetoric are tragic matters pertaining partly to the lives of individuals and partly to the state of the republic, whereas epideictic rhetoric leaves the living and the dead alone, and merely goes about painting the reputations and memories of others all over with praise and blame. Thus, just as the sight of two enemies wearing only their shirts and fighting one another with sharpened knives in hand-to-hand combat is no less pleasing for the wounds and the blood involved than is a match between two fencers who play their game with marvelous artfulness, so civil cases normally give us as much delight because of the subjects being treated as epideictic orations provide us with joy and solace through their verbal artistry. That's why it happens, as I was saying, that in the senate and the law court we willingly listen to mediocre orators, for their lack of art is easily compensated for by the subject being discussed, whereas if epideictic orations, just like poems, are not perfect, there is no one who would deign to see and hear them.

(Brocardo goes on to talk about Tuscan eloquence by explaining the study he once made of Petrarch and Boccaccio as literary models. He goes on to distinguish between the rhythms of prose and poetry and to insist that the rules for writing are different in Tuscan and Latin. At this point, he wishes to stop speaking.)

Brocardo. The speech of the orator is one thing, that of the rhetorician another: the first delights, while the second teaches. As a rhetorician, however, I am better suited for learning than teaching.

Valerio. You should at least teach me how to reply to the arguments of certain great men who may confess, as you've said, that rhetoric is an art that gives birth to pleasure and grace in our souls, but who then permit themselves to call it not a civic virtue, but perverse flattery, and to banish it as an evil-seeming vice from the state.

Brocardo. You're talking about Plato who, in the person of Socrates, not in order to speak the truth, but to try Polus and Gorgias, attacked rhetoric in the same spirit that he made Thrasymachus and Glaucon praise injustice.[17] Just as, according to him, music, an art more delightful than useful,

---

17. Brocardo alludes to two Platonic dialogues: the *Gorgias*, in which Socrates debates with Polus, Gorgias, and Callicles about the nature and value of rhetoric; and the *Republic*, in the first two books of which Thrasymachus and Glaucon defend the superiority of injustice and tyranny.

is necessary for the citizens and guardians of the Republic, so the learning and practicing of rhetoric, the joy and delight of the mind, is a good thing for them.[18] However, so that you will really grasp my meaning, you should know that among animals—from whom, as from more notable things, it's good to derive our examples—their senses are such that they feel happiness if the objects they are responding to are good and sadness if they are bad, that is, harmful to their lives. Thus, just as the dog takes pleasure in seeing and smelling and eating food that preserves him and dislikes animals that have already been slain, so the mind, which is filled with a desire for knowledge, naturally takes the greatest delight in truth, while abhorring falsehood, which is contrary to its desire. Surely, what food is for the stomach, truth is for the intellect, whereas a lie is a poison that destroys it and, although it is born immortal, makes it something worse than dead. Now, to return to the senses, man is certainly an animal nobler and better by nature than the beasts, a being who, raised out of the filth of the brutes, attends to things other than filling his maw and often suffers hunger and thirst in order to see a painting or hear a piece of music, choosing to feed his eyes and ears, not without harm to his person, rather than to fatten himself on the food of his kitchen. If this is true of the senses, then it is so of the mind, which must similarly be permitted occasionally to put aside the truth that nourishes it and to find delight in tasting that which gives it pleasure. In this case our human intellect is perhaps more divine than human, for insofar as it is human, that is, lacking in knowledge but eager to learn, it races to the truth that satisfies it, whereas, when it plays with verse and prose for its delight, it is very similar to the Intelligences, who, looking down beneath their feet, are eager to watch us there, not in order to know more than they already know, but for their pleasure.[19] For, if we are philosophers, then rhetoric and poetry are to us just like fruit on the tables of great lords who sometimes eat some of it after dinner when they are full as a courtesy and in order to please their palates. However, for those who are not yet, but are in the process of becoming, philosophers, the two arts I've just mentioned are the flowers that appear before the fruit of knowledge, so that the minds of those who desire to bear that fruit will first take delight in producing flowers just as spring has planned it for them. For the vulgar crowd of people, who know nothing and give no thought to knowledge and yet are still part of the state, orations and poems are all the food and fruit of their lives, for they do not have the virtue of being able to digest knowledge and to convert it to their own good, and they are accustomed to satisfy themselves by listening to orators who supply odors and images for them, and so they live and maintain themselves. Therefore, I don't see why rhetoric should be banished from the state, for it is an art that takes

18. See the *Republic*, II.xvii.376e–378e.
19. The Intelligences are the Angelic Intelligences, that is, the Angels.

our human activities as its subject, activities that constitute the origin of the state.

Although the orator delights and persuades his listeners with arguments that are merely probable and more uncertain than not, thereby judging and directing civic activities, nevertheless, his industry is really to be commended and considered something precious, for by its means our affairs are given perfect, proper treatment and consideration in a manner that is suitable for them. I say this presupposing that you know what is known to everyone, namely, that man is in the middle between the animals and the Intelligences, and therefore he knows himself in a middle way between the earthly knowledge that he has of the animals, and the faith, with which he adores God. This middle way of knowing involves the opinions that rhetoric generates and by means of which he takes pains to correct both his own will and that of others and to live in a civil manner with his relatives and friends in his country. For if at different times the same act can be forbidden or approved by the laws of the state and be thus considered a vice or a virtue, the reason for this situation is surely that our states are governed not by demonstrable knowledge that is true and certain for all time, but through prudence, by means of the opinions produced by rhetoric, opinions that are variable and changeable just as our activities and laws are. That's why Socrates, wrongly condemned by the ignorance of his judges, but obedient to the opinion of his country, willingly went to meet death, something he should have attempted to flee as a wicked and unjust punishment if he had argued the matter as a philosopher.[20]

Since the philosopher, who is accustomed to understanding nothing except that which comes through the senses and then finds a lodging in his intellect, tends to have less to do with matters of belief the more knowledge he acquires, and since he is also concerned about the works of Nature, which is eternal and unchangeable and produces its effects according to eternal laws, truly, such a man is badly suited to govern the state. For its laws are rightly made with respect to times and places, utility, the state's own power, and that of others, and they often change their forms and appearances from one day to the next, which is why magistrates are created to rule over the laws just as the laws are made to rule over us. The laws, then, are not true gods, like Nature and the Intelligences, but idols that are adored after they have been made by the very same people who used their art to fashion them. Therefore, it is proper that the orator of whom we are speaking should take pains to preserve those laws by means of his knowledge, a knowledge that is not necessary, but merely reasonable, not perfect, but perfectly suited to them. For if our intellect, when it understands something, comes to resemble the thing it has understood,

20. For Socrates' refusal to accept a proposal of flight from Crito, see Plato's *Crito*, 45a–54e.

how could a man, who is accustomed to contemplating the nature and habits of animals, be suited to ruling the state? Rather, we should believe what we see every day, namely, that such a person, who resembles the objects of his understanding, should go about seeking some solitary place and should bury himself there as he carries on his philosophical speculation. The orator does just the opposite, for his art, his rule, his habits, and his words are properly concerned with civic affairs, and what he says is not believed or known so much as it persuades us, giving us greater delight than does knowledge that is sure and demonstrable and that involves matters that are baser and pertain less to us—for it is a greater delight just to see or even to hear the words of a friend whom we love and hold dear than to see, hear, taste, and touch all the beasts in the world. Thus, when he produces this delight in the act of persuasion, the orator is able to generate out of himself the glory and salvation of his fellow citizens, just as the animals, with their carnal delights, generate one another without recourse to reason and thereby preserve their species.

(Brocardo admits that because the intellect is immortal, we should seek divine, not mortal knowledge, yet he argues that we know divine truth only through the things of this world, in relation to which rhetoric has an important role to play. He then turns to Valerio, asking him to speak, at which point the work suddenly breaks off: it seems that Speroni's son-in-law accidentally tore up several pages of the manuscript, and Speroni, angered by what had happened, refused to redo what was destroyed and continue his work to its conclusion.)

[12]

Jacques Amyot

The French bishop Jacques Amyot (1513–1593) was celebrated during his life as a classicist and a translator of the classics. Born in Melun, near Paris, he was the son of a haberdasher and was educated at the Collège du Cardinal Lemoine in Paris and at Bourges, where he became a reader in Greek and Latin in 1534. During the next decade he began working on a series of translations that would make him famous. His translation of the Greek romance *Aethiopica* by Heliodorus impressed the king, Francis I, who made him head of the Abbey of Bellozane in 1547. Between 1547 and 1552 Amyot was in Italy, where he studied manuscripts of Plutarch's *Lives* in the Vatican and in Venice; he also visited the Council of Trent, which had been called by the Church to deal with the threat posed to it by Protestantism. In 1557 he was appointed tutor to the two sons of Henry II, both of whom extended their patronage to him after they came to the throne, Charles IX making him his Grand Almoner in 1560, and Henry III appointing him bishop of Auxerre in 1570. Amyot published his most influential work, his translation of Plutarch's *Lives* (*Vies des hommes illustres*), in 1559. Amyot translated other works as well, including seven books of the *Histories* of Diodorus Siculus (1554), the Greek romance *Daphnis and Chloe* by Longus (1559), and Plutarch's *Moralia* (*Moral Essays,* 1572). He wrote his *Projet de l'éloquence royale, composée pour Henry III, roi de France* (*An Epitome of Royal Eloquence, Composed for Henry III, King of France*) most likely between 1570 and 1580. Amyot calls it a "projet," meaning a project or scheme or design or epitome; he thinks of his little book as a kind of shorthand summary containing all the basic knowledge of rhetoric a busy monarch needs. The *Projet* was first published in 1805 by Ph.-D. Pierres at Versailles; this translation of portions of it is based on that edition.

From *An Epitome of Royal Eloquence,
Composed for Henry III, King of France*

Chapter I

I have not undertaken to speak in praise of eloquence here and thus demon-strate how it would really be appropriate to work hard in order to acquire it. For eloquence itself is used to praise the other arts, and virtue in particu-lar, which people say has no greater or more agreeable reward. There is, in fact, nothing like knowing how to manage a multitude of men by means of rhetoric, how to arouse their emotions, master their wills and passions, in-deed, push them on and restrain them at one's pleasure as if, in a manner of speaking, one carried a spur and a bridle for them, hanging from the tip of one's tongue.[1]

I confess that it is grand to lead men by force to whatever conclusion one wishes, but that it is grander to conduct them there of their own free will, without striking a blow against them, without loss or danger, and to their satisfaction. King Archidamus once asked Thucydides, who in former times was an eminent person in his country, whether he or Pericles had more skill in wrestling.[2] "That would be difficult to judge," said Thucydides, "for as soon as I have cast Pericles down to earth by means of all my personal skill and force, he uses his eloquence to make those who have seen him believe that he has not fallen, so that he triumphs over me thanks to the cleverness of his tongue." Now, since we have been placed above all the animals and have, as by hereditary right, the gift of being able to talk and discourse among ourselves, revealing our thoughts to one another by means of lan-guage, we should certainly value that ability highly and should take pains to acquire this further advantage, namely verbal power, the very thing that, beyond all else, lets us triumph over the beasts, and that will be what allows us to triumph over other men.[3] Truly, there is nothing more desirable than to appear among an infinity of people as the only person, or as one with few to match him, who knows how to do better than the others what Nature has nevertheless granted to everyone. I recognize that the most eloquent men have been found in the ancient republics, for the first honors and the high-est dignities were given there by the people over whom one triumphed by means of eloquence.[4] In those republics they used to take counsel about peace and war and manage the entire government through public delibera-tions—and the latter were guided and ruled by the lively arguments and vehement persuasion of great orators. This is not seen in monarchies, where

1. Cf. Cicero, *De oratore,* I.viii.32, and Tacitus, *Dialogus,* v.4–6.
2. For this anecdote, see Plutarch, *Life of Pericles,* viii.3–4; it can also be found in Eunapius, *Lives of the Philosophers and Sophists,* 498. The Thucydides mentioned is not the historian, but Thucydides, the son of Melesias, who was Pericles' chief opponent.
3. Cf. Cicero, *De inventione,* I.iv.5, and *De oratore,* I.viii.32–33.
4. Cf. Tacitus, *Dialogus,* xxvi.2–8.

honors and dignities are in the hands of a single individual who distributes them according to his pleasure, and even though he gave everything to the most capable or to those who rendered him the most service, one sees nevertheless that it is done without much regard for eloquence. Still, I do not want for this reason to concede that the art and science of rhetoric should be less sought after and esteemed among us. I hold that it is honorable for everyone, but that it is greatly advisable, profitable, indeed necessary, for the ministers of a great king, and especially for the king, and that if he knows how to use it skillfully and with precision, he will be able to establish, preserve, and augment his state thanks to it, as much as, or more than, by any other means by which realms and seigniories are maintained.

Chapter II. How Useful and Necessary Eloquence Is

We have many examples that show how much this art can be of service to princes. For instance, there is Pyrrhus, who freely confessed that he had acquired more cities through the eloquence of his ambassador Cineas than he had conquered by arms.[5] And certainly, if he had had this virtue of speaking well, he would have deserved the surname of "Conqueror of cities" more than did Demetrius, the son of Antigonus, who had himself called that because of the number and the awe-inspiring grandeur of the machines that he used to batter and overpower cities.[6] For one should not, according to the ancient proverb, take the wolf by the ears; rather, one should take all the peoples and cities that way, for they let themselves be led in that manner by an eloquent prince.[7] Furthermore, just as the animals that most keep us company and are most loyal to us will cure all the wounds they have received if they can reach them with their tongues, so, by means of a sweet and agreeable word, a prince can remedy misfortunes when all other means would be useless. Moreover, there will be times when force has no place and persuasion has all the power. The army of Julius Caesar had revolted against him in the middle of his greatest enterprise.[8] At that time he had no recourse to his sword, since it would have benefited him little among so many thousands of weapons; so instead he fought and beat down that sedition with the cutting edge of his tongue, reducing his soldiers to reason so that they submitted of their own accord to whatever penalty and chastisement he might want, on the condition that he took them again into his favor. King Mithridates, who sustained a war for forty-three years against the Roman people, the conqueror of the rest of the world, was more revered by twenty-two

5. See Plutarch, *Life of Pyrrhus*, xiv.2.
6. See Plutarch, *Life of Demetrius*, xlii.6; when besieging Rhodes, Demetrius gave himself the name "Poliorcetes," which means "besieger of cities."
7. For the ultimate source of the proverb, see Terence, *Phormio*, 506; for a more immediate source, see Erasmus, *Adages*, I.v.25. "To take the wolf by the ears" is to put oneself foolishly in harm's way.
8. See Suetonius, *Divus Iulius*, lxx.

nations he commanded with his eloquence, speaking to each of them without an interpreter, than if he had had twenty-two armies to maintain their obedience.[9] Similarly, although the kings of Persia had ministers whom people called their eyes and ears because they went looking and listening everywhere in order to make their reports, they never once had any ministers whom people called their tongues. Rather, they always spoke themselves to their subjects and to foreigners, thinking, and not without reason, that the word of a king is the principal part of his power. I will not mention here our widely celebrated Gallic Hercules whom people followed, drawn by a cord from his tongue.[10] It will suffice for me to say that if eloquence is the queen of everything, as a certain poet has said in writing, there is no king, no matter how great and powerful, who should not desire to have her as his companion.[11]

Chapter III. That There Are Two Kinds of Eloquence

Now, so that you should not think that I want to send kings to some rhetoric school and make them descend from their royal seat in order to climb up to the rostrum and make declamations there, it is time to reveal what this eloquence is that I have undertaken to represent and describe. There are two kinds of eloquence one can see without difficulty in ancient orators: one is full of babbling and affectation like a courtesan; the other is adorned with sweetly grave language, with a bearing, a grace, and a natural beauty like a maid of honor. The first kind was used by rabble-rousers, all of whose efforts were aimed at flattering and pleasing the people; the second kind was made use of by the great and the powerful and by those who were most involved in the governing of republics and empires—and consequently this kind will be more appropriate for the present treatise. The first, which we will call vulgar eloquence, was certainly very effective in turning and whirling about the greatest city in the world to suit its pleasure. For instance, at one point the Roman people were assembled in the theater to see the games; at the arrival of Lucius Otho, who was deeply hated by the commoners because of some law of his, there arose such a noise, such a whistling and shouting, in response to him that the place seemed rather a stormy sea than a theater for putting on games. However, once the orator Cicero had delivered a harangue and reproved those commoners, in an instant all their

9. See Aulus Gellius, *Noctes atticae*, xvii.17; Gellius speaks of Mithridates knowing twenty-five languages, not twenty-two.

10. Amyot is referring to an account in Lucian's *Herakles* of the so-called Hercules Gallicus, or Gallic Hercules, a figure Lucian says was worshipped as the god Hermes, the god of eloquence, in a temple in Marseilles. The cord from Hercules' tongue to his followers' ears symbolizes the power of eloquence.

11. For the passage describing eloquence as a queen, see Quintilian, *Institutio oratoria*, I.xii.18, who attributes it to a "not ignoble tragic poet," thought in the Renaissance to be Euripides (see his *Hecuba*, 816). However, it is more likely that the passage in question is a fragment from Pacuvius's *Hermione*, which is also cited in Cicero, *De oratore*, II.xliv.187.

anger and ill will changed into a singular benevolence, such that with a clapping of their hands and cries full of joy, they forced themselves against their will to caress someone whom just a little while before they had received so badly and had insulted and reviled.[12] In this same city, during the civil wars of Marius and Sulla, some soldiers were sent to kill Marcus Antonius the orator. They had already drawn their swords and were ready to bathe them in his blood, but after having heard him speak so divinely, they did not have the force or the courage to touch him, and sheathing their swords again, they returned in complete astonishment to the place they had come from. Through these examples, one sees that there is nothing so hard that it may not be annealed and softened by eloquence, so that if we were asked even for our very lives, we would not have it in us to refuse the request. As evidence, consider how the philosopher Hegesias employed his eloquence in recounting all the miseries to which our life is subject, bringing them vividly to life before the eyes of his audience and kindling such a desire for death in their minds that several voluntarily killed themselves, so that the king, Ptolomy, was forced to forbid him most strictly from ever talking about such matters again.[13] If Hegesias's eloquence gave him power over the lives of the Egyptians, Pisistratus also had no less power over the liberty of the Athenians; for although Solon, considered the first of the twelve sages, vigorously opposed his designs and remonstrated with his fellow citizens that Pisistratus was only trying to enslave them, nevertheless the latter knew how to harangue them in such a way that Solon, despite all his wisdom and authority and the goodness of his cause, lost the battle completely.[14] But I have talked too much about this vulgar eloquence; I must come to that which belongs to princes and kings and must show what it consists of.

Chapter IV. What Royal Eloquence Consists Of

Man has two principal parts: understanding and language. Understanding is like a master who commands, and language like a servant who obeys. The understanding should have, like Neptune's trident, three prongs: one for finding out the things one must talk about; another for making judgments about the things one has found and choosing one out of many that seems most appropriate; the last, to wit memory, is the guardian and treasurer of all the riches of eloquence. As far as judgment and memory are concerned, you, Sire, have what one might wish in a most accomplished prince, and in that you have a marvelous advantage over those who have less, or none, of

12. For the story of Cicero and Lucius Otho, see Plutarch, *Life of Cicero*, xiii.2–4; the law referred to was one that gave members of the knightly class the first rows of seats at the public games. The following story about Marcus Antonius comes from Plutarch, *Life of Gaius Marius*, xliv.4.

13. The source of this story about Hegesias is Cicero, *Tusculan Disputations*, I.xxxiv.83.

14. Plutarch, *Life of Solon*, xxix–xxx.

these things. For, beyond the fact that they are necessary for eloquence and for all other arts, reason, like an anchor that stops a ship, is required in order to make a state secure, and as the anchor serves no purpose without chains and ropes, so reason has little effect without judgment, which makes it stay firmly in place once it has chosen and approved something. The same is true of your memory, whose excellence all admire, whether it's a matter of grasping and retaining all kinds of knowledge worthy of a king that is brought up and considered at every hour in your council, or of your recalling in detail an infinite number of people, recognizing them at once by sight, and knowing their names, qualities, and merits. This is one of the best and surest ways for a prince to win the hearts of his subjects, as the great king Cyrus demonstrated when he called by their names all the soldiers in his army, who were almost impossible to count, thereby retaining his hold on their hearts and disposing of them as he wished.[15] But I do not dare to speak further about either your judgment or your memory, because it is better to be silent than to say too little about them. We have yet to discuss what is involved in the third faculty of the soul—and the first part of eloquence—that is called invention, for which the promptness, vivacity, and agility of your mind are incomparable. Despite being occupied and distracted by the care and the continual thought that so many and such great affairs require, you will not disdain being provided with some commonplaces by means of which you may more easily discover the subject and the material about which you must speak.

Chapter V. What the Prince Talks About in His Very Short Periods of Leisure

The prince, like all men, speaks either for his profit or in order to enjoy himself. He gets pleasure from talking and chatting when, in the midst of his affairs, he wants to relax his spirit a bit because it is too tense, just as a musician does with several strings on a lyre in order to retighten them right afterward and put his lyre in tune even more than it was before. Since his talk should then be brief, like his leisure, it might seem in this case that eloquence is scarcely required, seeing that its property is to expand and amplify things by means of beautiful language. Nevertheless, those who in ancient times took away the prize for eloquence were also greatly esteemed for knowing how to speak briefly at a specific time and place, especially for knowing how to use appropriately words that are sharp and of noble appearance. In this, all princes who would follow your example should really know how to refrain from making witticisms that are too biting. For although a king may not only say, but also do, anything he likes, it is surely the case that in this situation, when he is seeking pleasure, there must also be a certain satisfaction in it for those to whom he is speaking, such that his

15. See Quintilian, *Institutio oratoria*, XI.ii.50, and Pliny, *Naturalis historia*, VII.xxiv.89.

words seem rather to tickle than to sting sharply, as much for the sake of retaining his authority and gravity, which such a thing would diminish, as because men are often very impatient about putting up with a mocking witticism even though it was hurled by a person against whom one dare not take revenge. Nevertheless, one might still sometimes touch someone to the quick under the cover of gentle words, as King Louis XI did to a certain bishop whom someone had named to him to be sent as ambassador to Venice. The person who had named the man and desired to help him advance because he was a relative said, when the king asked him which man it was, "He is the bishop of such a place, abbot of such an abbey, lord of such and such estates," reviewing all his qualities in petty detail. "Where there are so many titles," responded the king, "there is little learning." Captain Marasin approached the same king to inform him of what he had accomplished at Cambrai. The captain was wearing a rich golden necklace about his neck that people said had been made from relics taken from the churches of the aforementioned Cambrai, and when a gentleman wished to feel the necklace, the king said to him, "Be careful not to touch that; it's a sacred object."[16] Thus, one person was mocked by him as ignorant and the other reproved as sacrilegious, but it was done in such a way that there was more pleasure than bitterness in the mockery. Themistocles, captain general of the Athenians, did not mock the Erethrians any less pleasantly, although he did so more openly, when he reproached them for baseness and cowardice. "Those people," he said, "resemble the fish called the squid, for they have many swords, but no heart at all."[17] I do not want to stop to explain how and in how many ways one can make use of such sharp and stinging words, because it would be better to make a separate collection of them; I will just say that one must especially avoid having mockery turned back against its author, something that happened long ago to the emperor Augustus.[18] Someone told him that a stranger had come to Rome who resembled him perfectly. Augustus wanted to see the man, and thinking to play with him, he asked him if his mother had ever come to Rome. The stranger responded promptly to him: "Not my mother, for all I know, but my father has come here several times." Thus Augustus was paid with the same coin, and was constrained to take that reply in silence because he had started it and the stranger who had been assaulted had merely defended his honor and that of his mother. Princes should not, therefore, get angry in similar cases, but derive a double praise from them: one for their gentle, benign natures, and the other their true, royal magnanimity. For, as Fabius Maximus said, when his fellow citizens were criticizing him for having conducted the war too

16. Captain Marasin is most likely Guillaume Marasin, a follower of Louis XI, who made him bishop of Noyon. The battle of Cambrai occurred in 1476.

17. See Plutarch, *Sayings of Kings and Commanders* ("Themistocles," 14), in *Moralia*, 185e.

18. For this anecdote, see Macrobius, *Saturnalia*, II.iv.20.

coldly and slowly for their taste, "He who cannot endure a mocking witticism is more of a coward than he who flees before the enemy."[19]

(In the next three chapters Amyot says that when the prince is at leisure, he should read books about warfare, the histories of the noble families in his realm, and political history generally, all of which will help him embellish his speeches.)

Chapter IX. What the Prince Talks About When Conducting His Affairs

I have talked enough about the subjects a king can speak of for pleasure, so let's turn to the other reason for which nature gave language to man, that is, for profit. Since the principal end at which a good prince aims is nothing other than the welfare of his subjects and the good of his realm, it seems that the king will speak for his profit and for that of others, both at the same time, when there is some question involving his affairs. The variety of those affairs can be understood by considering the variety of the people involved. Neighboring kings and sovereign princes must be put first, because the power and dignity of royal eloquence are especially evident when rulers meet one another and parley together, as did your grandfather King Francis, the first of his name, and the emperor Charles V at Aiguesmortes.[20] Likewise, you yourself, Sire, at your return from your kingdom of Poland, allowed us to see how much the power of eloquence could accomplish with the rulers of Venice, the Duke of Savoy, and several other princes and potentates.[21] However, most princes do not seek out such interviews and parlays, but handle affairs through intermediaries, their ambassadors, who are normally select, knowledgeable, and eloquent people. For this reason, the prince who knows how to respond well to them himself derives greater praise from doing so—not that I want him to extend himself much in this, for there is less gravity in a long oration than in a tightly compressed utterance, and if ambassadors make use of harangues that are too long, he might say to them what Cleomenes, king of Lacedemonia, replied to the one delivered by the ambassadors of the Samians: "I no longer remember what you said at the beginning, which prevents me from understanding the middle; as for what you said at the end, I do not find it good."[22]

19. See Plutarch, *Sayings of the Romans* ("Fabius Maximus," 1), in *Moralia*, 195c; the war in question was the Second Punic War (218–201 B.C.), fought against Hannibal and the Carthaginians.

20. Francis I and Charles V, the Holy Roman Emperor, met in Aiguesmortes in 1538 to work on a peace settlement.

21. In 1574 Henry III left Poland in order to return to France and claim the throne after the death of his elder brother Charles IX; he traveled by way of northern Italy where, among other things, he delivered a celebrated speech before the Venetian Senate.

22. See Plutarch, *Sayings of Spartans* ("Cleomenes, Son of Anaxandridas," 7), in *Moralia*, 223d.

Jacques Amyot

Chapter X. On the Places from Which One Derives Arguments and Passions

In regard to the subjects the orator handles, he will most often consider whether the thing is profitable, honest, just, or the contrary, and to it, as to his goal and principal point, he will relate all his reasons and arguments, which he will look for in certain places of which I will speak only in passing while taking a few examples from them.[23] The first three are definition, division into parts, and etymology. An example of definition: he who commands a people by himself and with justice ought to be obeyed; the king is such a man; thus one ought to obey the king. An example of division into parts: a soldier in a battle is forced either to fight or flee or surrender to the enemy; it is base and cowardly to flee as well as to surrender; therefore a true soldier must fight to his last breath. An example of etymology: a prince who desires to maintain his state through good counsel must have good counselors near him. There are several other places, such as difference, genre, species, words that come from the same source, contraries, causes, and effects, but those that turn up most frequently are similarities and comparisons, which, in addition to their effectiveness in proving things, provide splendid ornaments for an oration. I omit examples of these things, however, for their number is infinite, nor are the arguments involved difficult to find. For just as a hunter, who has discovered the lairs of wild beasts and surrounded the forest with his nets, and has then entered it with his dogs and diligently lies in wait, cannot possibly fail to catch some of them, so, when one has carefully observed these places, which are the dens of arguments, and has surrounded them with one's thoughts, one cannot fail in one's quest to discover some that will be appropriate to support what we are alleging. Now, in order to persuade people, it is not sufficient to find and then make use of arguments, because that is something common to the philosopher as well as the orator; rather, one must, in addition, impress certain passions on the spirits of one's auditors, for they have much more power than arguments, and by their means people will allow themselves to be led and transported hither and thither wherever it seems good to an eloquent man. But insofar as that is done in certain parts of a speech, let's see now what they are and what the usual order is that one follows in them. There are normally four parts to an oration, of which two, to wit, the first and the last, serve to move the passions of the soul, and the two others to recount the case and to prove it with arguments.

(In chapter XI, Amyot briefly reviews the four parts of an oration, including the exordium, the narration or statement of the case, and the confirmation or arguments in favor of it. He ends with the peroration.)

23. The "places" are the "places of invention," that is, the general categories in which arguments are theoretically grouped and from which they may be "drawn" by the orator for use in specific cases.

Peroration.   If the entry of the oration has had a certain amount of grace and power so as to attract men's spirits to it, the exit must have yet more authority and force in order to ravish and transport them. However, in this part it would be appropriate to collect together and summarize the things that we have said—if not all of them, then at least the principal ones—in order to refresh the auditors' memory of them. Then the orator should release the bridle on his eloquence and let it run forward vehemently, stirring and moving men's emotions by means of amplification. Now, there are two sorts of passions: one kind is gentle, as are voluptuousness, love, hope; the other is sharper and more violent, as are fear, pity, hate, anger. One makes use of the first kind in the exordium, and of the second in the peroration, where they have often had so much power that the orator obtained by their means what he could not gain by arguments. Men thus let themselves be managed more readily by their passions than by reason. There are many precepts and commonplaces about this subject in rhetoric books that would take too long to explain at present.

(In chapter XII, Amyot explains how there are three kinds or levels of style: a simple one for narrating the case; a vehement one to move the emotions; and a moderate one to give pleasure.)

Chapter XIII. On Selecting Words and Joining Them Together

As for simple words, one must first select them and then connect and arrange them. In choosing them, we will take those that are fittest to signify the thing about which we wish to speak, those that seem the sweetest to us, that sound best to the ear, and that are most customarily found in the mouths of eloquent speakers. They will be good French words, not foreign ones, something that the emperor Tiberius observed carefully, especially in his edicts and ordinances, even to the point of making difficulties about using the word "strena," to wit, a New Year's gift.[24] In order to please him, the lawyer Capito said that that word was good Latin and that when it was not, it would become so if that were pleasing to Caesar. Then, a certain grammarian, standing up, said, "No, no, Caesar, you have the power to give the right of citizenship and naturalization papers to men, but you cannot naturalize a word." I would not, however, reject those foreign words that have been accepted for a long time and are, as it were, already rooted in our language, nor would I scorn those old words that one finds in romances. Rather, I would revive the use of a few of them, provided that that was done rarely and with discretion, and without seeking out words that are already

24. See Suetonius, *De grammaticis,* xxii. The lawyer was Ateius Capito; the grammarian, Marcus Pomponius Marcellus; and "strena" was a Sabine term. This passage does not identify "strena" as the offending term, however, although Suetonius reports Tiberius using it; see his *Tiberius,* xxxiv.

totally rancid and mildewed, to the point that, as Augustus said of Antony, his companion in empire, "Your speaking in such a way that you cannot be understood is enough to drive a man mad."[25] Moreover, one can sometimes make compound words whose composition is neither harsh nor too bold—our language is among the most fecund in producing these. Words that are figurative especially beautify and enrich one's language, so that I think, Sire, you ought to order someone to make a separate book for you about the figures and ornaments of oratory, with examples, for there is nothing that gives more luster and sparkle to both words and sentences. The words having been chosen, one must join and bind them together, in such a way that there are no hard conjunctures of words or syllables. And when the ear, to which one ought to refer, judges for us that a clause is too flat or too harsh, we should change the order of the words and arrange them differently, finally discovering which way will produce greater solidity and sweetness. Nor should we forget, either, to avoid rhyme, for it is a great vice in prose when several words, or the ends of clauses, have similar endings. Among other things, one must study not merely to connect, but to bind clauses together, and as much as possible to diversify and vary the conjunctions that hold them together, so that nothing is disjointed or interrupted, but everything flows, one thing after another, and all the parts are assembled like the members of a single body. Many other precepts touching on elocution could be given, but we have undertaken here only a simple epitome and summary discourse concerning each principal topic. Now let us go ahead and come to what remains.

Chapter XIV. On Memory and Delivery

After material has been found out and put in order, words have been chosen and well connected together, and the oration has all its ornamentation, then it is time to learn it by heart. Those people who have need of them will put into practice the teachings of artificial memory, but as for you, Sire, in this case nature does not require you to have anything to do with them.[26] Still, I have to say that if by chance some prince really distrusted his memory, he could follow the example of Augustus, who, once he ruled as emperor in peace, always read and recited his speeches, speaking thus by script, either because he feared he would break down for lack of memory, or because he did not have enough time to learn them. Now, so far we have considered only the body of eloquence, for delivery is its soul, as has been said elsewhere. Thanks to delivery alone, those who did not have a great

25. See Suetonius, *Divus Augustus*, lxxxvi.2.
26. Systems of "artificial memory," that is, systems of mnemonic devices, were composed throughout antiquity and the Middle Ages. In the Renaissance, such arts of memory as those of Peter of Ravenna (*Phoenix, sive artificiosa memoria*, 1491) and Giulio Camillo (*L'Idea del Teatro*, 1550) enjoyed enormous popularity.

ability to speak well have quite often been judged very eloquent, and on the contrary, about those who had acquired the other parts of the art, but lacked this one, people concluded that they said nothing of worth. For this reason, the great orator Demosthenes, when asked what part of eloquence he prized the most, replied, "Delivery"; asked forthwith what was the next one, he replied again "Delivery"; and he gave a similar response to the third question.[27] Delivery consists of three things: a good voice, a graceful face, and restrained gestures and bodily movements. A good voice comes from nature, although by means of application one can make it louder, fuller, and firmer, without losing its sweetness. For what Queen Parysatis, the mother of Cyrus, said—that one must use words of silk toward kings—can also be said of the voice of princes speaking to their subjects, for their sweet voice serves greatly to pacify the people when they are bitter and angry, or to comfort them when they see themselves afflicted and are complaining.[28] It is just like what one says about those afflicted with sciatica: when the rash torments them the most, if one plays some sweet aubade on the flute, they find their pain alleviated. However, this is not to say that one should not sometimes speak in a firmer manner, raising and reinforcing one's voice according to the subject matter and the occasion. A graceful face has no less power than the voice, nay rather, even more, for the face is the image of the soul, and in it the different emotions of the spirit are recognized, particularly in the eyes, which reveal on the outside everything that is inside, and imprint on those who look at them passions identical with those of the speaker. In this situation what happens to them is like what happens to the bird we call the oriole, which, on looking at those who have jaundice, takes on that same sickness directly. As for a good countenance, gestures, and movement of the body, it would not only be a loss of time and paper, but also a matter of presumption, to want to touch on these topics here.

(In his last chapter, Amyot stresses the importance of exercise, and says he thinks Henry III will learn more by studying actual orations than by learning the precepts taught by rhetoricians.)

27. For this anecdote, see Cicero, *Brutus*, xxxviii.142.
28. See Plutarch, *Sayings of Kings and Commanders* ("Parysatis"), in *Moralia*, 174a.

[13]

Anton Maria de' Conti

Anton Maria de' Conti (1514–1555), later known by his professional name of Marcantonio Maioraggio, was born in Milan. After having begun his education in Como in 1532, he returned to Milan where he studied mathematics and logic between 1534 or 1535 and 1540. He taught rhetoric in his native city for a while before going to Ferrara in 1543 in order to study law and philosophy, although he then returned to Milan in 1545, where he helped found the Accademia dei Trasformati and where he occupied the chair of rhetoric until his death. His publications were primarily legal and literary, including several interventions in the debate over Ciceronianism, a translation and commentary on Aristotle's *Rhetoric*, and several commentaries on rhetorical works by Cicero. The *De eloquentia dialogus* (*A Dialogue on Eloquence*) translated here was published posthumously in 1582 and is the counterpart to Conti's *De arte poetica* (*Art of Poetry*); both are apologies for the arts they discuss. Its interlocutors include two of Conti's relatives, Primo de' Conti and his brother Antonio de' Conti, as well as the unidentified Angelo Appiano. Primo de' Conti was a scholarly man who edited and published Anton Maria de' Conti's translation and commentary on Aristotle's *Rhetoric* in 1571. For the *Dialogus*, I have used the text in *Trattati di poetica e retorica del Cinquecento*, edited by Bernard Weinberg (Bari: Laterza, 1970), 3: 101–34.

FROM *A Dialogue on Eloquence*

It is often the case that our listless spirits can be revived by contemplating the variety of nature: the heavenly sphere inlaid with widely scattered stars that are like a kind of mosaic; the earthly sphere crowded with diverse animals and plants; the charm of growing meadows; the variegated colors of the flowers; and the great richness of the farms. Thus, when men who have been educated in the liberal arts assiduously cogitate about the vicissitudes of the material world and of history, they are easily led to experience the greatest wonder, with the result that the thought frequently occurs to them to seek out the causes of things, or at least, on the basis of what has been placed before their eyes, to hypothesize about celestial causes that they can in no way perceive while they are still alive.

We had retired into the garden of Saint Ambrose in which they say that famous African, Augustine, the light and ornament of Christendom, once bowed his spirit to belief in Christ and in that place, having been sprinkled with holy water, washed away the filth of original sin and his wicked mind.[1] Present there together with me at that time was Angelo Appiano, the head of the monastery, a man of the sweetest temperament, whose equal you will not easily find because of his exceptional moral integrity, the holiness of his life, and his enormous erudition in all the liberal arts. Also present was my most learned teacher Primo de' Conti, whose praiseworthy qualities I do not have the ability to unfold, although I hope that sometime a more suitable place will be found to speak of them. For who could describe in a brief oration how, in the classic authors who wrote in the three languages, there is almost nothing to be found that he has not diligently investigated, nothing in the liberal arts that he has not taught in the best way, nothing worthy of being remembered that he has not learned perfectly by heart?[2] I pass over in silence his most holy behavior, the strictness of his life, his continual thinking and talking of divine matters.

When we had seated ourselves beneath a certain leafy tree and were just planning to discuss our common studies, before anyone could begin, Primo's brother Antonio appeared. He was a young man filled with an intense thirst for learning and most knowledgeable about all the more refined kinds of writing. He was tied to me by a bond tighter than that which linked Pylades and Orestes, inasmuch as we were occupied by similar studies, had lived together practically since the time we started them, and served under the same master, Primo. If the same mother had given birth to us at the same time, we could not have been joined together by greater goodwill. When I saw him, I was marvelously cheered, for I had not seen him for almost twenty days, which had seemed to me longer than twenty years.

(Angelo opens the dialogue by asking the young Antonio to share his knowledge with them, but Antonio politely refuses and asks Primo to speak instead. The latter compares the garden they are in to paradise, declares that meditation on it should lead one to consider the joys of heaven and to practice virtue, and laments how much time men waste on base pursuits instead. Angelo praises Primo's speech and then switches the subject to eloquence.)

1. The Church of Saint Ambrose (Sant' Ambrogio) is one of the principal churches of Milan and contains the body of the saint for whom it is named. A Benedictine monastery was founded there in 784, though it was taken over by Cistercians in 1497. Both before and after his conversion, Augustine was taught by Ambrose; in his *Confessions*, IX.6, he recounts his baptism, which took place in this church in 387.
2. The "three languages" are Latin, Greek, and Hebrew.

"But I was really hoping that you would also say something about the study of the liberal arts and especially about eloquence. For I see these adolescents really laboring with all their strength in order to achieve just a little of it, a labor that seems to me to be unnecessary. Why it appears thus I will say later, after I have heard your opinion on the subject. Therefore, although you might talk about many other matters, you should unfold this one, so that these adolescents know what it seems they should be doing."

Then Primo said, smiling: "I know what you are up to, Angelo. You want to force me to say something about eloquence so that, using eloquence itself, which you say you do not approve of, you can reject all the reasons and arguments I use to defend it. For I have never known anyone more ardent than you in speaking or sharper in making refutations. Nevertheless, since you seem to want it, I will tell you my opinion. If you say something to the contrary, eloquence will still display itself in all its glory, for you cannot reject eloquence in any way without using it. You, however"—he indicated me and Antonio—"continue to go forward just as you have begun, applying all your energies to the study of eloquence, for of all things (excepting always divine matters) it is incontrovertibly the most excellent, and do not let Angelo throw you off balance and turn things upside down if he says anything to the contrary. Nay, rather, press forward. Of all things, only that one should be judged truly excellent and outstanding that is able to adorn and refine our better part, our mind, is capable of making men marvel, and offers the greatest utility to a great many people. For these reasons we esteem learning and the liberal arts and, finally, all the virtues, because by their means the human mind is perfected. Are gems, pearls, chrysolites, diamonds, and all the rest considered precious for any other reason than that men are accustomed to marvel at them? Indeed, silver and gold are esteemed so highly for the very reason that, thanks to the conventional arrangements and practices of men, they seem most suited to buying and selling. But no greater ornament of the mind can be found than refined and prudent speech, nothing capable of exciting greater wonder, nothing, finally, more useful for humankind.

"For what can be more beautiful than an individual who surpasses others in this one single thing by means of which men excel all the other animals?[3] What more honorable and becoming than to be able to govern your speech in such a way that you should seem to say nothing that is not elegant, prudent, and polished, nothing base and vulgar, but rather everything noble and splendid? What more marvelous than to be able to direct the minds of your auditors by means of speech in whatever direction you might wish? Although almost everyone knows how to speak, you alone would speak in

3. Cf. Cicero, *De inventione*, I.iv.5. The rest of this paragraph elaborates Cicero, *De oratore*, I.viii.32, and Tacitus, *Dialogus*, v.4–6.

such a way that the others would seem to know nothing at all. You would keep the minds of your auditors hanging and amaze them, so that you would force them, even unwilling, to cast their votes in favor of your opinions. Well, then, what is more useful than eloquence? What more liberal? By its means legal defense is offered to the accused, those who are afflicted are raised up, safety is given to the wretched, defendants are freed from dangers, cities are governed in the best manner, sedition and discord in the populace are calmed, and people are led to worship in holy religion. Now, if something is a real ornament of the mind, fills all men with wonder, and produces the greatest benefits, then that thing will be the most excellent of all. And since we have demonstrated that eloquence is no mediocre ornament of the mind, is particularly wonder-producing, and is most useful, no one can doubt that it is the most excellent of all things." When he had said these things, he stopped.

Angelo, however, said, "You have certainly handled me cleverly, seeking to alienate our listeners so that they will have no confidence in my words even before they have heard anything from me! Although I only asked for your opinion about eloquence, you yourself have so dazzled our eyes, despite their keen sight, with your arguments, or rather with certain juggling tricks, that you seem to have changed base lead into pure and, as they say, unalloyed gold. But I will get even with you, not indeed that I should wish to hide what is true, which is what you seem to me to have done, but more so that, once your tricks have been exposed, the truth will shine out on its own accord. But now we will clash in open war: although I could finish you off right away by cutting your throat—and even a dull sword, as they say, would suffice to do it—first let me unfold my position. If it were the case that great skill in speaking, obtained through study, could help a Christian to live well and blessedly, I would never really undertake to show how greatly I disapprove of it. For what can be thought or said with greater impudence than to condemn that which is not merely suited to our religious faith, but also most useful to it? But when I see that from the study of eloquence there derives not only no utility for Christians, but the greatest harm, why should I agree that so much labor ought to be devoted to it? Or rather, why should I not greatly disapprove of doing so? For what can one do that would be more pernicious than, having forsaken more serious studies, to use up good hours in learning by heart an empty hodgepodge of words? Especially since Christ himself, the founder of our religion, wanted us to be forbidden under his laws to speak much, for the reason that it is always possible for some sort of crime to occur when there is a lot of talk.[4] Not only are we not striving to the best of our ability to cut back in some

---

4. Angelo is most likely alluding to Matthew 6:5–7, a passage in which Christ tells his followers how not to pray and which precedes the one in which he teaches them the Lord's prayer.

way this vice of superfluous speech, which has come to possess almost all mortals, but—good lord!—we are actually sustaining our talkativeness by means of our studies.

"As for the fact that you say eloquence is marvelous because it fills your auditors with amazement, the same thing can be said about a rope-dancer, a juggler, or even a mountebank, and yet, such kinds of men are not said to be truly excellent for that reason. But when you claim that defendants are freed, cities governed, and people led to religion by means of eloquence, you seem to me to have argued more speciously than the facts warrant. For, first of all, who would concede to you that eloquence is useful on the grounds that it frees defendants from dangers? If they are bad, does it seem useful to you to free them? And if they are good, shouldn't they be freed because they are protected by their innocence rather than by someone's eloquence? Who freed that Hebrew woman Susanna from a false accusation? Was it not her silence (if we believe Ambrose)?[5] If, to defend herself, she had sought to employ an orator, she would not have seemed innocent at all, though she was. Should I bring up Socrates, the wisest of men in Apollo's judgment? To him, when he was in prison, the most eloquent orator Lysias is said to have brought an oration by means of which it seemed that the unfairly accused Socrates could be rescued, but that incredibly wise man preferred to be condemned unjustly than to be freed by the help of eloquence.[6] If eloquence defends the innocent and the guilty, although the former are not afraid because they are conscious of having done nothing wrong, while the latter seek legal protection, urged to it by their consciousness of their wicked deeds, then not only is eloquence not useful, but it is even pernicious since it defends those who ought to be suppressed.

"Moreover, as for the fact that you say cities are governed by eloquence, in my opinion you seem to have said that more for the sake of debate than because you think it to be the case. For I don't think you are ignorant of the fact that cities are ruled by the best laws and by the prudence of men, not by eloquence, which has been found to harm cities much more frequently than to benefit them. Who is ignorant of the great tumults in the Roman republic that the eloquence of the two Gracchi stirred up? of how many were caused by that of Saturninus? and of how many by that of Pisistratus in Athens?

"Your claim that people are drawn to religion through eloquence is by no means to be endured. For just what is that eloquence that you are praising? Is it really the one we find in Sacred Scripture? Who does not know that eloquence has been expelled as useless from it? Or are you talking about that

5. According to the thirteenth chapter of Daniel (a chapter considered apocryphal by Protestants), the beautiful and devout Susanna was spied on in her bath by two Jewish elders, then accused of adultery by them and condemned to death. She was saved by the intervention of Daniel who cross-examined and convicted the two men. Ambrose praises Susanna for remaining silent and depending on her modesty to protect her in his *Exhortatio virginitatis*, xiii.87.

6. This anecdote appears in Diogenes Laertius, *Socrates*, in *Lives of the Eminent Philosophers*, II.40–41.

eloquence by which Paul boasted he had converted the Corinthians when he says: 'And I, brethren, when I came to you, came not with excellency of speech or of wisdom, [but] declaring unto you the testimony of God.' And a little later: 'And my speech and my preaching was not with enticing words of man's wisdom, but in demonstration of the Spirit and of power, that your faith should not stand in the wisdom of men, but in the power of God.'[7] Does it seem to you that Paul is praising eloquence here, and not rather rejecting it? Then, it is not eloquence that draws men to religion, but the manifestation of the Spirit and the proclaiming of the Gospel.

"As for the fact that you say that eloquence is the greatest, most praiseworthy ornament of our minds, I will be absolutely consistent and flatly deny it. I will never say that there is any ornament of the human mind except virtue and an honest life, or that one should aim at anything beyond religion and knowledge of the One God through Sacred Scripture, which contains no eloquence. For what is to be aimed at except that which is useful? And indeed, what is useful to a Christian that is not likewise honorable? And yet no one will judge something honorable if it can be the common property of even the most wicked person—and eloquence is such that even the worst man can possess it. Therefore, eloquence is not honorable, and if not honorable, then not useful, and if truly not useful, then it seems that it should not only not be pursued, but actually avoided. Moreover, because it is to be avoided, it is necessarily pernicious. Therefore, not only should a Christian not conclude that eloquence is a really excellent thing—a conclusion you reached with anything but the best arguments—but actually that it is most pernicious."

After he had said these things, we waited in silence to see what Primo was going to say in opposition. The latter finally remarked: "Angelo, if I thought that your real views resembled your words, I would urge you with the greatest diligence to abandon such perverse opinions. Or, if you would not listen, I would brand you with the mark of ingratitude, you who, although owing so much to eloquence that no one, or perhaps very few, can match you at this time, nevertheless dare to attack it with its very own weapons. But since I know that you have said these things not from your heart, but for the sake of arguing and only in a superficial manner, I will say nothing about you or your ingratitude. I will simply strive, with my shield held on high, to protect and defend eloquence itself, so that you will seem to have been beating the air with your arguments. First, therefore, I will try to refute your statements, and then I will strive to assemble and unfold all those arguments useful for confirming my case.

"And so, let me begin right here and ask: what is more defective than that logical conclusion you maintained in your peroration as though it were

7. 1 Corinthians 2:1, 4–5. I have cited the King James Version, but have added the "but" needed to make better sense in the first verse cited.

absolutely valid? Indeed, on first hearing it, I was not a little confused; it seemed to me I was listening to one of those inexplicable sophistic arguments or logical conundrums of Chrysippus. However, after I had considered it more carefully, nothing seemed more inane to me. I believe you reasoned in this manner: nothing is useful that is not at the same time also honorable, and nothing is honorable that can be the common property of a wicked person. I might easily grant you these propositions, although that first one is not probable in many instances, but let's see what is connected to them: eloquence is such that even the worst man can possess it. What are you saying, Angelo? You should see that it is not sufficient for a dialectician either to be ignorant of definitions or to fail to consider those that are commonly known. The worst man can possess eloquence? Don't you see that this is as if you were saying, 'The most foolish man can be the wisest'? For what is eloquence other than wisdom speaking copiously? What is the orator other than a good man skilled in speaking?[8] Can a wicked man be either wise or good? Who in his right mind would dare to say this? And yet you, either in ignorance or perhaps actually knowing what you were doing, reached this conclusion. For whoever is eloquent must necessarily also be a wise and good man if in fact eloquence is defined as wisdom and the orator as a good man. On the contrary, if a wicked man is eloquent, will he likewise be wise and good? Who does not know that this can never be the case? Therefore, eloquence can never have any connection to an evil man. With this notion taken away, do you see how quickly you have been cut down in your argument? But it seems that these things need to be shown more clearly.

"What you think eloquence to be is of great importance, Angelo, for if you think it is only an empty hodgepodge of words, as you said, then you are right in condemning it, although you clearly err greatly in your definition. If, on the contrary, you really believe, as I think you do, that eloquence is something greater than a farrago of words, and that no man can be eloquent at all without knowing many things, both divine and human, how can I describe your actions when you blame such a praiseworthy thing—except to say you are acting very badly indeed? Insofar as you say it is not fitting to forsake weightier studies [in order to pursue eloquence], just what are those weightier studies, or what is it that we take pains with in our studies other than to increase our eloquence and, having assembled a multitude of arguments, to be able to help both ourselves and as many others as possible to live well and happily? Is there anyone who learns something who does not desire, once he has mastered it, to spread it abroad as much as possible? After all, nature has instilled in everyone the desire to know and to teach others what they know, and when they do so, who is he who does not

8. Conti's definition of the orator as a "good man skilled in speaking" repeats the classic phrase from Cato, which Quintilian quotes in the *Institutio oratoria,* XII.i.1.

desire to speak as well as possible? Thus, all our studies and all our zeal are directed to the end of becoming eloquent, for learning that is hidden away is worth little or nothing. In short, there can be no study that is weightier than the study of eloquence.

"But Christ, you say, has ordered us to speak little. For what reason, I ask you, do you assume that this was said against eloquence? Beware lest you also provoke the theologians by badly distorting the Gospel when you just want to make eloquent men into your enemies. You will not be equal to that battle, although you are very capable of dealing with the subject of theology, for if the Scotists once come down on you, you would not be able to extricate yourself very easily from their dark snares, nor will that really marvelous learning of yours be of any use to you against the clamoring of the Thomists and the Occamists.[9] But let me return to the point from which I digressed. In the passage alluded to earlier, Christ is blaming the long prayers of the heathen by means of which they trust they will be able to obtain what they desire from God. You, however, are quite the original interpreter and twist Christ's words against eloquence. For if it is bad to speak, why are we not perpetually silent? But if it is good, why shouldn't we strive to speak as well as we can whenever we do speak? For thus we would eliminate the vice of talkativeness, which you rightly say has come to possess almost all mortals, and we would say only those things that are worthy, utilizing speech that is most polished and at the same time most useful.

"And how wittily you joked about the rope-dancer and the juggler, as if a rope-dancer had anything to do with oratory or as if this comparison were not, as they say, 180 degrees off the mark! It seemed to me that, since you had nothing that you could say against eloquence, you invented such an absurd comparison just out of a desire to contradict. For what similarity does a tightrope walker have to eloquence? Although he performs certain quite ridiculous things that may seem marvelous, still he is not useful to himself or others, he is despised by all, and he is watched merely for the sake of amusement. By contrast, eloquence seizes and transforms the minds of men, forcing even the unwilling toward the most useful ends, and for this reason it seems absolutely divine. Indeed, it is inevitable that when someone has once heard an eloquent man, he will admire him greatly and revere a certain something in him that transcends the human. What sedition arising among the most ferocious people could be so great that an eloquent man, should he come upon it, could not calm it on the spot and bring enemies together in peace? And what is more savage than the sedition of the common people? Menenius Agrippa won over the plebeians, who were angry at the patricians, merely by means of a fable eloquently recited and wisely interpreted: how much more easily would he have accomplished that feat, if he

9. Conti here manifests a typical Renaissance disdain for the forms of argumentation and the Latin style of the followers of the Scholastic philosophers Duns Scotus, Thomas Aquinas, and William of Occam.

had reached down to the very fountainhead of eloquence? [10] What about the time when all of Greece rushed together for the debate between Demosthenes and Aeschines? [11] Do you think that those Greeks who came there did so for the sake of seeing jugglers? Or when certain people used to come from the farthest reaches of the world to hear Livy of Padua, don't they seem to you to have been admiring his eloquence, not treating it as an empty matter, which is what you call it, but as something really marvelous and almost divine? [12]

"But these things that you said on your own authority are easily refuted because they are slight, whereas what you quoted from Paul seems to create more of a difficulty for my argument. We will see about Susanna and Socrates afterward. Nevertheless, even that which Paul says is very easy to refute, since he does not attack eloquence, but seems merely to prefer instead the manifestation of the Spirit and power of God. For at the beginning when the Church was first being born, I confess that miracles were more necessary, since men could not be compelled to change their worship of the gods and the deeply rooted religion of their ancestors by means of eloquent persuasion alone, unless miracles were also present that proclaimed that what was happening was necessarily divine, not human. But after they had been converted to Christ, then eloquence alone was sufficient on a daily basis to strengthen the spirits of the weak and the infirm, to rouse the idle, to correct those who erred, and to inflame the fervent to even greater displays of zeal.

"Moreover, we also see that Paul wrote with great art, for although you pretend that he condemns eloquence, he is in fact most eloquent himself. To this fact, leaving aside what Paul's epistles reveal, Augustine bears witness, as he strives to display the embellishments of subject matter and style and the power of eloquence in Paul's writings. [13] Therefore, those words of Paul, which you cited just now, are not to be interpreted in the way you think and should not lead us to believe that he condemns the eloquence with which he was overwhelmingly endowed. But when he writes to the Corinthians, many of whom were being seduced by false prophets, he skillfully leads them to recall the manifestation and miracles of the Spirit to make them remember that they accepted the faith of Christ not so much through Paul's

10. Menenius Agrippa's fable, known as the fable of the belly, is a political allegory of the body in which the supremacy of the patricians in the state and their receipt of food during a time of scarcity are justified by their identification with the belly, which does not just receive the food, but distributes it to the other members, including the plebeians. Livy recounts the story and explains how it did indeed pacify the Roman plebeians; see his *Ab urbe condita*, II.xxxii.8–12.

11. The debate between Aeschines and Demosthenes is probably the one that took place in 330 B.C. over the proposal to award a crown to Demosthenes in recognition of his services to Athens.

12. Livy's fame for eloquence was so great that a man from Gades in Spain supposedly traveled to Rome just to hear him speak.

13. See Augustine, *De doctrina christiana*, IV.vii.11–14.

words as through the power and miracles of the Gospel. Nor has eloquence really been expelled from Sacred Scripture, as you say. Nay rather, it is more credible to believe that it had its beginning there and then gradually increased because of the studies of the wisest men. For it cannot be the case that such a divine thing took its origin from any other place than Sacred Scripture, especially since we see many speeches in the Holy Bible that we surely know are most eloquent in the Hebrew language and that even in translation display a kind of image of elegance. One has to believe that those whom we call prophets, whose eloquence I admire in greater measure when I read their writings in Hebrew, were nothing other than the most fluent orators whom God elected out of the multitude to be the ones who would lead the people to religion.

"When one of them, Daniel, saw that the innocent Susanna was being led to punishment, he freed her by means of his eloquence, and although, as you say, Ambrose thought it right that she proved her own innocence by her silence, nevertheless, if she had not been aided by Daniel's speech, which God admonished him to make, there would have been no impediment to have prevented her from undergoing the most unworthy punishment. Moreover, you say Socrates preferred to perish rather than to be saved by the speech of Lysias. Let me grant that, to be sure. Did Socrates thereby condemn eloquence? He said that that oration seemed to him unworthy of the man because it was perhaps insufficiently eloquent. He did not make a judgment about the whole of eloquence—unless perhaps you believe that one who scorns the gold that covers copper also rejects gold that is pure and refined. But what Socrates thought about eloquence his disciple Plato intimates when he brings him on everywhere discoursing most eloquently. Thus, you see that you have adduced these examples in vain.

"Moreover, there's no point in speaking about the Gracchi, Saturninus, and Pisistratus, since these were seditious citizens, whereas we declare that no one is eloquent unless he is a good man. Even though those men had a certain amount of eloquence, nevertheless such a great virtue does not seem worthy of condemnation for that reason, nor should the vices of wicked men be entirely transferred to it, for not it, but their evil deeds fall into the category of vice.

"As for the fact that you say it seems to you that cities are governed by laws and prudence, not by eloquence, I would say, by your leave, that you yourself separate eloquence from these things in a manner that is not sufficiently prudent and lawful, for you are not ignorant of the fact that laws and prudence can in no way exist without eloquence. After all, who do you think first found out the laws—let us trace things back to their roots here— by means of which cities are ruled, or who persuaded the people that they should not refuse to obey the laws? Does it seem to you that it was someone totally incapable of speech and entirely unequipped with eloquence? Does it make sense that they would have obeyed a person who, because of his inability to speak, could not supply an explanation as to why the laws might seem good? Or did an uncivilized people, most desirous of living freely, place the laws like a yoke on its own neck? It really seems to me more likely that it was a most eloquent man who explained why it was best to live in one city together and to use laws as the best means to do so, thus softening the spirits of the people with most eloquent speech and transforming them so that he forced them to obey his will.[14]

"And yet, after they came together in a single town, they surely began to be ruled no less by eloquence than by the laws they had accepted. For when they listened to the most prudent men discoursing on equity and justice, they were seduced by eloquence and judged that they ought to obey those things that seemed best to them. And so, I think that if we had not had eloquence first, we would not have had laws at all. Nor is eloquence, like a limb from its body, to be separated from prudence, for that is said to be the part of eloquence to which all liberal studies are devoted. And if it is the role of a prudent man to embrace liberal studies, why would it not seem to you the role of a prudent man to master eloquence, which is, as it were, the light and adornment of all studies? How much more easily and advantageously might the rulers of cities impel their people to embrace justice and avoid wickedness if they also joined great eloquence to prudence!

"What is to be said about the publishing of Christ's message, for which I think eloquence is as necessary as knowledge of Sacred Scripture? And why? Don't we frequently see that the most learned men on the theological faculty preach so insipidly, because they are destitute of eloquence, that they do not move their listeners at all, although they pour out a great many words. Instead, shouting at the top of their lungs, they waste almost the entire time they are speaking on empty, trifling questions, which should really have been buried under a great silence. For, of what use to the people are those things that Scotus and fellows of his ilk have dreamed up, by means of which people are not in the least inspired to religion, but when they have listened to them, are made much more reluctant to embrace divine matters? How much better would it be for men to apply themselves with all their energy to eloquence, after having studied Sacred Scripture, and, having rejected the sophisms of the dialecticians in which they will drown as if they had just crashed on the rocks of the Sirens, to obtain through study such great eloquence that they can transform, propel, drag, and force the minds of their auditors to pursue what is honest? They will be able to pursue, condemn, defeat, and exterminate the worst vices there are, place future punishments before the eyes of the wicked, scare the life out of people with threats, reveal to them the region of the damned, and bring to light the torments, tortures, and punishments of the wicked. But virtue, since it is most

14. In this paragraph and the one that follows, Conti rehearses the myth of the orator as civilizer found in Cicero, *De inventione*, I.ii.2–4; Quintilian, *Institutio oratoria*, II.xvi.9; and Horace, *Ars poetica*, 391–401.

worthy, they will praise to heaven, describing in detail its rewards, beauty, immortality, glory, and blessedness. Thus, they will speak in such a way that the minds of their auditors will be inflamed in greater measure by a desire for those things; they will be made to grieve, fear, hope, and complain bitterly about the time that has passed by them in vain; they will decide to reject all lusts and passions in the future and to expend all their efforts on virtue alone.

"If anyone follows this method persistently, how much burning desire for what is honest will he awaken, how much marvelous, fiery striving for virtue will he arouse in the minds of mortals, how easily will vices seem to vanish like smoke while the purer flame of virtue is pursued! But I would run out of time if I tried to unfold the universal power of eloquence. I think you see—unless you don't wish to see, or have been made blinder than Hipsaea—how much utility eloquence possesses.[15] Lack of time (for I see evening approaches) forces me to be brief, but unless you abandon your opinion, you should expect a much longer and more elegant speech at some other time in the future."

Here Angelo smiled and said: "Today we have seen Primo speak extemporaneously beyond all our expectations. What if he had come prepared? What if he should happen to speak a second time about eloquence? But that is not really necessary, for I have already voted in favor of your opinion." These things having been said, we departed a short while later.

15. For the phrase "blinder than Hipsaea," see Horace, *Sermones*, I.ii.91, where it is used for a lover who cannot see the defects of his beloved. We do not know who Hipsaea was.

[14]

Peter Ramus

Pierre de la Ramée (1515–1572), usually referred to as Peter (or Petrus) Ramus, was responsible for the most important attempt to transform rhetoric during the Renaissance. At the University of Paris, where he completed an M.A. in 1536, he heard the German educator Johann Sturm lecture on Rudolph Agricola's *De inventione dialectica*, a decisive event that led him to argue that two of the traditional five parts of rhetoric—invention and disposition—really belonged to dialectic or logic, leaving only the other three—elocution or style, delivery, and memory—for rhetoric. He presented his views in two works published in 1543 in which he also attacked the authority of Aristotle, who was central to the heavily Scholastic curriculum at the University of Paris, which had Ramus's teaching and writing banned as a result. His response was to write, alone or with Omer Talon, his collaborator after 1544, a series of works extending his attacks to Cicero and Quintilian and refining and defending his views on logic, rhetoric, and grammar. When Henry II came to the throne in 1547, he was persuaded to lift the ban on Ramus, who was made a regius professor at Paris in 1551, eventually becoming dean of the regius professors in 1565. He converted to Protestantism in 1561 and was killed in 1572 when Catholics throughout France murdered Protestants in what is known as the Saint Bartholomew's Day Massacre. The intellectual revolution Ramus produced stemmed from his transformation of logic and rhetoric into simplified, schematized, and universalized disciplines that could be easily mastered by students. Invention, the finding out of arguments, was limited to just ten places—general categories such as causes, effects, subjects, and adjuncts—from which all arguments concerning all subjects could theoretically be generated. Ramus also argued that disposition or arrangement consisted of propositions, syllogisms, and what he called the method of art and the method of prudence. The first method arranged arguments so that one moved from the most universal to the most specific, always proceeding by means of definitions and divisions or dichotomies and thus producing sets of tree diagrams that he thought mapped the structures of both the mind and the world. This way of mapping knowledge—Ramus called it "method"—was the most important and influential element in his thought during the Renaissance because it promised a supposedly sure way to reach absolute truth. The fact that it was easily visualizable also allowed Ramus to claim that he had a superior memory system, and thus effectively appropriate another traditional part of rhetoric for his dialectic. The method of prudence, despite Ramus's efforts to distinguish it from rhetoric, looks very much like that art, as the excerpt translated below reveals. In his scheme, the province of rhetoric was reduced to style and delivery—or really just style, since he gave delivery very short shrift—and style was further simplified so that all tropes, for instance, were reduced to just four: metaphor, synecdoche, metonymy, and irony. Like rhetoricians before and after him, Ramus saw tropes and figures as the means to provoke emotional reactions in the reader and as a source of pleasure, but he distrusted and denigrated them, preferring a plain style, a preference that would later be shared by the Puritans and by exponents of the New Science. The excerpt translated here is taken from Ramus's French *Dialectique* (*Logic*) published in Paris in 1555 and reprinted in *Gramere* (1562), *Grammaire* (1572), *Dialectique* (1555) (Geneva: Slatkine Reprints, 1972).

FROM *Logic*

(In the first book of this work, which is concerned with invention, Ramus explains how all the material for one's arguments may be derived from just ten places. The subject of the second book he calls judgment, since judgment is involved in making the correct disposition or arrangement of the propositions found out by means of invention. That judgment has three forms: the enunciation or proposition, in which one thing is expressed by another, the syllogism, and what Ramus calls method. After reviewing different sorts of propositions, moving from simple ones such as "fire is hot" to more complex ones such as "all men are healthy or someone is ill," he treats the various forms the syllogism can have. He then states a brief conclusion about it.)

Now, then, when we undertake to resolve some great dispute, if the question is a proposition open to doubt, the syllogism will bear great fruit, and we will be able to demonstrate what is to be concluded firmly and boldly; it provides the true scales of justice when we are examining the correctness or incorrectness of a controversial matter. Finally, we should remember that the syllogism is a rational law, truer and more just than all the laws that Lycurgus and Solon ever made, in which a judgment about a proposition open to doubt is established by a necessary and immutable verdict. It is a rational law, I say, one that is proper to man, it being in no way shared with the other animals, as the first judgment [about propositions] could be to some degree, albeit only in relationship to things perceived by the senses and pertaining to their body and corporeal existence.[1] However, the body, together with all its senses, could not complete a single syllogism, even though Epicurus were presiding in their case. And spiders and ants do what is natural to them, like touching, never conceiving anything by reasoning with a third [term], so far are they from being able to conclude a single syllogism by applying and manipulating that term. And certainly this part of man [i.e., reason] is the image of some sort of divinity. But like our first judgment [of propositions], so our second one [of syllogisms] is often troubled and deceived by errors of opinion, for we quite often reach conclusions through love, hate, envy, fear, desire, and other deceiving emotions rather than through the solid, firm judgment of the syllogism. Therefore, we must animate and raise up this great act of mental judgment and establish it by means of the certainty and truth provided by the syllogism; otherwise our conclusion will be light and erroneous, a matter of temerity rather than judgment.

Method

Method is arrangement, according to which, among several things, the first one that can be known is put in the first place, the second in the second, the third in the third, and so on; this word fits all subjects in the curriculum and treatises of all sorts, although it is commonly taken to mean a path and a direct route.[2] Using this metaphor, the Greeks and Latins put it into practice in the schools, and when they were also speaking of rhetoric, they called it arrangement, using the term for the general category, and under this word no instruction concerning propositions or syllogisms was given in rhetoric, but they only talked about method.

The Method of Nature. Method is either of nature or of prudence. Cicero and Quintilian divide arrangement thus.[3] Aristotle also teaches its parts

---

1. Ramus's point here is that animals can "judge" propositions such as "fire is hot" by means of sensory experience, whereas since only human beings have reason, only they can "judge" things by constructing syllogisms.

2. "Method" for Ramus is a way of teaching as well as a way of constructing arguments, and it involves starting with the most general and universal notions and moving to the most particularized ones. Its virtue is that it is eminently teachable because of its simplicity and directness—hence, the importance of its metaphorical meaning as a path and direct route. *Méthodos* in Greek means a pursuit, a following after, or a way through.

3. Ramus is most likely referring to the fact that Cicero and Quintilian both say that in the exordium or prologue of a case, one can either state things clearly and directly, if the case is unproblematic, or use *insinuatio*, indirection and dissimulation, if it is not; see Cicero, *De inventione*, I.xv.21 and xvii.23–25, and Quintilian, *Institutio oratoria*, IV.i.42–48.

From *Logic*

similarly. The method of nature is the one in which what is clearest and most manifest is placed first; it is what Aristotle calls in the first book of his *Posterior Analytics* either something more manifest by nature or something that has precedence by nature, insofar as what is clearer by nature should come first in the orderly explanation of what is taught, as causes come before effects and, consequently, also what is used to symbolize them, and just as the general and universal come before the special and the particular.[4]

This method is also called the method of art because it has been preserved in the tradition of the arts and of university teaching, and it corresponds in terms of the quality of the judgment involved to propositions that are shown to be necessary and syllogisms that have been properly concluded. Now, then, although in all true disciplines all rules are general and universal, nevertheless they have distinct degrees, and to the extent that one is more general, to that extent it will precede the others, and the most general will be the first in rank and order, for it is the first in clarity and comprehensibility. The subordinate ones will follow, for they are next in clarity, and of those, the more manifest ones will precede, while the less manifest ones will follow. And finally, examples, which are most specialized, will be put in the last position. This method has a singular and unique place in subjects that are taught well, for it is singular and unique and starts with the things that are the antecedents of all the others and are absolutely the clearest and most manifest so that it can clarify and make manifest those things that follow and are obscure and unknown. Thus all the ancients, such as Hippocrates, Plato, and Aristotle, have approved of this method. Hippocrates said one should begin with things that are greater and easier, greater in terms of their usefulness and power, and easier to be grasped by the senses and the understanding, as Galen truly interprets it.[5] Plato, in the *Philebus*, speaks of how all the arts, although they have been discovered and found out through induction that goes from individual things and mounts up to generalities, nevertheless must be deduced by moving in the contrary way, descending from the highest genus to the infinite multitude of the species.[6] And he says so again in the *Phaedrus*, when he teaches that in the method of art one must consider two ideas, the first being the definition of the genus, the second its distribution into its species. He teaches a similar thing in the *Charmides* with the example of doctors who do not begin to cure the part that is sick unless they have first cured the entire body. Aristotle followed this carefully in the first book of his *Posterior Analytics* when he teaches that all true learning and knowledge must proceed from general things and descend degree by degree to particular ones and that it is not at all possible to

4. Aristotle, *Posterior Analytics*, I.ii.71b30–72a8.
5. Claudius Galenus, *Ars medica*, in *Opera omnia*, ed. C. G. Kühn (Leipzig, 1821; reprint, Hildesheim: Georg Olms Verlag, 1964), 1: 305–9.
6. See *Philebus*, 16c–17a. For the references in the next three sentences, see *Phaedrus*, 265d–265e and 270d; *Charmides*, 156b and 157a; and Aristotle, *Posterior Analytics*, I.xxiv.85a13–86a30.

establish an art in any other way, as we have demonstrated more fully in the ninth book of our *Remarks* against Galen and against the interpreters of Aristotle.[7] In short, this method of art seems to me to be like a long golden chain, such as the one Homer imagines, whose rings are those degrees that thus depend one on the other and are all linked so precisely together that none of them may be removed without breaking the order and continuity of the whole.[8] But so that something so great may be made more familiar, we must also make use of a familiar example.

Let's suppose that all the definitions, divisions, and rules of grammar have been found, each one having been judged truly, and that all these precepts have been written on different tickets, which have been turned about all together and mixed up higgledy-piggledy in an urn as in the game of blanks.[9] Here I ask what part of logic would be able to teach me to arrange these precepts that are thus confused and to put them back in order. In the first place, we will not have need of the places of invention, for everything has already been found out, each particular proposition having been tested and judged, and we do not need to make the first judgment of the proposition, or the second one of the syllogism. Only method remains: the sure way of putting things together. Thus, by the light of the method of nature, the logician will choose the definition of grammar from the urn, for that is the most general thing, and he will put it in the first place: grammar is the science of speaking well. Then he will seek in the same urn for the divisions of grammar, and he will put them in the second place: the parts of grammar are two, etymology and syntax. Then, in this same vase he will separate out the definition of the first part and will add it as the third stage after the two preceding ones. Thus, by defining and dividing things he will descend to the most particularized examples and will put them in the last place. And he will do the same for the other part of grammar—just as we have taken pains up to now to arrange the precepts of logic, the most general first, the subordinate ones following, the most particular examples last.

Now this method is not only applied to the materials of the arts and sciences, but to everything that we want to teach with ease and clarity. Thus, it is common to orators, poets, and all writers. Orators desire to follow this order in their prologues and narrations, confirmations, and perorations, and call it then the order of art and nature, and sometimes they practice it more carefully, as Cicero has done in this accusation, first making a statement, and second dividing it. "For the last fourteen years," he says, "you have been the quaestor of the consul Gnaeus Papirius, and I call in judgment what you have done from that time up to now: no hour will be found free of larceny,

7. Ramus is referring to his *Scholae dialecticae* (*Lectures on Dialectic*) of 1543, a book that was originally entitled *Aristotelicae animadversiones* (*Remarks on Aristotle*).

8. See Homer, *Iliad*, VIII.19–27.

9. Apparently a kind of lottery game, the game of blanks is one of those played by Gargantua; see Rabelais, *Gargantua*, chap. 21.

wickedness, cruelty, villainy."[10] Here is his statement and description of the entire accusation. The division follows. "These years have been spent in the office of quaestor and in the Asian embassy, as the praetor of the city and of Sicily. Consequently, my accusation will follow this same four-part division." Afterward he treats these four parts each in its rank and place—a procedure he affected in all his other speeches insofar as it was possible.

(Ramus goes on to supply similar examples from the poets, including Vergil and Ovid. He then insists that one should not merely indicate the order one follows, but briefly summarize what one has said at each step while anticipating the next one, and again he supplies examples from Cicero and the poets.)

This is thus the method of nature and of instruction; it is easy to teach, but quite hard to apply and put into practice, as Socrates says in Plato's *Philebus*, and not without cause.[11] For no one can make good use of this method who is not first able to use the places of invention and the first and second kinds of judgment. Moreover, it is infinitely greater and more difficult to arrange and position things well by means of this method of art than to find them out and to make good judgments about propositions and syllogisms. And without a doubt, the art involved here is much more excellent than it was in the first case with propositions and the second with syllogisms. This can be understood by means of the wonderful example of all the arts and sciences, for in them many things have been perfectly judged by the first and second kinds of judgment, but no art, not even the elements of Euclid, whose method has been thought the most perfect, has been judged and arranged by means of this method of art with sufficient care, as will be shown more fully some day when these same elements will be arranged by this means.[12] "And consequently," as Socrates says in the same place, "the light of this method is a gift of the gods, granted to men by a Prometheus with a shining, resplendent fire. Thus the ancients, who are more perfect than we and closer to the gods, have taught us this truth." Through this statement of Socrates we can recognize the antiquity and excellence of such a way of ordering things.

The Method of Prudence. There follows the method of prudence in which the things that come first are not entirely and absolutely the clearer, but nevertheless are more suitable for the person whom one must teach and

---

10. *Against Verres*, II.xii.34. Gaius Verres was prosecuted by Cicero on behalf of the people of Sicily during the late summer of 70 B.C. for extortion and other crimes while he was praetor there. Quaestors were magistrates, some of whom managed the pecuniary affairs of the state and others of whom conducted criminal trials; praetors were also magistrates charged with administering justice.

11. See *Philebus*, 16c.

12. Ramus published a translation of Euclid in 1544 and his own treatise on arithmetic in 1555.

more likely to induce and lead him to go where we want him to.[13] It is called the arrangement of prudence by the rhetoricians, because it lies largely within men's prudential judgment more than in the art and precepts of teaching, for if the method of nature is a judgment about knowledge, that of prudence is a judgment about matters of opinion. Still, this method has been somewhat followed by philosophers, poets, and orators, for we can mention here what Aristotle calls *crypsis*, that is, a hidden and deceptive insinuation, of which he has spoken in the second book of his *Prior Analytics*, the eighth of his *Topics*, and the first of his *Elenchs*, making several declarations, which are, in sum: to begin in the middle, and not to declare our intention at the start or deduce the remaining parts from it; to seek from far away the means and antecedents of what we are attempting, and that principally by means of similitudes and parables; and to pursue them straightway if the party we are dealing with is imprudent, for such spirits allow themselves to be straightway surprised.[14] If the man is astute and shrewd, one should not show one's pieces straightway one after the other, but change and mingle them frivolously: pretend the contrary, correct oneself, give no appearance of thinking about the matter; say it's a common and customary thing, hurry up, grow angry, flounder about, proceed with great boldness, and at the very last gasp, reveal and execute the ambush such that one's adversary, astonished, says, "To what end is all this going?" Aristotle has observed these moves in his master Plato in the dialogues where Socrates frequently employs such ruses again the sophists who do not want to be taught by him. And consequently, when their foolish opinions have thus been refuted, they become angry at Socrates and call him an electric ray in one place, a Daedalus in another, now an enchanter, now a sophist, as if he had numbed them by that method, abused them by means of a phantom, charmed and deceived them by means of some mask and mere appearance of reason. The poet who often excels in all the parts of logic is even more wonderful in using this part. He aims at teaching the people, that is, that beast with many heads, and he therefore deceives them in many ways.

(Ramus goes on to cite Horace's Ars poetica *and its notion that the good poet can start in the middle of an action, and he then discusses examples of such procedures in Vergil's* Aeneid *and Terence's play* The Eunuch.*)*

The wisdom of this method has been similarly noted by the orators when they recommend that in the prologue, before stating or narrating the case in question, one must gain, beyond the understanding, the good will and

13. The method of prudence differs from that of nature and art in that it does not systematically start with what is clearest and then proceed to what is less so by a simple series of definitions and distinctions.

14. See *Prior Analytics*, II.xix.66a25, *Topics*, VIII.i.156a8–157a14, and *On Sophistical Refutations* (*Elenchs*), I.164a20–165a38.

attention of the auditor, and that during the speech one must hold him by means of changing the subject and by repetitions, and that in the peroration one must move him to favor us totally. For, as Aristotle says in the third book of his *Rhetoric*, such prologues and perorations are not needed at all to teach effectively a good auditor who loves and seeks the truth of his own accord.[15] In short, everything people use that goes beyond the method of teaching is often blamed by Aristotle in his *Organon*, but both he and the rhetoricians nevertheless prudently recommend it on the occasion when one deals with an auditor, and the rhetoricians have further recommended that in a case that is dishonest and yet admirable, one should not enter on the true road except by some circuitous insinuation and that one should not put at the start either one's proposition or its division into parts, any more than the surgeon shows the lancet to a fearful person before he has made an incision, as you will see in Quintilian.[16] Thus Cicero, speaking of arrangement, suggests that there is nothing greater in a speaker's judgment than, after he has seen what is good and ill in a case, that he should embrace the good, enrich and augment it, remain entirely focused on it, attaching himself to it and fleeing its contrary. Indeed, he should sometimes say nothing in response to a troublesome and difficult argument, although in such a way that he does not seem to flee and abandon his arms, but rather that he seems to act with bravado not out of any sort of fear, but in order to occupy a more suitable place in order to fight better.[17]

(Ramus shows how Cicero uses this method in the openings of his second and third speeches De lege agraria ["On the Agrarian Law"]. He then notes how Cicero often displayed various emotions in order to move his auditor.)

In short, all the tropes and figures of style and all the graces of delivery, which constitute the entirety of true rhetoric—something separate from logic—serve no other purpose than to lead the troublesome and stubborn auditor, whom we must deal with, through this method [of prudence], and they have been used for no other reason than that auditor's stubborn resistance to authority and his perversity, as Aristotle truly teaches us in the third book of his *Rhetoric*.[18] Thus, we see how this method of prudence has been taught and practiced by philosophers, poets, and orators, and we know through their precepts and examples how great this prudence is. However, we will understand it much better through the daily affairs and business of men among whom this clever insinuation will easily obtain the first place whenever it is necessary to persuade someone about something

15. See *Rhetoric*, III.xiv.7–9.
16. See *Institutio oratoria*, IV.i.42–46.
17. See *De inventione*, I.xv.20–xvi.23.
18. The third book of Aristotle's *Rhetoric* treats style and arrangement, but at no point does it say that tropes and figures must be used because of the auditor's perversity.

he does not wish to grasp. For this reason, if the entryway to the path of truth and art is closed, the logician will make another way for himself by dint of his wits and his prudence, and because he is deprived of any help from [the method of] teaching, he will seek everywhere else for every kind of usual and customary assistance. And because he cannot maintain the correct course, he will change his sails and will lead his ship, safe and sound, to port by such winds as he is able to use. Just as in times past the Spartans were praised among their citizens for stealing things secretly, so indeed without comparison that person will receive even more praise for having gained by means of this method of prudence the consent of another person who is rebellious and resistant.

(In the final portion of his work, Ramus argues for the importance of exercise and practice if one wishes to be a distinguished logician.)

•

[15]

John Jewel

John Jewel (1522–1571), an educator and preacher, was one of the chief defenders of English Protestantism and the religious settlement of Elizabeth I. Educated at Merton College, Oxford, he was elected a Fellow of Corpus Christi College there in 1542. During the reign of Edward VI (1547–1553), Jewel became a leader of the party that wished to extend the reforms that Henry VIII had started when he broke with the Church of Rome. After Mary was crowned in 1553, Jewel fled the country and settled in Frankfurt where he began to play the role he would later assume once Elizabeth began her reign in 1558: spokesman for the Church of England as a mean between the extremes of Catholicism and continental Protestantism. After his return to England, Jewel was one of the official disputants who spoke publicly against supporters of Rome in 1559, and he was appointed bishop of Salisbury the next year. In 1562 he produced his *Apologia ecclesiae Anglicanae* (*Apology for the English Church*), the first comprehensive defense of the Church of England against the Church of Rome. The *Oratio contra rhetoricam* (*Oration against Rhetoric*), which is translated here, was composed while Jewel was a prelector, that is, a reader or lecturer, at Oxford sometime between 1544 and 1552, although it was not published until 1848. It is possible that he never actually delivered it. Even though Jewel attacks rhetoric in the *Oration,* as a student he strove to perfect his speaking style, and he was later known for his eloquence and valued as a teacher and a preacher. Moreover, Jewel taught Cicero, and although he admired Erasmus and doubtless shared Erasmus's anti-Ciceronianism, the extreme nature of the attacks in the *Oration* suggests that the work may be ironic. The text of the *Oration* on which this translation is based comes from his *Works,* edited by John Ayre, for the Parker Society (Cambridge, 1850), 4: 1283–91.

John Jewel

ORATION AGAINST RHETORIC[1]

I know, most learned auditors, in what low opinion those people are held, especially nowadays, who frequently change the course of their studies and from time to time select new kinds of learning for themselves. For our dignity requires that we keep things, which are already established, just as we wish them to be and that we choose things for ourselves from which we will not be separated and led away. It is, moreover, a characteristic of light and inconstant men to be carried about everywhere as if by wind and storm, at one moment to profess themselves poets and at another philosophers, now to be mathematicians, now theologians. Although I am really afraid that this fault might be assigned to me, considering that I have spent so much time studying eloquence and reading philosophy, I am nevertheless going to devote myself to the poets because of a sudden change of heart. Still, since most of us are born with a weak judgment so that we can easily be deceived and err in selecting a mode of life, and since whatever I do, I do it for your utility, I am led to hope that my decision, which has been made for your sake, will easily be approved by all of you. For no one ever undertook the study of letters with such good fortune that either experience or some accident did not frequently turn all the plans of his former life upside down. We are not Januses, nor do we have eyes behind us enabling us to see whatever is going to happen, or to anticipate the future in our minds. For this reason Homer, the wisest of poets, has called us "partial" because we contemplate just one side, as it were, of each thing, not being able to examine it from all angles with our eyes and embrace it as a whole.[2] Thus, if one plan has not succeeded at first, the thing to do next is to correct matters by a change of course. Who among you has not heard that Marcus Cato, a man who was a senator and a censor and in his sixties, undertook the study of Greek letters, which he always hated up till then, in his advanced old age?[3] Who does not know how Aristotle, after he had learned that the word of Isocrates was held in great honor and was made much of even by his own followers, suddenly changed practically his entire method of teaching, abandoning his former plans and casting philosophy aside, although he was an old, gray-haired man and a philosopher? Why need I say more? So great is the weakness and blindness of our reason that we do not see what is most fitting for us and

1. The full title of Jewel's work is: "The Oration against Rhetoric of Master Jewel, Prelector of Humanities in Corpus Christi College, Oxford, Delivered Publicly in the Hall of That College Before All Its Students."
2. See Homer, *Iliad*, I.250 and IX.390, and *Odyssey*, XX.49. The Greek word that Jewel uses here, *méropas*, really means "articulate," but the rest of the sentence suggests that he is confusing it with the noun *méros*, from which it is derived, and which means the "part" of something; hence, the translation of it as "partial."
3. See Quintilian, *Institutio oratoria*, XII.xi.23. For Aristotle in the next sentence, see Cicero, *De oratore*, III.xxxv.141.

what will be most valuable for us in the future, and we repeatedly slip into certain kinds of studies before we can discern what would be best. As far as I am concerned, I seek to serve your interests, and I would really prefer to be prudent rather than praised for constancy because I thoughtlessly held fast to what I once proposed. For if I were to respond by saying just one thing—namely that I want to look after the talents and profit of so many choice youths—what fair judge would reprehend me for what I seek to accomplish?

Truly serious and substantial causes have moved me to change my direction at this time, for finally I see, I really do see, that the entire time that I have spent thus far on eloquence has been wasted in a useless, base pursuit. I know that many of you marvel when you hear such things said by me, especially about myself, but it is as I say, and I do not see why I should engage in pretenses since I am seeking to be of help to you. Would that the time I have spent playing in school up until the present could be called back in its entirety! For a long time now I have known from experience that rhetoric confers on us neither benefits nor dignity. The entire pursuit of eloquence, I say, which so many Greek and Latin writers enriched, which I myself embraced so eagerly, and into which I drove you with my encouragement—I openly proclaim here that it offers neither dignity nor benefit, and is entirely idle, empty, futile, and trifling. Now I will expound this matter briefly and in a few words. Since it is your concern, something which I have always placed ahead of all my own interests, I beseech you to pay close attention, as you are accustomed to do, and you may well conclude that this concern with speaking is empty and of little moment and that you could turn your minds more fruitfully to another course of studies. I do not promise to say here all those things that can be said about rhetoric, nor do I think they can be said in so brief a space of time by anyone anywhere unless he is a garrulous orator indeed.

Since many things—nay rather, all things—in this art are empty and trivial, the very profession of speaking seems to me idle and utterly absurd. For nothing shows narrowness of mind and childish shallowness so much as the pursuit of beauty and elegance in speaking and the devotion of all one's care and thought to verbal ornamentation and a nimble tongue. Without doubt it should shame a man who has a spirit, mind, and heart to polish only his tongue and turn his complete attention to adorning it, while leaving those superior things, which are by far the greatest of all, unfortified, uncultivated, neglected. What was the meaning of that lengthy silence of the Pythagoreans, those wisest of men, what was the meaning of the brevity and plainness of speech of the Spartans, unless they considered it ridiculous and unworthy of a serious person to overflow with a multitude of words? Why are words called "winged" by Homer except that they seemed to that divine poet to be borne about as if on wings, to be tossed around by the wind, to have nothing solid and firm about them, to be incapable of ever standing still or stopping anywhere.[4] These are the grave concerns and weighty matters of orators who are totally involved with the sound of words and with trivialities; no one is so stupid or dim-witted that he does not understand what to think about these studies or what they are fit for.

We have all been taught to speak well enough by nature, for we learned it long ago on our own initiative without a master or a teacher, and by this gift of nature alone we excel the wild beasts and the dumb cattle.[5] We do not surpass them by our spiritual virtues or the strength of our bodies, nor by any specific virtue such as prudence, cleverness, reason, or cunning, but by the sole power of speech. Although infants and boys may suffer from a weakness of the tongue and jaws, which prevents them from producing words and forcing speech out of themselves, nevertheless they often cry and wail, emitting broken and confused sounds as they struggle and strain their bodies, so that even then they seem to be saying something. Never was a nation so barbarous, a people so wild, or the citizens of a state so uncivilized and undeveloped that they were not formed in some manner by nature to acquire the habit of speech. Different nations may have different educational programs, intellectual capacities, and customs, but language and the ability to speak it are innate, imprinted on the spirits and hearts of all as if engraved there. Therefore, those who have composed so-called arts of speaking, which they claim they are going to teach, behave no less imprudently and absurdly than if they had composed and professed arts of seeing, hearing, and walking. Why do they think there is a greater discipline for the tongue than for the feet, the eyes, or the ears? Why do they drum things into our ears that no one was ever so dense as to remain ignorant of if he really wished to know them? Perhaps these wicked men are afraid that we are going to be mute unless they themselves teach us to prattle. And yet men spoke and managed the greatest affairs among themselves before those gods of theirs, Cicero and Demosthenes, were born.

Therefore, there is no need to reduce speech, through infinite and childish labor, to some undefinable art and its set of precepts. What insolence to usurp for oneself alone among all men the one thing that is given equally to all! To credit what has always been shared by everyone just to libidinous, prattling rhetors! For, if what we seek in speaking is to be understood by the others with whom we are dealing—and surely this is what we seek—then what kind of speech is better than that which is open, clear, and distinct? Why do we need art or puerile ornaments? If we are speaking in schools, acumen is more to be sought than elegance of speech, or if we stand before the bench in court, an angry judge will tolerate anything more willingly than copiousness of speech, for he is concerned with how probable our

4. For Homer's "winged words," see, for example, *Odyssey,* IV.550.
5. For examples of this comparison, see Cicero, *De inventione,* I.iv.5, and *De oratore,* I.viii. 32–33.

argument is, not with its verbosity and abundance. In fact, if a speech were to become too copious and fluent, he would suspect that it concealed some deceit beneath it and that a trap was being laid for him. For the truth is clear and simple and has little need to be protected by the tongue and by eloquence. If something is clear and distinct, it has enough support in itself and does not need the allurements of polished speech, whereas if it is obscure and unattractive, it will not be discovered despite all the clamor and flood of words. After two orators have striven with one another and each one has begun to sprinkle that learned dust about, if the judge focuses on their art, the nimbleness of their tongues, the strife and noise of their words, their clamor and audacity and elegance, he will have nothing on which to base a decision and reach his verdict. Orators frequently produce many things that are light, empty, harmful, and contradictory, and like the individual cups of a balance, they incline to the side where you pour in the most. For they are moved not by piety, love, justice, and religion, but by booty, rewards, gifts, and bribes. If in an intricate and slippery case it is sufficient for a loud-mouthed ranter to bark for several hours by the clock, what is the use of having benches, tribunals, laws, rights, traditional statutes, and old established rules? What purpose is served by senators, praetors, judges, and magistrates? Why do we depend on the authority of witnesses, records, statements both oral and written, examinations, and experts in law? What an excellent idea, to bring into court, whenever we are debating matters of justice and equity, not an interpreter of the law from the senate, but a rhetor from the school; or to think that a case will stand if an orator is shouting, but totter and fall if he becomes hoarse and grows silent!

In truth, orators are only summoned to cases that are forsaken and hopeless, just as doctors are to men who are sick and feeble. Where no justice or equity or good can be seen, there they sharpen their tongues to produce a whirlwind of words, there they really get fired up. Just as fishermen who hunt for eels capture nothing unless they spread night, as it were, on their nets so as to confuse the fish and turn everything upside down, so, if orators do not take away all the light—which is the one thing they seek to do—they try at least to render their subject, and the truth, as obscure as possible. Did I say "obscure"? But what if they tell lies? And what if they do nothing else? What if they actually *plan* to do so? For in what other way could Protagoras make the worse case appear the better?[6] How else could Carneades speak in Rome against justice and prove that the highest virtue was the worst plague of states? When Pericles had been cast down and conquered publicly by his adversary and when the crowd around him had seen it, nevertheless he persuaded those standing about him by means of his elegant language that he

6. See Aulus Gellius, *Noctes atticae*, V.iii.7. For the anecdote about Carneades in the next sentence, see Pliny, *Naturalis historia*, VII.xxx.112; for the next one about Pericles, see Plutarch, *Life of Pericles*, viii.3–4.

had won, so that the people were moved more by what he said than by what they had just seen.

Rhetors shape their lives through lies, nor is that truly surprising since they have Mercury as their patron and household god. They may glory that they have him as the discoverer and prince of elegant language, but, good lord, what a deity! He is the one who first introduced the customs of fraud, deception, robbery, theft, lying, and perjury, who took through trickery Tireisias's cattle, Mars's sword, Vulcan's tongs, Apollo's arrows, Venus's girdle, and finally, the scepter of Jove himself. And this god they venerate as their father; to this god they make sacrifices! From this teacher they have learned how to be bold, to trick, to cheat, to perjure themselves, and by means of tricks, slanders, and flattery, how to confuse and darken the truth, laws both divine and human, equity, and justice. These things the orators both profess and undertake, and they have only as much right on their side as they have verbal skill and impudence. After all, if they were confident of the truth and justice of their cause, why would they disdain a simple, ordinary manner of speech? Why would they pursue so many verbal enticements, so many obscurities and absurdities? Why would they contrive feet, rhythms, and fetters of this sort for free and flowing prose? Why would they fight by means of hints, conjectures, opinions, fables, and rumors? Why would they prepare so many snares to capture our ears? What would they want with those figures, forms, schemes, and what they call "lights" (although they rather seem like darkness to me): epanorthoses, antimetaboles, suspensions, catachreses, enigmas, extenuations, premunitions, exclamations, aposiopeses, apologies, circumlocutions, diminutions, and hyperboles?[7] Why is the forum filled with so many shouts, yells, and tears? Why are the gods called down from heaven, the dead roused up from the underworld? Why are buildings, temples, columns, tombs, and stones caused to speak? What do they want with those faces they make, that tossing about and contracting of the body, that thrusting out of the arms, that beating of the thigh, that stamping of the foot? Why don't they speak with their mouth, tongue, and jaws, instead of with their hands, their fingers, their limbs, their arms, their faces, their entire body? Idlers have devised all these things for themselves, and they rely much more on them as a defense than they do on their subject itself or on the truth. Oh you sweet triflers, you will never find that game insufficient, I know, throughout your entire lives!

Now, truly, if a bad cause should not be adorned with inappropriate rhetorical figures and allurements, nor a good one rendered obscure in the same manner, what place do we imagine would be left for rhetoric? Moreover, what about the fact that rhetors disagree among themselves and destroy the truth with one set of lies or another just as executioners and doc-

7. These are all figures of speech.

tors cut the throats of people by all sorts of schemes and methods? Still, it is amazing to me that, although rhetoricians disagree about how to teach those tricks of theirs, they nevertheless manage to harmonize together wonderfully—in lying. Tisias does not approve of Corax, Theophrastus of Tisias, Demetrius of Theophrastus, Hermagoras of Theophrastus. Then Aristotle, lest he might seem to know too little, condemned all the precepts of former rhetoricians. Cicero departed from Aristotle, Fabius [Quintilian] from Cicero, and Hermogenes from Fabius. But why do I speak of them? Today, when there are more than six hundred rhetoricians, you will still not find anyone in that entire number who agrees with anyone else about the right method of instruction. Either they are simply all deceivers, or, since they teach contrary and clearly contradictory things, one can scarcely claim that all of them are teaching the truth.

Should I mention that one kind of speech has been pleasing to one group or another of them, and that since some prefer a rich style for themselves, others a dry one, others a luxuriant one, others a graceful one, others a sharp and vehement one, and others a modest and sober one, the result is that there have never been two orators up to now who were really similar to each other and shared the same rhetorical system? To Cicero, some speakers seem too rich, others too dry, some too cheery, others too sad, some too swollen and verbose, others too bloodless and arid. Why continue? That most eloquent man, that supreme orator Demosthenes, is despised by Aeschines and criticized as a barbarian. Cicero himself is disdained by his fellow citizens; Cicero himself, I say, the father of Latin eloquence, after he had traveled through almost the entirety of Greece for the sake both of the language and of eloquence and had introduced into his fatherland a great number of foreign words, was nevertheless booed from the stage by other orators as weak and feeble, as too relaxed, as an emasculated Asiatic.[8] And yet all those who want to be considered somewhat elegant propose to imitate him alone; with all their zeal and spirit, they fix their gaze on him alone whenever they write, or compose, or say anything. Although they may be flowing with an abundance of the choicest words, they nevertheless so interrupt themselves as they polish their speech, so hesitate, so waver in doubt, so stop to reject one word, seek out another, and replace yet another, so correct and torture themselves, that although they wish to appear elegant Ciceronians, nothing seems more affected than their speech, and nothing is heard with greater disgust. As if Cato, Varro, Caesar, and Terence spoke inadequate Latin or even in a completely barbarous manner, these people follow Cicero alone with total religious reverence. They repeat every tiny distinction he makes, pad their sentences with rhymes, and, as if they had no minds of their own, think nothing unless Cicero thought it first—they taste

8. See Tacitus, *Dialogus*, xviii.5, and Quintilian, *Institutio oratoria*, XII.x.12.

more with the palate of another than with their own. They read no poet or physician or historian; they have no contact with civil or common law, with any record of antiquity, with geometers, mathematicians, or philosophers. They have pitched the tent of their life in Cicero alone; in him they seek neither learning nor the knowledge of things nor judgment, but just letters, accents, vowels, elegant phrases, and verbal abundance. But even if they did reproduce him perfectly—something that so far not even the most loquacious among them has accomplished, for no one has ever been so dissimilar from others as Cicero is from himself—they would seem weak, enervated, Asiatic; and if they failed to reproduce him, they would seem rustic, dull, unpolished, and barbarous. Moreover, who are the judges of all this verbal abundance; whose judgment and ears do these orators slavishly follow? Those of the wise? But the wise are few and far between, and are captivated more easily by anything other than eloquence. Rather, it is fitting that so much labor, sleeplessness, and study should be judged according to the opinion of fools, for eloquence was discovered and brought into being for their ears. It does not seek wise auditors, grave men, and philosophers, but the filth of the people, the followers of mountebanks, and street corner crowds. Pallas [Athena] herself, the goddess of polished speech, takes delight not in the councils of the elders and the senate, but in the mob and the common people. Without these judges, that is, without these cobblers, tailors, servants, fishermen, and muleteers, even Cicero himself would never have been sufficiently eloquent. Here is where eloquence revels; here it reigns and triumphs. O beautiful and magnificent faculty, which seeks the ignorant approval of the uninformed masses while shrinking from the grave judgment of the wise!

I know that what I have discussed so far seems weighty and serious in your judicious estimation, but it is slight and trivial when compared with what I will now say. For when I have shown how states have been overturned by the most eloquent men and great empires converted into great wastelands, all the things that you have heard so far—which are certainly very serious matters—will be thought to be nothing. It seems to me that whoever first introduced eloquence into human affairs gave the worst advice possible. I will not speak of how oaths have been called into doubt—violating them is equivalent to maliciously tearing up the foundations of the state—nor will I mentions sedition, factions, plots, treason, wars, and conflagrations. For who among us has not heard of the lamentable plundering of that greatest and most ancient of cities, Athens, which, although said to be the Hellas of Hellas and the epitome of all Greece, was nevertheless leveled to the ground and almost completely uprooted and destroyed thanks to the eloquent tongue of Demosthenes? Who will believe that the city of Rome, girded with so many walls, fortified with so many moats, and established by the prudence of so many kings, could have been conquered by any human force, no matter how long it worked? But when Marcus Cato bestirred himself and sent Augustus against Antony,[9] although the Roman state had stood for so many centuries thanks to the united will of its citizens and the devotion and good services of the entire world, it fell straightway in the briefest time through the work of a single orator. That state, I say, which had flourished amidst the victories, the trophies, and the triumphs of so many great emperors and generals, which fortune itself had adorned with the spoils of all tribes and nations, and which neither Gracchus, nor Carbo, nor Marius, nor Sulla, nor the madness of Catiline, nor the infinite force of its enemies, nor all the barbarians, could destroy—that state, with its countless ramparts, citadels, and walls, its temples to the gods, its shrines, hearths, and altars, a single orator, Marcus Cicero, using not his wisdom but his tongue, not his prudence but his eloquence, not his reason but his speech, in a brief time demolished and utterly destroyed, taking along with it practically all its people and its name. Where now are those who are accustomed so often to complain and cry out how the might of states is overthrown by avarice, luxury, and lust? Eloquence is really the one responsible; this is the disaster, the plague, the destroyer of states; wherever it appears, ruin, tempests, and conflagrations follow. Why should I speak of men like the Gracchi, Brutus, Cassius, Critias, and Alcibiades, when I have spoken of their ringleader and prince, Demosthenes? What can we hope for from the common herd of orators when we see what the greatest among them have done? And what would the life of men be like if we were all orators, seeing how just a few individual ones have toppled great states?

There was once a certain little woman from Kent who came to London and chanced upon a great number of noble youths who were engaged in studying the common law. She asked who they were and what they were pursuing, and when she found out that they were law students and in just a short time would be lawyers and advocates, she said, "Oh, what a waste! Oh, this poor, unhappy country!" Asked why she, a lowborn woman and a stranger, should be so disturbed, she replied, "In our district a single lawyer has long since plundered the fortunes of all the people and exhausted the region, so what will all of these do who have been made arrogant by their education and training and have been fashioned to be cheats from their tender youth?" What would that woman have said if she had seen a comparable group of orators? For lawyers, to be sure, do seem to be selling their credibility and their intelligence as well as the laws, edicts, oaths, and decrees of the senate, when they mislead men through fraud and defend cases by means of unjust arguments. But orators try to sell their faces, their gestures, their words—all the greatest trifles—when they promise they can do everything. That is why we see that they have been condemned by the considered judgment of the most ancient states. The Lacedemonians ordered

9. This is an error on Jewel's part, since Marcus Cato (Cato of Utica) was dead well before Augustus broke with Antony.

Ctesiphon, who claimed he could speak for an entire day, to be driven out into exile. By a decree of the Senate, the Romans expelled all orators not only from the city, but from the whole of Italy.[10] See, by the immortal gods, how the wisest and gravest men have regarded this species of people! Actors, flute players, panders, parasites, and whores were held in the highest regard by senators and elders, who did not allow orators even to loiter in the outskirts of the city, or to linger in obscure corners and hidden recesses, lest their contagion should spread to others. And these things were decreed by the judgment and authority not of light Greeks, barbarians, or the ignorant multitude, but by that of Cato, the elders, the entire state. This is why the more skilled one is in speaking, the more awkwardly and disgracefully embarrassed he is when beginning his speech.[11] His conscience and knowledge of his crimes do not permit him to stand easy; he shakes with fear thinking of the laws, tortures, sentences, chains, and exile. Why did reason and speech suddenly desert Plato when he was going to speak on behalf of his teacher Socrates—the best of cases?[12] Why did Theophrastus disgracefully become mute in a public harangue, something that even intelligent boys are unaccustomed to do? Why did the greatest orator Demosthenes lose his mind, his reason, his very self when he stood before Philip? What is the meaning of all this trepidation, pallor, hesitation, confusion, and shaking? If the case is good, why are they afraid? If it is bad, why do they take it on?

Let us set aside the authority of states and of the ancients, since it may be judged insufficient, and ask why orators are not moved by the examples of the wise, of philosophers, of the gods. If the immortal gods ever say anything, they do so in the ordinary manner of speaking and with the fewest words. That divine man Socrates, judged the wisest being by Apollo, when he was fighting for his life and fortune, did not wish to be defended by a clever oration.[13] Gymnosophists, bards, and philosophers, when they were establishing their workshops of wisdom and devoting the greatest care to acquiring knowledge of an infinite number of things, still never cultivated this study, not because these wisest and least busy of men lacked either the time or the talent for it, but because they judged it to be a trifling and childish matter not consistent with philosophical gravity.[14] But why do I call to mind the ancients? In recent times, when certain men of ours had not acquired even the shadow, I will not say of eloquence, but of pure Latin speech; when Cicero still lay scorned and rejected in the dirt and darkness;

10. I have not been able to find a source for the expulsion of Ctesiphon by the Lacedemonians. The Romans banished orators in 161 B.C. at the urging of Cato the Censor, and again in 92 B.C.; see Suetonius, De rhetoribus, i.

11. Cf. Cicero, De oratore, I.xxvi.119–xxvii.123.

12. See Diogenes Laertius, Socrates, in Lives of the Philosophers, II.41. For the failures of Theophrastus and Demosthenes noted in the following sentences, see Aelian, Varia historia, viii.12.

13. See Diogenes Laertius, Socrates, in Lives of the Philosophers, II.40-41, and Cicero, De oratore, I.liv.231.

14. The Gymnosophists were an ascetic sect in India.

when Scotus possessed the entrances to all the schools and the pathways to learning; when those philosophers of ours did not understand themselves sufficiently and were thought to rave and rage by people who were not learned in such mysteries—still, how richly learned, how acutely philosophical, how gravely theological did those men seem! How great then was the admiration for good learning! What a crowd of studious youths! This place was the seat, the shrine, of learning; here was the fountain, the head, of all humanity! How fortunate the university then! O happy times! Then nothing was done except when we judged it proper: we could make peace, incite sedition, restrain war, unite princes together; we strove to inculcate reverence for the divine will, piety, and religion; and everything we decreed was fair, good, just, and right. But once Cicero, like Cerberus from hell, had been brought from the darkness into the light by I know not what means, the study of letters was snuffed out, the ardor of men's spirits languished, the number of students dwindled on each successive day, colleges were deserted, all the glory and splendor of the university were eclipsed. Cicero has brought all these evils to you; Cicero has given you this mortal blow, this wound; Cicero has ravaged all our study rooms; Cicero has extinguished the light and glory of the entire university.

I see that time is running out and that while I am criticizing the worthlessness and foolishness of oratory, I am being judged by you as being worthless and foolish myself. I shall add only this one important thing, something I scarcely understand myself: why, when they are feigning that zeal of theirs, do rhetors hold that the main point of their discipline is to cover up their beauty, art, and eloquence as if they were just so many roots and stalks? This is not the behavior of good men, but of degenerate thieves, for there has never been an artisan, no matter how common or base, who is ashamed of his art. Tailors, medicine peddlers, and bawds seek crowds in the light, showing their merchandise openly and freely in public. Only the orator does not dare to parade his skill, but behaves in such a way that, just when he is making the maximum use of the art of his tongue, he seems then to be the farthest away from art and utterly inarticulate, as if he had learned nothing. Why do we need to seek greater examples and look for other witnesses and authorities when orators actually condemn themselves with their own mouths? Why are they afraid of the light and of being in public view? Why are they ashamed of their profession? Why do they simulate one thing, but do another? What sort of faith could we have in them to deal with others' affairs when they lie about themselves and their art? What must we imagine they do in their own homes if they do not hesitate to perjure themselves when people are watching them? These are the individuals on whom the health of the state depends; we run to them, defer our cases to them, make them the emperors of our lives and deaths, commit to them our fortunes, our wives, our children, our dignity, and our safety—yet they are ashamed to have learned their art and to profess it. I will not say more. For

I do not doubt that you all understand sufficiently in your own minds what eloquence can do in every respect and just how great a scope it should have.

Therefore, learned youths, do not expend so much time and effort on something that is ridiculous and vain and confers no utility or benefit on our common life; that nature itself has already implanted in the spirits and minds of all; that renders good causes obscure and adorns evil ones and makes them resplendent; that teaches treachery, fraud, and lying; that was found out and brought into existence for the sake of error, for profit, for popular recklessness; that flees away from the grave vision of the wise; that has overturned the greatest commonwealths; that the most ancient states have booed from the stage; that philosophers of all ages and nations have repudiated; that our ancestors despised; that destroyed the old, ancestral glory of this school; and that, finally, rhetors themselves are ashamed to profess after they have learned it. It is inconsistent with your dignity and your talents to waste all your energies on easy matters and to be unable to raise your eyes to better kinds of learning. Let such studies be for those who have nothing else to do; your talents and your years urge me in another direction. For you have not been exhausted by age or thoughtlessly exposed to the disorderly mob of men. You are young men, I say, young men with the greatest talents and the highest hopes, born to achieve unparalleled knowledge and attainments in the arts, for which you have been trained continually. Others have established different schemes of life and learning for themselves, but we take pleasure in the knowledge of those things to which we have given ourselves with total commitment since boyhood. This is the purpose of all these schools, all these splendid buildings, all these magnificent colleges, all these heroic establishments. This is why we have undertaken such long journeys and have come from so far away to Oxford, to this marketplace of disciplines and arts; upon this way our ancestors set forth to seek the highest fame for virtue and learning. Let us look to them, contemplate them, strive to imitate and resemble them, walk in the footprints they left behind them. For we are not going to be travelers, or heralds, or criers, or ranting lawyers. Therefore, if the utility involved or the thought of your own dignity is worth anything to you, let us despise the pointless fluency of words and the nonsense of eloquence. Let us direct our thoughts, our industry, and our intelligence toward the knowledge of profound matters. Finally, with all our diligence, let us apply ourselves so as to gain that knowledge, lest we later grieve that we have wasted our time and misspent our youth. I have spoken.

[16]

Thomas Wilson

The Englishman Thomas Wilson (ca. 1524–1581) was an accomplished humanist scholar and politician. Born in Lincolnshire, he entered Eton in 1537 and then went on to Cambridge where he studied with some of the most famous humanists of the day, including John Cheke and Roger Ascham. After receiving his B.A. in 1547 and his M.A. in 1549, he earned a living by teaching and tutoring, but sought to make a name for himself by translating classical works and ideas into the vernacular. In 1551 he published *The Rule of Reason*, a logic manual, which brought him a certain degree of fame. When his patron, John Dudley, earl of Warwick, suggested sometime in 1551 or 1552 that Wilson write a similar work on rhetoric, he composed *The Art of Rhetoric* and published it in 1553. Wilson's accomplishments would have gained him some sort of preferment at court, but when the young king Edward VI died suddenly that year and was succeeded by the Catholic Mary, Wilson's patrons were either imprisoned or banished, and he himself fled to the continent. After narrowly escaping death at the hands of the Inquisition in Rome in 1558, and having been made a Doctor of Civil Law in Ferrara in 1559, he returned to England the next year and saw a second edition of his *Rhetoric* through the press. He was then elected a member of Parliament every year between 1563 and 1581, held a series of administrative and judicial posts, and served as ambassador to various European states. He reached the pinnacle of his success in 1579 when he was made secretary of state. In addition to his works on logic and rhetoric, he produced a *Discourse on Usury* in 1569 and translations of Demosthenes in 1570. His books on logic and rhetoric were both highly successful, going through a number of printings during and after Wilson's lifetime. *The Art of Rhetoric* is a complete rhetoric on the Ciceronian model: the first of its three books is devoted to invention, as is most of the second, which also treats disposition; and the third is concerned with elocution or style, taking up memory and delivery briefly at the end. The excerpts included here are taken from the edition of the *Rhetoric* of 1560, edited by G. H. Mair (Oxford, 1909); I have emended it at times after consulting later editions.

FROM *The Art of Rhetoric*

To the Right Honorable Lord John Dudley, Lord Lisle, Earl of Warwick, and Master of the Horse to the King's Majesty: Your Assured to Command, Thomas Wilson

When Pyrrhus, King of the Epirotes, made battle against the Romans and could neither by force of arms, nor yet by any policy[1] win certain strongholds, he used commonly to send one Cineas (a noble orator and sometimes scholar to Demosthenes) to persuade with the captains and people that were in them that they should yield up the said hold or towns without fight or resistance.[2] And so it came to pass that through the pithy eloquence of this noble orator divers strong castles and fortresses were peaceably given up into the hands of Pyrrhus, which he should have found very hard and tedious to win by the sword. And this thing was not Pyrrhus himself ashamed in his common talk, to the praise of the said orator, openly to confess, alleging that Cineas through the eloquence of his tongue won more cities unto him than ever himself should else have been able by force to subdue. Good was that orator that could do so much, and wise was that king which would use such a mean. For if the worthiness of eloquence may move us, what worthier thing can there be than with a word to win cities and whole countries? If profit may persuade, what greater gain can we have than without bloodshed achieve to[3] a conquest? If pleasure may provoke us, what greater delight do we know than to see a whole multitude, with the only talk of a man, ravished and drawn which way he liketh best to have them? Boldly then may I adventure, and without fear step forth, to offer that unto your Lordship which for the dignity is so excellent and for the use so necessary that no man ought to be without it which either shall bear rule over many or must have to do with matters of a realm. . . .

Eloquence First Given by God, and After Lost by Man, and Last Repaired by God Again

Man (in whom is poured the breath of life) was made at his first being an ever-living creature unto the likeness of God, endued with reason, and appointed lord over all other things living. But after the fall of our first father,

---

1. **policy** statecraft, diplomacy, ingenious stratagem, trick.
2. See Plutarch, *Life of Pyrrhus*, xiv.
3. **achieve to** achieve.

sin so crept in that our knowledge was much darkened, and by corruption of this our flesh, man's reason and intendment[4] were both overwhelmed.[5] At what time God, being sore grieved with the folly of one man, pitied of his mere[6] goodness the whole state and posterity of mankind, and therefore (whereas through the wicked suggestion of our ghostly[7] enemy, the joyful fruition of God's glory was altogether lost), it pleased our heavenly father to repair mankind of his free mercy and to grant an ever-living inheritance unto all such as would by constant faith seek earnestly hereafter. Long it was ere that man knew himself, being destitute of God's grace, so that all things waxed savage, the earth untilled, society neglected, God's will not known, man against man, one against another, and all against order. Some lived by spoil; some like brute beasts grazed upon the ground; some went naked; some roamed like woodwoses;[8] none did anything by reason, but most did what they could by manhood. None, almost, considered the ever-living God, but all lived most commonly after their own lust.[9] By death they thought that all things ended; by life they looked for none other living. None remembered the true observation of wedlock; none tendered the education of their children; laws were not regarded; true dealing was not once used. For virtue, vice bare place; for right and equity, might used authority. And therefore, whereas man through reason might have used order, man through folly fell into error. And thus for lack of skill and for want[10] of grace evil so prevailed that the devil was most esteemed, and God either almost unknown among them all, or else nothing feared among so many.

Therefore, even now when man was thus past all hope of amendment, God still tendering[11] to his own workmanship, stirred up his faithful and elect[12] to persuade with reason all men to society, and gave his appointed ministers knowledge both to see the natures of men and also granted them the gift of utterance, that they might with ease win folk at their will and frame them by reason to all good order. And therefore, whereas men lived brutishly in open fields, having neither house to shroud[13] them in, nor attire to clothe their backs, nor yet any regard to seek their best avail,[14] these appointed of God called them together by utterance of speech and persuaded them what was good, what was bad, and what was gainful for mankind. And although at first the rude could hardly learn, and either for the strangeness of the thing would not gladly receive the offer, or else for lack of knowledge could not perceive the goodness, yet being somewhat drawn and delighted with the pleasantness of reason and the sweetness of utterance, after

4. **intendment** understanding.
5. Wilson is elaborating here his Protestant version of the myth of the orator as civilizer that was widespread in antiquity; see, for example, Cicero, *De inventione*, I.ii.2–3; Quintilian, *Institutio oratoria*, II.xvi.9; and Horace, *Ars poetica*, 391–401.
6. **mere** absolute, complete.   7. **ghostly** spiritual.   8. **woodwoses** wild men of the woods.   9. **lust** desire, appetite.   10. **want** lack.   11. **still tendering** always pitying.   12. **elect** The elect were, according to Protestant, and particularly Calvinist, teaching, those saved by God from all eternity.   13. **shroud** shelter.   14. **avail** help, advantage.

a certain space they became through nurture and good advisement, of wild, sober; of cruel, gentle; of fools, wise; and of beasts, men. Such force hath the tongue and such is the power of eloquence and reason, that most men are forced even to yield in that which most standeth against their will. And therefore the poets do feign that Hercules, being a man of great wisdom, had all men linked together by the ears in a chain, to draw them and lead them even as he lusted.[15, 16] For his wit was so great, his tongue so eloquent, and his experience such, that no one man was able to withstand his reason, but everyone was rather driven to do that which he would and to will that which he did, agreeing to his advice both in word and work in all that ever they were able.

Neither can I see that men could have been brought by any other means to live together in fellowship of life, to maintain cities, to deal truly, and willingly to obey one another, if men at the first had not by art and eloquence persuaded that which they full oft found out by reason. For what man, I pray you, being better able to maintain himself by valiant courage than by living in base subjection, would not rather look to rule like a lord than to live like an underling, if by reason he were not persuaded that it behooveth every man to live in his own vocation and not to seek any higher room than whereunto he was at the first appointed? Who would dig and delve from morn till evening? Who would travail[17] and toil with the sweat of his brows?[18] Yea, who would for his king's pleasure adventure and hazard his life, if wit had not so won men that they thought nothing more needful in this world, nor anything whereunto they were more bounden, than here to live in their duty and to train their whole life according to their calling. Therefore, whereas men are in many things weak by nature and subject to much infirmity, I think in this one point they pass all other creatures living that have the gift of speech and reason. And among all other, I think him most worthy fame, and amongst men to be taken for half a god, that therein doth chiefly and above all other excel men wherein men do excel beasts.[19] For he that is among the reasonable of all most reasonable, and among the witty of all most witty, and among the eloquent of all most eloquent—him think I among all men not only to be taken for a singular man, but rather to be counted for half a god. For in seeking the excellency hereof, the sooner he draweth to perfection, the nigher he cometh to God, who is the chief wisdom, and therefore called God because he is most wise, or rather wisdom itself.

Now then, seeing that God giveth his heavenly grace unto all such as call

15. **lusted** desired.

16. Wilson is speaking of the figure of the Hercules Gallicus whom Lucian described in his *Herakles* as being identified with Hermes, the god of eloquence, and who, as a symbol of the power of eloquence, had chains of gold and amber stretching from his tongue to the ears of his followers.

17. **travail** labor, work.

18. For the "sweat of his brows," see Genesis 3:19.

19. Cf. Cicero, *De inventione*, I.iv.5, and *De oratore*, I.viii.32–33.

unto him with stretched hands and humble heart, never wanting to those that want not to themselves, I purpose by his grace and especial assistance to set forth precepts of eloquence, and to show what observation[20] the wise have used in handling of their matters, that the unlearned by seeing the practice of others may have some knowledge themselves, and learn by their neighbor's device what is necessary for themselves in their own case.

The End of Rhetoric

Three things are required of an orator: to teach, to delight, and to persuade.[21] First, therefore, an orator must labor to tell his tale that the hearers may well know what he meaneth and understand him wholly, the which he shall with ease do, if he utter his mind in plain words, such as are usually received, and tell it orderly, without going about the bush. That if he do not this, he shall never do the other. For what man can be delighted or yet be persuaded with the only hearing of those things which he knoweth not what they mean? The tongue is ordained to express the mind that one might understand another's meaning: now what availeth to speak when none can tell what the speaker meaneth? Therefore, Favorinus the philosopher (as Gellius telleth the tale) did hit a young man over the thumbs very handsomely for using overold and overstrange[22] words. "Sirrah," quoth he, "when our old great ancestors and grandsires were alive, they spake plainly in their mother's tongue and used old language such as was spoken then at the building of Rome. But you talk me such a Latin, as though you spake with them even now that were two or three thousand years ago, and only because you would have no man to understand what you say. Now, were it not better for thee a thousandfold, thou foolish fellow, in seeking to have thy desire, to hold thy peace and speak nothing at all? For then by that means, few should know what were thy meaning. But thou sayest, the old antiquity doth like thee best, because it is good, sober, and modest. Ah, live, man, as they did before thee, and speak thy mind now as men do at this day. And remember that which Caesar saith, 'Beware as long as thou livest of strange words, as thou wouldest take heed and eschew great rocks in the sea.'"[23]

Of Delighting the Hearers and Stirring Them to Laughter

Considering the dullness of man's nature, that neither it can be attentive to hear, nor yet stirred to like or allow any tale long told, except it be refreshed or find some sweet delight, the learned have by wit and labor devised much

20. **observation** observant care.
21. The three ends of rhetoric, according to classical theorists, were to teach, to delight, and to move; see, for example, Quintilian, *Institutio oratoria,* III.v.2. Wilson is essentially equating moving with persuading.
22. **overstrange** overly foreign.
23. See Aulus Gellius, *Noctes atticae,* I.x.1–4.

variety.[24] Therefore, sometimes in telling a weighty matter, they bring in some heavy tale and move them to be right sorry, whereby the hearers are more attentive. But after, when they are wearied either with tediousness of the matter or heaviness of the report,[25] some pleasant matter is invented both to quicken them again and also to keep them from satiety. But surely few there be that have this gift: in due time to cheer men. Neither can any do it whom nature hath not framed and given an aptness thereunto.

Some man's countenance will make pastime though he speak never a word. Yea, a foolish word uttered by an apt man or a gesture strangely used by some pleasant body sets men full oft upon laughter. And whereas some think it a trifle to have this gift, and so easy that every varlet or common jester is able to match with the best, yet it appeareth that they which wittily can be pleasant and when time serveth can give a merry answer or use a nipping taunt, shall be able to abash a right worthy man and make him at his wit's end through the sudden, quick, and unlooked frump[26] given. I have known some so hit of the thumbs that they could not tell in the world whether it were best to fight, chide, or to go their way. And no marvel, for where the jest is aptly applied, the hearers laugh immediately, and who would gladly be laughed to scorn? Some can prettily by a word spoken take occasion to be right merry. Other can jest at large[27] and tell a round tale pleasantly, though they have none occasion at that time given. But assuredly, that mirth is more worth which is moved by a word newly spoken than if a long tale should pleasantly be told. Forasmuch as both it cometh unlooked for and also declares a quickness of wit worthy commendation. . . .

The occasion of laughter and the mean that maketh us merry . . . is the fondness,[28] the filthiness,[29] the deformity, and all such evil behavior as we see to be in other. For we laugh always at those things which either only or chiefly touch handsomely and wittily some especial fault or fond behavior in some one body or some one thing. Sometimes we jest at a man's body that is not well proportioned, and laugh at his countenance if either it be not comely by nature, or else he through folly cannot well see it. For if his talk be fond, a merry man can want no matter to hit him home, ye may be assured. Some jest is made when it toucheth no man at all, neither the demander, neither the standers-by, nor yet any other, and yet delighteth as much the hearers as any the other can do. Now when we would abash a man for some words that he hath spoken and can take none advantage of his person or making of his body, we either dolt him at the first and make him believe he is no wiser than a goose, or else we confute wholly his sayings with some pleasant jest, or else we extenuate and diminish his doings by some pretty means, or else we cast the like in his dish[30] and with some other device dash him out of countenance, or last of all, we laugh him to scorn outright, and

24. Cf. Cicero, *De oratore*, II.liv.216–lxxi.290, and Quintilian, *Institutio oratoria*, VI.iii.1–112.
25. **report** statement, account.   26. **frump** flout, mockery.   27. **at large** at length.
28. **fondness** foolishness.   29. **filthiness** moral corruption, vileness.   30. **cast . . . in his dish** reproach him.

sometimes speak almost never a word, but only in countenance show ourselves pleasant. But howsoever we make sport, either the delight is uttered
by countenance, or by pointing to some thing, or showed at large by some
tale, or else occasion taken by some word spoken. . . .

Assuredly, it behooveth a man that must talk much evermore to have regard to his audience, and not only to speak so much as is needful, but also
to speak no longer than they be willing to hear. Even in this our time, some
offend much in tediousness, whose part it were to comfort all men with
cheerfulness. Yea, the preachers of God mind so much edifying of souls that
they often forget we have any bodies. And therefore, some do not so much
good with telling the truth as they do harm with dulling the hearers, being
so far gone in their matters that oftentimes they cannot tell when to make an
end. Plato, therefore, the father of learning and the well of all wisdom, when
he heard Antisthenes make such a long oration that he stark wearied all his
hearers, "Fy, for shame man," quoth he, "dost thou not know that the mea-
suring of an oration standeth not in the speaker, but in the hearers."[31] But
some perhaps will say unto me, "Pascite quantum in vobis est," to whom I
answer, "Estote prudentes."[32] And now because our senses be such that in
hearing a right wholesome matter we either fall asleep when we should
most hearken, or else are wearied with still[33] hearing one thing without any
change, and think that the best part of his tale resteth in making an end, the
witty and learned have used delightful sayings and quick sentences even
among their weighty causes, considering that not only good will is got
thereby (for what is he that loveth not mirth?), but also men wonder at such
a head[34] as hath men's hearts at his commandment, being able to make them
merry when he list,[35] and that by one word speaking, either in answering
something spoken before or else oftentimes in giving the onset, being not
provoked thereunto. Again, we see that men are full oft abashed and put
out of countenance by such taunting means, and those that have so done
are counted to be fine men and pleasant fellows, such as few dare set foot[36]
with them.

Thus, knowing that to move sport is lawful for an orator or anyone that
shall talk in any open assembly, good it were to know what compass[37] he
should keep that should thus be merry, for fear he take too much ground
and go beyond his bounds. Therefore, no such should be taunted or jested
withal that either are notable evil livers and heinous offenders, or else are
pitiful caitiffs[38] and wretched beggars. For everyone thinketh it a better
and a meeter deed to punish naughty packs[39] than to scoff at their evil de-
meanor, and as for wretched souls or poor bodies, none can bear to have

31. I have not been able to locate the source of this quotation.
32. "Pascite . . . est": 1 Peter 5:2, "Feed them [i.e., the audience] as much as is in you." "Estote
prudentes": Matthew 10:16, "Be prudent."
33. **still** constantly.   34. **head** person (with respect to intelligence).   35. **list** desires.   36. **set foot** engage in combat.   37. **compass** bounds, limits.   38. **caitiffs**
miserable, wretched persons.   39. **packs** set of persons, usually of low character.

them mocked, but think rather that they should be pitied, except they foolishly vaunt themselves. Again, none such should be made any laughingstocks that either are honest of behavior or else are generally well beloved. As for others, we may be bold to talk with them and make such game and pastime as their good wits shall give good cause. But yet this one thing we had need ever to take with us, that in all our jesting we keep a mean, wherein not only it is meet to avoid all gross bourding[40] and alehouse jesting, but also to eschew all foolish talk and ruffian manners, such as no honest ears can once abide, nor yet any witty man can like well or allow.

Of Apt Choosing and Framing of Words and Sentences Together, Called Elocution

And now we are come to that part of rhetoric, the which above all others is most beautiful, whereby not only words are aptly used, but also sentences are in right order framed. For whereas invention helpeth to find matter and disposition serveth to place arguments, elocution getteth words to set forth invention and with such beauty commendeth the matter, that reason seemeth to be clad in purple, walking afore[41] both bare and naked. Therefore Tully [Cicero] saith well, "To find out reason and aptly to frame it is the part of a wise man, but to commend it by words and with gorgeous talk to tell our conceit,[42] that is only proper to an orator."[43] Many are wise, but few have the gift to set forth their wisdom. Many can tell their mind in English, but few can use meet terms and apt order, such as all men should have and wise men will use, such as needs must be had when matters should be uttered. Now then, what is he at whom all men wonder and stand in amaze at the view of his wit, whose doings are best esteemed?[44] Whom do we most reverence and count half a god among men? Even such a one assuredly that can plainly, distinctly, plentifully and aptly utter both words and matter, and his talk can use such composition that he may appear to keep an uniformity and (as I might say) a number[45] in the uttering of his sentence. Now an eloquent man being smally learned can do much more good in persuading by shift[46] of words and meet placing of matter than a great learned clerk[47] shall be able with great store of learning, wanting words to set forth his meaning. Wherefore I much marvel that so many seek the only knowledge of things, without any mind to commend or set forth their intendment, seeing none can know either what they are or what they have without the gift of utterance. Yea, bring them to speak their mind and enter in talk with

40. **bourding** jesting.   41. **walking afore** that walked before.   42. **conceit** idea, conception.

43. Cicero, *Orator*, xiv.

44. See Cicero, *De oratore*, III.xiv.53.

45. **number** rhythm.   46. **shift** clever manipulation, cunning trick.   47. **clerk** someone who has been to university.

such as are said to be learned, and you shall find in them such lack of utterance, that if you judge them by their tongue and expressing of their mind, you must needs say they have no learning. Wherein methinks they do like some rich snudges,[48] that having great wealth go with their hose out at heels, their shoes out at toes, and their coats out at both elbows. For who can tell if such men are worth a groat when their apparel is so homely and all their behavior so base? I can call them by none other name but slovens that may have good gear, and neither can nor yet will once wear it cleanly. What is a good thing to a man if he neither know the use of it, nor yet (though he know it) is able at all to use it? If we think comeliness and honesty to set forth the body with handsome apparel, and think them worthy to have money that both can and will use it accordingly, I cannot otherwise see but that this part deserveth praise which standeth wholly in setting forth matter by apt words and sentences together, and beautifieth the tongue with great change of colors and variety of figures. . . .

Among all other lessons, this should first be learned, that we never affect any strange inkhorn[49] terms, but so speak as is commonly received, neither seeking to be over-fine, nor yet living over-careless, using our speech as most men do and ordering our wits as the fewest have done. Some seek so far for outlandish English that they forget altogether their mother's language. And I dare swear this, if some of their mothers were alive, they were not able to tell what they say, and yet these fine English clerks will say they speak their mother tongue if a man should charge them for counterfeiting the king's English. Some far-journeyed gentlemen at their return home, like as they love to go in foreign apparel, so they will powder their talk with oversea language. He that cometh lately out of France will talk French English and never blush at the matter. Another chops in with English Italianated and applieth the Italian phrase to our English speaking, the which is as if an orator that professeth to utter his mind in plain Latin would needs speak poetry and farfetched colors[50] of strange antiquity. The lawyer will store his stomach with the prating of peddlers. The auditor in making his account and reckoning cometh in with "sise sould" and "cater denere" for *six sous* and *quatre deniers.* The fine courtier will talk nothing but Chaucer. The mystical wise men and poetical clerks will speak nothing but quaint proverbs and blind allegories, delighting much in their own darkness, especially when none can tell what they do say. The unlearned or foolish fantastical that smells but of learning (such fellows as have seen learned men in their days) will so Latin their tongues that the simple cannot but wonder at their talk and think surely they speak by some revelation. I know them that think rhetoric to stand wholly upon dark words, and he that can catch an inkhorn term by the tail, him they count to be a fine Englishman and a good rhetorician. . . .

48. **snudges**   misers.   49. **inkhorn**   pedantic.   50. **colors**   rhetorical figures.

Now whereas words be received, as well Greek as Latin, to set forth our meaning in the English tongue, either for lack of store[51] or else because we would enrich the language, it is well done to use them, and no man therein can be charged for any affectation, when all others are agreed to follow the same way. There is no man aggrieved when he heareth "letters patent," and yet "patent" is Latin and signifieth "open" to all men. The communion is a fellowship or a coming together, rather Latin than English; the king's prerogative declareth his power royal above all others, and yet I know no man grieved for these terms, being used in their place, nor yet anyone suspected for affectation when such general words are spoken. The folly is espied when either we will use such words as few men do use or use them out of place when another might serve much better.

51. **store**   a sufficient or abundant supply.

[17]

Francesco Patrizi

The Italian philosopher and scholar Francesco Patrizi (1529–1597) was born in Dalmatia and studied in Padua and Venice. For a number of years he traveled, going as far away as Spain and Cyprus, but did not secure an appointment, to teach philosophy at the University of Ferrara, until 1578. He moved to Rome in 1592, where he taught until his death. In all his writings, most of which concern philosophy, poetics, and rhetoric, he took positions against Aristotle, basing his thinking instead on Plato, various Neoplatonic philosophers, and Longinus. He began work on a vast poetics in 1555 and published the first two parts of it in 1586, arguing that poetry required divine inspiration, not obedience to rules derived from Aristotle. He later added another section to this work in which he defended Ariosto against Tasso because of the latter's Aristotelianism. His *Discussiones peripateticae* (*Peripatetic Discussions*), published in 1571 (revised edition, 1581) is essentially a polemic against Aristotle, and his *Nova de universis philosophia* (*New Universal Philosophy*) of 1591 constitutes a kind of *summa* of Renaissance Platonism and includes elements of Hermeticism as well as Zoroastrianism. Patrizi's *Della retorica dieci dialoghi* (*Ten Dialogues on Rhetoric*) was published in 1562. In it he displays a hostility toward rhetoric similar to Plato's, critiquing its claim to be able to treat any subject, its supposed nobility, the notion that it has any particular subject matter that belongs to it rather than to some other branch of learning, and the idea that its appeal is to the wise rather than the masses. Imitating Plato's style, Patrizi presents his work as ten dialogues between various people and himself in which he plays the role of Socrates. Besides Patrizi, the other speaker in the seventh book, most of which is translated here, is a certain Florio Maresio, who appears to be a minor Italian humanist who was active in Tuscany. This translation is based on the 1562 Venice edition of Patrizi's work.

Francesco Patrizi

FROM *Ten Dialogues on Rhetoric*

Book VII. Maresio, or On the Qualities of the Orator

Maresio. Now, what is it you said, Patrizi: that there is little room in the world for orators nowadays? How can that be true?

Patrizi. I said that?

Maresio. Yes, you certainly did.

Patrizi. I don't remember it. And if I did say it, I really marvel at myself, for the thought never crossed my mind to do so. Nor do I know if the idea is true. In fact, I think I believe the exact opposite because of a powerful argument that has persuaded me.

Maresio. Because of what argument? and how so?

Patrizi. Because of what Cicero said: that the profession of the orator always flourished and was the master in every free people and especially in quiet, tranquil cities.[1] Also it seems to me that Longinus said the orator has always been held in high esteem and considered of great worth among the people.

Maresio. And this seems the exact opposite of what you were saying you now believe.

Patrizi. How is it the opposite?

Maresio. It certainly is, for nowadays there are very few states governed by the people, so what you said at first now turns out to be true.

Patrizi. Then you understand the words of Cicero and Longinus to be referring to government by the people?

Maresio. I certainly do, nor should they be understood in any other way.

Patrizi. I thought they were referring just to plebeians. But let's see whether my belief or yours is closer to the truth.

Maresio. Please, let's do.

Patrizi. But where should we begin?

Maresio. Wherever seems best to you.

Patrizi. Let's start with that remark of Cicero's, that orators began to appear after the tyrants had been removed in Sicily and the people began to take one another to court over the property taken from them by both the tyrants and their neighbors.[2]

Maresio. That's the very place to start from in my opinion.

Patrizi. How so?

1. See *De oratore*, I.viii.30. For Longinus in the next sentence, see *On the Sublime*, xliv.1–3.
2. *Brutus*, xi.46. In this passage, Cicero credits this idea about the origin of rhetoric to Aristotle.

From *Ten Dialogues on Rhetoric*

Maresio. Because once the tyrants had been chased out, the people controlled the state in Syracuse and in other cities that were made subject to them.

Patrizi. From this perspective, the argument is yours, but from the other one, I don't know who will win.

Maresio. From what perspective?

Patrizi. From this one—that we should see in which cities the most ancient and the most famous orators once flourished.

Maresio. Well said.

Patrizi. Cicero recounts that the most ancient orators, according to what is recorded about them, were Pisistratus and Solon.[3]

Maresio. And these men also lived in a city governed by the people.

Patrizi. Yes? But when Demosthenes, Aeschines, and those other marvelous men flourished there afterward, what sort of state was it?

Maresio. Similarly, one governed by the people.

Patrizi. Then I'm wrong?

Maresio. It seems so to me.

Patrizi. But in Rome, when did they flourish?

Maresio. Not under the kings, that's for sure.

Patrizi. But in the time of the Republic?

Maresio. At that time.

Patrizi. And was the Republic a form of government by the people?

Maresio. It was.

Patrizi. And were there no orators under the emperors?

Maresio. Yes, there were, while there remained any vestige of the Republic, but it fell into a continuous decline, and together with its last vestige, they too disappeared.

Patrizi. Well, now I'm aware of my error.

Maresio. And the same thing occurred in the cities of Asia, which had many orators as long as they were ruled by the people, but once they came under the power of Rome, little by little all of them disappeared.

Patrizi. You have certainly made a good argument, and I am forced to agree with you, since I feel the power of your argument within me, constraining me to do so. But tell me, my beloved leader, in order to free me from every doubt: doesn't the profession of orators involve their arguing one against the other?

Maresio. It surely does.

3. *Brutus*, vii.27.

Patrizi. And it is equally the job of both to speak in terms of probabilities and to say contrary things that are semblances of the truth?

Maresio. This too.

Patrizi. And it happens sometimes that the same man will say one thing is true in one case and will affirm precisely the opposite in another?

Maresio. That happens.

Patrizi. And yet the truth in all cases is one and the same?

Maresio. It is one and the same.

Patrizi. And the truth never was, nor is, nor could be in the future, contrary to itself.

Maresio. Certainly not.

Patrizi. Thus, someone who speaks the truth will never affirm two contrary things both to be true.

Maresio. No, never.

Patrizi. And who does such a thing either does not know the truth about what he says, or knowing it and saying the opposite, he seeks to deceive others.

Maresio. One of these two conclusions is necessary.

Patrizi. And will you say that someone who has no knowledge of the truth of things is anything other than ignorant?

Maresio. That's what he is.

Patrizi. And can anyone who deceives others intentionally be called anything other than an evil man?

Maresio. He appears to be so at first sight. But it may be that one person deceives another for the good of the person deceived.

Patrizi. That's a good observation. But if one person deceives another for the good of the deceiver, what do you say he is?

Maresio. He's certainly an evil man.

Patrizi. Now look: weren't we just saying that the orator often says two contrary things about the same subject?

Maresio. We did.

Patrizi. Then it's necessarily the case that either he allows deception to go on out of ignorance, or he wants to deceive others.

Maresio. That's reasonable.

Patrizi. And if he's ignorant, he's a base sort of person and utterly worthless.

Maresio. Without a doubt.

Patrizi. But if he's a deceiver, he is also an evil and dangerous man.

Maresio. If he deceives others for his own benefit.

Patrizi. Now, shall we see by means of what sort of deception he deceives others?

Maresio. Let's see.

Patrizi. Now, what does the true orator talk about?

Maresio. About what happens in public consultations and in the law courts, and for that reason he is truly praised as a sophist.

Patrizi. And is the subject matter of consultations anything other than what is useful and what is harmful?

Maresio. It is surely that.

Patrizi. And is what is taken up in the law courts anything other than questions of justice and injustice?

Maresio. Nothing else.

Patrizi. Then the orator, speaking on both sides of the issue about these subjects, either does not understand them and is ignorant, or he's a deceiver.

Maresio. Necessarily.

Patrizi. And between us we've reached the conclusion today that if he deceives others for his own benefit, he's a wicked man.

Maresio. We did.

Patrizi. But what's the situation with that other sort of deception?

Maresio. Let's see.

Patrizi. First let's consider the kind of deception used in the law courts.

Maresio. Whichever one pleases you the most.

Patrizi. Consider this: if in the law courts he wants to deceive others, will he direct his deception either at the judge or at his adversary or at the audience?

Maresio. Principally at the judge, and then perhaps at the others.

Patrizi. And his deception will concern justice or injustice?

Maresio. One of the two, or both.

Patrizi. And if the judge lets himself be deceived so that he believes that what is just is unjust, or vice versa, then he will not know what the truth is in either case—and that's what he has to reach a verdict about.

Maresio. He will not know what the truth is.

Patrizi. And if he knew what the truth was, he would not let himself perpetrate a deception, for he would want to be an upright judge.

Maresio. That's right.

Patrizi. Then from this viewpoint, the judge who lets himself be deceived is ignorant about justice and injustice.

Maresio. He is.

Patrizi. But the orator who deceives him, why does he do it?

Maresio. Who knows?

Patrizi. What if he should perhaps do it to win his case?

Maresio. It appears that he does not do it for any other reason.

Patrizi. And isn't winning the case done for the benefit of his client?

Maresio. Yes.

Patrizi. And isn't it also for his own benefit?

Maresio. It doesn't seem to be that way.

Patrizi. Do you think any orator would devote himself to speaking in order to win a case for his client if he did not hope to get from it either some practical benefit or some pleasure in the form of fame and reputation?

Maresio. Perhaps no one would.

Patrizi. And when that didn't happen to him, I think he'd quit his profession.

Maresio. I think so, too.

Patrizi. Then he is moved to speak more for his own benefit than for that of others?

Maresio. Yes.

Patrizi. And then to win the lawsuit?

Maresio. Yes.

Patrizi. Therefore, if he devoted himself to speaking in order to lose the lawsuit and with it the right and sometimes the life and honor of his clients, would you think that this man was anything other than insane?

Maresio. What could he say in his own defense?

Patrizi. And if it should happen that he lost all of his lawsuits, one would perhaps believe that that was due to ignorance or disloyalty or both?

Maresio. That's true.

Patrizi. Both of those things would deprive him of benefits and of his good reputation.

Maresio. Very true.

Patrizi. Therefore, the orator always strives for victory.

Maresio. That's for certain.

Patrizi. And for the sake of that, he doesn't care about justice or duty.

Maresio. How so?

Patrizi. Because if he sees that justice is on the side of his adversary, he makes every effort to attack and beat him in order to gain the victory.

Maresio. I see it's like that.

Patrizi. But isn't a person who fights against justice unjust himself?

Maresio. He certainly is.

Patrizi. And isn't a person who is unjust nothing less than a wicked, evil man?

Maresio. No less.

Patrizi. Then, if the orator fights against justice for the sake of a victory, serving his own benefit or pleasure, he's a wicked man.

Maresio. It's correct that he seems to be a barbarian, but that is actually not the case in reality.

Patrizi. How is it then?

Maresio. The orator may well be defending a just case while his adversary defends an unjust one.

Patrizi. And what is he because of that?

Maresio. He who defends a just case is not a wicked man because he does not seek to deceive the judge, but to make justice appear clear to him.

Patrizi. You've spoken very well and have completely consoled me, for it really was weighing heavily on my mind that the orator had become an evil man through our discussion. But with what you've said being the case, we've now found some of them among the good, and it is a very dangerous thing to offend a person of such great repute. And with this consolation in mind, tell me: if an orator would never undertake to defend anything other than a just case and would always prosecute unjust ones, would he always be acting justly in doing so?

Maresio. He would.

Patrizi. Just as, on the contrary, one who always undertook to prosecute a just case and to defend an unjust one would always be working against justice.

Maresio. That's true.

Patrizi. And such a man is wicked.

Maresio. He is, without a doubt.

Patrizi. But if there were an orator who defended cases that went beyond both justice and injustice, and prosecuted in similar cases, he would sometimes be good and sometimes evil?

Maresio. That's the way it appears.

Patrizi. And he who is truly good is always good and never changes no matter what he does?

Maresio. No.

Patrizi. And the subtle, wicked person never changes from being that way.

Maresio. Certainly not.

Patrizi. Then the orator is a man in between good and evil.

Maresio. I grant your argument.

Patrizi. And because of this middle position, he will act equally to defend and to prosecute a just man, as he will an unjust one.

Maresio. It seems that way.

Patrizi. Therefore, if he were moved to defend justice because he loved it, he would never do the opposite.

Maresio. Certainly not.

Patrizi. And thus he'd be a just man, and a good one.

Maresio. He would.

Patrizi. But because he also undertakes the defense of injustice, he does not seem to feel any love for justice.

Maresio. No.

Patrizi. And when he's moved to do that, he's not moved by love.

Maresio. No.

Patrizi. But for the sake of winning, as we've said.

Maresio. For that purpose.

Patrizi. Always.

Maresio. Always.

Patrizi. And he forces himself to win either for the fee he will receive from his clients or for the sake of glory.

Maresio. For these reasons.

Patrizi. Then glory and gain are dearer to him than justice is.

Maresio. They certainly are.

Patrizi. Always.

Maresio. Always.

Patrizi. Then the orator always aims at his own advantage and for that reason at victory, whether in a just cause or not.

Maresio. That's right.

Patrizi. And one who does not care about justice cannot be called a just man.

Maresio. He can't.

Patrizi. And if by defending an unjust man and prosecuting a just one for the sake of glory and money a man can be said to be wicked, can't it be said that the orator is wicked, too?

Maresio. It can.

Patrizi. But if for that reason he does not merit such a bad name, still, by the same token, he cannot be called a good man.

Maresio. Truly not.

Patrizi. But perhaps he will be a man in between good and evil.

Maresio. That's the way he is.

Patrizi. And if that's the way he is, we shouldn't consider him worth very much.

Maresio. And why not?

Patrizi. Because I've heard tell that good men must be valued, loved, and honored because of their goodness.

Maresio. That's true.

Patrizi. And the wicked should be judged according to the hatred and fear one feels toward them.

Maresio. And the orator?

Patrizi. The orator, then, from this perspective, is not a man to be valued.

Maresio. It seems he is not.

Patrizi. But it seems, from another perspective, that he is a man to be feared, and is therefore worth something.

Maresio. From what perspective?

Patrizi. That as long as he hopes for victory, he will not restrain himself from using force on the judge.

Maresio. In what way?

Patrizi. When, by disturbing the judge's mind, he tears the judgment out of his hands as if by violence—just as in some passage Cicero boasts he has done.[4]

Maresio. Now I understand you.

Patrizi. And won't you say that someone who uses force on others is to be feared?

Maresio. Yes, I would.

Patrizi. And won't someone who does so against duty and justice be wicked?

Maresio. That's right.

Patrizi. And so, from this perspective, the orator is a violent man and the descendant of tyrants.

Maresio. Yes.

Patrizi. But if he deceives the judge, what sort of lineage do you think he has?

Maresio. I don't know.

Patrizi. What do you call someone who affirms something to be true when it isn't?

Maresio. A liar.

Patrizi. And that man who says something is good just when it is exactly the opposite, and who does so for money?

Maresio. Perhaps he's a con man.

---

4. One of the speakers in Cicero's *De oratore* (II.xviii.74) mentions the notion of tearing verdicts from the hands of judges by the force of eloquence.

Patrizi. From these two perspectives, then, the orator is a liar and a con man.

Maresio. That seems to be the case.

Patrizi. And from the other two, he's a base or tyrannical man.

Maresio. Yes, he is, if he did such things out of malice, but if he acted on other motives, he perhaps would be worthy of being excused by others and of not being accounted so evil.

Patrizi. For what other reason can he act?

Maresio. For this one: because it might not be clear through written statements or other evidence just what the true perspective on justice was.

Patrizi. Now this relates to what he knows. So tell me, if he didn't know anything at all about the case he's prosecuting or defending, would he speak about it in some random manner?

Maresio. No, unless he were crazy.

Patrizi. And if he knew the case perfectly, then he would know the truth within it?

Maresio. Yes, he would.

Patrizi. And someone who knows the truth about a subject is said to know the subject itself.

Maresio. That's very true.

Patrizi. And, on the contrary, someone who doesn't know the truth about a subject doesn't know the subject.

Maresio. That's right.

Patrizi. And one who doesn't know it, likewise doesn't know the truth about it.

Maresio. This also is very true.

Patrizi. Now, if someone knows the truth about a subject and doesn't say it because he intends to deceive others, or if he says the opposite, there's no doubt he has a wicked spirit.

Maresio. He certainly does.

Patrizi. But someone who does not know the truth and yet speaks of it, is speaking of something he doesn't know.

Maresio. He is.

Patrizi. And someone who doesn't know a subject is ignorant of it.

Maresio. He is.

Patrizi. Then the orator is ignorant if he does not know whatever subject he may be discussing.

Maresio. Necessarily.

Patrizi. For a variety of reasons, then, the orator cannot escape being either wicked or ignorant.

Maresio. He certainly can't. Now, Patrizi, in a marvelous manner you have made us reach the worst conclusion thanks to all your clever subtleties.

But it seems to me they shouldn't be carried so far that they perpetrate such a serious offense, for you have pierced the honor of that great man too deeply.

Patrizi. You're certainly right; I know I've acted badly. But when I'm in the process of speaking, I'm like an unbridled horse that doesn't slow down at all no matter how much the rider pulls on the reins until it goes headfirst into a wall or something and breaks its neck. I'm filled with grief that Nature has given me such ardent spirits that transport me against my will so that I offend myself as well as others. I thank you sincerely for having restrained me, for now I see I've spoken incorrectly.

Maresio. In what way?

Patrizi. In this way: is it true or not that someone who doesn't know a subject or the truth about it may be ignorant of that subject and its truth, and yet not be ignorant about all other subjects?

Maresio. It's very true.

Patrizi. And therefore he should not be called ignorant, but ignorant about the thing he doesn't know.

Maresio. Just about that.

Patrizi. And therefore, when the orator doesn't know about a deed that is just or unjust, he is ignorant about it and nothing else. If perhaps he really could not tell in every case whether something was just or unjust, then he would be ignorant of his entire profession.

Maresio. He would be.

Patrizi. And do you think he's really like that?

Maresio. I don't believe he's so bad as that.

Patrizi. And yet Gorgias, the father of all the teachers of oratory, was content that orators should not know what they were talking about, merely that they should know how to give the appearance of knowing it to others.

Maresio. And from whom do you know this?

Patrizi. From Plato.[5]

Maresio. If Gorgias was content with that situation, that does not mean all the others were.

Patrizi. Yes, they were, too, or Plato is lying.

Maresio. Not so, but where does he say it.

Patrizi. In the *Phaedrus*.[6]

Maresio. That's very strange.

Patrizi. In fact, it's approved by the testimony of Cicero who was both a great teacher of orators and the greatest orator.

5. See *Gorgias*, 459a–460b.
6. See *Phaedrus*, 259e–262a.

Maresio. From what testimony?

Patrizi. From this one: "For we also talk among those who are ignorant and we talk about things we ourselves don't know. And so people think and judge differently about the same subjects, and we often speak about opposed cases"—and so on and so forth.[7]

Maresio. Now they're harming themselves by condemning themselves.

Patrizi. But perhaps all this applies solely to the genre of judicial rhetoric and not also to that of consultation.

Maresio. Perhaps.

Patrizi. Therefore it will be good if we at least try to free that kind of rhetoric from the imputation of such a bad reputation.

Maresio. Let's try to do so in every way possible, and let's not fail if we can help it in any way.

Patrizi. Aren't consultations, of which we were just speaking, concerned with what is useful or harmful to the public—or with something else?

Maresio. Not with something else.

Patrizi. And what is good or bad for the public is considered by those who are running the state.

Maresio. Yes.

Patrizi. And if consultations are undertaken, are they anything other than a search for what will produce good results and avoid bad ones?

Maresio. They're nothing other than that.

Patrizi. And whoever is searching for something, as long as he's still searching for it, can't affirm it as if he'd already found it.

Maresio. It doesn't seem to me that he can.

Patrizi. And doesn't the person who produces orations of this sort affirm that the things he talks about are either good or evil?

Maresio. He certainly does.

Patrizi. Then he is not searching for those things.

Maresio. No.

Patrizi. Then he's not engaged in consultation.

Maresio. What?

Patrizi. We shouldn't be talking about the rhetorical genre of consultation here.

Maresio. Then what should we be talking of?

Patrizi. Perhaps that of deliberation.

Maresio. That's what teachers of rhetoric call it.

Patrizi. Isn't it the case that whoever engages in deliberation, after having searched for something, explains it and then establishes it?

7. *De oratore,* II.vii.30.

Maresio. It is.

Patrizi. And isn't he establishing a state?

Maresio. Yes.

Patrizi. Then he's not an orator, and that's not his manner of speaking.

Maresio. Explain why not.

Patrizi. Why his manner of speaking should be called deliberation?

Maresio. Patrizi, you're confusing everything.

Patrizi. I am? No, may it please God; rather, it's you.

Maresio. And how am I doing so, for the love of God?

Patrizi. Because I merely ask, while you, in responding, make affirmations, and thereby bring my questioning to an end.

Maresio. Well, I will take this burden on myself in order to please you.

Patrizi. But it's not shameful to affirm the truth.

Maresio. Then what we've been saying is the truth?

Patrizi. Up to now it seems to be. But if we want to avoid all doubt, we should see what sort of state is established as a result of the orator's speech.

Maresio. Let's see whatever you want, since it's necessary to let everything be directed by your questions.

Patrizi. Let me put it this way: perhaps a tyrant will not want to listen to the orator.

Maresio. Why not?

Patrizi. Since he looks only at what benefits him, he will not want to listen when others talk to him of justice.

Maresio. That's true.

Patrizi. Nor of injustice.

Maresio. And why not of that?

Patrizi. Because he perpetrates injustice on his own account without having another persuade him, by dint of speech, to do so.

Maresio. This is also true. But we were speaking of the second kind of oratory, not the first.

Patrizi. You're right, but it seems to me that not even in the case of the first would he lend an ear to others.

Maresio. Why not?

Patrizi. Because what is beneficial for the public is harmful for the tyrant and is something that he, as the master of things, doesn't want to hear.

Maresio. No.

Patrizi. And there's no need for people to persuade him to do what is harmful to the public in his city, since he is really ready to do that of his own free will.

Maresio. You speak the truth. But won't he want to hear people persuade him about what is beneficial to him?

Patrizi. Yes, he will, but they won't be orators.

Maresio. Why not?

Patrizi. Because orators practice their profession by shouting out loud and making long speeches, whereas he wants talk that's quiet so that the people will not hear his consultations, which he engages in to do them harm.

Maresio. That's a reasonable assertion.

Patrizi. Nor will a king want to hear the orator speak.

Maresio. Why not?

Patrizi. Because if the king were one of those "best men"—the ones who don't exist, but whose portrait has been drawn by Plato—he would estimate things according to his own perfect prudential judgment, something he'd possess to a greater degree than any orator would.[8]

Maresio. The judgment of that king may be like that, but such kings do not exist.

Patrizi. Well said. But if he's a king of the usual type, he will have his secret council in which people don't shout out loud, but business is carried on in subdued tones and among just a few, those few being such that they would perhaps laugh at the orator.

Maresio. Let the king be of this sort.

Patrizi. In a state run by the optimates, what need is there of a person who doesn't understand what he's talking about?

Maresio. Then, you're making the orator ignorant about everything?

Patrizi. I? No. But Cicero and Plato are, according to what we've seen. Moreover, he's also ignorant about the future toward which consultations are directed, for only the most divine and inspired men have ever known about that.

Maresio. It seems to me that it's you now who are wandering off as though inspired.

Patrizi. That could be. However, a state run by just a few will not tolerate orators either.

Maresio. Why?

Patrizi. Because these few are also tyrants who rule according to what pleases and benefits them.

Maresio. Let's also allow this to be the case.

Patrizi. What remains, then, is that the orator finds a place only among the

8. Patrizi is referring to the philosopher king in Plato's *Republic;* see V.xvii.473d–473e.

crowd of common people and not elsewhere—which is what Longinus and Cicero said.

Maresio. And why is that?

Patrizi. Because the common people do not understand things and allow themselves to be taken by the appearance of reason and by the passions, and those two things make the orator seem marvelous to them. But it would perhaps be much better if we made a distinction among orators.

Maresio. What distinction?

Patrizi. That some orators are concerned with lawsuits and others, as we said, with consultations.

Maresio. Why do we have to make this distinction now? Hasn't it already been made?

Patrizi. Perhaps because the two kinds are not the same, and perhaps because neither one group nor the other should be called orators.

Maresio. Now this is a great deal stranger than anything you've said before.

Patrizi. Perhaps not so much stranger. For the two groups are in fact distinguished in some cities, since there are those who are in the senate and others who appear before judges. And the latter would not know how to say a word among senators, while the former could not do so in front of the judges, nor could the two exchange the subject matters they work with.

Maresio. Perhaps this is not a defect in the art of oratory, but in orators.

Patrizi. Perhaps it is, as you say. But aren't their subject matters distinct?

Maresio. Yes.

Patrizi. And the topics they use?

Maresio. They are.

Patrizi. And their styles of speech?

Maresio. In what way?

Patrizi. Judicial speeches are more contentious and involve moving the emotions.

Maresio. Yes.

Patrizi. Therefore, it would be appropriate to give the two kinds of orators different names, for their activities differ from one another in almost every way.

Maresio. Perhaps.

Patrizi. But let's put aside the matter of their names and consider their essential characters.

Maresio. Let's do it.

Patrizi. There have been republics ruled by the people that have had no need of orators in the law courts.

Maresio. Which ones would they be?

Patrizi. Florence, Lucca, and Genoa for a while, and nowadays the Germans, the Swiss, and Dubrovnik.[9]

Maresio. You are certainly telling the truth. But what's the explanation for this situation?

Patrizi. I believe there are two.

Maresio. What are they?

Patrizi. One is that they make judgments according to written laws, either those of the Empire, or those they've made themselves.[10]

Maresio. And the other?

Patrizi. Because the multitude of the common people do not have power over the judges.

Maresio. And what difference does that make?

Patrizi. A lot, because the multitude is ignorant.

Maresio. And if that's the way it is?

Patrizi. That means it does not understand the laws.

Maresio. That's true, and it's best that they don't.

Patrizi. And someone who doesn't understand something, whatever it may be, can't make a correct judgment about it.

Maresio. He certainly can't.

Patrizi. Then it turns out not to be a good idea to let the common people make judgments in those states where one judges things according to the laws.

Maresio. No.

Patrizi. That's why, in places where judgments are based on the laws of the Empire, they have formed tribunals composed of men who understand those laws, men whom the people call Doctors.

Maresio. That's right.

Patrizi. And if it happened that all republics and all states were governed in such a way that everything were judged according to written laws, then judicial orators would never have appeared.

Maresio. It seems not.

Patrizi. But because states were not run that way, those orators appeared in mobs in the ancient world.

Maresio. How were those states run then?

9. Florence, Lucca, and Genoa were all republics up until the sixteenth century. Various German and Swiss states were famous for republican governments in the period. Dubrovnik (in the former Yugoslavia) was nominally under Venetian, then Hungarian, and finally Turkish rule during the late Middle Ages and the Renaissance, but managed to maintain a form of republican self-government.

10. The Empire is the Holy Roman Empire.

Patrizi. In order to gain money through the salaries paid to judges, the common people wanted to fill those offices, with the result that judges were elected from the body of the people.

Maresio. In what way were they able to be judges, since they were ignorant?

Patrizi. They said they did so according to equity and according to the justice that God had written in their hearts.

Maresio. And they understood things?

Patrizi. I don't know, but they were reduced to judging according to their own opinions, which were guided for the most part by blind ignorance and muddied by the angry passions of their spirits. Those passions always make things appear other than they really are, and either more or less than what is truly just. In this business the orator has infinite power, for he has never judged things according to what is right.

Maresio. Tell me: didn't Plato want his ideal king to judge things not according to written laws, but according to his own opinion?

Patrizi. Yes he did, but he also wanted that king not to be a man of the people in terms of his knowledge, but excellent and prudent beyond all others.

Maresio. Plato's desire was the best.

Patrizi. And someone who is really prudent cannot be said to be disturbed by the passions of the spirit so as not to be able to discern what is just and right.

Maresio. That's true.

Patrizi. And the world would be in the best condition if the most prudent men judged disputes.

Maresio. It would without fail.

Patrizi. Just as, on the contrary, it would be the worst if a man of the people were the judge.

Maresio. Also true.

Patrizi. Because the majority is foolish and in its heart has a wild beast with many heads that are always barking and that completely deafen its spirit, dazing it so that it cannot see the light or discern the truth.

Maresio. Very true.

Patrizi. And the master orator always has the power to awaken that beast and to make it bark from whichever one of its heads he pleases.

Maresio. Thus it is.

Patrizi. And if that is the case, then there's no doubt that the orator will always stimulate whatever head he knows or believes will be helpful in his quest for victory.

Maresio. No doubt.

Patrizi. This kind of judgment is really bad, then, since it is always, or almost always, determined by the will of the speaker who is the best competitor.

Maresio. It is really bad, without question.

Patrizi. And wouldn't you say that where the judges were taken from the people, even if there was just one of them, that the orator then was exercising his profession among the people?

Maresio. Why do you say this?

Patrizi. Because the minds of the people are ignorant and controlled by the emotions.

Maresio. True.

Patrizi. And such a mind will always be plebeian even if joined to a noble body and has a grand lineage.

Maresio. It will always be thus.

Patrizi. If the orator is in the law courts, then his place is among judges from the common people.

Maresio. Nowhere else.

Patrizi. And in consultations, since neither the king nor the tyrant nor the optimates nor the powerful nor those people who govern themselves according to laws want to listen to him, his only function would be to move and upset the worst part of the common people.

Maresio. That's true, insofar as it's been shown.

Patrizi. Then that's the situation with law courts and consultations.

Maresio. It is.

Patrizi. But perhaps he will want to enter into the consultations of the best people.

Maresio. Perhaps—for these and only these are the places left for him.

Patrizi. And in this case he would be doing so with the greatest ignorance.

Maresio. Why?

Patrizi. Because men have the greatest ignorance about the future.

Maresio. True.

Patrizi. And especially orators, who, according to the testimony of Cicero and Gorgias, are and must be ignorant about what they are saying.

Maresio. Right.

Patrizi. Then, if some god with the power to do so should banish from the world all democratic states and every government run by the common people, the orator would exist in vain.

Maresio. Truly in vain.

Patrizi. Just as we have actually seen.

Maresio. When was that?

Patrizi. When states came under monarchical control.

Maresio. I don't understand you.

Patrizi. I will explain. As long as there were kings in the first age of the world, and even after they had disappeared and their sons, the tyrants, ruled, there is no record of any orator in all of antiquity.

Maresio. That's true.

Patrizi. But when after many years kings and tyrants were done away with in a few countries and the people came to power in the government, orators began to be heard in the squares and tribunals whenever they found ears fit to receive their din. And this, according to Aristotle, happened in Sicily before anywhere else. And according to others, in Athens, after the descendants of Theseus had been chased out and the people took over the government.[11] Among these, the most famous were Pisistratus and Solon. The former truly knew how to create a din so that the childish people, dazed by his shouting, made him its master. From there the study of rhetoric developed, since the cleverest Athenians were aware of its power and indeed put it into practice. Thus arose among them that famous crew of orators who were extinguished later under the first or second kings who succeeded Alexander [the Great].

Maresio. These things you recount are very true.

Patrizi. And at Rome, it's certain that when the kings reigned, there was no talk of orators.

Maresio. That's certain.

Patrizi. And when the kings had been chased away and the optimates had taken the state, there was no need of orators then.

Maresio. There wasn't.

Patrizi. But later, when the people rose up to rule and introduced a time of license, then orators arose to make themselves heard and to achieve greatness. However, when the state had been changed into the monarchy of the emperors, as long as the shades of that first republic endured, the shades of the orators did so, too. And when the shades of the former had completed faded away after a time, those of the latter also disappeared. Nor have they ever risen again after thousands of years and centuries. Nor will they rise again until the monarchies have been extinguished and the people once again take over the government.

Maresio. This has been quite a story, Patrizi, and seemingly a true one.

Patrizi. As far as that goes, I've heard Cicero say, "This one thing has always particularly flourished and has always ruled in every free people and especially in peaceful, tranquil cities."[12]

Maresio. Patrizi, you understand rhetoric in a way that is very different from that of all the other people who pursue eloquence, the number of

11. See note 2.
12. See note 1.

whom is infinite nowadays—although for all that, there's still no one who's a complete orator.

Patrizi. And you shouldn't hope for one, as long as the world continues on this course, and here's why. Although Petrarch, when he found Cicero's books, awoke the spirits of the orators and all the other *literati*, who had been buried, thanks to the monarchs and the barbarians, and although after him many others undertook the task of adding breath and life to them, no one has been able to make them leave the area around their tombs, in which they were put by the monarchs and around which they are still forced to wander like spirits not yet purged of their sins.[13] Nor will they ever be freed until the power of the people comes to untie the bonds of the laws that keep them bound.

Maresio. Quite a grand new interpretation, Patrizi, and one with such an appearance of truth that it cannot help but be believed—and as far as I'm concerned, I'm disposed to do so.

(Like Plato, Patrizi ends this dialogue by rehearsing a myth in order to explain why orators, who are so unsavory, are still held in high esteem. In the myth, the goddess Fame, the winged daughter of Words, reveals the plot of the Titans against Jupiter, who punishes them and rewards her with the ability to go everywhere, to confuse truth and falsehood, and to reward orators, as the kin of Words, with fame and immortality.)

13. Petrarch discovered several volumes of Cicero's familiar letters in Verona in 1345.

[18]

George Puttenham

The English courtier George Puttenham (ca. 1529–1590) is generally acknowledged to be the author of *The Art of English Poesy*. According to statements in that work, he was perhaps educated abroad, and he most likely visited Flanders and other countries on the continent sometime between 1563 and 1578. Puttenham matriculated at Cambridge in 1546, but never took a degree, and was admitted to the Middle Temple to study law in 1556. Tied to one important family through his mother, he allied himself with another when he married Lady Elizabeth Windsor around 1560. His brother-in-law Sir John Throckmorton paid Puttenham's debts and rescued him from prison in 1569, when he was charged with conspiring to murder the bishop of London, and again in 1570, after he was arrested for having criticized the queen's counselors too freely. In 1587 Puttenham wrote *A Justificacion of Queen Elizabeth in Relacion to the Affair of Mary Queen of Scots*, a tract that circulated anonymously and for which he was rewarded by Queen Elizabeth in 1588. He wrote a large number of works, most of which are lost except for the *Justificacion*, the *Art*, and *Partheniades*, a collection of poems praising Elizabeth and intended as a New Year's gift, probably in 1581–1582. *The Art of English Poesy*, which appeared anonymously in 1589, is divided into three books. The first defines poetry and the poet, traces the history of poetry from the ancient world, and reviews the different kinds or genres of poetry. Book II treats questions of meter, rhythm, rhyme, and stanzaic patterns, while Book III discusses ornamentation, including language and style, figures of speech, and faults in writing. It ends with a lengthy treatment of the all-important subject of decorum. Although his work is technically a poetics, rather than a rhetoric manual, much of what Puttenham says about poetry derives from or is identical with classical and Renaissance teachings about rhetoric. The portions of the *Art* included here are taken from a facsimile of the 1589 edition published in London by Richard Field and reprinted, with introduction by Baxter Hathaway by The Kent State University Press (Kent, Ohio, 1970).

George Puttenham

FROM *The Art of English Poesy*

The First Book. Of Poets and Poetry

Chapter III. How Poets Were the First Priests, the First Prophets, the First Legislators and Politicians in the World

The profession and use of poesy is most ancient from the beginning, and not as many erroneously suppose, after, but before any civil society was among men. For it is written that poesy was the original cause and occasion of their first assemblies, when before the people remained in the woods and mountains, vagrant[1] and dispersed like the wild beasts, lawless and naked, or very ill-clad, and of all good and necessary provision for harbor[2] or sustenance utterly unfurnished, so as they little differed for their manner of life from the very brute beasts of the field.[3] Whereupon it is feigned that Amphion and Orpheus, two poets of the first ages, one of them, to wit Amphion, built up cities and reared walls with the stones that came in heaps to the sound of his harp, figuring thereby the mollifying of hard and stony hearts by his sweet and eloquent persuasion. And Orpheus assembled the wild beasts to come in herds to hearken to his music and by that means made them tame, implying thereby how by his discrete and wholesome lessons uttered in harmony and with melodious instruments, he brought the rude and savage people to a more civil and orderly life, nothing, as it seemeth, more prevailing or fit to redress and edify the cruel and sturdy courage[4] of man than it. And as these two poets, and Linus before them, and Musaeus also and Hesiod in Greece and Arcadia, so by all likelihood had more poets done in other places and in other ages before them, though there be no remembrance left of them by reason of the records by some accident of time perished and failing. Poets therefore are of great antiquity. Then forasmuch[5] as they were the first that intended[6] to the observation of nature and her works, and especially of the celestial courses, by reason of the continual motion of the heavens, searching after the first mover and from thence by degrees coming to know and consider of the substances separate and abstract, which we call the divine intelligences or good angels (*Daemones*), they were the first that instituted sacrifices of placation,[7] with invocations and worship to them as to gods, and invented and established all the rest of the observances and ceremonies of religion, and so were the first priests and ministers of the holy mysteries. And because for the better execution of that high charge and function, it behooved them to live chaste and

1. **vagrant** wandering.   2. **harbor** shelter.

3. In this passage, Puttenham is recounting a version of the myth of the orator as civilizer, which occurs in a number of ancient texts, including Cicero, *De inventione*, I.ii.2–3; Quintilian, *Institutio oratoria*, II.xvi.9; and Horace, *Ars poetica*, 391–401. Horace mentions Orpheus and Amphion.

4. **courage** spirit, liveliness.   5. **forasmuch** insofar.   6. **intended** devoted attention.   7. **placation** propitiation.

in all holiness of life and in continual study and contemplation, they came by instinct divine and by deep meditation and much abstinence (the same assubtiling[8] and refining their spirits) to be made apt to receive visions, both waking and sleeping, which made them utter prophecies and foretell things to come. So also were they the first prophets or seers, *Videntes,* for so the Scripture termeth them in Latin after the Hebrew word, and all the oracles and answers of the gods were given in meter or verse, and published to the people by their direction. And for that they were aged and grave men, and of much wisdom and experience in the affairs of the world, they were the first lawmakers to the people and the first politicians, devising all expedient means for the establishment of commonwealth to hold and contain the people in order and duty by force and virtue of good and wholesome laws, made for the preservation of the public peace and tranquillity, the same peradventure not purposely intended, but greatly furthered by the awe of their gods and such scruple of conscience as the terrors of their late invented religion had led them into.

Chapter IV. How the Poets Were the First Philosophers, the First Astronomers and Historiographers and Orators and Musicians of the World

Utterance also and language is given by nature to man for persuasion of others and aid of themselves, I mean the first ability to speak. For speech itself is artificial[9] and made by man, and the more pleasing it is, the more it prevaileth to such purpose as it is intended for; but speech by meter is a kind of utterance more cleanly couched[10] and more delicate to the ear than prose is, because it is more current[11] and slipper[12] upon the tongue, and withal tunable and melodious, as a kind of music, and therefore may be termed a musical speech or utterance, which cannot but please the hearer very well. Another cause is, for that it is briefer and more compendious and easier to bear away and be retained in memory, than that which is contained in multitude of words and full of tedious ambage[13] and long periods. It is beside a manner of utterance more eloquent and rhetorical than the ordinary prose, which we use in our daily talk, because it is decked and set out with all manner of fresh colors and figures, which maketh that it sooner inveigleth[14] the judgment of man and carrieth his opinion this way and that, whithersoever the heart by impression of the ear shall be most affectionately[15] bent and directed. The utterance in prose is not of so great efficacy, because not only it is daily used, and by that occasion the ear is overglutted with it, but is also not so voluble and slipper upon the tongue, being wide and loose and nothing numerous,[16] nor contrived into measures and sounded with so gallant

8. **assubtiling** rendering more subtle or fine. 9. **artificial** artful, the product of art. 10. **cleanly couched** artfully expressed in words. 11. **current** flowing, fluent. 12. **slipper** easily uttered or pronounced. 13. **ambage** roundabout or indirect speech, periphrasis. 14. **inveigleth** blinds, beguiles, deceives. 15. **affectionately** by the emotions. 16. **numerous** rhythmic.

and harmonious accents, nor in fine[17] allowed that figurative conveyance,[18] nor so great license in choice of words and phrases as meter is. So as the poets were also from the beginning the best persuaders and their eloquence the first rhetoric of the world, even so it became that the high mysteries of the gods should be revealed and taught by a manner of utterance and language of extraordinary phrase, and brief and compendious, and above all others sweet and civil as the metrical is. The same also was meetest[19] to register the lives and noble gests[20] of princes and of the great monarchs of the world, and all other the memorable accidents[21] of time, so as the poet was also the first historiographer. Then forasmuch as they were the first observers of all natural causes and effects in the things generable[22] and corruptible, and from thence mounted up to search after the celestial courses and influences,[23] and yet penetrated further to know the divine essences and substances separate, as is said before, they were the first astronomers and philosophists and metaphysicks.[24] Finally, because they did altogether endeavor themselves to reduce the life of man to a certain method of good manners and made the first differences between virtue and vice and then tempered all these knowledges and skills with the exercise of a delectable music by melodious instruments, which withal served them to delight their hearers and to call the people together by admiration[25] to a plausible[26] and virtuous conversation, therefore were they the first philosophers ethic[27] and the first artificial musicians of the world. Such was Linus, Orpheus, Amphion, and Musaeus the most ancient poets and philosophers, of whom there is left any memory by the profane writers. King David also and Solomon his son and many other of the holy prophets wrote in meters and used to sing them to the harp, although to many of us ignorant of the Hebrew language and phrase, and not observing it, the same seem but a prose. It cannot be therefore that any scorn or indignity should justly be offered to so noble, profitable, ancient, and divine a science[28] as poesy is.

The Third Book. Of Ornament

Chapter I. Of Ornament Poetical

As no doubt the good proportion of any thing doth greatly adorn and commend it, and right so our late remembered proportions[29] do to our vulgar[30] poesy, so is there yet requisite to the perfection of this art another manner of

17. **in fine** in the end, in short.   18. **figurative conveyance** expressing of thought in figures of speech.   19. **meetest** fittest.   20. **gests** deeds, feats.   21. **accidents** events.   22. **generable** capable of being generated.   23. **courses and influences** i.e., of the planets.   24. **philosophists and metaphysicks** philosophers, i.e., lovers of wisdom, and metaphysicians.   25. **admiration** wondering, marveling.   26. **plausible** praiseworthy, laudable.   27. **philosophers ethic** moral philosophers.   28. **science** art, branch of knowledge.
29. "late remembered proportions": Puttenham's second book was concerned with "proportion," that is, with meter, rhyme, and stanzaic patterns.
30. **vulgar** vernacular.

George Puttenham

[206]

exornation,[31] which resteth in the fashioning of our maker's language and style to such purpose as it may delight and allure as well the mind as the ear of the hearers with a certain novelty and strange manner of conveyance, disguising it no little from the ordinary and accustomed, nevertheless making it nothing the more unseemly or misbecoming,[32] but rather decenter[33] and more agreeable to any civil ear and understanding. And as we see in these great madams of honor, be they for personage or otherwise never so comely and beautiful, yet if they want[34] their courtly habiliments,[35] or at leastwise such other apparel as custom and civility have ordained to cover their naked bodies, would be half ashamed or greatly out of countenance to be seen in that sort, and perchance do then think themselves more amiable in every man's eye when they be in their richest attire, suppose of silks or tissues[36] and costly embroideries, than when they go in cloth or in any other plain and simple apparel. Even so cannot our vulgar poesy show itself either gallant or gorgeous if any limb be left naked and bare and not clad in his kindly[37] clothes and colors, such as may convey them somewhat out of sight, that is, from the common course of ordinary speech and capacity of the vulgar judgment, and yet being artificially handled must needs yield it much more beauty and commendation. This ornament we speak of is given to it by figures and figurative speeches, which be the flowers as it were and colors that a poet setteth upon his language by art, as the embroiderer doth his stone and pearl or passements[38] of gold upon the stuff of a princely garment, or as the excellent painter bestoweth the rich orient colors upon his table[39] of portrait, so nevertheless, as if the same colors in our art of poesy (as well as in those other mechanical arts) be not well tempered, or not well laid, or be used in excess, or never so little disordered or misplaced, they not only give it no manner of grace at all, but rather do disfigure the stuff and spill[40] the whole workmanship, taking away all beauty and good liking from it, no less than if the crimson taint, which should be laid upon a lady's lips or right in the center of her cheeks, should by some oversight or mishap be applied to her forehead or chin, it would make, ye would say, but a very ridiculous beauty, wherefore the chief praise and cunning[41] of our poet is in the discreet using of his figures, as the skillful painter's is in the good conveyance[42] of his colors and shadowing traits of his pencil, with a delectable variety, by all measure and just proportion, and in places most aptly to be bestowed.

Chapter II. How Our Writing and Speeches Public Ought to Be Figurative, and If They Be Not Do Greatly Disgrace the Cause and Purpose of the Speaker and Writer

31. **exornation** adornment. 32. **misbecoming** unbecoming. 33. **decenter** more decorous. 34. **want** lack. 35. **habiliments** attire. 36. **tissues** rich kind of cloth, often containing gold or silver threads. 37. **kindly** natural. 38. **passements** lace trim. 39. **table** board on which a picture is painted. 40. **spill** spill; spoil. 41. **cunning** knowledge, skill. 42. **conveyance** managing.

But as it hath been always reputed a great fault to use figurative speeches foolishly and indiscreetly, so is it esteemed no less an imperfection in man's utterance to have none use of figure at all, especially in our writing and speeches public, making them but as our ordinary talk, than which nothing can be more unsavory and far from all civility. I remember in the first year of Queen Mary's reign a knight of Yorkshire was chosen speaker of the Parliament, a good gentleman and wise in the affairs of his shire, and not unlearned in the laws of the realm, but as well for some lack of his teeth, as for want of language, nothing well-spoken, which at that time and business[43] was most behooveful[44] for him to have been; this man after he had made his oration to the queen, which ye know is of course to be done at the first assembly of both houses, a bencher of the Temple[45] both well learned and very eloquent, returning from the Parliament house, asked another gentleman his friend how he liked Mr. Speaker's oration: "Mary,"[46] quoth the other, "Methinks I heard not a better alehouse tale told this seven years."[47] This happened because the good old knight made no difference between an oration or public speech to be delivered to the ear of a prince's majesty and state[48] of a realm, than he would have done of an ordinary tale to be told at his table in the country, wherein all men know the odds[49] is very great. And though grave and wise counselors in their consultations do not use much superfluous eloquence, and also in their judicial hearings do much mislike[50] all scholastical[51] rhetorics, yet in such a case as it may be (and as this Parliament was) if the Lord Chancellor of England or Archbishop of Canterbury himself were to speak, he ought to do it cunningly and eloquently, which cannot be without the use of figures, and nevertheless none impeachment[52] or blemish to the gravity of their persons or of the cause—wherein I report me to them that knew Sir Nicholas Bacon, Lord Keeper of the Great Seal, or the now Lord Treasurer of England, and have been conversant with their speeches made in the Parliament house and Star Chamber.[53] From whose lips I have seen to proceed more grave and natural eloquence than from all the orators of Oxford or Cambridge, but all is as it is handled, and maketh no matter whether the same eloquence be natural to them or artificial

43. **business** busy season. 44. **behooveful** necessary (it behooved him). 45. **bencher of the Temple** lawyer (the Temple contained lawyers' offices and was one of the establishments in which they were trained). 46. **mary** an oath: by Mary.

47. The "knight of Yorkshire" was Sir John Pollard (d. 1557), who was Speaker of the first session of the House of Commons under Mary, 1553–1555; although a branch of the Pollard family was established in Yorkshire, Sir John was born in Devonshire and was elected as a member of the House for Oxfordshire.

48. **state** rulers, government. 49. **odds** difference. 50. **mislike** dislike. 51. **scholastical** pertaining or belonging to the school. 52. **impeachment** hindrance, detriment.

53. Nicholas Bacon (1509–1579) became Lord Keeper of the Great Seal in 1558. The lord treasurer was William Cecil, Lord Burghley (1520–1598), who held that post from 1572 on. The Star Chamber was a room in Westminster Palace in which the monarch's council met and in which, in the fifteenth century, it began to serve as a court for dealing with criminal cases; in the Renaissance it was an effective instrument for carrying out the policies of the monarch and was regarded by many during the reigns of James I and Charles I as synonymous with tyranny.

(though I think rather natural), yet were they known to be learned and not unskillful[54] of the art when they were younger men; and as learning and art teacheth a scholar to speak, so doth it also teach a counselor, and as well an old man as a young, and a man in authority as well as a private person, and a pleader[55] as well as a preacher, every man after his sort[56] and calling as best becometh.[57] And that speech which becometh one, doth not become another, for manners of speeches, some serve to work in excess, some in mediocrity,[58] some to grave purposes, some to light, some to be short and brief, some to be long, some to stir up affections, some to pacify and appease them, and these common despisers of good utterance, which resteth altogether in[59] figurative speeches, being well used whether it come by nature or by art or by exercise,[60] they be but certain gross ignorants of whom it is truly spoken *scientia non habet inimicum nisi ignorantem.*[61] I have come to the Lord Keeper Sir Nicholas Bacon, and found him sitting in his gallery alone with the works of Quintilian before him; indeed, he was a most eloquent man, and of rare learning and wisdom, as ever I knew England to breed, and one that joyed as much in learned men and men of good wits. A knight of the queen's privy chamber once entreated a noble woman of the court, being in great favor about her majesty (to the intent to remove her from a certain displeasure, which by sinister[62] opinion she had conceived against a gentleman his friend), that it would please her to hear him speak in his own cause and not to condemn him upon his adversaries' report. "God forbid," said she, "he is too wise for me to talk with. Let him go and satisfy such a man" (naming him). "Why," quoth the knight again, "had your Ladyship rather hear a man talk like a fool or like a wise man?" This was because the lady was a little perverse and not disposed to reform herself by hearing reason, which none other can so well beat into the ignorant head as the well-spoken and eloquent man. And because I am so far waded into this discourse of eloquence and figurative speeches, I will tell you what happened on a time, myself being present, when certain doctors of the civil law were heard in a litigious cause betwixt a man and his wife. Before a great magistrate who, as they can tell that knew him, was a man very well learned and grave, but somewhat sour and of no plausible utterance, the gentleman's chance was to say, "My Lord, the simple woman is not so much to blame as her lewd[63] abettors, who by violent persuasions have led her into this willfulness." Quoth the judge, "What need such eloquent terms in this place?" The gentleman replied, "Doth your Lordship mislike the term 'violent,' and methinks I speak it to great purpose, for I am sure she would never have done it, but by force of persuasion, and if persuasion were not very violent, to the mind of man it could not have wrought so strange an effect as we read

---

54. **unskillful** ignorant. 55. **pleader** lawyer. 56. **sort** kind, quality, rank. 57. **as best becommeth** as is most appropriate. 58. **mediocrity** moderation. 59. **resteth . . . in** consists of. 60. **exercise** practice. 61. **scientia . . . ignorantem** "knowledge has no enemy except an ignorant man." 62. **sinister** prejudicial, malicious. 63. **lewd** wicked.

that it did once in Egypt"—and would have told the whole tale at large,[64] if the magistrate had not passed it over very pleasantly. Now to tell you the whole matter as the gentleman intended, thus it was. There came into Egypt a notable orator, whose name was Hegesias, who inveighed so much against the incommodities of this transitory life, and so highly commended death the dispatcher of all evils, as a great number of his hearers destroyed themselves, some with weapon, some with poison, others by drowning and hanging themselves to be rid out of[65] this vale of misery, insomuch[66] as it was feared lest many more of the people would have miscarried by occasion of his persuasions, if king Ptolomy had not made a public proclamation that the orator should avoid[67] the country and no more be allowed to speak in any matter.[68] Whether now persuasions may not be said violent and forcible to simple minds in special,[69] I refer it to all men's judgments that hear the story. At leastways, I find this opinion confirmed by a pretty devise or emblem that Lucian allegeth he saw in the portrait of Hercules within the city of Marseilles in Provence, where they had figured a lusty old man with a long chain tied by one end at his tongue, by the other end at the people's ears, who stood afar off and seemed to be drawn to him by the force of that chain fastened to his tongue, as who would say, by force of his persuasions.[70] And to show more plainly that eloquence is of great force and not, as many people think amiss, the property and gift of young men only, but rather of old men, and a thing which better becometh hoary hairs then beardless boys, they seem to ground it upon this reason: age (say they and most truly) brings experience, experience bringeth wisdom, long life yields long use and much exercise[71] of speech, exercise and custom[72] with wisdom make an assured and voluble[73] utterance; so is it that old men more then any other sort speak most gravely, wisely, assuredly, and plausibly,[74] which parts are all that can be required in perfect eloquence, and so, in all deliberations of importance where counselors are allowed freely to opine and show their conceits,[75] good persuasion is no less requisite then speech itself, for in great purposes to speak and not to be able or likely to persuade is a vain thing. . . .

Chapter IV. Of Language

Speech is not natural to man, saving for his only ability to speak, and that he is by kind apt to utter all his conceits with sounds and voices[76] di-

---

64. **at large** completely, from start to finish. 65. **rid out of** free oneself of. 66. **insomuch** insofar. 67. **avoid** leave.

68. On Hegesias, see Cicero, *Tusculan Disputations*, I.xxxiv.83.

69. **in special** especially.

70. Puttenham is referring to an account in Lucian's *Herakles* of the so-called Hercules Gallicus, or Gallic Hercules, a figure Lucian says was worshipped as Hermes, the god of eloquence, in a temple in Marseilles. Puttenham may be taking his account not from Lucian directly, but from an emblem ("devise") book, such Andrea Alciati's *Emblemata* (Augsburg, 1531), that included a visual representation along with a description of the figure.

71. **exercise** practice. 72. **custom** habitual use. 73. **voluble** fluent. 74. **plausibly** in a praiseworthy manner. 75. **conceits** ideas, conceptions. 76. **voices** utterances.

versified many manner of ways, by means of the many and fit instruments he hath by nature to that purpose, as a broad and voluble[77] tongue, thin and movable lips, teeth even and not shagged,[78] thick ranged,[79] a round, vaulted palate, and a long throat, besides an excellent capacity of wit[80] that maketh him more disciplinable[81] and imitative than any other creature. Then, as to the form and action of his speech, it cometh to him by art and teaching, and by use or exercise. But after a speech is fully fashioned to the common understanding and accepted by consent of a whole country and nation, it is called a language and receiveth none allowed alteration, but by extraordinary occasions by little and little, as it were, insensibly bringing in of many corruptions that creep along with the time, of all which matters we have more largely spoken in our books of the originals and pedigree of the English tongue.[82] Then, when I say language, I mean the speech wherein the poet or maker writeth, be it Greek or Latin or, as our case is, the vulgar English, and when it is peculiar unto a country, it is called the mother speech of that people—the Greeks term it *idioma*—so is ours at this day the Norman English. Before the conquest of the Normans, it was the Anglo-Saxon, and before that the British, which, as some will, is at this day the Welsh, or as others affirm, the Cornish. I for my part think neither of both, as they be now spoken and pronounced. This part in our maker or poet must be heedily[83] looked unto, that it be natural, pure, and the most usual of all his country, and for the same purpose rather that which is spoken in the king's court, or in the good towns and cities within the land, than in the marches and frontiers, or in port towns, where strangers haunt for traffic sake,[84] or yet in universities where scholars use much peevish affectation of words out of primitive[85] languages, or finally, in any uplandish[86] village or corner of a realm, where is no resort but of poor, rustical, or uncivil people; neither shall he follow the speech of a craftsman or carter,[87] or other of the inferior sort, though he be inhabitant or bred in the best town and city in this realm, for such persons do abuse good speeches by strange accents or ill-shaped sounds and false orthography.[88] But he shall follow generally the better brought up sort, such as the Greeks call *charientes*, men civil and graciously behaviored and bred. Our maker therefore at these days shall not follow [Langland's] *Piers Plowman*, nor Gower, nor Lydgate, nor yet Chaucer, for their language is now out of use with us. Neither shall he take the terms of northernmen, such as they use in daily talk, whether they be noblemen or gentlemen, or of their best clerks[89] all is

---

77. **voluble** fluent.   78. **shagged** rough.   79. **thick ranged** densely arranged, abundant.   80. **wit** intelligence.   81. **disciplinable** teachable.

82. Puttenham's *Originals and Pedigree of the English Tongue* is lost.

83. **heedily** heedfully, with attention.   84. **strangers haunt for traffic sake** foreigners resort to frequently for the sake of business.   85. **primitive** original, ancient (i.e., Greek and Latin).   86. **uplandish** outlandish, rustic, foreign.   87. **carter** peasant.

88. For the requirements that the poet's speech be natural, pure, and usual, see, among others, Cicero, *De oratore*, III.x.37–39.

89. **clerks** learned men who had been to the university.

a matter,[90] nor in effect any speech used beyond the river of Trent; though no man can deny but that theirs is the purer English Saxon at this day, yet it is not so courtly nor so current as our southern English is, no more is the far westernman's speech. Ye shall therefore take the usual speech of the court and that of London and the shires lying about London within 60 miles, and not much above. I say not this, but that in every shire of England there be gentlemen and others that speak, but especially write, as good Southern as we of Middlesex or Surrey do, but not the common people of every shire, to whom the gentlemen and also their learned clerks do for the most part condescend,[91] but herein we are already ruled by the English dictionaries and other books written by learned men, and therefore it needeth none other direction in that behalf. Albeit peradventure some small admonition be not impertinent, for we find in our English writers many words and speeches amendable, and ye shall see in some many inkhorn[92] terms so ill-affected[93] brought in by men of learning, as preachers and schoolmasters, and many strange terms of other languages by secretaries and merchants and travelers, and many dark[94] words and not usual nor well-sounding, though they be daily spoken in court. Wherefore great heed must be taken by our maker in this point, that his choice be good. And peradventure the writer hereof be in that behalf no less faulty than any other, using many strange and unaccustomed words and borrowed from other languages, and in that respect himself no meet[95] magistrate to reform the same errors in any other person, but since he is not unwilling to acknowledge his own fault and can the better tell how to amend it, he may seem a more excusable corrector of other men's; he intendeth[96] therefore for an indifferent[97] way and universal benefit to tax himself first and before any others.

Chapter VII. Of Figures and Figurative Speeches

As figures be the instruments of ornament in every language, so be they also in a sort abuses or rather trespasses in speech, because they pass the ordinary limits of common utterance and be occupied[98] of purpose to deceive the ear and also the mind, drawing it from plainness and simplicity to a certain doubleness, whereby our talk is the more guileful and abusing.[99] For what else is your metaphor but an inversion of sense by transport;[100] your

90. **all is a matter** it's all the same.   91. **condescend** lower oneself graciously (to speak with in their language); condescension is not implied.   92. **inkhorn** pedantic.   93. **ill-affected** diseased.   94. **dark** obscure.   95. **meet** fitting.   96. **intendeth** aims at.   97. **indifferent way** neutral, impartial, middling (manner of speech).   98. **occupied** taken, possessed, seized.

99. Puttenham's definition of figurative speech is derived from classical ones; see Aristotle, *Rhetoric*, III.ii–x; Cicero, *De oratore*, III.xxxviii.155–xl.161; and Quintilian, *Institutio oratoria*, VIII.vi.

100. **transport** transformation ("metaphor" literally means "transport," i.e., the transporting of the meaning of a word from one sense to another).

allegory by a duplicity of meaning or dissimulation under covert and dark intendments;[101] one while speaking obscurely and in riddle called enigma; another while by common proverb or adage called paremia; then by merry scoff called irony; then by bitter taunt called sarcasm; then by periphrasis or circumlocution when all might be said in a word or two; then by incredible comparison giving credit, as by your hyperbole, and many other ways seeking to inveigle and appassionate[102] the mind—which thing made the grave judges Areopagites, as I find written, to forbid all manner of figurative speeches to be used before them in their consistory of justice[103] as mere[104] illusions to the mind and wresters of upright judgment, saying that to all such manner of foreign and colored[105] talk to make the judges affectioned, were all one as if the carpenter before he began to square his timber would make his squire[106] crooked, insomuch as the straight and upright mind of a judge is the very rule of justice till it be perverted by affection.[107] This no doubt is true and was by them gravely considered, but in this case because our maker or poet is appointed not for a judge, but rather for a pleader, and that of pleasant and lovely causes and nothing perilous, such as be those for the trial of life, limb, or livelihood, and before judges neither sour nor severe, but in the ear of princely dames, young ladies, gentlewomen, and courtiers, being all for the most part either meek of nature or of pleasant humor, and that all his abuses tend but to dispose the hearers to mirth and solace by pleasant conveyance and efficacy of speech, they are not in truth to be accounted vices but virtues in the poetical science very commendable. On the other side, such trespasses in speech, whereof there be many, as give dolor[108] and disliking to the ear and mind, by any foul indecency[109] or disproportion of sound, situation,[110] or sense, they be called, and not without cause, the vicious[111] parts or rather heresies of language, wherefore the matter resteth much in the definition and acceptance of this word decorum, for whatsoever is so cannot justly be misliked.[112] In which respect it may come to pass that what the grammarian setteth down for a viciosity in speech may become a virtue and no vice; contrariwise his commended figure may fall into a reproachful fault, the best and most assured remedy whereof is generally to follow the saying of Bias: *ne quid nimis*.[113] So as in keeping measure and not exceeding nor showing any defect in the use of his figures, he cannot lightly do amiss, if he have besides, as that must needs be, a special regard to all the circumstances of the person, place, time, cause and purpose

---

101. **intendments** understandings.   102. **appassionate** impassion, fill with emotion. 103. **consistorie of justice** courtroom.   104. **mere** absolute, total.   105. **colored** rhetorical (figures of speech are the "colors" of rhetoric).   106. **squire** square.

107. The Areopagites were members of the Areopagus, the supreme tribunal of Athens. Puttenham's source for this information is Aristotle, *Rhetoric*, I.i.5.

108. **dolor** sadness, sorrow.   109. **indecency** lack of decorum, inappropriateness. 110. **situation** the placement or arrangement of words.   111. **vicious** faulty.   112. **misliked** disliked.   113. **ne quid nimis** Nothing too much. (The source of this saying is doubtful; see Erasmus, *Adages*, I.vi.96.) Bias was one of the proverbial Seven Sages of Greece.

he hath in hand, which being well observed it easily avoideth all the recited inconveniences, and maketh now and then very vice go[114] for a formal virtue in the exercise of this art.

Chapter XXIII. What It Is That Generally Makes Our Speech Well Pleasing and Commendable, and of That Which the Latins Call Decorum

In all things to use decency[115] is it only that giveth everything his good grace and without which nothing in man's speech could seem good or gracious, insomuch as many times it makes a beautiful figure fall into a deformity, and on the other side, a vicious speech seem pleasant and beautiful; this decency is therefore the line and level for all good makers to do their business by. But herein resteth the difficulty: to know what this good grace is and wherein it consisteth, for peradventure it be easier to conceive than to express, we will therefore examine it to the bottom and say that everything which pleaseth the mind or senses, and the mind by the senses as by means instrumental, doth it for some amiable[116] point or quality that is in it, which draweth them to a good liking and contentment with their proper objects. But that cannot be if they discover any ill-favoredness[117] or disproportion to the parts apprehensive,[118] as, for example, when a sound is either too loud or too low or otherwise confused, the ear is ill-affected;[119] so is the eye if the color be sad[120] or not luminous and recreative,[121] or the shape of a membered[122] body without his due measures and symmetry, and the like of every other sense in his proper function. These excesses or defects or confusions and disorders in the sensible objects are deformities and unseemly to the sense. In like sort the mind for the things that be his mental objects hath his good graces and his bad, whereof the one contents him wondrous well, the other displeaseth him continually, no more nor no less than ye see the discords of music do to a well-tuned ear. The Greeks call this good grace of everything in his kind, *to prepon*, the Latins decorum; we in our vulgar call it by a scholastical term decency; our own Saxon English term is seemliness, that is to say, for his good shape and utter appearance well pleasing the eye; we call it also comeliness for the delight it bringeth coming towards us, and to that purpose may be called pleasant approach, so as every way seeking to express the *prepon* of the Greeks and decorum of the Latins, we are fain in our vulgar tongue to borrow the term which our eye only for his noble prerogative over all the rest of the senses doth usurp, and to apply the same to all good, comely, pleasant, and honest things, even to the spiritual objects of the mind, which stand no less in the due proportion of reason and dis-

---

114. **go** pass.   115. **decency** appropriateness, fitness, propriety.   116. **amiable** worthy of being loved.   117. **ill-favoredness** ugliness.   118. **parts apprehensive** parts capable of apprehension or perception.   119. **is ill-affected** perceives it badly.   120. **sad** dull.   121. **recreative** refreshing.   122. **membered** having members.

course[123] than any other material thing doth in his sensible beauty, proportion, and comeliness.[124]

Now because this comeliness resteth in the good conformity[125] of many things and their sundry circumstances with respect one to another, so as there be found a just correspondence between them by this or that relation, the Greeks call it analogy or a convenient[126] proportion. This lovely conformity, or proportion, or conveniency between the sense and the sensible hath nature herself first most carefully observed in all her own works, then also by kind grafted it in the appetites of every creature working by intelligence to covet and desire, and in their actions to imitate and perform, and of man chiefly before any other creature as well in his speeches as in every other part of his behavior. And this in generality and by an usual term is that which the Latins call decorum. So albeit we before alleged that all our figures be but transgressions of our daily speech, yet if they fall out decently to the good liking of the mind or ear and to the beautifying of the matter or language, all is well; if indecently and to the ear's and mind's misliking, be the figure of itself never so commendable, all is amiss: the election is the writer's, the judgment is the world's, as theirs to whom the reading appertaineth. But since the actions of man with their circumstances be infinite, and the world likewise replenished[127] with many judgments, it may be a question who shall have the determination of such controversy as may arise whether this or that action or speech be decent or indecent. And verily, it seems to go all by discretion, not perchance of everyone, but by a learned and experienced discretion, for otherwise seems the decorum to a weak and ignorant judgment than it doth to one of better knowledge and experience, which showeth that it resteth in the discerning part of the mind, so as he who can make the best and most differences of things by reasonable and witty[128] distinction is to be the fittest judge or sentencer of decency. Such generally is the discreetest man, particularly in any art the most skillful and discreetest, and in all other things for the more part those that be of much observation and greatest experience. The case then standing that discretion must chiefly guide all those business,[129] since there be sundry sorts of discretion all unlike, even as there be men of action or art, I see no way so fit to enable a man truly to estimate of decency as example, by whose verity we may deem the differences of things and their proportions and by particular discussions come at length to sentence[130] of it generally, and also in our behaviors the more easily to put it in execution. But by reason of the sundry circumstances

123. **discourse** discursive understanding.
124. Puttenham's thinking on decorum is indebted to Cicero, *Orator*, xxi.70–xxii.74, and *De oratore*, III.lv.210–212.
125. **conformity** congruity of parts.   126. **convenient** appropriate, fitting.   127. **replenished** filled.   128. **witty** clever, intelligent.   129. **business** activities.
130. **sentence** judgment.

that man's affairs are, as it were, wrapped in, this decency comes to be very much alterable and subject to variety, insomuch as our speech asketh one manner of decency in respect of the person who speaks, another of whom we speak, another of what we speak, and in what place and time and to what purpose. And as it is of speech, so of all other behaviors.

Chapter XXV. That the Good Poet or Maker Ought to Dissemble His Art, and in What Cases the Artificial Is More Commended Than the Natural, and Contrariwise

And now, most excellent Queen, having largely[131] said of poets and poesy and about what matters they be employed, then of all the commended forms of poems, thirdly of metrical proportions, such as do appertain to our vulgar art, and last of all set forth the poetical ornament consisting chiefly in the beauty and gallantness of his language and style, and so have appareled him to our seeming[132] in all his gorgeous habiliments, and pulling him first from the cart to the school, and from thence to the court, and preferred him to your Majesty's service in that place of great honor and magnificence to give entertainment to princes, ladies of honor, gentlewomen and gentlemen, and by his many modes of skill[133] to serve the many humors of men thither haunting and resorting, some by way of solace, some of serious advice, and in matters as well profitable as pleasant and honest.[134] We have in our humble conceit sufficiently performed our promise, or rather duty, to your Majesty in the description of this art, so always as we leave him not unfurnished of one piece that best beseems that place of any other and may serve as a principal good lesson for all good makers to bear continually in mind in the usage[135] of this science: which is, that being now lately become a courtier, he show not himself a craftsman and merit to be disgraded[136] and with scorn sent back again to the shop or other place of his first faculty[137] and calling, but that so wisely and discreetly he behave himself as he may worthily retain the credit of his place and profession of a very courtier, which is, in plain terms, cunningly to be able to dissemble.

(Puttenham goes on to provide a number of examples of the different ways that courtiers feign illness and the like in order to protect themselves and their reputations.)

These and many such like disguisings do we find in man's behavior, and especially in the courtiers of foreign countries, where in my youth I was brought up and very well observed their manner of life and conversation, for of mine own country I have not made so great experience. Which parts,

131. **largely** at length. 132. **to our seeming** in our opinion. 133. **modes of skill** skillful modes.
134. In the first part of this sentence, Puttenham sums up what he has covered in the three books of his work; the Queen is Elizabeth I.
135. **usage** customary use. 136. **disgraded** degraded, lowered in rank socially.
137. **faculty** occupation, profession.

nevertheless, we allow not now in our English maker, because we have given him the name of an honest man, and not of an hypocrite. And therefore, leaving these manner of dissimulations to all base-minded men and of vile[138] nature or mystery,[139] we do allow our courtly poet to be a dissembler only in the subtleties of his art; that is, when he is most artificial, so to disguise and cloak it as it may not appear, nor seem to proceed from him by any study or trade[140] of rules, but to be his natural; nor so evidently to be descried,[141] as every lad that reads him shall say he is a good scholar, but will rather have him to know his art well and little to use it.[142]

138. **vile** base.   139. **mystery** craft, occupation.   140. **trade** practice.   141. **descried** discovered.

142. For Puttenham's notion that the poet must hide his art, see Baldesar Castiglione, *The Book of the Courtier*, I.xxvi, a passage that is based on ideas presented throughout the first book of Cicero's *De oratore*.

[19]

Michel de Montaigne

The French author Michel Eyquem de Montaigne (1533–1592) was one of the most original thinkers of the Renaissance. The son of a wealthy merchant, he was born into a France in the throes of religious war and in a region that was strongly Protestant. Although a brother and a sister converted to the new religion, Montaigne remained a Catholic, but a moderate one who advocated tolerance. He received an ideal humanist education, first from a tutor who taught him Latin years before he learned French, and then from leading humanists at the Collège de Guyenne in Bordeaux. After studying law between 1546 and 1550, Montaigne became a counselor in the Parlement of Bordeaux in 1557. However, when his father died in 1568 and his best friend did so as well a year later, he resigned his office and retired to his estate where he began to write his essays. He was occasionally drawn out of retirement to serve as an intermediary in the religious wars, and in 1580–1581 he made a journey to Germany and Italy, which he recorded in his *Journal du voyage* (*Diary of His Voyage*). Upon returning home, he discovered that he had been elected mayor of Bordeaux, a position he held until 1585. He died at his estate at Montaigne, and it seems likely that had he lived to see Henry IV's coronation in 1594, he would have been offered a position in the government. The first edition of his *Essais* (*Essays*), which contained the first two of its eventual three books, appeared in Bordeaux in 1580. A second edition came out in Paris in 1588, adding the third book as well as many passages interpolated into the first two. In 1595 a posthumous final edition appeared, which included additions Montaigne had written in the margins of his book. The term "essai" means trial or attempt: each individual essay is a trial both of the subject it discusses and of Montaigne's judgment. Although credited with the invention of the essay, he did not refer to individual essays that way, but used the term in the plural for the entire collection. His earliest essays are marked by an inclination toward Stoicism, but most display his characteristic skepticism as well as his tolerance and openness. In them, he evinces a special hostility to the emphasis contemporary education placed on the study of languages rather than the training of the intellect and the judgment. His critical attitude toward rhetoric, evident in "On the Vanity of Words," the fifty-first essay of Book II of the *Essais*, is consistent with his view of education, his insistence on honesty, and the self-revelatory nature of his writing. This translation of that essay is based on the text in his *Essais*, edited by J.-V. Le Clerc (Paris, 1875), I: 459–464.

On the Vanity of Words

A rhetorician from times past used to say that his profession was to make little things appear and be thought to be great ones: that's a shoemaker who knows how to make large shoes for a little foot.[1] They would have had him whipped in Sparta for professing a tricky and lying art, and I believe that Archidamus, who was king there, did not hear without astonishment the response of Thucydides, whom he asked whether he or Pericles was better at wrestling. "That," said he, "would be difficult to determine, for when I've brought him to the ground in wrestling, he persuades those who've seen it that he didn't fall, and he wins the match."[2] Those who mask and make up women do less evil, for not seeing them in their natural condition is a matter of little loss, whereas those others make a profession of deceiving not our eyes, but our judgment, and bastardizing and corrupting the essence of things. Commonwealths that have maintained themselves in a regulated and orderly state, like the Cretan and Lacedemonian ones, have held orators to be of little account.

Ariston wisely defines rhetoric as the art of persuading the people; Socrates and Plato, as the art of deceiving and flattering.[3] The Mohammedans forbid their children to be taught it because of its uselessness.[4] And the Athenians, perceiving to what extent its employment, which had great credit in their city, was pernicious, ordered that the principal part of it, which is the moving of the emotions, should be removed from it, together with the prologues and the perorations.[5]

It is a tool invented to manipulate and stir up a mob and an unruly populace, a tool that is employed only in sick states, like medicine; in states,

1. The saying comes from Plutarch, *Sayings of the Spartans* ("Agesilaus the Great," 3), in *Moralia*, 208c.
2. See Plutarch, *Life of Pericles*, viii.3–4; note that Thucydides is not the historian, but Thucydides the son of Melesias, who was the chief conservative opponent of Pericles in Athens.
3. For Ariston, see Quintilian, *Institutio oratoria*, II.xv.19; for Plato, see *Gorgias*, 462e–466a.
4. From Guillaume Postel, *Histoire des Turcs* (Poitiers, 1560), 36.
5. See Aristotle, *Rhetoric*, I.i.4–6, and Quintilian, *Institutio oratoria*, II.xvi.4.

such as those of Athens, Rhodes, and Rome, where the crowd, where the ignorant, where all the people had power over all things, and where things were in a perpetual tempest, there the orators flooded in. And in truth, one sees few people in those states who forced their way to great reputations without the aid of eloquence. Pompey, Caesar, Crassus, Lucullus, Lentulus, Metellus drew from it the great support needed in order to climb up to the heights of authority they finally arrived at, and they helped themselves by its means more than by means of arms—something contrary to the opinion of the best times. For L. Volumnius, speaking in public in favor of the election of Q. Fabius and P. Decius as consuls, said, "These are people born for war, great in deeds, clumsy in the combat of babbling, truly consular spirits. Those who are subtle, eloquent, and knowledgeable are good to stay in the city as praetors to administer justice."[6]

Eloquence flourished most at Rome when affairs were in the worst condition and were disturbed by the storm of the civil wars, just as a field that is free and untamed bears the strongest weeds. From that it seems that the governments that depend on a monarch have less need of it than do others, for the foolishness and pliability that are found in the common people and that make them subject to manipulation and to being led about by the ears to the sweet sound of that harmony, without weighing things and coming to understand the truth about them through the force of reason, this pliability, I say, is not found so easily in a single individual, and it is easier to protect him by means of a good education and good counsel from being affected by that poison. One has never seen an orator of renown come out of Macedonia or Persia.

I have said these words on this subject prompted by an Italian with whom I have just been talking and who served the late Cardinal Carafa as chief steward until his death. I made him tell me about his post. He made a speech for me about the art of the gullet with a gravity and magisterial countenance as if he had been speaking about some important point in theology. He deciphered the different appetites for me: the one we have before eating; the one we have after the second and third course; the means, now of simply pleasing it, now of arousing and stimulating it; the ordering of his sauces, first generally, and then particularizing the qualities of their ingredients and their effects; the differences among salads according to the season, the one that must be warmed, the one that must be served cold, the way to adorn and embellish them to make them even more pleasant to the sight. After that, he started on the order of the service, full of beautiful and important considerations,

6. Livy, *Ab urbe condita*, X.xxii.6–7. Lucius Volumnius Flamma was a Roman general who led the army against the Samnites; he was consul in 307 and 296 B.C. Quintus Fabius Maximus Rullianus and Publius Decius Mus were also generals; the first served as consul in 322, 310, 297, and 295 B.C., while the second did so in 308, 297, and 295 B.C., dying heroically in this last year fighting the Samnites.

> and truly it does make a great difference
> how you cut up hares and how, a hen.[7]

And all this puffed up with rich and magnificent words, and those the same ones we use to treat the governing of an empire. He made me think of a man of mine:

> "That's too salty; that's burnt; that's not cleaned enough;
> That's just right; remember to do it thus another time."
> I advise them as I can with what wisdom I have.
> Finally, Demea, I order them to look into the dishes
> As into a mirror, and teach them what they should do.[8]

To be sure, even the Greeks greatly praised the order and arrangement that Aemilius Paulus observed at the feast that he made for them on his return from Macedonia.[9] But I am not talking at all about actions here; I am talking about words.

I don't know if it happens with others as it does with me, but when I hear our architects swell up with those fat words, such as pilasters, architraves, cornices, Corinthian and Doric work, and similar words from their jargon, I cannot prevent myself from immediately taking possession of the palace of Apollidon in my imagination—and in reality I find that these are the wretched parts of the door to my kitchen.[10]

When you hear people say metonymy, metaphor, allegory, and other such names in grammar, doesn't it seem they mean some rare and exotic kind of language? These are terms that apply to the babbling of your chambermaid.

It's a deception close to this one to call the offices of our state by the proud titles of the Romans, although there is no similarity in responsibilities, and still less in authority and power.[11] And this one, too—which will one day serve, in my opinion, as evidence for the singular ineptitude of our century—of unworthily using the most glorious surnames for whoever seems good to us, surnames with which antiquity honored one or two people during several centuries. Plato won the epithet of "divine" by universal consent, and no one ever sought to begrudge it him; and the Italians, who boast, and with reason, of generally having livelier minds and sounder rational faculties than the other nations of their time, have just bestowed the term as a gift on Aretino, in whom, except for a style of speech that is bloated and

---

7. Juvenal, *Saturae*, V.123–24.

8. Terence, *Adelphoe* (*The Brothers*) III.415–29. These lines are spoken by a servant to Demea, an old man who is one of the two brothers of the title.

9. See Plutarch, *Life of Aemilius Paulus*, xxviii.4.

10. The palace of Apollidon, created by a necromancer, is described in *Amadís de Gaula*, II.i and IV.ii.

11. For instance, magistrates in the Parlement of Paris called themselves *sénateurs*.

bubbling over with witticisms, truly ingenious, but far-fetched and fantastic—in short, beyond his eloquence, such as it may be—I do not see there is
anything that transcends the ordinary authors of his century, so far is he
from approaching the divinity of the ancients. And the epithet of "great":
we attach it to princes who have nothing above the greatness of the common
people.

[20]

Henry Peacham

The Englishman Henry Peacham (1546–1634) entered the ministry in 1574 and obtained the living of North Mimms in Hertfordshire, where his son, also named Henry and the author of *The Compleat Gentleman*, was born in 1578. In that year, Peacham acquired the living of North Leverton in Lincolnshire, where he apparently remained until his death. He brought out the first edition of *The Garden of Eloquence* in 1577 and a second edition in 1593. He is also considered the author of "A Sermon on the Last Three Verses of the Book of Job," which appeared in 1590. The *Garden* is a manual of style consisting of a list of figures of speech, each of which is defined and illustrated, and is then followed (in the 1593 edition) by two sections, one specifying the uses to which the figure may be put, and a second one, the "caution," warning of the dangers attendant upon its use. The structure of the *Garden* follows that of Joannes Susenbrotus's *Epitome troporum ac schematum grammaticorum et rhetoricorum (An Epitome of the Tropes and Schemes of Grammarians and Rhetoricians)*, which was published in 1540, although Peacham adds material from classical writers such as Cicero and Quintilian, and from Renaissance ones, including Trapezuntius, Erasmus, and Melanchthon. Peacham classifies all figures of speech as either tropes, which alter the sense of a word, or schemes, which are concerned with the arrangement of words, and he then creates further divisions and subdivisions for each category. The last two subdivisions of the schemes (Peacham calls them "orders"), namely schemes that create the impression of vehemence and emotion, and schemes that amplify one's speech, take up the most space in Peacham's book. Peacham's organization of his work in terms of binary oppositions and his use of definitions and illustrations for individual figures all suggest he was affected by Ramus's methods as well as his redefinition of rhetoric that limited it to style. The following excerpts from the *Garden* are taken from the facsimile reproduction of the 1593 edition that was published with an introduction by William G. Crane (Gainesville, Fla.: Scholars' Facsimiles and Reprints, 1954).

Henry Peacham

From *The Garden of Eloquence*

(Peacham opens his book with a dedication to Sir John Puckering, Lord Keeper of the Great Seal.)

The argument whereof [i.e., of this book], albeit I confess it subject to the exceptions of many, and peradventure to the reprehensions of some which seem to make a divorce between nature and art and a separation between policy[1] and humanity, yet Cicero, being both a most excellent orator and prudent politic,[2] doth mightily support and defend it against all objections, as we may plainly see in one short sentence of his (among many other tending to this purpose) where he saith: "Ut hominis decus est ingenium, sic ingenii lumen est eloquentia."[3] That is: as wit is man's worship, or wisdom man's honor, so eloquence is the light and brightness of wisdom, in which sentence he both expresseth the singular praises of two most worthy virtues and also enforceth the necessity and commendeth the utility of their excellent conjunction. And true it is that if we join with this prudent orator in a diligent inquisition and contemplation of wisdom, and in a deliberate consideration of art, we shall see that verified which he hath here affirmed. For if we inquire what wisdom is, we shall find that it is the knowledge of divine and human things; if whose gift it is, we shall be certified that it is the gift of God; if we consider the inventions thereof, they are wonderful; if the works, they are infinite; if the fruits, they are in use sweet, in nature necessary, both for the search of truth and for the direction of human life. Briefly, this virtue is the loving and provident mother of mankind, whom she nourisheth with the sweet milk of prosperity, defendeth against manifold dangers, instructeth with her counsel, and preferreth to the imperial dominion over all earthly creatures. And lest dissenting with himself he should by his own contention work his own confusion, she deviseth laws to support equity and appointeth punishments to repress injury; she inventeth the art and skill of war to resist violence offending against peace; she maintaineth the one and directeth the other, and is the mighty empress of them both.

Finally, by her the true felicity of man is found out and held up; without her it falleth by a sudden and woeful ruin. By her his honor is highly advanced; without her it sinketh into shame and reproach and is utterly confounded. By her he is endowed with a blessed state of life; without her he perisheth in misery and death. Now, lest so excellent a gift of the divine goodness (as wisdom here appeareth to be, and is) should lie suppressed by silence and so remain hid in darkness, almighty God, the deep sea of wisdom and bright sun of majesty, hath opened the mouth of man, as the mouth of a plentiful fountain, both to pour forth the inward passions of his heart

---

1. **policy**   prudence; a prudent course of action.   2. **politic**   politician.
3. *Brutus*, xv.59: "As intelligence is the glory of man, so the light of intelligence is eloquence." (Peacham translates Cicero's statement in his next sentence.)

and also as a heavenly planet to show forth by the shining beams of speech the privy thoughts and secret conceits of his mind. By the benefit of this excellent gift—I mean of apt speech given by nature and guided by art—wisdom appeareth in her beauty, showeth her majesty, and exerciseth her power, working in the mind of the hearer partly by a pleasant proportion and as it were by a sweet and musical harmony, and partly by the secret and mighty power of persuasion after a most wonderful manner. This then is the virtue which the orator, in his praise before mentioned, calleth eloquence and the brightness of wisdom, so that by the mean hereof, as well the rare inventions and pleasant devises as the deep understanding, the secret counsels, and politic[4] considerations of wisdom are most effectually expressed and most comely beautified. For even as by the power of the sunbeams the nature of the root is showed in the blossom and the goodness of the sap tasted in the sweetness of the fruit, even so the precious nature and wonderful power of wisdom is by the commendable art and use of eloquence produced and brought into open light. So that hereby plainly appeareth both the great necessity and singular utility of their conjunction before commended, for the one without the other do find both great want and show great imperfection. For to possess great knowledge without apt utterance is as to possess great treasure without use; contrariwise, to affect eloquence without the discretion of wisdom is as to handle a sweet instrument of music without skill. But the man which is well furnished with both—I mean with ample knowledge and excellent speech—hath been judged able and esteemed fit to rule the world with counsel, provinces with laws, cities with policy, and multitudes with persuasion. Such were those men in times past who by their singular wisdom and eloquence made savage nations civil, wild people tame, and cruel tyrants not only to become meek, but likewise merciful.[5] Hence it was that in ancient time men did attribute so great opinion of wisdom to the eloquent orators of those days that they called them sacred, holy, divine, and the interpreters of the gods. For so doth Horace commending Orpheus; his words be these:

> Agrestes homines sacer interpresque deorum,
> Caedibus, et foedo victu deterruit Orpheus:
> Dictus ob id, lenire tigres rigidosque leones.[6]

The poet here under the name of tigers and lions meant not beasts but men, and such men as by their savage nature and cruel manners might well be

4. **politic** political, i.e., pertaining to the state; shrewd, prudent.
5. Peacham here rehearses the myth of the orator as civilizer found in numerous ancient texts; for examples, see Cicero, *De inventione*, I.ii.2–3, Quintilian, *Institutio oratoria*, II.xvi.9, and Horace, *Ars poetica*, 391–401.
6. *Ars poetica*, 391–93: "Orpheus, seer and interpreter of the gods, turned savage men from murder and a shameful way of life, whence it is said that he tamed tigers and fierce lions." (Note that modern editions of Horace have a slightly different version of these lines.)

compared to fierce tigers and devouring lions, which notwithstanding, by the mighty power of wisdom and prudent art of persuasion, were converted from that most brutish condition of life to the love of humanity and politic government.[7] So mighty is the power of this happy union—I mean of wisdom and eloquence—that by the one the orator forceth and by the other he allureth and by both so worketh that what he commendeth is beloved, what he dispraiseth is abhorred, what he persuadeth is obeyed, and what he dissuadeth is avoided, so that he is in a manner the emperor of men's minds and affections and next to the omnipotent God in the power of persuasion by grace and divine assistance.[8] The principal instruments of man's help in this wonderful effect are those figures and forms of speech contained in this book, which are the fruitful branches of elocution and the mighty streams of eloquence, whose utility, power, and virtue I cannot sufficiently commend, but speaking by similitude, I say they are as stars to give light, as cordials to comfort, as harmony to delight, as pitiful spectacles to move sorrowful passions, and as orient colors to beautify reason. Finally, they are as martial instruments both of defense and invasion, and being so, what may be either more necessary or more profitable for us than to hold those weapons always ready in our hands, wherewith we may defend ourselves, invade our enemies, revenge our wrongs, aid the weak, deliver the simple from dangers, conserve true religion, and confute idolatry? For look what the sword may do in war, this virtue may perform in peace, yet with great difference, for that with violence, this with persuasion, that with shedding of blood, this with piercing the affections, that with desire of death, this with special regard of life. . . .

(Peacham opens his book by distinguishing between tropes and schemes. He then begins his presentation of individual figures of speech with tropes of words, that is, with tropes involving just single words, the first of which is metaphor.)

Metaphora

Metaphora is artificial translation[9] of one word from the proper signification to another not proper, but yet nigh and like.

The Efficient Cause of a Metaphor. It is apparent that memory is the principal efficient[10] of a metaphor, for being the retentive power of the mind, it is the treasure house of man's knowledge, which as it possesseth the forms of known things, so is it ready at all times to present them to man's

---

7. **politic government** lawful or constitutional and orderly rule.

8. Cf. Cicero, *De oratore*, I.viii.30–32.

9. **artificial translation** the artful transferring of something from one place to another. (Note that *translatio* is the Latin word for metaphor and that Peacham uses "metaphor" and "translation" interchangeably.)

10. **efficient** the cause that makes effects to be what they are.

use, as often as occasion and cause doth necessarily require. As, for example, he that hath seen a caterpillar eating and devouring the tender buds and blossoms of trees and plants, and after this shall see an idle person living by the spoil of other men's labors, is put in mind to call him a caterpillar. He that hath seen a gulf or gaping sink[11] swallowing a continual stream or mighty quantity of water, and afterward shall see a man consuming his substance and patrimony in prodigality and riot,[12] is put in mind to call him a gulf of patrimony or a sink of wealth.

It is to be confessed, notwithstanding, that memory worketh not all alone in the framing of translations, but hath exact judgment always to help her, for memory presenteth the former part of the comparison and judgment applieth the latter. For a man may easily remember what he hath seen, but yet if he want[13] discreet judgment, he cannot aptly compare to it the thing that he now seeth, although there be some fit similitude between them and also some necessary occasion to use it. And therefore ample knowledge, perfect memory, and exact judgment joining together in one mind are the principal and special causes of all apt and excellent translations. . . .

The Use of Metaphors.   All metaphors have their manifold fruits, and the same both profitable and pleasant, which is a thing well known to men of learning and wisdom. First, they give pleasant light to dark things, thereby removing unprofitable and odious obscurity. Secondly, by the aptness of their proportion and nearness of affinity, they work in the hearer many effects: they obtain allowance of his judgment, they move his affections, and minister a pleasure to his wit. Thirdly, they are forcible to persuade. Fourthly, to commend or dispraise. Fifthly, they leave such a firm impression in the memory as is not lightly forgotten.

The Comparison of Metaphors.   Metaphors in respect of their perspicuity and light which they give may well be compared to the stars of the sky, which are both the comfort of the night and the beauty of the firmament. 2. In respect of their aptness to make descriptions, they are not only as pleasant colors of all kinds, but also as ready pencils to line out and shadow any manner of proportion in nature. 3. In respect of their firm impression in the mind and remembrance of the hearer, they are as seals upon soft wax or as deep stamps in long-lasting metal.

The Caution.   In the choice and use of translations heed ought to be taken that these faults be not found in metaphors. First, that there be not an unlikeness instead of a likeness, as if one should say, the bull barketh, which is very unlike. Secondly, that the similitude be not far-fetched, as from strange

11. **sink** a conduit or drain carrying things away; a place where things are swallowed or lost.   12. **riot** wanton or wasteful living.   13. **want** lack.

things unknown to the hearer, as if one should take metaphors from the parts of a ship and apply them among husbandmen which never came at the sea, he shall obscure the thing that he would fainest make evident. Thirdly, that there be no unclean or unchaste signification contained in the metaphor, which may offend against modest and reverent minds. Fourthly, that the similitude be not greater than the matter requireth, or contrariwise less.

(After discussing seven other tropes of words, Peacham turns to tropes of sentences, of which he identifies ten, beginning with allegory.)

Allegoria

Allegoria, called of Quintilian *Inversio*, is a trope of a sentence, or term of speech, which expresseth one thing in words and another in sense.[14] In a metaphor there is a translation of one word only; in an allegory, of many, and for that cause an allegory is called a continued metaphor.

The Use of This Figure. The use of an allegory serveth most aptly to engrave the lively images of things, and to present them under deep shadows to the contemplation of the mind, wherein wit and judgment take pleasure, and the remembrance receiveth a long-lasting impression. And there as a metaphor may be compared to a star in respect of beauty, brightness, and direction, so may an allegory be fitly likened to a sign compounded of many stars, which of the Grecians is called *astron*, and of the Latins *sidus*, which we may call a constellation, that is, a company or conjunction of many stars.

The Caution. In speaking by allegories, strange similitudes and unknown translations ought to be avoided, lest the allegory, which should be pleasant, become peevish and altogether unprofitable. Also, unlikeness of the comparisons do make the allegory absurd.

(After finishing his discussion of tropes, Peacham turns to schemes, dividing them into three groups or orders. The first order is concerned with individual words and contains twenty-five different figures, beginning with epanaphora.)

Epanaphora

Epanaphora, or anaphora, is a form of speech which beginneth diverse members still with one and the same word. . . .

The Use of This Figure. The use hereof is chiefly to repeat a word of importance and effectual signification, as to repeat the cause before his singular effects, or contrariwise, the effect before his several causes, or any other

14. For Quintilian's translation of the Greek *allegoria* as *inversio*, or inversion, see *Institutio oratoria*, VIII.vi.44.

word of principal account. It serveth also pleasantly to the ear, both in the respects of the repetition and also of the variety of the new clause.

The Caution. Although this figure be an exornation[15] of great use, yet it may be too often used in an oration. Secondly, the repetitions ought not to be many; I mean the word ought not to be repeated too oft, as some do use it in a most wearisome tautology. Thirdly, heed ought to be taken that the word which is least worthy or most weak be not taken to make the repetition, for that were very absurd.

Figures of Sentences

Figures of sentences are those by which either our affections are elegantly expressed or matters mightily magnified. The difference between the figures of words and the figures of sentences is great, found both in their forms and effects. For the figures of words are as it were effeminate and musical; the figures of sentences are manly and martial. Those of words are as it were the color and beauty; these of sentences are as the life and affection, which are divided into figures of affection and figures of amplification.

The Second Order

Figures of the second order are such as do make the oration not only pleasant and plausible, but also very sharp and vehement, by which the sundry affections and passions of the mind are properly and elegantly uttered, and that either by the figures of exclamation, moderation, consultation, or permission.

(Peacham supplies fifty-six figures of the second order, including philophronesis, which falls into the suborder of figures of moderation, and parrhesia, which falls into that of figures of permission.)

Philophronesis

Philophronesis, in Latin *benevolentia* and *exceptio benigna*, is a form of speech by which the speaker, perceiving the might of his adversary to be too great and too strong against him, useth gentle speech, fair promises, and humble submission to mitigate the rigor and cruelty of his adversary.[16] We have a notable example hereof in Jacob, who, fearing the malice and might of

---

15. **exornation**   decoration, embellishment.
16. *Benevolentia* means "good will," and *exceptio benigna,* "a favorable restriction or interpretation."

his brother Esau, used this means to appease his rage and cruelty.[17] He cometh before his family; as soon as he saw Esau, he showed a sign of dutiful submission: he bowed himself seven times most humbly before he came near to him, calling him his lord, and himself his servant. His family, also children, came likewise in seemly and suppliant order, and humbled themselves at his presence, yielding obeisance and reverence unto him, by means whereof the fiery and flaming wrath of Esau was turned into tears of compassion. . . .

The Use of This Figure. The use of this figure is of a singular virtue, both in respect of civil policy and spiritual wisdom. In respect of civil policy it often appeaseth the malice of enemies, mollifieth the cruel hearts of tyrants, saveth the life of innocents, and preventeth the destruction of cities and countries, which the histories of times do sufficiently confirm. In respect of spiritual wisdom, this form of humble submission of man to his high judge and imperial prince moveth compassion, turneth away his heavy displeasure, and obtaineth grace and mercy. If Ahab being a wicked man found favor in God's sight to escape present punishment due to his iniquity only by humbling himself before Him, how much more shall good men in the true and contrite humility of repentance prevail with the same God, who never desireth the death of a sinner, but rather that he may convert and live?[18]

The Caution. The counterfeit submission of hypocrites is opposed to the true use of this figure which is well observed by Jesus Sirach who described it thus: "There is some," saith he, "that being about wicked purposes do bow down themselves and are sad, whose inward part burn altogether with deceit."[19] And also he showeth that such a one under color of humble submission will execute his malice upon thee before thou shalt be able to prevent him.

Parrhesia

Parrhesia is a form of speech by which the orator, speaking before those whom he feareth or ought to reverence, and having somewhat to say that may either touch themselves or those whom they favor, preventeth the displeasure and offense that might be taken, as by craving pardon aforehand, or by some other like form of humble submission and modest insinuation. . . .

17. See Genesis 33:1–4.
18. For Ahab, see 1 Kings 21:27–29.
19. See Ecclesiasticus, or the Wisdom of Jesus Son of Sirach 19:26. Ecclesiasticus was considered one of the apocryphal books of the Bible by most Renaissance Protestants, but the Church of England accepted its being read in church, while denying that it had the same authority as Scripture. In the Anchor Bible, the verse is translated: "There is the wicked who is bowed in grief, but is full of guile within"; see *The Wisdom of Ben Sira*, trans. Patrick W. Skehan, intro. Alexander A. Di Lella (New York: Doubleday, 1987).

The Use of This Figure.   This figure serveth to insinuate, admonish, and reprehend, and may fitly be called the herald or ambassador of speech, which is the only form that boldly delivereth to great dignities and most high degrees of men the message of justice and equity, sparing neither magistrates that pervert laws, nor princes that do abuse their kingdoms.

The Caution.   This figure doth best beseem a man of wisdom and gravity, who is best able to moderate the form of his speech and to restrain it from that rude boldness which doth more hurt than good, from whence there oft springeth a malice in the hearer against the speaker, a contempt of his doctrine, and sometimes a punishment of his person, for now and then a rude *Vae vobis* doth cause a *Coram nobis*.[20] As for the prophets, they were extraordinary men, and therefore their examples in this respect are not to be imitated.

(In the last part of his book Peacham discusses the third order of figures of sentences, that is, figures of amplification, a category that contains seventy different figures, including prosopopeia.)

Amplification: What It Is

Amplification is a certain affirmation very great and weighty, which by large and plentiful speech moveth the minds of the hearers and causeth them to believe that which is said.

The Use of Amplification.   This exornation was first devised to increase causes and to augment the oration with words and sentences, whereby the hearers might the sooner be moved to like of that which was spoken. And indeed it is a singular art and mighty to delight and persuade the minds of men to the purpose and drift of the speaker. It is full of light, plenty, and variety, causing the orator to teach and tell things plainly, to amplify largely, and to prove and conclude mightily. For being well furnished with skill and habit of this figure, he may prevail much in drawing the minds of his hearers to his own will and affection; he may wind them from their former opinions, and quite alter the former state of their minds; he may move them to be of his side, to hold with him, to be led by him, as to mourn or to marvel, to love or to hate, to be pleased or to be angry, to favor, to desire or to be satisfied, to fear or to hope, to envy, to abhor, to pity, to rejoice, to be ashamed, to repent, and finally, to be subject to the power of his speech whithersoever it tendeth.[21] The orator by help hereof either renteth all in

20. *Vae vobis* means "woe unto you"; *Coram nobis*, "in our presence," is a phrase used by a superior commanding an inferior to appear in his presence at once.
21. Cf. Cicero, *De oratore*, I.viii.32.

pieces like the thunder, or else, by little and little, like the flowing water, creepeth by gentle means into the consent of his hearers.

Prosopopeia

Prosopopeia, the feigning of a person, that is, when to a thing senseless and dumb we feign a fit person or attribute a person to a commonwealth or multitude. This figure orators do use as well as poets. The orator by this figure maketh the commonwealth to speak, to commend, to dispraise, to ask, to complain, also life and death, virtue and pleasure, honesty and profit, wealth and poverty, envy and charity to contend and plead one against another. And sometimes he raiseth again as it were the dead to life and bringeth them forth complaining or witnessing what they knew. Sometimes to cities, towns, beasts, birds, trees, stones, weapons, fire, water, lights of the firmament, and such like things he attributeth speech, reason, and affection, and to no other end than to further his purpose and to confirm and make his cause evident. . . .

The Use of This Figure. This figure is an apt form of speech to complain, to accuse, to reprehend, to confirm, and to commend, but the use of it ought to be very rare, then chiefly when the orator, having spent the principal strength of his arguments, is as it were constrained to call for help and aid elsewhere, not unlike to a champion, having broken his weapons in the force of his conflict, calleth for new of his friends or of such as favor his person and cause, or to an army having their number diminished or their strength enfeebled, to crave and call for a new supply.

The Caution. It is not convenient that the orator should use the help of feigned persons without some urgent cause compelling him thereunto. Secondly, it is necessary to provide that the person feigned may speak to the purpose of the matter propounded and give strength to the fainting cause and also minister a pleasure to the hearer. For otherwise, this figure shall be used without cause, speak without profit, and be applied without pleasure.

[21]

Juan de Guzman

Juan de Guzman was most likely born in Seville before or during the middle years of the sixteenth century. He studied with the celebrated professor Francisco Sanchez de la Brozas at Salamanca and eventually taught humanities in Pontevedra in Galicia and then in Alcalá. It is likely that he made several trips to the Americas where he probably saw service as a soldier. He was best known in the Renaissance for his annotated translation of Vergil's *Georgics, Las Georgicas de Virgilio*, published in Salamanca in 1586. His rhetoric treatise, *La Primera parte de la Rhetorica (The First Part of Rhetoric)*, appeared three years later. It consists of a prologue, in which he explains that he is writing only about the first part of rhetoric, that is, deliberative rhetoric, although he claims that it is the principal part from which all the others may be derived. The prologue is followed by fourteen dialogues, each of which he calls a "combite," that is, a convivium or symposium, a kind of dialogue that stresses informality of mood and discussion. He says he decided to write this way in order to avoid the dryness of most treatises as well as to imitate the ancients. The dialogues, which cover almost all the aspects of rhetoric, have just two speakers, the teacher Master Fernando de Boan, who was a fellow professor at Pontevedra, and Don Luis Gaytan, whom Guzman identifies as a nobleman who was his pupil. The extract translated below comes from the first convivium, which is generally concerned with the nature and purpose of rhetoric. It is based on the edition of the work published in Alcalá de Henares in 1589.

FROM *The First Part of Rhetoric*

Convivium I[1]

Master Fernando. Rhetoric, according to Aristotle in the first book of his *Rhetoric* and Cicero in the first book of his *On Invention*, is the faculty or

1. The rest of the title reads: "Concerning Orators, in which is discussed what rhetoric is, its goal, material, utility, and how many kinds of cases there are and what material they

art of speaking well whose end is to persuade, although it's true that Saint Isidore in the first chapter of the second book of his *Etymologies* defines it as an art.[2] In reality any one of those three terms truly squares well with rhetoric. Its being an art suits it because of the close connection it has with dialectic, or logic, for these two terms are often confused, and that is why our most learned Brocense did not hesitate to entitle his art of rhetoric *The Instrument of Dialectic.* And although I have to admit that logic treats things at greater length—for which reason they call it an art—than rhetoric does, and that rhetoric is much briefer in this case when compared to logic, I say that in the same way that someone who has the skill to make a logical proposition is considered a logician, this art [of rhetoric] should quite simply be considered an art, since it accomplishes many things that are counted as belonging to the art of logic. Furthermore, we know that Zeno made logic and rhetoric such close relatives, when he compared logic to a closed hand or fist and rhetoric to an open hand.[3] And if logic is called an art because it contains precepts, there is no reason why the word won't suit rhetoric, since it has so many of them and such good ones, so that if men observe the order it teaches and make sure to practice it, they will be able to discuss any subject proposed to them in so orderly and harmonious a manner that they will cause everyone else to marvel. Nor do others err who call rhetoric a faculty, since it is a certain virtue and power that nature has given to men in order to reveal themselves. Thus, I find there is a difference between those who have studied the art of rhetoric and those who have not learned it, namely that rhetoricians discuss things in an orderly and harmonious manner, in such a way that they very seldom merit reproach, whereas those who lack this art always turn things upside down, for all that they may be logicians and learned men. Although they may have very good intellects, they will err because of the fear they carry with them of not knowing this art and understanding whether things are arranged in a good and harmonious order. Thus, all those who lack what this art teaches go about like blind men, feeling their way with a cane. This business of arrangement in rhetoric is so very difficult that I cannot fault someone who might scold Cicero about the organization of his material.[4] For this reason, the student of eloquence should devote the greatest diligence to the arrangement of his subject. Thus, if someone were well trained in this art and knew how to maintain the correct order when he speaks and to use the true method of composition, he would always amplify his discourse, would proceed from the

---

require. Also, what an Idea is, how this faculty may be acquired, the qualities one must have in order to be a perfect orator, and of the benefits of writing and the antiquity of eloquence."

2. See Aristotle, *Rhetoric,* I.ii.1; Cicero, *De inventione,* I.i.2 and I.v.6; and Isidore of Seville, *Etymologiae,* II.i.1.

3. See, for example, Quintilian, *Institutio oratoria,* II.xx.7.

4. See Quintilian, *Institutio oratoria,* XII.i.22.

lesser to the greater aspects of his subject, and would skillfully make use of a certain praiseworthy clarity. Therefore, one may conclude from this how marvelous this art is, as we have seen in Demosthenes, Cicero, and other truly eloquent men, who, because they knew how to make use of it, astounded the world.

Don Luis. I would like you to resolve a few doubts for me about things I do not understand in this subject. For I would say, considering the definition you gave of rhetoric and the end you determined for it—which is to persuade—that Cicero is not a rhetorician since in some orations he failed to persuade.

Master Fernando. That Cicero failed to persuade and is thus no rhetorician is not a good argument, because in the same way that the doctor who applies the necessary remedies his art teaches him to illnesses is not to blame if he fails to make a sick person healthy—even if the latter should die— nor does the doctor lose the name of doctor, since the humors [of the patient] were corrupted to such a degree that human remedies were of no avail, so the orator does not stop being an orator if he has spoken about his subject in a well-ordered and harmonious manner, even if he never persuades anyone, as Aristotle teaches us in the first book of his *Topics*.[5] On the contrary, he will be a consummate orator, according to our way of speaking, if he doesn't omit any item from among all the things that seem to be necessary in order to persuade—which should be the proper office and goal of the orator.

Don Luis. I think I could disprove this doctrine about the office of the orator, and here's my argument. A person who has good graces and beauty attracts people to himself and persuades them merely by means of his looks, and these pleasant, delightful meadows right here are now doing the same thing, as do those that are described for us in Tempe in Thessaly.[6] And what can we say about the lodestone that draws and "persuades" iron to come to it, or about the aetites stone, called the eagle stone by the common people, which, when shaken, seems to make a sound from within, and which, when placed in the navel, is known to persuade the baby not to come out of the womb, but placed lower, makes it move down and come out?[7] In the same way, the simple folk have found out many other things that medicine has accepted and that have their own functions that are appropriate to them. Thus, persuasion isn't an office just proper to the orator, since it pertains to other things besides orators.

5. Aristotle, *Topics*, II.iii.110a23–111a8; cf. Quintilian, *Institutio oratoria*, II.xvii.18.
6. The Vale of Tempe was a beautiful valley sacred to Apollo between Mounts Olympus and Ossa in Thessaly; for one of many references, see Ovid, *Metamorphoses*, I.568–82. Guzman commented on Tempe in his annotated translation of Vergil's *Georgics*; see n. 46 on the second book in *Georgicas de Virgilio* (Salamanca, 1586), fol. 133–34.
7. The aetites stone, a hollow pebble with a loose nucleus, derived its popular name from supposedly being found in eagles' nests and had various magical and medical properties attributed to it; see Pliny, *Naturalis historia*, X.iv.12, and XXXVI.xxxix.49–51.

Master Fernando. I'm very happy that you're arguing with me, because that way you'll understand my reasoning better. One must make certain distinctions concerning the office of persuasion in terms of what is and is not proper to it: its proper use involves arguments about oppositions and similarities, comparisons, witnesses, and authorities, which are the things that actually persuade people. Thus this office will belong solely to the orator, since he alone uses it in this manner. The mode that other things, such as beauty and freshness and the rest of the things you mentioned, employ to persuade others is also called persuasion, except that that usage is not proper insofar as their persuading is done by means of the silent power of attraction that those things possess within themselves.

Besides pursuing the end of rhetoric, which is persuasion, this faculty [of eloquence] also possesses a material on which it exercises its powers. For just as a carpenter practices his art on a piece of wood, which is his material, and the surgeon practices his on wounds, which are likewise his material, so, no more no less, the material serving the art of oratory or rhetoric will be everything that that art chooses to handle. Consequently, the difference I see between this art and the rest is that the others have their determined boundaries in the same way that water does which does not exceed the point fixed for it by divine commandment, while rhetoric is like the air, which, situated beneath the hollow of the moon and the element of fire, totally surrounds what serves as its boundary and passes through and penetrates it and transforms itself into all things created here. This is just what our Guzman explained in his annotations on the fourth book of the *Georgics*, that Proteus in its etymological sense meant the primal matter, which is that which is converted into all the things created in this lower world, and because this was such a lofty secret, there was no learned man among the ancients who did not write about it, as Homer did in the fourth book of the *Odyssey*, and Ovid in the fight of Python and Apollo and in the fable of Hermaphroditus.[8] So I say that, in exactly the same way, rhetoric is like another Proteus, which transforms itself into everything it desires and takes everything as its material. If it handles medicine, rhetoric takes over all the doctrines medicine possesses, and those are its material. If it handles philosophy, it does exactly the same thing, just as it does with mathematics or theology. Consequently, if one or another of those subjects was to be discussed by someone, and he presented them using a good arrangement that was in conformity with reason, while observing the true method of composition and

8. Proteus was a sea deity, to whom Poseidon, the god of the sea, gave the power to change his shape and to utter prophecies; on him see Homer, *Odyssey*, IV.383–570, and Vergil, *Georgics*, IV.387–529. Python (or Pytho) was a serpent generated from the slime of the earth after the flood and was slain by Apollo; see *Metamorphoses*, I.438–44. Hermaphroditus, the son of Hermes and Aphrodite, was loved by the nymph Salmacis, who wanted to be united with him forever and who got her wish as the two of them were transformed into a single being; see *Metamorphoses*, IV.285–388.

displaying discretion, dexterity, and elegance, we would say he was an eloquent man. But at the moment in which some defect were found in him—if he were crude, put things upside down, and spoke with a poorly ornamented style—he would not be called eloquent or merit the name of orator.

Don Luis. How can we understand the division of the genres of oratory, since I have seen that there are controversies about this subject?

Master Fernando. The poet Hesiod suggested an answer in his *Theogony* through the figure of Chimera, saying that this animal has three heads, those of a lion, a goat, and a dragon, which are epideictic, deliberative, and judicial rhetoric.[9] The interpreter of Hesiod said the head of the lion was judicial rhetoric in the allegorical sense, because this involves an action that disturbs everyone and practically renders them speechless, whether they are prosecuting or defending a case. Thus, Cicero became so enraged in his speech in favor of Milo that he did not say a word.[10] Judicial rhetoric is well represented by this animal, because with its ferocity it terrifies those who are in its presence. The head of the goat indicates epideictic rhetoric, in which the orator proceeds, filled with vehement desire, to the eulogies he is thinking of making, in the same way that we also see that animal acting out of excessively vehement desire and lust. The head of the dragon is a figure for deliberative oratory for many reasons. First, because this animal is composed of many colors, and so, precisely, this kind of rhetoric is composed of a great variety of subjects. Second, because of the manner in which this animal, in order to go from place to place, must move by making great revolutions with its body, just as the man who is to persuade others of something finds it necessary to use large circumlocutions, as we will see when we discuss his art, something that nowadays is practiced in the pulpit, no matter how much they may say more and more that they don't want to admit that kind of speech and insist that the modes of ancient oratory cannot be adapted to the modes of our sermons.

The third reason is that this animal has very acute vision and can see great distances, which signifies that the orator who practices this genre of oratory must keep the sight of his understanding sharp without ignoring anything that he should do in connection with his subject. We see that because the animal has these attributes the poets have celebrated it, writing that a dragon watched the garden of the Hesperides, another the Golden Fleece, and another was the guard of the Castalian Spring.[11] And because

9. Hesiod says that Chimera, the offspring of Hydra who was the daughter of Echidna, was a fire-breathing monster with three heads, those of a lion, a goat, and a snake or dragon; see *Theogony*, 304–26.

10. See Plutarch, *Life of Cicero*, xxxv.4.

11. The garden of the Hesperides, containing a tree with golden apples, belonged to the Titan Atlas, who set three nymphs, the Hesperides, and a dragon to guard it; see Ovid, *Metamorphoses,*

the art that embraces the three genres that I have spoken about is wrapped about by a variety of precepts, Hesiod said that Chimera was engendered by Echidna, which is the same thing as the viper, and that animal, thanks to its ability to coil itself up, signifies the art that always revolves around itself with its precepts. And the fire that they say issues from the mouth of this monster is nothing other than the vehemence of this faculty, although it's true that the fable does not allegorize it thus. By contrast, Saint Isidore in his *Etymologies*, in chapter 39 of Book I, says it signifies the three ages of man, and Nicander of Colophon also says it signifies rivers, and there are various other allegories about the Chimera.[12] This should not be astonishing since it is customary for poets to produce extremely fecund fictions. Finally, I say that in regard to deliberative rhetoric, it is the sole basis for all the genres and embraces the rest. And even if it does not do so completely, I say that it embraces judicial rhetoric when we impugn vices and things worthy of condemnation, and it embraces epideictic rhetoric when we exalt the attributes of virtue, exhorting the audience to embrace them.

(Master Fernando goes on to discuss a number of the subdivisions of the three rhetorical genres, then talks about how difficult it is to define, let alone achieve, ideal eloquence. He explains that this difficulty is due in part to the impossibility of ever realizing the Platonic Idea of anything here on earth and in part to what he sees as the decline in people's abilities since the ancient world.)

Master Fernando. But even if we appear in a certain way to be incapable of achieving either perfect eloquence or that which flourished in other ages and which we now admire so much, for all that we should still hold in great esteem that which can be achieved now. We should spend time with it, and we will achieve honors, dignities, and riches, and we will provide great benefits for our country and ourselves. And if someone is pronounced most eloquent, he is most eloquent, not in any absolute sense, but with respect to his having come quite close to that ideal perfection, as I have explained.

Don Luis. Now tell me: what qualities must one have in order to be perfectly eloquent?

Master Fernando. To achieve perfect eloquence, it's necessary to be perfect in everything pertaining to the orator, in the same way, as I have already said, that in order to have a perfectly round circle, it must not be one made

IV.646–48. The Golden Fleece, which was hung in a sacred grove in Colchis, was guarded by a dragon that Jason put to sleep using magical herbs given to him by Medea; see *Metamorphoses*, VII.149–53. The Castalian Spring is named for a nymph, Castalia, who was pursued by Apollo and, according to Pausanias, was turned into a spring; see Pausanias, *Description of Greece*, X.viii.9–10.

12. See Isidore, *Etymologies*, I.xl.4.

by the hands of mortal men, but one imagined in our minds. Thus, it's necessary for the true orator who is perfectly eloquent to have a memory just
like the one Charmidas had, whom Pliny talks about, for he could recite
again by heart all the books he went through just as if he had actually read
them.[13] This is necessary so that he can have at the ready not only the material about which he will speak, but also all the sayings and maxims that
have been in all sorts of authors, the majority of whom he will have to
read at least once in his life. It's necessary that the perfectly eloquent man
should have the copiousness of another Cicero, and much more; that he
should have a greater command of brevity than Sallust, and even more;
that he should be more ingenious than Lysias; more florid than Pliny [the
Younger]; more varied than Saint Jerome; graver than Seneca or Statius;
more graceful than Martial; simpler than Terence; sharper than Quintilian or Hyperides. In mildness and freedom from affectation he should
be like another Caesar, and he should surpass Isocrates in sweetness.
The sound of his voice should thunder much louder than did that of
Aeschines, in vehemence he should have the advantage over Demosthenes, and he should be so perfect and complete that not only does he
lack all the things in which any defect can be found, but he maintains
everything in a state of the highest perfection. The orator who did all this
would be pronounced perfect according to our way of thinking and
would conform to the one we are able to imagine.

Don Luis. It's certain that the more you discuss this faculty, the more I find
myself enthralled by it, indeed more enthralled by it than Antiochus, the
son of Seleucus, king of Asia, was by his stepmother Stratonice.[14]

Master Fernando. Then let's seek a remedy just as the doctor Erasistratus—
or the mathematician Leptines, according to others—sought one on his
behalf. But what would it be like, Don Luis, if the rest of the Spanish nobility felt such a desire as you do and then acted on it? It's a certainty, and
something evident to all the world, that not only have men of low condition come to be famous through learning alone, men such as Socrates, the
son of a midwife, Demosthenes, whose father was unknown, and Euripides, who did not know who had been his mother, but even those who
were held to be illustrious because of their ancestors shone with a much
brighter light merely for studying the arts. As we know, among our kings
Don Alfonso of Aragon was worthy of great praise for learning even
though it was after his fiftieth year that he devoted himself to the teaching of his master Lorenzo Valla, and Don Alfonso of Castile, surnamed the
Wise, was held in greater esteem for the immense learning he achieved,
something he displayed in his *Alphonsian Tables* that he abandoned

13. See *Naturalis historia,* VII.xxiv.89.
14. For this story, see Valerius Maximus, *Ditorum et factorum memorabilium libri novem,*
V.7.Ext.1.

because the astrologers were quarreling about them and not because of his regal condition. And if it were necessary to inspire us with other examples, who would omit king Zoroaster, for he was a man of the greatest learning in astrology, and Mithridates, king of Pontus, for we know well that he spoke the twenty-two languages of as many more provinces of which he was king?[15] And who can be silent about those who feel the greatest incentive to study, namely, women? Aspasia was a teacher of rhetoric in her homeland of Miletus, Arete of Cyrene, the daughter of Aristippus, was immensely learned, and Hypocracia, the disciple of Myrtis, in addition to having written five books of famous epigrams, beat the great Pindar, prince of the lyric poets, five times in public contests.[16]

Don Luis. Was the labor great that you endured in order to acquire this art?

Master Fernando. On the contrary, it was a particular delight for me.

Don Luis. In what way?

Master Fernando. In this one: the sound of the words and phrases, when I pronounced them as I was arranging them, seemed to me to have a song-like sweetness of the most perfect and harmonious sort that humans could achieve. But tell me, what line of poetry can be found, no matter how much more artful and lofty it may be, that closes with more concord and harmony, than does a perfectly rounded-off clause in prose?

Don Luis. Who was the inventor of those perfectly composed clauses?

Master Fernando. Thucydides was the first among the Greeks, and he and the other eloquent men provide more pleasure and contentment than do famous actors when they are going to go onto the stage. Is there anything perchance that can equal the orator when he is discreetly and prudently discussing things that concern us? What is more exquisite than the frequent use of clever sayings? What provokes greater marvel than something we adorn with majestic words? And what can be found that is as rich and copious as the conversation of an eloquent man that is filled with a great variety of material? This faculty [of eloquence] has many marvelous properties: it can handle what it takes as its subject with the greatest gravity; it produces marvelous advice and praiseworthy counsel; it raises up the weak and the downcast. And even if someone has faults of the sort that are tolerable, by using this faculty he will have marvelous success in winning the wills of the people with whom he is engaged in discussion, as Ovid suggests:

Non formosus erat, sed erat facundus Ulysses
& tamen aequoreas torsit amore deas.

15. See Quintilian, *Institutio oratoria,* XI.ii.50.

16. For Hypocracia's victories over Pindar, see Aelian, *Varia historia,* xiii.25, and *The Suda* (a Greek lexicon compiled at the end of the tenth century and formerly referred to as *Suidas,* as if the name of a person), "Korinna."

> Ulysses was neither handsome nor attractive,
> All he had was his eloquence,
> And thus he had at his command
> Goddesses descended from the god of the moist trident.[17]

Don Luis. By what means may one acquire such great riches and that phoenix that seems so difficult to catch?

Master Fernando. The most beneficial and effective thing to do is to write, and to do so continually. And the reason is clear why this is the best of all exercises and the one which, by itself, suffices to make us quite skillful men. For if one has the chance to think a bit about the speech one is making, it always has a great advantage over something offered on the spot, and so, how much more will a composition resulting from uninterrupted labor surpass this impromptu kind of talk? It's certain that in the time we spend composing our writings, time we spend contemplating things with all our care, there can be no tiny little point that presents itself in relation to our subject that will not eventually be revealed to us, for our memory will provide us with it without our knowing how it does so. From the exercise of writing one acquires a marvelous benefit, and it's this: for the most part the things one says are similar to those that were written beforehand, for if it should happen that one is to discuss some topic that one has written about first, normally what will be said will resemble that which was written. In the same way, as Cicero says in his books on the orator, a galley, propelled by the force of its oars, is accustomed to maintain its course and movement for a while even though the oars have been raised up.[18]

Don Luis. Ulysses did not marvel at the singing of the Sirens so much as I do when I consider your opinions about the exercise of writing, for throughout your life you have spoken to me about it in the hope that I might be inclined to practice it.

Master Fernando. What I can tell you is that this exercise alone tries the forces of the mind: it holds back the unbridled movements of the spirit, stimulates the understanding, awakens the memory of the things we've seen, read, and heard, alters opinions, clarifies what is obscure, and unties the tongue and the hand. It is the guardian of studies, the declarer of thoughts, the ambassador of things entrusted to the memory and to the memory of the arts, and a sweet companion both for those at leisure and those who are working. These and many other things are recounted by Cicero and by Jacobus Ludovicus [Strebaeus], about the benefits of writing, all of which I have experienced.

17. *Ars amatoria*, II.123–24. The translation is Guzman's. The "god of the moist trident" is Poseidon or Neptune, god of the sea.
18. *De oratore*, I.xxxiii.153. On the importance of writing as an exercise for the orator, see *De oratore*, I.xxxiii.150–53, and Quintilian, *Institutio oratoria*, XI.ii.40.

Don Luis. Little by little I've been surmising that except for divine matters— for they must be placed ahead of everything—there is nothing that gives more pleasure in my opinion than the practice of eloquence, since I never get tired or irritated while listening to you. . . .

Master Fernando. If this [i.e., eloquence] were not a matter of enormous sweetness, both for the one who practices it and the one who hears it, how could it have happened that when humans were wandering through the fields in the manner of wild animals, sustaining themselves in the very way that the beasts do, and governing themselves not according to what reason dictates but what each one could do by means of his own power, I say, how could it have happened that they were brought together and led to live in towns and cities?[19] And, leaving aside the liberal arts and sciences, if this art did not celebrate the friendships that have been so famous in this world, such as that of Damon and Pythias, in which the first dared take the place of the second as a pledge for his life made to Dionysius of Syracuse, so that if Pythias did not return within a certain time, Dionysius could impose the justice on Damon that he would have imposed on his friend—if this divine art did not celebrate such things, it's certain they would remain forever in obscurity, as would be the case with Orestes and Pylades.[20] Therefore, when the poet Aristides considered deeply the good things that flowed from this faculty, he did not hesitate to contradict Plato who was seeking to defame rhetoric, and thus he fashioned that elegant fiction in which Prometheus, who interceded with Jupiter on behalf of men, grieved to see the human race wasting away in the desert without any defense and persecuted by the beasts, and he begged Jupiter to send a remedy to the world. Nothing seemed better or more effective to Jupiter than to send his son Mercury, the god of eloquence, so that by distributing that faculty among men, the human race might be preserved.[21]

Don Luis. Since you've touched on the story of Prometheus, by any chance is this faculty as ancient in the world as you are suggesting?

Master Fernando. There's no doubt but that it goes back many years and that the antiquity of the Romans is nothing compared to that of the Greeks who distinguished themselves greatly by its means, as did Gorgias, Prodicus, Thrasymachus of Chalcedon, Protagoras, and Hippias. And if we go back a bit farther to those who were the shining lights of this faculty in Greece, we must come to Isocrates and Demosthenes, and if we seek even greater antiquity, we cannot help but sail to the age of Cleisthenes, Solon,

19. Guzman is recounting a version of the myth of the orator as civilizer that occurs in a number of ancient texts, including Cicero, *De inventione,* I.ii.2–3; Quintilian, *Institutio oratoria,* II.xvi.9; and Horace, *Ars poetica,* 391–401.

20. The story of Damon and Pythias can be found in a number of ancient sources; see, for example, Cicero, *De officiis,* III.x.45.

21. See Aristides, *To Plato: In Defense of Oratory,* 395–98 (133d–134d).

and Pisistratus, though still much greater than all of those were Thucydides and Pericles. And what if we talk about ages even more ancient, such as to imagine those many thousands of years ago when the Trojan War was taking place? I am sure that if this divine art did not exist in the world at that time, Homer would never have exalted so greatly or given so much praise to the eloquence of Ulysses, or raised up so high that of the immensely wise Nestor. In conclusion, I say that if the enormous number of things that occur to me concerning this particular subject had not all come crowded together into my mind and if I could find an exit for them of the sort I desire, it might even be possible for me to say more things from which you would receive pleasure.

[22]

Guillaume du Vair

Guillaume du Vair (1556–1621) was a French lawyer and writer who was admired by his contemporaries for his prose style and whose philosophical mixture of Christianity and Stoicism was widely influential. Born in Paris, he became clerk-counselor of the Parlement there in 1584. During the religious wars then raging in France, du Vair was valued for his conciliatory style, and his work for the cause of peace endeared him to Henry IV, whose ascent to the throne in 1589 brought the wars to an end. Du Vair was sent to England in 1596 as Henry's ambassador in order to negotiate a treaty against Spain, was later sent to restore order in Provence, and became the first president of the Parlement of Aix. In 1616 he was made keeper of the seals, and in 1617, bishop of Lisieux. His writings include numerous works on ethics, religion, and philosophy as well as politics. His *La Philosophie des Stoïques* (*The Philosophy of the Stoics*) and *De la constance et consolation ès calamités publiques* (*On Constancy and Consolation in Public Calamities*) influenced such thinkers as Descartes and Pascal. The following extract comes from his treatise *De l'Eloquence françoise, et des raisons pourquoy elle est demeuree si basse* (*On French Eloquence and the Reasons Why It Has Remained So Inferior*), which appeared in 1594. It served as an introduction to four orations, three of which du Vair translated from Aeschines, Demosthenes, and Cicero, and the fourth of which he wrote himself. The text of this treatise is taken from the edition of du Vair's *Oeuvres*, edited by René Radouant (Paris, 1907; reprint, Geneva: Slatkine Reprints, 1970), 133–67.

FROM *On French Eloquence and the Reasons*
Why It Has Remained So Inferior

Several Greek and Latin authors have left us complaints about the decline of their century, and some among them were quite astonished to see the honor of the arts, and specifically of eloquence, so reduced in their times.[1] They sought to discover the reasons for this and have left us beautiful, elegant discourses about it. For my part, I have never thought that our nation had a reason to make this complaint, because I believe—and it is surely true—that French eloquence has never mounted higher than it is now and that those who lived before us have left us nothing in our language that is worthy of being preferred to the writings of our contemporaries. But I have sometimes really been astonished how, although this kingdom has been so great and flourishing, eloquence has been cultivated here with so little success that all previous centuries have not left us evidence of a single man whom one could rightly call eloquent. Like us, Greece had its infancy, but after having stuttered a while, it formed its voice in full, perfect speech and produced orators admired by all subsequent ages. Rome did the same, and it seems that fortune wanted to raise its eloquence as high as its empire. France has not yet been unable to untie its tongue, and like children born when the moon is on the wane, has not been able to start its proper growth. Perhaps I am making this judgment too boldly; others who want to show themselves more zealous than I about French honor will tax my temerity in judging something about which I have no sure knowledge. I will never grant them that they have more affection than I do for the glory of their country: if they think that my judgment takes something away from the praise that France merits here, I am ready to hear their reasons, and I will always be pleased to learn something from them that makes me change my opinion. My country cannot win a victory that I do not share in its trophies. But as I am quite straightforward—and very French for that reason—saying freely what I think, and not conceding more to the opinion of others than what I can understand rationally, I am constrained to confess that from all the evidence we have, whether in writing or in memory, about the men of our nation who have been thought the most eloquent, there is nothing that persuades me they have ever reached the level of excellence of the ancients.

If those who wrote in our language more than forty years ago had a certain simplicity and a pure style that decorously adhered to the nature of the things they were describing, I do not want to deprive them of praise for that. That is certainly the case with some of them, just as one finds beautiful, upright, sturdy plants in a good, fertile plot of land, although it has never been tilled or cultivated—their fruit, however, is quite different from that which has been sweetened by the careful hand of a diligent, knowledgeable laborer. As for those who have lived during the last forty years, they are a bit more awake and have tried to enrich our language with the spoils of Greek and Latin and to imitate the art of those noble ancients. But who among them has acquired great glory in this art? What work have they left us that

1. Du Vair is thinking of such works as Tacitus's *Dialogus* and Longinus's *On the Sublime*.

has survived them and that is still in our hands and much prized and esteemed? I see almost nothing at all. And of all those works that remain, the most artfully perfected ones may acquire praise for them as accomplished rather than eloquent.[2] If there is anything worth a greater recommendation, it has been produced in the last twenty years, something I have seen confessed by those who have examined both this period and the preceding one. Still, I could say almost the same thing about everyone I have seen in the time I have lived among men and their affairs.

I will not speak about those who are living nowadays: the praise I would give them would seem flattery, and the faults I would note, envy. I want as much to avoid the suspicion of both as I am far away from feeling them. Their time will come, and it will give them the praise they are due—and there are some who merit a lot of it. I will speak only for the time being about those who are dead and whose memory and writings are still completely fresh among us.

(In the next pages of his treatise, du Vair reviews the limited achievements of a few of his predecessors.)

If I had not said I was not going to speak about those who are alive today, I would mention one of them whom I have always valued greatly and who has acquired, not without reason, a great reputation in this profession, because he has a marvelously nimble and judicious mind, has created a very pure and elegant style for himself, and is most skilled in making himself understood and explaining what seems most obscure and confused. If eloquence consisted only of clarity, purity, and lucidity of speech, containing nothing but what Isaeus and Lysias sought in it, I would compare him freely to the ancients and think that he would almost put our language on a par with theirs. But that grand, divine eloquence to which the first place of honor is due and that Aeschines and Demosthenes among the Greeks, and Cicero and Hortensius among the Latins, have found out, that shapes itself in whatever style it desires and such as its subject requires, that is fully ornamented and dynamic, that does not lead the auditor, but drags him along, that reigns among the people and establishes a violent empire over men's spirits—that eloquence transcends everything that all the people I have spoken about have been able to achieve. This leads me to conclude—with reason, I think—that even though the people of our time have greatly surpassed all our older countrymen who have dabbled in speaking or writing, they have still remained beneath the ancient Greeks and Latins whom they have followed only from quite a distance. This is what I am troubled about and seek an explanation for.

2. Cf. Cicero, *De oratore*, I.xxi.94.

Could one not throw the blame back on nature, as some of the ancients did for the infertility of their soil, and accuse her of having reserved us for the end of the world when her fecundity, exhausted by the excellence of past centuries, produces nothing anymore except totally defective, unsound spirits who reflect the aged condition of their mother?[3] Or could one not say, in the words of a famous person, that states and empires have their greatness bounded by certain limits that do not permit them to excel in many things at once, and that our kingdom, having had the honor of arms as its share, has not been able to acquire that of letters? I would believe this willingly, if I did not see clearly that for the last hundred years our France has blossomed more than any other nation on earth with all sorts of arts and has borne men comparable to the most learned of the ancients. Moreover, those who have most carefully reviewed the natural inclinations of peoples have given the southern nations the honor of having invented the abstruse sciences, such as philosophy, mathematics, and other contemplative arts, and have left to the middle and temperate regions, among which our nation is found, the political sciences and, in particular, the grace of speaking well.[4]

(Du Vair goes on to note all the ancient Gauls who excelled in speaking either Latin or their native tongue during the time of the Roman Empire.)

Beyond our natural inclination [toward eloquence], we have had the teaching of antiquity, which has furnished us with so many good precepts and beautiful examples of this art that one can rightly judge our century happy in that the preceding ones have almost all exerted themselves to educate and instruct it. What then? Have our Frenchmen judged eloquence to be a thing not worth burning the midnight oil in order to study? Or have they abandoned it as good husbandmen would do with a field that is more delightful than profitable, more suitable for gardening than plowing, more fit to bear flowers than fruit? I cannot believe they have made such a judgment. The majesty of eloquence, its august dignity, its great utility—or rather necessity—display themselves only too evidently in every aspect of civic life and have produced too many signal effects in the course of ages past to be unknown to them. And just as language makes man more excellent than the other animals, so eloquence makes him more excellent than other men.[5] For eloquence is nothing other than the perfection of speech and a more exquisite means of communicating our words and thoughts. In short, it is the rudder of souls that arranges manners and emotions as though they were certain musical notes, tempering them in such a way that it causes them to produce infinitely melodious harmonies. If this universe,

3. Cf. Columella, *De re rustica*, I.Pr.1–3.
4. Cf. Jean Bodin, *Les six livres de la Republique* (Paris, 1577), V.i.522.
5. Cf. Cicero, *De inventione*, I.iv.5, and *De oratore*, I.viii.32–33.

as Plato said, and before him the Pythagoreans, is nothing other than harmony, and if that entire harmony is something divine, how much more will eloquence be so, since it produces the harmonies and is the art that forms and tempers them?[6] Thus, the ancient poets, who enveloped the sacred mysteries of wisdom in their fables, wanting it to be understood that Tantalus had been the first to give men the celestial grace of eloquence, said at the start that he stole the nectar of the gods in order to give it to men. In this matter we can certainly believe that he really took something divine from heaven, but not, as they pretend, that he was punished for it.[7] For it would be unworthy of divine goodness to envy men the blessing of eloquence by means of which they have been made capable of recognizing and serving that goodness. For my part, I believe that there is nothing in this world that pleases God so much as well-ordered assemblies of people and communities tied together by the knot of just and holy laws. And I certainly think it was eloquence that first softened the manners of men, tempered their savage emotions, and brought them together with their different wills in civil society. It is she without doubt who built cities, established kingdoms and empires, and inspired good laws there as their soul and the source of their life. It is she who impels and inspires nations to do beautiful and noble deeds, turns them away from evil and injustice, and pacifies people possessed by fury, leading them back to peace and repose. It is the lyre of Amphion that drags forests, rocks, and rivers after it. It is the caduceus of Mercury that enables him through persuasion to command the powers of heaven, earth, and hell.[8]

Thus, if nothing other than this recommended it, those who are of noble birth and love their country would still devote long hours and all their labors to it. Beyond this, I would say that of all the arts for which we consume the best years of our lives, there is none that brings the person who studies it more individual honor, utility, or pleasure.[9] What greater honor in the world can one imagine for oneself than, without arms and troops, to command those with whom you live, to be master not only of their persons and their goods, but of their very wills? It is a perpetual empire that does not need guards and escorts. What in this world is more regal than to answer the prayers of the afflicted, to succor them in their calamity, to deliver them from danger, to procure their safety, and to serve as the common refuge for

6. For Plato's view, see, perhaps, *Gorgias*, 507e–508a.

7. See Philostratus, *Life of Apollonius*, III.xxv. Tantalus was punished by being placed in a lake that receded whenever he sought a drink and by having trees bear their fruit just out of his reach; see Homer, *Odyssey*, XI.582–93.

8. In this passage, du Vair is recounting a version of the myth of the orator as civilizer, which occurs in a number of ancient texts, including Cicero, *De inventione*, I.ii.2–3; Quintilian, *Institutio oratoria*, II.xvi.9; and Horace, *Ars poetica*, 391–401. Horace mentions Amphion, the legendary builder of Thebes, whose music is credited with having made the rocks rise up to form the walls of the city.

9. This and the following sentences are based on Cicero, *De oratore*, I.viii.32; and Tacitus, *Dialogus*, v.4–6.

oppressed innocents? What is more magnificent than to see those who are prosperous seek your friendship, honoring and revering you as the defender and protector of their good fortune? What is more majestic than to see, when you get up to speak, how all become quiet, prick up their ears attentively, and fix their eyes on you, and then to see the feelings and inclinations of the people turn about with your words and the opinions of the judges and decisions of the senate bend beneath your voice? What do your citizens admire more than an eloquent man? What is there that foreigners desire more to see in a city when they arrive there? What does more to extend and protect the reputation and glory of men, especially after death, than eloquence? Pericles performed many noble feats of arms, but we impute everything to his eloquence, and of all the praise given to him, there is nothing that makes his name resound on high or honors him more than our hearing these words of praise accorded him: the goddess of Persuasion erected her temple on his lips.[10]

If someone is not sufficiently stimulated to pursue this subject for the sake of honor and seeks some other kind of profit from his labors, he may conclude without difficulty that no art can benefit him so much as eloquence can. What other art can more easily win over and preserve more faithfully the friendship of princes than this one?[11] There is no one about whom they make so much ado than those who they see have been recognized as possessing the grace of speaking well. Nor can princes have more useful or necessary instruments for keeping the people beneath the yoke of obedience, contenting the nobility, negotiating with other princes, and handling happily all sorts of affairs. Eloquence also acquires the friendship of individuals by using its good offices to do them an infinite number of favors, and in the train of such friendships and favors, it brings a flood of goods and riches to those who desire them.

But may God prevent such an excellent kind of knowledge from having such a base and abject end in view! A noble spirit who directs his labors to achieve perfection in eloquence will be sufficiently encouraged to work on it with a ready will when he realizes that oratory reigns among men and bends everything to do its will. He will look for the fruit of his labor not in his purse and in a mercenary salary, but in the contentment of his spirit and the contemplation of his virtue. From that source will flow a perpetual course of pleasures, which will accompany all of his actions and will make him enjoy a truly divine happiness whose cause and source lie within those who possess it.[12] Unless one has experienced it oneself, one could not estimate, let alone express, the satisfaction a person receives when, in the midst of a large and illustrious assembly, he sees the aged love him, the young admire him, and everyone put aside their own feelings in order to espouse his.

10. See Quintilian, *Institutio oratoria*, X.i.82.
11. Cf. Tacitus, *Dialogus*, viii.2–4.
12. This paragraph recalls Tacitus, *Dialogus*, vi.

What sweetness beyond this do you think a person will feel from whose mouth this Attic honey flows—that is, a speech that is elaborated to perfection, adorned with grave and wise ideas, and made beautiful by its words, and in which reason and truth, made lustrous by their own richer adornment, shine with marvelous splendor? Believe me, there is no sort of song or harmony that touches our souls more sweetly and more voluptuously. If what one says about music is true, namely that he who sings gets more pleasure from his singing than does his audience, you should have no doubts at all that of the great number of pleasures the orator gives to those who listen to him, he gets the principal and most agreeable portion. In my opinion, I do not doubt that if a person has enjoyed real success in some great debate and, as he leaves it, hears the applause of his audience and their soft murmur of praise for him, he will feel totally ravished within, and his heart will blossom at the rising of this joy, like a new rosebud at the first ray of a bright, cheerful sun. Therefore, I cannot think it is because of scorn for this art, which by itself is capable of making life honorable, rich, and happy, that Frenchmen have profited so little from it.

I think that someone, stricken by a fever of austerity, might propose getting rid of the art as a danger to the government of states and to one's judgment of affairs and as something that wicked men have customarily abused in order to overturn laws, trouble the peace of the country, and accomplish their wicked designs.[13] In defense of his opinion, that person will readily allege the practice of the Areopagites who, before giving audience to orators, used to have a court usher forbid them to move the judges, because they thought that a judge who was stirred up by the movements of eloquence could no more determine what was right and reasonable than a passionate lover could judge beauty.[14] And he will fortify himself with the saying of Plato who maintained that there was nothing in the world so eloquent as truth.[15] Indeed, one cannot deny that many wicked men have made bad use of eloquence and have diverted its employment to the ruin of their countries. But it should never be concluded from this fact that one should reject or neglect it. It has in common with all the most excellent things in the world the potential to turn out well or ill, depending on how the person who possesses them is disposed. Most men abuse their understanding: who would say that, because they do so, they should not have one? Thus, one can say of all things that they have two handles, and a person who seizes them by one handle will use them well, and by the other, ill. Who would want to say that using arms to defend oneself justly against violence was wicked because there are people who use them in unjust attacks on the innocent? If there

13. For these arguments, see Quintilian, *Institutio oratoria*, II.xv–xvi.

14. See Aristotle, *Rhetoric*, I.i.5. The Areopagites were members of the Areopagus, the supreme tribunal of Athens.

15. This is less a reference to a specific passage in Plato than a general summary of what he argues in the *Gorgias*.

were nothing else that counseled us to work to become eloquent, we should certainly do so to arm virtue against vice, truth against deception and calumny. For, since we can't prevent malice and wickedness from taking possession of eloquence and using its assistance to execute pernicious plots, what other remedy remains for us to defend ourselves with except arms that are similar to those with which others wish to assault us? What if we abandon them and present ourselves naked for combat, would we not be betraying virtue and truth, and would we not merit the same bad reputation that a soldier in the militia of the ancient world would get if he abandoned his shield. Truth, you say, will defend itself well enough by itself. That would be very true in a place where spirits were pure and free of every passion, but since the common run of men is predisposed to passion and possessed by it from the start, partly because of human nature, partly because of bad customs, and partly because of our artfulness, one must necessarily act like those who soften iron in fire before tempering it in water, passing the spirits of one's auditors through the heat and movements of eloquence before they receive the tempering of truth. Eloquence usually finds those with whom she deals so deranged that they would hardly let her open her mouth unless she appeared in grave and magnificent clothing and showed that she had the means to seize by force what they would not at all want to grant her by reason. The condition under which she enters into the lists is that she must fight for us by fighting against us, using violence against us to make us embrace equity and justice. To take away her force and leave her naked in this combat would be, it seems to me, tremendously imprudent, as would thinking she is worth more without arms than with them—something contrary to Providence, which will never be so unjust toward its creations as to prefer the infirm and weak to the strong and powerful.

Now, since it cannot be scorn for eloquence that has caused us Frenchmen to derive so little profit from it, we must seek out other reasons that could have prevented it from taking root in our soil and flourishing as it could have done in the springtime and prosperity of this state. In this meticulous search—for my overly great leisure gives me the right to be meticulous now—what first presents itself to me is that beautiful notion of Plato's, who said that all of men's actions were carried out and governed by two great and powerful Daemons, desire for gain and fear of suffering.[16] All sorts of arts are nourished by the milk of sweet hope and elevated through the worthy recompense given for the honest labor of those who busy themselves with them. Just as the pantarba stone, by means of a secret power, draws to itself everything that comes near it, so honor and glory raise noble men up to virtue and like a sharp spur urge them to make haste toward it.[17] By contrast, contempt and scorn are like a harsh, rough bridle for them that stops

16. See Plato (?), *Hipparchus, or Lover of Gain*.
17. The pantarba stone, a magnet, is described in Philostratus, *Life of Apollonius*, III.xlv–xlvi.

them when they are running fastest. In states where eloquence served as a ladder for men to climb up to the highest dignities, as in Athens and Rome, the best minds aimed their flight at it and strove with all their might to acquire praise for it.[18] By making himself pleasing in public meetings, the least of the inhabitants of a city could assure himself he would have the greatest, most important responsibilities, and great authority was given to those who were the most eloquent, the marks of power appearing more in the artfulness of their speech than in the maces carried by the lictors and the sergeants, so that a person who had acquired a reputation for eloquence held something like a perpetual magistracy among his fellow citizens. Thus, those cities used to have marvelous orators, principally in periods when the government was run by the people. Liberty nourished a courageous grandeur in men and gave them the means to develop their capacities. In this liberty, those who had the grace of speaking well and sought to stir up the people's noble strivings in the service of their country appeared in the floods of popular meetings and public assemblies like a great wind that rises up in the middle of the sea, heaps up waves one upon the other, and sweeps away everything that appears before it. Such were the words of Ulysses, as described by Homer in this passage:

> When his voice rose up from the depths of his chest,
> It was like a flood from a ravine of water
> That dragged along with it whatever it encountered:
> Nothing human could impede its course.[19]

From its birth our French state has been governed by kings whose sovereign power drew the authority of ruling to itself and has truly delivered us from the miseries, calamities, and confusions that are ordinarily found in states run by the people. However, it has also deprived us of an exercise noble spirits could have engaged in and of the means to be involved in the handling of affairs. For the prince, vigilant in devoting his cares to our safety and placing himself as a constant guard over us, has slowed down the progress of our spirits, relegating them, as it were, to the care and conduct of their individual families so that, like a noble horse held by a tight rein, they have not been able to show what force and vigor they possess.[20] Eloquence has, among other things, a certain something it can manifest only about a subject that merits it, so that it is difficult for an orator to provide grave and magnificent words if he does not have an argument similarly grave and magnificent.[21] It should not be surprising if we are unable to con-

18. See Cicero, *De oratore*, I.iv.13–15; Tacitus, *Dialogus*, xxxvi.2–8; and Longinus, *On the Sublime*, xliv.2–6.

19. This is du Vair's free translation of the *Iliad*, III.221–23.

20. Cf. Tacitus, *Dialogus*, xxxix.2.

21. Cf. Cicero, *Orator*, xxxiii.119–122, and for this and the following sentence, Tacitus, *Dialogus*, xxxvi–xxxvii.

ceive and bring forth anything comparable to what those ancient Romans did, since their exercises consisted of orating in a senate that seemed a consistory of kings, defending provinces from oppression, accusing the governors who had trod them down, and deliberating about peace and war for the entire world. It was quite easy to conceive something grand in such a grand business: rich words would easily follow from such lofty and grave ideas. Alexander was certainly able to point this out, for when someone judged Callisthenes highly for having been eloquent in praise of the Macedonians, he responded with this passage from Euripides: "It is not difficult to speak nobly / When one has a rich, splendid subject." [22]

Just as eloquence has changed its subjects in our state, so have the people who cultivate it, and this is, in my opinion, one of the principal reasons why it remains so inferior and faded and produces almost no fruit anymore. When an ancient Roman was pleading nature's case against the idle complaint of his contemporaries, who blamed it because the earth was no longer so fecund in bearing fruit as she had been in the time of their ancestors, he replied that that was because the earth felt herself neglected, no longer being cultivated except by servile hands, whereas in ancient times she had been managed by the greatest and most valiant captains with their very own hands when, filled with joy, they returned from their military triumphs to till her. The earth, he said, rejoiced then under the victorious hands of those magnificent captains, gloried in feeling a cart crowned with laurels and a triumphant plowman upon her, opened her breast more liberally then, and spread her favors more prodigally. [23] Thus we could say today that when eloquence was handled and worked even by emperors and by the greatest men, she breathed a greater and fuller majesty. For no one who has even glanced at history from afar can be ignorant of the fact that the greatest men in all of Greece and the entire Roman Empire were those who were the most meticulous in the practice of eloquence. It is strange that even Pompey the Great, who was celebrated for so many victories, took up the practice of declaiming again and continued to do so when the war raged the hottest. [24] And as for Augustus and Antony, they declaimed almost every day while they were waging war near Modena. The other emperors who followed them did not neglect this exercise either. That's why we find it written by an ancient that Tiberius did not lack eloquence any more than Gaius [Caligula] and Claudius did, and one notes that Nero was the first of the emperors who needed assistance to speak in public. [25] Titus himself, having become emperor, made a public profession of eloquence and thought that one of the greatest honors he could have was to be considered an orator. [26]

22. Plutarch, *Life of Alexander*, liii.3. The reference to Euripides is to *Bacchae*, 260.
23. See Pliny the Elder, *Naturalis historia*, XVIII.iv.19.
24. For this anecdote and the ones that follow, see Suetonius, *De rhetoribus*, i.
25. See Tacitus, *Annales*, XIII.3
26. See Pliny the Elder, *Naturalis historia*, Pr.5, 11, and Suetonius, *Life of Titus*, iii.

In France eloquence has always been almost scorned by our princes and by our old nobility: they persuaded themselves that good deeds were worth more than good words and, content with the rank granted them by birth or valor, they did not seek any other honor at all except that of arms in war and of running their households in peace. As a result, the only use remaining for eloquence is either before the bar in the parlements, or in public pulpits, and it has always been in the hands of mean individuals who have come from base and inferior stock, been taught manners less than noble, and educated with little care and inappropriately, so that they have brought nothing to the management of such a valuable and worthy art that might enable it to grow and advance. It is certain—make no doubt about it—that the seeds of nobility or baseness pass to children from their fathers and that a set of behaviors is formed at men's birth that are recognized later on in what they undertake to do. This is something Homer pointed out when, speaking of Telemachus, the son of Ulysses, he said: "The virtue of your father has flowed into you."[27]

If this good and noble French aristocracy, whose valor produces both wonder and fear in all the nations of the earth, and whose spirits demonstrate everywhere that they have enormous vigor and worth, had not neglected the Muses and left them prey to the basest, most servile minds, in my opinion French eloquence would be much more advanced today, and the position and dignity of the nobility more assured. Eloquence is certainly a precious jewel that is more important than one thinks and is worthy of being entrusted to hands that are skillful and loving. May it please God that one might do with this subject what Alexander did with his portraits and statues![28] And yet he did not have so much of an opportunity to choose those he permitted to make his portrait and to forbid others from undertaking it, as kings and princes would have to choose those who ought to be instructed in eloquence and speak in public. Those people do not merely paint their characters on the tablets of our hearts, but imprint there, indeed, with burning fire, the liveliest and most violent emotions that are capable of entering them and that, being placed there by a malignant or imprudent hand, will ruin and deform in strange ways our entire civil society.

Although these are the most apparent reasons for the little progress eloquence has made in France, one may say in truth that the difficulty of this art in and of itself is the principal cause, for mastery of it can be acquired only through incredible labor and a happy conjuncture of several quite necessary things. The common nature of man bears with difficulty his submission to continual work and stubbornly resists things that are only acquired with great trouble and over a long time. It is almost easier for him to work a great deal than to work a long time, great perseverance being found in few

27. *Odyssey*, II.271.
28. See Plutarch, *Life of Alexander*, iv.1–2.

individuals. But in particular, we French are such that we cannot command ourselves to be patient, and it seems that nature, which gave us great promptness and vivacity, envied giving us constancy, for fear that if these two things were joined together, they would raise the honor of our nation higher than humanity is permitted to go. For, to tell the truth, if we had as great an ability to endure things as we have wit and nobility, the other nations of the earth would have to yield us the prize in any endeavor to which we chose to devote ourselves. Now, one can say indeed that there is no art in the world that involves so much trouble and labor as eloquence. To obtain it, in addition to having a natural inclination for it, one must engage in serious study that involves running through almost all the other arts, and one must acquire a general acquaintance with everything as well as a particular knowledge of the laws, customs, manners, and passions of the people with whom we live.[29] In addition, to all this one then has to add broad experience and the usual exercises, so that if there is any art whose difficulty makes one say that human life is short, this is it. As for those who have thought that eloquence merely consisted of a flood of empty, well-arranged words that would tickle people's ears and that those individuals were eloquent who were chatterers and charlatans, who entertained and dazzled their auditors with vain babbling, they have, in the judgment of the wise, really deceived themselves and done a great wrong to eloquence. Do not think that without a great knowledge of all sorts of liberal arts one could produce an oration worthy of praise. Philostratus writes in one place that the image of Memnon that was in Egypt would begin to speak when the sun shone on its mouth—through which I believe he wanted to indicate nothing other than the effect of knowledge and erudition, which brings the tongue and lips to life in those people who have something grand and divine to say, without which words are only wind and lost sounds.[30]

Those who want to encourage sloth say it is sufficient for the orator to borrow, to the extent that he will deal with such things, what the other arts possess that is appropriate to the subject he wants to treat, and that he should not spend so much time in other kinds of learning, which a person who has to speak in public will rarely use. It is as if they do not know what the difference is between that which is our own and that which we borrow, how we have different uses for the one and the other, and how people recognize right away what is really ours and what has been lent to us. Furthermore, do we not discover every day that we are so pressed by the lawsuits and debates with which we are burdened that we scarcely have the leisure to collect our thoughts and choose words fit for the subjects involved?[31] What would happen then if we had to go to the other arts for counsel in order to

---

29. Cf. Cicero, *De oratore*, I.v.17–18; *Orator*, xxxiii.116–xxxiv.121; and Tacitus, *Dialogus*, xxx–xxxi.
30. Philostratus, *Life of Apollonius*, VI.iv.
31. Cf. Quintilian, *Institutio oratoria*, X.vii.2.

seek some assistance in what we have undertaken? Do you not remember how greatly antiquity praised the judgment of Alexander who cashiered one of his soldiers for repairing the cord on his javelin when the army was in battle formation because the man was preparing his arms when he should have been using them?[32] Is there a good household manager, I ask you, who has ever undertaken to erect a great building, and who, before beginning to build, has made no provision of wood, stone, lime, and other appropriate materials, for fear that, having already significantly advanced with his work, he would be forced to leave everything go if he happened to lack some necessary item? Consider also that wood, stone, and lime, which have been chopped, cut, and cooked at the right moment, produce greater benefits and certainly have more firmness and solidity than if, on the contrary, they are used too soon, for then they crack, crumble apart, and flake off. You will surely perceive that when those who speak in public present you with learning that is badly digested and inventions that have not been warmed up in a long, profound meditation, there are gaps everywhere, and many things buckle and throw themselves out of their true, correct alignment. By contrast, those who bring forth nothing except what comes from their stomachs, where they have, through careful study, turned into the blood and sap of life what they have learned from the other arts and sciences—those individuals will produce a work resembling that of nature itself, something that grows all of a piece, is wonderfully proportioned in shape, and shines throughout with an unaffected beauty.[33] Thus, he who would acquire glory through eloquence will behave as good, rich household managers do, who, long before they will use them, will provide themselves not only with necessary things, but also with those that serve merely for pleasure, and this in such abundance that they could lend things rather than be constrained to borrow them. That person will fill his mind with a great variety of beautiful material that he will keep in reserve, and in the gardens of philosophy he will do what the noble nursling of Hypsipyle did, who "went gathering with a tender little hand many a little flower, his child's heart not being able to eat its fill of such booty."[34] For it is really easy afterward to extract a sweet and savory honey from such a storehouse of soft, fragrant flowers. As philosophers say that from the potency of matter is drawn the perfection of form, so one can say that from an abundance of learning and knowledge the orator draws that verbal beauty by means of which he acquires honor and glory.

Now, although a knowledge—if not perfect, then at least a middling one—of all the arts is necessary for the orator, because they are all so linked

32. See Plutarch, *Sayings of Kings and Commanders* ("Alexander," 13), in *Moralia*, 180d.
33. Cf. Cicero, *Orator*, xxiii.76.
34. In Euripides' *Hypsipyle*, of which only fragments remain, Hypsipyle is blamed for the death of her son, her "nursling," who was killed by the bite of a viper in the garden of Nemea; du Vair's source for this quotation is Plutarch, *On Having Many Friends*, 2, in *Moralia*, 93d.

together that it is difficult to have exact knowledge of one of them without having some knowledge of the others, still there are two he cannot in any way do without and that seem to have been made entirely for him. They are moral philosophy and logic.[35] For the orator's end being to move and persuade, how can he move people if he does not have perfect knowledge of the things that stir our emotions and move our wills? A careful and diligent doctor will never order a remedy for a sick person if he is not well informed not only about that person's sickness, but also about his humor and complexion, his manner of living, what he loves and what he abhors. The orator is the true doctor of our spirits whose concern is to do what Theophrastus said, to cure the bite of vipers with the music of flutes: that is, to cure the calumnies of the wicked with the harmony of reason. How can he do this if he does not know the character of those who have been stricken, what objects move them, what things excite fear, hope, indignation, pity, envy, and the other passions in them?[36] Shouldn't he know the tones of their souls and what sounds they make at each spot where they are touched? And shouldn't he know what produces passion in the young and the old, the poor and the rich, this nation here or that one there? Quite often it is even necessary for the orator first to put on the passions with which he wants to affect others, that he receive the blow in himself with which he wants to hit his listeners, just as Brasidas drew the dart out of his own wound and used it to kill his enemy.[37] All the force and excellence of eloquence truly consist of moving the passions: through these instruments, like a strong militia, it manages its sovereign empire, turns and bends men's wills, and makes them serve its designs. For the passions, being conceived in our hearts, form themselves directly in our words, and issuing from us by means of these words, enter others and, through a subtle, lively contagion, make an impression there similar to the one we feel ourselves. The force of words that are chiefly animated by the passions is truly a strange thing. For you would almost say that it mixes and kneads souls, or that it is a glowing fire, which, encountering another body, lights it and makes it burn, no matter how far away it may be, just like naphtha that begins to burn at the mere sight of fire.[38] I have often observed men who, not with eloquent words, but with those that are scarcely suitable, no, not with those that are suitable, but with those that are scarcely articulated and intelligible, and without any hint of rational discourse, have put their listeners into a fury just by their presence—so easily are the passions communicated through words and pass from the speaker to those who hear him. What will it be like when the passions of the orator

35. Cf. Cicero, *De oratore*, I.xv.68.

36. See Tacitus, *Dialogus*, xxxi.2–3.

37. For the "contagion theory" of moving the passions, see Cicero, *De oratore*, II.xlv.189– 90, and Quintilian, *Institutio oratoria*, VI.ii.27–36. Brasidas, a Spartan commander in the Peloponnesian War, died in 422 B.C.; see Plutarch, *On the Delays of Divine Vengeance*, in *Moralia*, 548a– 548e.

38. On naphtha's propensities, see Plutarch, *Life of Alexander*, xxxv.

are also aided and elevated by the art of eloquence? Who will be able to protect himself from them then? This is a great and powerful force that rouses the passions in the souls of those who listen. To handle it with dexterity the orator must necessarily have a great knowledge of moral philosophy and of the character of the human soul.

Now, to persuade and force one's auditor by means of logic to believe what one proposes to him, is it not necessary to be practiced in that art that suggests arguments to us and assists invention through certain places or reservoirs in which we can examine those arguments and that teach us what makes them powerful and sure? Should we not know this art, which also shows us the method by which we must arrange our arguments so that they have more weight and force, and which, beyond all this, reveals the general order we must preserve throughout the entire body of our speech? If order is the father of ornamentation and beauty, and beauty is born from order, and order is taught by this art, then this art can be called the chief mistress of eloquence. Thus I believe that if someone has not tarried with it a while and has not been well instructed in it, he will be of no help to himself, having little grace and making as little true use of eloquence as a blind man does of a mirror.

The eloquent man has need of many things with which to instruct and equip himself. These things eloquence must find elsewhere, and since their acquisition is very vexing and tiresome, it should not be surprising that few people want to undertake the task of perfecting eloquence. But if eloquence were not prevented from cultivating what grows in her own field and bringing to perfection her own particular work—which consists of elocution and delivery—do you think she would still have only a little to keep her busy? Do you think that the beautiful face of a speech, composed of well-chosen words properly arranged and falling in a perfect cadence, a face that gleams and has the tint and color of eloquence, is a common thing that is easy to find, and that the person who finds it can then give it life through a grave, unaffected delivery, in which one sees the face, hands, and body of the orator speaking together with his mouth, following with their movements the movements of his mind? How many people have been found in an entire century who have acquired a reputation for having reached this height? Therefore, it should not be surprising that in such a difficult affair human beings, who are free and resist being subjected to constant labor have made so little progress, especially considering that neither the subject itself nor any reward for it has invited them to pursue it.

(Du Vair goes on to say he thinks that the best way for his countrymen to acquire eloquence is to study and imitate the speeches of those who have excelled in it. To that end, he has translated orations by Aeschines, Demosthenes, and Cicero and has written one of his own. He praises the speeches by Aeschines and Demosthenes for their artful arrangement and elegant style, and then turns to their use of metaphors, or "borrowed words.")

I would prefer that you imitate the purity of those orators who borrowed words with such care that one can never blame them for extravagance and excess. In them you will not find a single soft, effeminate connecting and re-peating of words, something that smacks of an idle mind more concerned with words than with what is being said. If you do find some of these words at times, it will be in a passage where their use is immediately apparent and where you see the repetition as a recharging and doubling of a blow just at the point where it is necessary to strike and impress something of conse-quence deep into the memory of the auditor. Every allusion those orators make has its importance, nor do they ever play with words unless they are dealing some dangerous blow to their enemies. And truly, in great and cel-ebrated debates, who would tolerate spirits so dissolute and careless that, when it is a matter of the property, honor, and lives of men, would amuse themselves by picking over words, fitting them properly together, and tick-ling the ears of the auditor as a simpering courtesan would do in a scene from a comedy? In those two orators [i.e., Aeschines and Demosthenes] you will certainly see that they have sought great variety and avoided the repe-tition of similar words, because repetition surfeits and irritates the ear whereas variety wakes it up and delights it. But you will especially observe in them that the words are so arranged that they are normally magnified by degrees, something that greatly beautifies the face of the speech and pro-duces a much desired gravity in it, causing it to gleam as it represents the forward movement of nature through a series of words. After their choice and selection of words, you will remark their composition and structuring of clauses whose members are kept distinct from one another so that there is nothing obscure in them and everything follows from what comes before it. The length of each clause is measured so that it does not exceed at all what the breath can handle or what the mind of the listener can conceive and un-derstand without difficulty. In short, this kind of speech is like a beautiful, healthy body: it is not swollen and puffy, and in it, on the other hand, the nerves do not appear, nor do the bones pierce the skin, but it is full of blood and spirits, in good condition, with its muscles in good relief, its skin pol-ished, and its color rosy.[39] In my opinion, if someone saw those words brought to life by a speaker who had a clear, full, distinct voice that got louder and softer by degrees and represented through its stresses the pas-sions the orator feels or feigns, and who used gestures involving every part of his body to accompany his voice and imitate his emotions in their move-ments—if someone saw all this, he would surely believe what authors have written about the power of eloquence those ancient orators possessed and would confess that their commands are no less violent than those of tyrants surrounded by their guards and attendants.[40] I hope that, although they

39. Cf. Tacitas, *Dialogus,* xxi.8.
40. Cf. Plato, *Gorgias,* 466c.

have been stripped of their most beautiful ornaments and speak a foreign language, they will still please you, make you regret that you cannot understand them in their native language, and desire to imitate the little bit of grace derived from the original subject that I have been able to produce in this portrait.

Everything I have told you about these two may also be understood to apply to that great Roman orator [i.e., Cicero]. There was no absence of people in antiquity who did not merely compare him, but preferred him, to those Greeks. This is a judgment I do not wish to make; I am content to admire all of them and to let each person love them according to his taste. But I will say one thing: that noble spirit, truly worthy of the grandeur of the empire in which he was born, seems to me to have a style less suited and proportioned to our manners and our ears than those Greeks had. That eloquence of his, so very full and bold, could not be deployed, it seems, except in the expanses of such a powerful and flourishing state as the Roman republic. The confidence he had in his credit and authority and the grandeur of the courage in which he was nourished permitted him to do many things that it would not be seemly for us to do. Still, one cannot fail, when practicing this art, by choosing the loftiest goal, for if the weakness of our natures cannot carry us that high, we will at least come as close to it as we possibly can, and we will raise what is too humble and low in our spirits by means of the counterweight of such a noble example.

[23]

Francis Bacon

Francis Bacon (1561–1626) was a politician and a thinker whose original ideas had a profound impact on the development of the New Science in the seventeenth century. The youngest son of Sir Nicholas Bacon, a civil servant and courtier under Elizabeth I, he went to Cambridge in 1573, and three years later began the study of law at Gray's Inn. When the death of his father in 1579 left him without means, Bacon began a political and legal career. He was elected to Parliament in 1584 and admitted to the bar in 1586, but began his real rise to prominence when James I came to the throne in 1603. He was knighted that year, became a member of James's privy council in 1616, and was made Baron Verulam in 1618 and Viscount St. Albans in 1621. In 1618 he became lord chancellor, a post he held until 1621, when he was turned out of office after being convicted of having accepted gifts from favor seekers. Bacon's most important works include the *Essays; The Advancement of Learning;* the *Novum Organon (The New Organon),* which was to be part of an incomplete larger work he called the *Instauratio Magna (Great Instauration);* and *The New Atlantis.* Bacon felt that philosophy had made little progress since ancient times because of the uncritical acceptance of received ideas, and he was hostile to Scholasticism as well as to much Renaissance thinking, including Ramism, because they lacked critical distance from the past and relied on deductive logic and syllogistic forms of disputation. Instead, Bacon advocated a method involving observation, experimentation, and the use of inductive reasoning, a method that would be important later for the practitioners of the New Science. Bacon recognized the existence of a problematic split between thought and language, and distrusted, but did not reject, rhetoric as a result. The following excerpts come from *The New Organon* (1620), in which Bacon discusses what he sees as the impediments to understanding; *The Advancement of Learning* (1605), in which he first discusses the Renaissance infatuation with language, but later presents a qualified argument for rhetoric; and the chapter on Typhon from the *De sapientia veterum* (*On the Wisdom of the Ancients*, 1609), a work in which he demonstrates how the mythological fables of antiquity contain hidden meanings. All the texts are based on those in Bacon's *Works*, edited by James Spedding, R. L. Ellis, and D. D. Heath (London, 1857–1874).

FROM *The New Organon*

XXXVIII

The idols and false notions which are now in possession of the human understanding, and have taken deep root therein, not only so beset men's minds that truth can hardly find entrance, but even after entrance obtained, they will again in the very instauration of the sciences[1] meet and trouble us, unless men being forewarned of the danger fortify themselves as far as may be against their assaults.

XXXIX

There are four classes of Idols which beset men's minds. To these for distinction's sake I have assigned names—calling the first class *Idols of the Tribe*; the second, *Idols of the Cave*; the third, *Idols of the Market-place*; the fourth, *Idols of the Theater*.

XL

The formation of ideas and axioms by true induction is no doubt the proper remedy to be applied for the keeping off and clearing away of idols. To point them out, however, is of great use; for the doctrine of Idols is to the Interpretation of Nature what the doctrine of the refutation of Sophisms is to common Logic.

XLI

The Idols of the Tribe have their foundation in human nature itself, and in the tribe or race of men. For it is a false assertion that the sense of man is the measure of things.[2] On the contrary, all perceptions as well of the sense as of the mind are according to the measure of the individual and not according to the measure of the universe. And the human understanding is like a false mirror, which, receiving rays irregularly, distorts and discolors the nature of things by mingling its own nature with it.

1. **instauration of the sciences** restoration or establishment of the arts or kinds of knowledge.
2. For this saying of Protagoras, see Diogenes Laertius, *Protagoras*, in *Lives of the Philosophers*, IX.51.

XLII

The Idols of the Cave are the idols of the individual man. For every one (besides the errors common to human nature in general) has a cave or den of his own, which refracts and discolors the light of nature, owing either to his own proper and peculiar nature; or to his education and conversation with others; or to the reading of books, and the authority of those whom he esteems and admires; or to the differences of impressions, accordingly as they take place in a mind preoccupied and predisposed or in a mind indifferent and settled; or the like. So that the spirit of man (according as it is meted out to different individuals) is in fact a thing variable and full of perturbation, and governed as it were by chance. Whence it was well observed by Heraclitus that men look for sciences in their own lesser worlds, not in the greater or common world.[3]

XLIII

There are also Idols formed by the intercourse and association of men with each other, which I call Idols of the Market-place, on account of the commerce and consort of men there. For it is by discourse that men associate, and words are imposed accórding to the apprehension of the vulgar. And therefore the ill and unfit choice of words wonderfully obstructs the understanding. Nor do the definitions or explanations wherewith in some things learned men are wont to guard and defend themselves, by any means set the matter right. But words plainly force and overrule the understanding, and throw all into confusion, and lead men away into numberless empty controversies and idle fancies.

XLIV

Lastly, there are Idols which have immigrated into men's minds from the various dogmas of philosophies and also from wrong laws of demonstration. These I call Idols of the Theater; because in my judgment all the received systems are but so many stage-plays, representing worlds of their own creation after an unreal and scenic fashion. Nor is it only of the systems now in vogue, or only of the ancient sects and philosophies, that I speak; for many more plays of the same kind may yet be composed and in like artificial[4] manner set forth, seeing that errors the most widely different have nevertheless causes for the most part alike. Neither again do I mean this only of entire systems, but also of many principles and axioms in science, which by tradition, credulity, and negligence have come to be received. . . .

3. For Heraclitus's opinion, see Sextus Empiricus, *Against the Logicians*, I.131–34.
4. **artificial**   artful.

LIX

But the *Idols of the Market-place* are the most troublesome of all: idols which have crept into the understanding through the alliances of words and names. For men believe that their reason governs words, but it is also true that words react on the understanding, and this it is that has rendered philosophy and the sciences sophistical and inactive. Now words, being commonly framed and applied according to the capacity of the vulgar, follow those lines of division which are the most obvious to the vulgar understanding. And whenever an understanding of greater acuteness or a more diligent observation would alter those lines to suit the true divisions of nature, words stand in the way and resist the change. Whence it comes to pass that the high and formal discussions of learned men end oftentimes in disputes about words and names, with which (according to the use and wisdom of the mathematicians) it would be more prudent to begin, and so by means of definitions reduce them to order. Yet even definitions cannot cure this evil in dealing with natural and material things, since the definitions themselves consist of words, and those words beget others, so that it is necessary to recur to individual instances, and those in due series and order, as I shall say presently when I come to the method and scheme for the formation of notions and axioms.

LX

The idols imposed by words on the understanding are of two kinds. They are either names of things which do not exist (for as there are things left unnamed through lack of observation, so likewise are there names which result from fantastic suppositions and to which nothing in reality corresponds), or they are names of things which exist, but yet confused and ill-defined, and hastily and irregularly derived from realities. Of the former kind are Fortune, the Prime Mover, Planetary Orbits, Element of Fire, and like fictions which owe their origin to false and idle theories. And this class of idols is more easily expelled, because to get rid of them it is only necessary that all theories should be steadfastly rejected and dismissed as obsolete.

But the other class, which springs out of a faulty and unskillful abstraction, is intricate and deeply rooted. Let us take for example such a word as *humid*, and see how far the several things which the word is used to signify agree with each other, and we shall find the word *humid* to be nothing else than a mark loosely and confusedly applied to denote a variety of actions which will not bear to be reduced to any constant meaning. For it both signifies that which easily spreads itself round any other body; and that which in itself is indeterminate and cannot solidise; and that which readily yields in every direction; and that which easily divides and scatters itself; and that which easily unites and collects itself; and that which readily flows and is put in motion; and that which readily clings to another body and wets it; and that which is easily reduced to a liquid, or being solid easily melts. Accordingly, when you come to apply the word—if you take it in one sense, flame is humid; if in another, air is not humid; if in another, fine dust is humid; if in another, glass is humid. So that it is easy to see that the notion is taken by abstraction only from water and common and ordinary liquids, without any due verification.

There are however in words certain degrees of distortion and error. One of the least faulty kinds is that of names of substances, especially of lowest species and well-deduced (for the notion of *chalk* and of *mud* is good, of *earth* bad); a more faulty kind is that of actions, as *to generate, to corrupt, to alter;* the most faulty is of qualities (except such as are the immediate objects of the sense) as *heavy, light, rare, dense,* and the like. Yet in all these cases some notions are of necessity a little better than others, in proportion to the greater variety of subjects that fall within the range of the human sense.

FROM *The Advancement of Learning*

From *Book I*

Now I proceed to those errors and vanities[5] which have intervened[6] amongst the studies themselves of the learned, which is that which is principal and proper to the present argument; wherein my purpose is not to make a justification of the errors, but by a censure and separation[7] of the errors, to make a justification of that which is good and sound, and to deliver that from the aspersion[8] of the other. For we see that it is the manner of men to scandalize and deprave[9] that which retaineth the state and virtue[10] by taking advantage upon that which is corrupt and degenerate: as the Heathens in the primitive church used to blemish and taint[11] the Christians with the faults and corruptions of heretics. But nevertheless I have no meaning at this time to make any exact animadversion[12] of the errors and impediments in matters of learning which are more secret and remote from vulgar opinion; but only to speak unto[13] such as do fall under, or near unto, a popular[14] observation.

There be therefore chiefly three vanities in studies, whereby learning hath been most traduced. For those things we do esteem vain, which are either false or frivolous, those which either have no truth or no use; and those

---

5. **vanities** worthless activities.   6. **intervened** come in as something extraneous. 7. **censure and separation** critical assessment and discrimination.   8. **aspersion** damaging report.   9. **scandalize and deprave** malign and defame.   10. **state and virtue** original condition and inherent strength.   11. **blemish and taint** stigmatize and tarnish. 12. **exact animadversion** precise criticism.   13. **unto** about.   14. **popular** general (as opposed to learned).

ᗷ.esoteric

ᗷexoteric

persons we esteem vain, which are either credulous or curious;[15] and curiosity is either in matter or words: so that in reason[16] as well as in experience, there fall out to be these three distempers[17] (as I may term them) of learning; the first, fantastical[18] learning; the second, contentious learning; and the last, delicate[19] learning; vain imaginations, vain altercations, and vain affectations; and with the last I will begin.

Martin Luther, conducted (no doubt) by an higher Providence, but in discourse of reason[20] finding what a province[21] he had undertaken against the Bishop of Rome and the degenerate traditions of the church, and finding his own solitude,[22] being no ways aided by the opinions of his own time, was enforced to awake all antiquity and to call former times to his succors to make a party[23] against the present time, so that the ancient authors, both in divinity and in humanity,[24] which had long time slept in libraries, began generally to be read and revolved.[25] This by consequence did draw on a necessity of a more exquisite travail[26] in the languages original wherein those authors did write, for the better understanding of those authors and the better advantage of pressing[27] and applying their words. And thereof grew a delight in their manner of style and phrase, and an admiration of that kind of writing; which was much furthered and precipitated[28] by the enmity and opposition that the propounders of those (primitive[29] but seeming new) opinions had against the schoolmen;[30] who were generally of the contrary part, and whose writings were altogether in a differing style and form; taking liberty to coin and frame new terms of art[31] to express their own sense and to avoid circuit of speech,[32] without regard to the pureness, pleasantness, and (as I may call it) lawfulness of the phrase or word.[33] And again, because the great labor then was with the people (of whom the Pharisees were wont to say, "Execrabilis ista turba, quae non novit legem")[34] for the winning and persuading of them, there grew of necessity in chief price[35] and request eloquence and variety of discourse, as the fittest and forciblest access into the capacity of the vulgar sort.[36] So that these four causes concurring, the admiration of ancient authors, the hate of the schoolmen, the exact study of languages, and efficacy of preaching, did bring in an affectionate[37] study of eloquence and copie[38] of speech, which then began to flourish. This grew

---

15. **curious** fussy, overly precise.   16. **reason** theory.   17. **distempers** diseases.
18. **fantastical** fanciful.   19. **delicate** affected, overly refined.   20. **discourse of reason** process of reasoning.   21. **province** sphere of action.   22. **solitude** intellectual isolation.   23. **make a party** take sides.   24. **humanity** secular (vs. theological) studies.
25. **revolved** considered.   26. **exquisite travail** painstaking labor.   27. **pressing** impressing (upon the mind).   28. **precipitated** brought about.   29. **primitive** ancient.
30. **schoolmen** the scholastic philosophers.   31. **terms of art** technical terms.
32. **circuit of speech** circumlocutions.

33. Although Bacon has been speaking of the Reformation, his attack will become one on Renaissance Ciceronianism.

34. John 7:49: "This multitude which knoweth not the law are accursed."

35. **price** value.   36. **vulgar sort** common people.   37. **affectionate** zealous; affected.   38. **copie** copiousness (from Latin *copia*).

speedily to an excess, for men began to hunt more after words than matter, and more after the choiceness of the phrase, and the round and clean[39] composition of the sentence, and the sweet falling[40] of the clauses, and the varying and illustration[41] of their works with tropes and figures, than after the weight of matter, worth of subject, soundness of argument, life of invention, or depth of judgment. Then grew the flowing and watery vein of Osorius, the Portugal bishop, to be in price. Then did Sturmius spend such infinite and curious pains upon Cicero the orator and Hermogenes the rhetorician, besides his own books of periods[42] and imitation and the like. Then did Carr of Cambridge, and Ascham, with their lectures and writings almost deify Cicero and Demosthenes, and allure all young minds that were studious unto that delicate and polished kind of learning. Then did Erasmus take occasion to make the scoffing echo; "Decem annos consumpsi in legendo Cicerone," and the echo answered in Greek, óne, Asine.[43] Then grew the learning of the schoolmen to be utterly despised as barbarous. In sum, the whole inclination and bent of those times was rather towards copie than weight.

Here therefore is the first distemper of learning, when men study words and not matter: whereof though I have represented an example of late times, yet it hath been and will be "secundum majus et minus" in all time.[44] And how is it possible but this should have an operation[45] to discredit learning, even with vulgar capacities, when they see learned men's works like the first letter of a patent or limned book,[46] which though it hath large flourishes,[47] yet it is but a letter? It seems to me that Pygmalion's frenzy is a good emblem or portraiture of this vanity, for words are but the images of matter, and except they have life of reason and invention, to fall in love with them is all one[48] as to fall in love with a picture.[49]

But yet notwithstanding it is a thing not hastily to be condemned, to clothe and adorn the obscurity even of philosophy itself with sensible and plausible elocution.[50] For hereof we have great examples in Xenophon, Cicero, Seneca, Plutarch, and of Plato also in some degree; and hereof likewise is there great use; for[51] surely to the severe inquisition of truth and the deep progress into philosophy, it is some hindrance, because it is too early

39. **round and clean** polished and smooth. 40. **sweet falling** syntactic parallelism involving words with similar endings. 41. **illustration** making lustrous or splendid. 42. **periods** sentences, prose units.

43. "I have spent ten years reading Cicero," and Echo answers "óne," which is "ass" in Greek ("asine" in Latin); see Erasmus, "Echo," in *Colloquia*, in *Opera omnia*, ed. J. Leclerc (Leiden, 1703–6), I: 818b.

44. "more or less."

45. **operation** effect. 46. **patent or limned book** official document or illuminated book (first capitals in such books were ornamented). 47. **flourishes** ornamental forms. 48. **all one** the same.

49. Pygmalion fell in love with the statue of a woman he had created; see Ovid, *Metamorphoses*, X.243–297.

50. **sensible and plausible elocution** style (i.e., "elocutio") that is full of sense and worthy of praise. 51. **for** notwithstanding.

satisfactory to the mind of man and quencheth the desire of further search before we come to a just period;[52] but then if a man be[53] to have any use of such knowledge in civil occasions,[54] of conference,[55] counsel, persuasion, discourse,[56] or the like; then shall he find it prepared to his hands in those authors which write in that manner. But the excess of this is so justly contemptible, that as Hercules, when he saw the image of Adonis, Venus's minion,[57] in a temple, said in disdain, "Nil sacri es," so there is none of Hercules's followers in learning, that is, the more severe and laborious sort of inquirers into truth, but will despise those delicacies and affectations as indeed capable of no divineness.[58] And thus much of the first disease or distemper of learning.

From *Book II*

Now we descend to that part [of knowledge or learning] which concerneth the Illustration of Tradition,[59] comprehended in that science which we call Rhetoric, or Art of Eloquence; a science excellent, and excellently well labored. For although in true value it is inferior to wisdom, as it is said by God to Moses, when he disabled[60] himself for want of this faculty, "Aaron shall be thy speaker, and thou shalt be to him as God."[61] Yet with people it is the more mighty, for so Solomon saith, "Sapiens corde appellabitur prudens, sed dulcis eloquio majora reperiet,"[62] signifying that profoundness of wisdom will help a man to a name or admiration, but that it is eloquence that prevaileth in an active life. And as to the laboring of it, the emulation of Aristotle with the rhetoricians of his time, and the experience of Cicero, hath made them in their works of Rhetorics exceed themselves.[63] Again, the excellency of examples of eloquence in the orations of Demosthenes and Cicero, added to the perfection of the precepts of eloquence, hath doubled the progression in this art, and therefore the deficiencies which I shall note will rather be in some collections which may as handmaids attend the art, than in the rules or use of the art itself.

Notwithstanding, to stir the earth a little about the roots of this science, as we have done of the rest: the duty and office of Rhetoric is *to apply Reason to Imagination* for the better moving of the will. For we see Reason is disturbed in the administration thereof by three means: by Illaqueation[64] or Sophism,

---

52. **period** stopping point.   53. **be** needs.   54. **civil occasions** public life.
55. **conference** conversation.   56. **discourse** formal discussion in speech or writing.
57. **minion** darling.

58. Erasmus, *Adages*, I.viii.37: "You are no divinity."

59. **Illustration of Tradition** elucidation of discourse (but also the "making it lustrous or more splendid").   60. **disabled** pronounced incapable.

61. Exodus 4:16.

62. Proverbs 16:21: "The wise in heart shall be called prudent but he that is eloquent shall attain greater things."

63. For Aristotle's rivalry with the rhetoricians, see Cicero, *De oratore*, III.xxxv.141.

64. **Illaqueation** sophism, an entangling in argument.

which pertains to Logic; by Imagination or Impression,[65] which pertains to Rhetoric; and by Passion or Affection, which pertains to Morality.[66] And as in negotiation[67] with others men are wrought[68] by cunning, by importunity,[69] and by vehemency, so in the negotiation within ourselves men are undermined by Inconsequences,[70] solicited and importuned by Impressions or Observations, and transported by Passions. Neither is the nature of man so unfortunately built, as that those powers and arts should have force to disturb reason, and not to establish and advance it: for the end of Logic is to teach a form of argument to secure reason, and not to entrap it; the end of Morality is to procure the affections to obey reason, and not to invade it; the end of Rhetoric is to fill the imagination to second[71] reason, and not to oppress it: for these abuses of arts come in but *ex obliquo*,[72] for caution.

And therefore it was great injustice in Plato, though springing out of a just hatred of the rhetoricians of his time, to esteem[73] of Rhetoric but as a voluptuary art, resembling[74] it to cookery that did mar wholesome meats[75] and help unwholesome by variety of sauces to the pleasure of the taste.[76] For we see that speech is much more conversant in adorning that which is good than in coloring that which is evil, for there is no man but speaketh more honestly than he can do or think, and it was excellently noted by Thucydides in Cleon that because he used to hold on[77] the bad side in causes of estate,[78] therefore he was ever inveighing against eloquence and good speech, knowing that no man can speak fair of courses sordid and base.[79] And therefore as Plato said elegantly, that "virtue, if she could be seen, would move great love and affection," so seeing that she cannot be shewed to the Sense by corporal shape, the next degree is to shew her to the Imagination in lively representation, for to shew her to Reason only in subtlety of argument was a thing ever derided in Chrysippus and many of the Stoics, who thought to thrust virtue upon men by sharp disputations and conclusions, which have no sympathy with the will of man.[80]

Again, if the affections in themselves were pliant and obedient to reason, it were true there should be no great use of persuasions and insinuations[81] to the will, more than of naked propositions and proofs, but in regard of the continual mutinies and seditions of the affections—

---

65. **Impression** influence.   66. **Morality** moral philosophy.   67. **negotiation** dealings.   68. **wrought** influenced, shaped.   69. **importunity** persistency.   70. **undermined by Inconsequences** confused, deceived by false or illogical arguments.   71. **second** support (serve as a "second" to).   72. **ex obliquo** obliquely.   73. **esteem** judge, think.   74. **resembling** comparing.   75. **meats** foods.

76. See *Gorgias*, 462e–465e.

77. **hold on** support.   78. **causes of estate** political affairs.

79. See Thucydides, *History of the Peloponnesian War*, III.40.

80. See Plato, *Phaedrus*, 250d. For Chrysippus, see Cicero, *De oratore*, II.xxxviii.159; *De finibus*, IV.vii.18–viii.19; and *Tusculan Disputations*, II.xviii.42.

81. **insinuations** indirect arguments (orators were supposed to use *insinuatio* at the start of speeches to gain their auditors' good will).

Video meliora, proboque;
Deteriora sequor[82]

—reason would become captive and servile if Eloquence of Persuasions did not practice[83] and win the Imagination from the Affection's part, and contract a confederacy between the Reason and Imagination against the Affections. For the affections themselves carry ever an appetite to good, as reason doth; the difference is, that "the affection beholdeth merely the present; reason beholdeth the future and sum of time"; and therefore, the present filling the imagination more, reason is commonly vanquished; but after that force of eloquence and persuasion hath made things future and remote appear as present, then upon the revolt of the imagination reason prevaileth.[84]

We conclude therefore, that Rhetoric can be no more charged with the coloring of the worse part, than Logic with Sophistry, or Morality with Vice. For we know the doctrines of contraries are the same, though the use be opposite.[85] It appeareth also that Logic differeth from Rhetoric, not only as the fist from the palm, the one close the other at large,[86] but much more in this, that Logic handleth reason exact and in truth, and Rhetoric handleth it as it is planted in popular opinions and manners.[87] And therefore Aristotle doth wisely place Rhetoric as between Logic on the one side and moral or civil knowledge on the other, as participating of both, for the proofs and demonstrations of Logic are toward all men indifferent and the same; but the proofs and persuasions of Rhetoric ought to differ according to the auditors:

Orpheus in sylvis, inter delphinas Arion:

which application, in perfection of idea, ought to extend so far, that if a man should speak of the same thing to several persons, he should speak to them all respectively[88] and several ways: though this *politic part of eloquence in private speech* it is easy for the greatest orators to want,[89] whilst by the observing their well-graced forms of speech they leese the volubility[90] of application. . . .[91]

82. Ovid, *Metamorphoses*, VII.20–21: "I see what is better and approve it, but I follow the worse."
83. **practice** conspire.
84. Cf. Aristotle, *De anima*, III.x.433b5.
85. For the "doctrine of contraries," see Aristotle, *Rhetoric*, I.i.12–13; Aristotle's notion is that orators must know how to argue contrary positions, but that they should do so not in order to prove what is false or wrong, but to be able to refute such arguments.
86. **at large** extended.
87. For Zeno's comparison of dialectic to a closed fist and rhetoric to an open hand, see Cicero, *Orator*, xxxii.113, and Quintilian, *Institutio oratoria*, II.xx.7.
88. **respectively** in terms adapted to them. 89. **want** lack. 90. **leese the volubility** lose the versatility.
91. See Aristotle, *Rhetoric*, I.ii.7. Vergil, *Eclogues*, VIII.56: "An Orpheus in the woods, among the dolphins an Arion."

FROM *On the Wisdom of the Ancients*

Typhon, or the Rebel

The poets tell us that Juno, being angry that Jupiter had brought forth Pallas [Athena] by himself without her help, implored of all the gods and goddesses that she also might bring forth something without the help of Jupiter, to which when wearied with her violence and importunity they had assented, she smote the earth, which quaking and opening gave birth to Typhon, a huge and hideous monster.[92] He was given to a serpent by way of foster-father to be nursed. As soon as he was grown up he made war upon Jupiter, whom in the conflict he took prisoner, and bearing him on his shoulders to a remote and obscure region, cut out the sinews of his hands and feet, and carrying them away, left him there helpless and mutilated. Then came Mercury, and having stolen the sinews from Typhon gave them back to Jupiter, who finding his strength restored attacked the monster again.[93] And first he struck him with a thunderbolt, which made a wound the blood whereof engendered serpents; then, as he fell back and fled, threw upon him the mountain Etna and crushed him beneath the weight.

The fable has been composed in allusion to the variable fortune of kings and the rebellions that occur from time to time in monarchies. For kings and their kingdoms are properly, like Jupiter and Juno, man and wife. But it sometimes happens that the king, depraved by the long habit of ruling, turns tyrant and takes all into his own hands, and not caring for the consent of his nobles and senate, brings forth as it were by himself; that is to say, administers the government by his own arbitrary and absolute authority. Whereat the people aggrieved endeavor on their part to set up some head of their own. This generally begins with the secret solicitation of nobles and great persons, whose connivency being obtained, an attempt is then made to stir the people. Thence comes a kind of swelling in the State, which is signified by the infancy of Typhon. And this condition of affairs is fostered and nourished by the innate depravity and malignant disposition of the common people, which is to kings like a serpent full of malice and mischief; till the disaffection spreading and gathering strength breaks out at last into open rebellion; which because of the infinite calamities it inflicts both on kings and peoples is represented under the dreadful image of Typhon, with a hundred heads, denoting divided powers; flaming mouths, for devastations by fire; belts of snakes, for the pestilences which prevail, especially in sieges; iron hands, for slaughters; eagle's talons, for rapine; feathery body,

92. Bacon could have pieced together his myth of Typhon from various classical sources, including Apollodorus, *The Library*, I.vi.3, the Homeric *Hymn to Pythian Apollo*, 191–98, and Hesiod, *Theogony*, 820–68. However, he most likely used a Renaissance mythographer; see, for example, Natale Conti, *Mythologiae* (Venice, 1567; reprint, New York: Garland Press, 1976), V.xxii.305–8.
93. Mercury is the patron deity of thieves as well as being the god of eloquence.

for perpetual rumors, reports, trepidations,[94] and the like. And sometimes these rebellions grow so mighty that the king is forced, as if carried off on the shoulders of the rebels, to abandon the seat and principal cities of his kingdom, and to contract his forces, and betake himself to some remote and obscure province, his sinews both of money and majesty being cut off. And yet if he bears his fortune wisely, he presently by the skill and industry of Mercury recovers those sinews again; that is to say, by affability and wise edicts and gracious speeches he reconciles the minds of his subjects, and awakens in them an alacrity to grant him supplies, and so recovers the vigor of his authority. Nevertheless, having learned prudence and caution, he is commonly unwilling to set all upon the toss of fortune, and therefore avoids a pitched battle, but tries first by some memorable exploit to destroy the reputation of the rebels: in which if he succeed, the rebels feeling themselves shaken and losing their confidence, resort first to broken and empty threats, like serpent's hisses, and then finding their case desperate take to flight. And then is the time, when they are beginning to fall to pieces, for the king with the entire forces and mass of his kingdom, as with the mountain Etna, to pursue and overwhelm them.

94. **trepidations** confusions and alarms.

[24]

Nicholas Caussin

Nicholas Caussin (1583–1651) was a French Jesuit who taught rhetoric in Rouen, La Flèche, and Paris before deciding, around 1620, to devote himself to preaching. He delivered sermons frequently at court and was eventually appointed confessor to Louis XIII in 1637, although he held that position for less than a year, for, when he allied himself to Mlle. de La Fayette and opposed Richelieu's foreign policy, he was briefly imprisoned and then exiled to Quimper in Brittany. He remained there until 1643 when, after the deaths of Richelieu and Louis XIII, he was recalled to Paris where he spent his remaining years. Caussin composed many works in both Latin and the vernacular. In 1618, while he was teaching at La Flèche, he published a hermetic work that in later editions was called *De symbolica Aegyptiorum sapientia* (*On the Symbolic Wisdom of the Egyptians*) and that argued that ancient Egyptian hieroglyphs were representations of divine wisdom. His five sacred tragedies in Latin, inspired by Seneca, appeared in 1620. Among Caussin's works in French was *La Cour sainte* (*The Holy Court*) of 1624, an attempt to define an ideal Christian courtier. His major work on rhetoric, *De eloquentia sacra et humana* (*On Sacred and Profane Eloquence*), first appeared in 1619. It grew to over a thousand pages in length by the time of its last edition, including thirteen books devoted to profane and three to sacred eloquence. Despite this seeming disproportion, sacred eloquence is still presented as being superior to its profane counterpart. Although written for adults, the *De eloquentia* contains many elements of the schoolbook, including detailed explications of texts, Latin translations for most Greek passages, and much repetition of basics. The excerpts translated here come from the third edition of the work published in Paris in 1630.

Nicholas Caussin

FROM *On Sacred and Profane Eloquence*

Book I: Of Ancient Eloquence

Preface: On the Best Kind of Eloquence and the Plan of This Work

In the minds of certain people an opinion has taken root that is perhaps very harmful, but that has been defended very pugnaciously by men of uncommon learning, namely that eloquence just bubbles up out of us, having nature and natural talent as its resources, rather than being a matter of rules derived from art. It must be confessed that to have been blessed with an exceptional natural talent counts for a great deal in all the arts, and for even more in eloquence, especially when it has been strengthened through assiduous exercise. But without the polish provided by art and training, that talent will very frequently result in thoughtless errors. You should not think that, since precepts exist for even the least of the arts, there are none for eloquence, which alone reigns as queen over the other disciplines, for it has lasted a long time and has been celebrated in all its glory by so many remarkable geniuses—unless, perhaps, we judge men such as Aristotle, Demetrius, Cicero, and Fabius [Quintilian] to be foolish, when they were truly prudent and judicious men endowed with the keenest intelligence. They presented the whole art of eloquence with great brilliance, nor would they have done so if they had thought that it did not involve the rules of art. On the other hand, I freely admit that the multitude of ignorant writers, who have wanted to call themselves learned rhetoricians, have harmed this discipline greatly, for, although lacking the resources of mature eloquence, they have discussed in tedious detail all sorts of minutiae, cramming all of it into their stupid, childish books.

For a long time now I have given a great deal of serious thought to producing this work. I determined that if I dismissed the old songs sung in the schools and paid attention to the opinions of the most illustrious authors about the best manner of speaking, I could unfold the art of eloquence and enrich it with examples from the most famous monuments of the Greeks and Latins. Thus, I concluded that my work, brought to perfection with what I have gathered from all those great minds and all those ages, and having been made into a single, unified whole, would reach a broad audience and find favor with it.

In order to make the scheme of this book clearer, let me speak in general terms and divide all of eloquence into three types, which I will explain more fully and clearly later on. The first is divine eloquence, not that which is learned in schools, but that which is stirred up by the spirit of Almighty God who alone can make even the most inarticulate into orators. This is the really sublime form of eloquence; its origin is celestial, and what it produces is wonderful and truly golden. This eloquence has not pandered to delicate ears with flowery little words; instead, it has made men into its subjects,

inflaming their deepest feelings by means of a kind of divine fire. This eloquence has tamed kings, and having repudiated errors, it has enticed cities,
provinces, and finally the entire world to accept the yoke of Christ. This eloquence, very different from the one used by Orpheus in the fables, has made
lambs lie down with wolves; that is, it has led the pagans, whose spirits once
were savage, to love religion, self-control, and mildness.[1] Through this eloquence Moses gained a wonderful renown in religion. According to the
opinions of Origen and Saint Gregory, he was considered eloquent chiefly
in that eloquence in which men excel, for he was liberally educated from the
start of his childhood at the court where his noble talents were cultivated
and refined.[2] However, after he began to bring God's inspiration into his
speeches, he seemed to himself practically the most inarticulate of all when
he compared what he said to divine eloquence and wisdom. Finally, having
been divinely educated in the heavenly school, or rather the holy temple, he
wrote down things that appeared wonderful to the most consummate
rhetoricians among the pagans. For when Longinus, the author of a book on
sublime eloquence, reads Moses, he does not marvel at some empty dance
of words, but, as he puts it, at the overwhelming and abundant wisdom of
the ideas. Moses stood out, he said, because of this accomplishment: the famous lawgiver of the Jews was not a common man, for he recognized the
worthy concept of divine power and explained it in words.[3]

By means of this same eloquence, Isaiah triumphed, hurling down the
thunderbolts of God, and Saint Paul, whom Nicetas names "God's rhetor"
and the inhabitants of Lystra called, though with too base a term, a Mercury,
did not depend on flattering, painted language, but on the power and
knowledge of God.[4] And Paul said and did things we have read about in
which I think more eloquence is present—even in one sentence—than in all
the pomp and circumstance of the Greeklings' rhetorical periods. For this is
the tongue of the angels; . . . this eloquence is the gift God has poured down
on men and is hardly to be derived from the teachings of art.

The second kind of eloquence is the heroic, since Longinus names those
men "heroes" whose eloquence goes beyond the common kind of speech.[5]
It is called heroic, because it is a conflation of the human and the divine, for
this eloquence is not simply inherent in people; even when it is sustained by
human effort, at the same time it is fertilized by a kind of heavenly rain, so
that it blooms with the greatest beauty. Such is the eloquence of the Fathers,

1. Orpheus's ability to charm animals with his song was interpreted by Horace (*Ars poetica*,
391–401) as a sign of the power of eloquent language, an idea many Renaissance rhetoricians
found appealing.

2. See Origen, *Homily* III (on Exodus 4), and (probably) Gregory Nazianzus, *Oratio* IX.

3. See Longinus, *On the Sublime*, ix.9.

4. I cannot locate the phrase Nicetas supposedly uses for Paul, although he does call him
"God's herald"; see Nicetas Acominatus Choniates, *Historia*, in *Corpus Scriptorum Historiae By-
zantinae*, ed. Immanuel Bekker (Bonn, 1835), 35: 461. Lystra was a city in the Roman province of
Galatia; Paul's reputation as a Mercury is mentioned in Acts 14:12.

5. See *On the Sublime*, iv.4, xiv.2, and xxxvi.2.

such as Saints Basil, Gregory Nazianzus, John Chrysostom, Cyprian, and others, who from childhood directed their minds to eloquence so that, when later they were filled by those heavenly streams, they would overflow like great torrents, bearing with them all the marvelous richness and fecundity of the Church.

The third kind of eloquence is the human one, although it is virile, wise, lofty, full of power and juice, blood and beauty, as was the eloquence of Demosthenes, Cicero, and the older orators who pursued a chaster and more studied kind of speech. I do not put in the category of such weighty speech that childish talkativeness that can now be found in many orators and that is full of vanity and almost pointless nonsense. For many insubstantial men and Greeklings, who on account of the deficiencies of their minds were not able to master this lofty kind of speech, which is the offspring of a noble spirit, have devoted themselves entirely to quibbling about letters, phrases, and rhetorical periods, behaving no differently than boys who, since they do not know the value of gold and pearls, collect colored stones by the shore and are marvelously delighted by them. Eloquence is no such thing. It is not what it is thought to be by many: a mere fabric woven out of phrases, a ring of periods cleverly turned out on the lathe. Eloquence is a river flowing from the lofty part of the mind, and it is composed of things and feelings rather than little words. However, just as those gardens, which are called the gardens of Adonis and are hung from windows in little pots, delight people in a humble fashion who do not have a great deal of money, so those who have been brought up on these almost childish seductions have not been able to approach, even at the conceptual level, the grandeur of true eloquence. . . .[6]

I. On the Dignity of Eloquence: The Similarity of God, the Soul, and Eloquence

Eloquence is truly a heavenly seed and a ray taken from the fountain of eternal light. Thanks to it, those who excel in everything else approach nearer to the divine and seem to have an almost direct connection to it. Let me say it more clearly and plainly: as the human mind has an affinity with God, so eloquence, the queen of the earth, claims the same affinity for itself with the mind. The mind is the image of God; God is the mind; eloquence is divine. As God is in the world, and the mind is in the body, so eloquence is in civil life. God has been separated from any mortal materiality; the mind is entirely spirit; eloquence is the bright offspring of a special mind. God sees all things, nor is He seen; the mind discerns all things, nor is it discerned; eloquence takes possession of all things, nor does anything really take possession of it. God flows into things with the speed of the winds; the mind does

6. On the gardens of Adonis, see Julian the Apostate, *The Caesars*, 329c–329d. The expression was proverbial for things that perish quickly.

so on the wings of love; but all the power of persuasion is carried by the emotions as by a vehicle, and it penetrates and permeates the breast. God has been diffused through all the regions of the universe; the mind has been distributed through all the parts of the body; but eloquence, having tied all the arts and disciplines together by means of a certain common chain, glides through all of them. The first has His kingdom in heaven; the second in the heart; the last in the brain. The heavens worship God, the souls of the dead observe Him, He makes the world turn, causes the sun to shine, rules the world, treads on the damned. The highest parts of the body submit to the mind, while the lowest ones are its slaves; the head moves the muscles as though they were taut strings, kindles the light of the eyes, bends the body, and is lord over all the members. But kings fear eloquence, and subjects stand in awe of it; it curbs the wills of men, adorns geniuses, administers cities, and looks down on all things as inferior to itself.

We have fashioned many arts after what the brute animals do and share many in common with them—I will say nothing here of brickmakers, stone-cutters, bedmakers, and architects—for through the example of the beasts we have learned to sing with our voices and to make music with strings, to dye wool, weave cloth, make medicine, wage war, and administer empires. But truly, to speak—that is, to speak copiously, ornately, and wisely, some-thing which is great in and of itself—that belongs exclusively to us. The mute herds cannot join the society of those who have this praiseworthy quality, and the angels themselves grant us our palm of victory, although they would strive with us for it if they were confined within the frame of the human body. For this reason, the ancients believed eloquence was invented by the gods; the Greeks ascribed it to Mercury, whom Orpheus calls "the minister of speech" and the French identify with their Hercules Ogmios—though it would be better if all of them said they got it from God, the foun-tain of knowledge.[7]

II. On the Beauty of Eloquence, Compared with the Pantarba Stone

Although the dignity of eloquence is very great, its beauty and sweetness are certainly no less, and they are things that tickled the senses of the bar-barians and gave them incredible pleasure. Here it occurs to me to mention what Iarchas says in Philostratus about the Pantarba stone.[8] That little stone is as distinguished for its beauty as it is admirable for its power, for it burns with a certain soft light, and when its rays just touch the eyes, it creates day-light even in the middle of the night. But what you should marvel at is that

7. The citation from Orpheus is from the *Orphic Hymns*, 27 (*To Hermes*), 4. For the French identification of Hermes or Mercury with Hercules Ogmios, see Lucian, *Herakles*, 1. It is not cer-tain who Ogmios is, although there is an Ogmos who appears in later Celtic mythology and may be the figure with whom Hercules is being conflated.

8. In Philostratus's *Apollonius of Tyana*, Iarchas, a Brahmin Apollonius met during his travels in India, describes the pantarba stone; see III.xlvi.

this same light is a spirit so powerful that it can bring stones together that are located far away from one another. And as far as its force spreads—a force that cannot be explained adequately by means of words—it obtains control and drags up heaps of stones just like bees in a swarm. But nature, lest such a precious boon be despised, has not only hidden it away in the secret bowels of the earth, but has also made it so that it will slip out of the hands of those trying to seize it, unless it is being held by one who is prudent and reasonable. All of these attributes of the stone are marvelously suited to eloquence. If light is at issue, what shines brighter than eloquence? If force, what is more powerful? If being hidden away, what is more hidden from sight? For not only does eloquence shine, but it fills those over whom it rules with the clear light of knowledge and ennobles them as well through the glory of its exalted authority. Moreover, so great is its power that when it insinuates itself into the heart by means of a certain gentle, though absolute rule, no war machines can force it out. Note, however, that this grand, sinewy kind of speech, driven by powerful emotions, is not available to everyone. Just as nature has surrounded the rose with thorns, so it has placed a rampart of enormous difficulties around this exceptionally beautiful faculty, as about all other things, in order to keep men away from it.

III. On the Usefulness of Eloquence

There are two things that can accomplish a great deal in civic life, namely, military science and learning, and both need more than just the average assistance of eloquence. As far as the military is concerned, Onasander bears witness to how much help it gets from eloquence, even to the point of counting eloquence as the chief among the eleven qualities in a good general.[9] From it, he says, an army derives the greatest and most extraordinary advantages, since soldiers who have been cheered up and excited by their general's vehement oration will eagerly undertake difficult and terrifying things and will act as one, fighting bravely for the glory and the victory he has imagined for them. Nor does their hearing the shrill sound of war trumpets sharpen and excite their spirits for battle as much as a speech will urge them on to virtue and glory. It fills the mind with the power to resist the dangers lying in the way; nay rather, by means of its steady encouragement, it gives strength to those who are almost prostrate with fear. For this reason, that perspicacious blind man [Homer], the father of poets, especially commends eloquence in leaders and glorifies the sweetness of Menelaus, the honey river of Nestor, and the force and gravity of Ulysses. Nor is there any doubt that a certain artful and diligent mode of speaking conferred a great deal of splendor on a general in those heroic times, so that in the days of the Greeks and Romans, that mode grew and spread so far that rare were the generals who had no knowledge of civic eloquence. Civic eloquence, I say,

9. Caussin is paraphrasing Onasander, *The General*, I.13.

for I do not think that a general should affect the kind of polished speech that comes from the schools and is limited to the little flowers of the rhetoricians, but the kind that is grand, vehement, lofty, the kind that, animated by the energies of the best talents, takes something of its polish from art, from the refined judgment of the best men, from experience in affairs of state, and from the daily habit of associating with those who are well-spoken.

Of preachers and lawyers, who enjoy the most splendid reputation among the *literati*, it is not my concern to speak, for all know how much help they have found in eloquence. The species of fire, which permeates everything, cannot ignite the other parts of the universe by means of its mysterious power as readily as the force of speech can kindle fires in all the arts and disciplines; without it they would not only languish, but would of necessity waste away completely.[10]

IV. On the Power of Eloquence

Eloquence is a procuress and can effectively seize and bind people's spirits, especially when it is joined as a companion to wisdom and moral integrity. Carried on its wings, as it were, the orator's soul flows into the very hearts of his auditors, and he purchases them for himself in a form of slavery that is most pleasing to all. Once he has entered them, what does he bring to pass? Are spirits to be inflamed? He lights the fire. To be stung into action? He sharpens his goad. Enlightened? He spreads light all around. Consoled? He sprinkled on Nepenthe.[11] Restrained? He puts on the brakes. Healed? He supplies Panacea. Allured? He turns into a little Siren. In short, one cannot say how many gentle juggling tricks this pandering eloquence possesses, how many and how admirable its effects. A person would hardly err who said, in the words of Philo Judaeus, that eloquence is the "siege-engine of the soul." Not unwisely the emperor Julian compares it to the rod of Mercury. "Has it sounded its thunder? All the cattle, the birds, and wild animals grow silent, / And the curved treetops look weary with sleep. / Nor is the sound of the raging river the same, the shuddering of the ocean / fades, and the sea, resting against the earth, grows quiet."[12]

Are you interested in the power of the sweet kind of eloquence? You can see it in Aristides.[13] When Smyrna, the richest city-state in Ionia during the

10. Caussin cites a lengthy passage at this point on the power and glory of oratory from Tacitus, *Dialogus*, v.4–6.

11. Nepenthe was a drug or potion reputed by the ancients to eliminate sorrow and induce oblivion. Panacea, referred to a little later, was an herb the ancients thought able to cure all diseases.

12. For the quotation from Philo Judaeus, see *The Decalogue*, 63 (2.191). The emperor Julian (Julian the Apostate) identifies eloquence with Mercury's rod, or caduceus, in his second letter to the Neoplatonic mystic Iamblichus; this letter is now considered spurious. The verse passage cited comes from Statius, *Silvae*, III.iv (*Somnus*), 3–6. The first word in the excerpt, "Increpuit" ("it made a sound," "it thundered"), has "eloquence" as its implied subject; the word is not, however, in Statius's poem.

13. This anecdote about Aristides comes from Philostratus, *Lives of the Sophists*, IX.582.

rule of Marcus Antoninus [Antoninus Pius], had collapsed because of an earthquake and lay piteously prostrate, Aristides wrote a monody to the emperor inviting him to repair the ruins of the wretched city-state, in which, after describing the former beauty of the flourishing city, he brought the passage to an end with "But now the west winds blow through the desolation." At these words, Antoninus testified to his sorrow with sighs and tears and immediately sent Theodosius, the prefect of Asia, to rebuild Smyrna.

Are you interested in that crafty form of persuasion that conquers heroes and is increased through the ingenious tricks of the orator himself? Alexander [the Great] had determined to destroy Lampsacus completely because its inhabitants were partisans of the Persians, and he was ready for combat, spurred on by sword and fury, when Anaximenes, the teacher of the great Alexander, was sent by his fellow citizens of Lampsacus to plead with Alexander and to offer an excuse for their fault. Having learned of this plan, the king, persisting in his anger, vowed to do everything contrary to what Anaximenes asked for. This exceptional orator, however, rather cunningly calmed the furious spirit of the young man, by saying: "I have not come, Alexander, as you think, in order to excuse a fault, but to propose justice. The people of Lampsacus acted wickedly and are guilty of high treason. This, then, I ask of you: sell their wives and children into slavery, burn their temples, and raze their city to the ground." Alexander, who had said he was going to do the opposite of what his teacher requested in every detail, saw that he was conquered, and smilingly issued a complete pardon.[14]

Are you interested in the juggling kind of eloquence? Consider Eustathius, whom Eunapius of Sardis recalls in his life of Aedesius when he discusses Eustathius's legation to [the Persian king] Sapor in detail.[15] Sapor, a haughty man, was difficult to approach and was consumed with a desire for fame. Nevertheless, after Eustathius had gained access to the king in the customary manner of a legation, Sapor was surprised to see his modest appearance and the attractive serenity of his look, and tried to terrify the man by various means. But once he had easily grasped the man's words as well as the arguments he reviewed modestly and expeditiously, Sapor ordered him to go outside for a little while. Soon thereafter, through his chamberlains, the king called him within to his public table, and Eustathius obeyed. Fashioned by nature to move in a properly obedient manner and to have every regard for courtesy, he came to the regal banquet, and while everyone was drinking, he delivered a discourse advocating contempt for worldly honor that inspired so much loathing in Sapor for his royal position and its trappings that the king, having already taken off his necklace of precious stones, practically cast off his crown and exchanged his purple robe for Eustathius's traveling coat. However, the king's in-laws prevented that from happening, saying repeatedly that the philosopher was a pure con man.

14. This anecdote comes from Pausanias, *Description of Greece*, VI.xviii.3–5.
15. See Eunapius, *Lives of the Philosophers and Sophists*, 466.

With this same tricky eloquence, Gaius Gracchus forced tears out of his enemies, Demosthenes proclaimed war, Cicero crushed Catiline, [Marc] Antony blunted the swords the assassins had drawn across his throat, and Cineas captured cities.

> It loves to walk surrounded by its attendants
> And, more powerful than a lightning bolt, to shatter rocks.[16]

V. On the Origin and Progress of Eloquence

The origin of eloquence is very ancient. States are held together by two things in particular, justice and speech. Hence, eloquence began with the founding of towns and the forming of societies by men who came in together from the countryside. Aristides tells how there was great confusion in the cradle of the world at its birth.[17] Almost all the animals surpassed man, who was naked and defenseless, in many ways, and they harassed him, causing him all sorts of troubles and anguish, which he was forced to put up with because he lacked counsel. And men themselves, like wild beasts, lived in the most disgusting chaos. Pitying this condition, Prometheus, as fables tell, went up to heaven to bring back help to make man safe as well as to enhance his dignity. In response, Jupiter, partly allured by Prometheus's charm and partly moved profoundly by the misery of men, who were in a daily state of decay, sent Rhetoric to the world under Mercury's escort and ordered her to give abundantly of herself to mortals. Nevertheless, he did not want her lavishly bestowed on everyone in promiscuous fashion, like money flung in a theater; instead, he wanted her to select certain truly choice and noble minds and to enrich them with the resources of superior knowledge, both for their own benefit and for that of many others. Hence, the first societies, characterized by industry, deliberation, cunning, art, and wealth, began to flourish.

Aristides cites this charming fable in order to commend the antiquity and necessity of rhetoric. It is certainly the case that the word rhetoric is most ancient and existed long before that of philosopher, for Homer recalls it in the first book of the *Iliad* where he refers to Phoenix, who was sent to Achilles by his father Peleus, as a master of eloquence and guide to conduct, expressly calling him "a speaker of words and a doer of deeds."[18] Homer showed that already in his days a mastery of eloquence in meetings was zealously pursued, for he sang the praises of ancient heroes because of their linguistic facility, assigning subtle brevity to Menelaus, honeylike sweetness to Nestor, but to Ulysses, a copiousness similar to the snows of winter,

16. Horace, *Odes*, III.xvi.9–11. Caussin has suppressed the initial word in the first line of this quotation, "aurum" ("gold"), thus transforming Horace's indignation over the power of gold into a celebration of the power of eloquence.

17. See *To Plato in Defense of Oratory*, 133d–136d (394–399).

18. See *Iliad*, IX.453; Caussin gets the line slightly wrong and places it in the wrong book.

to wit, "the words drifted down like winter snows."[19] But they also maintain that Paris himself had a really splendid natural talent, and his father ordered that he be given instruction at Antandros in the arts of the Greeks, including the discipline of eloquence, with the result that he turned out to be eloquent beyond the natural genius of his race. He wrote works in honor of Venus, her girdle, and other things of that sort (if we believe Athenaeus), and afterwards his fame was increased because of the judgment of the goddesses and the victory of Venus.[20] Also, Pausanias says in his book about Corinth that Pitheus, the maternal grandfather of Theseus and king of Argolis, not only made just decisions, as befitted his public office, but also taught the art of speaking and left posterity a book on rhetoric, from which you can infer that before the time of Hercules there were books on rhetoric here and there.[21]

But since these beginnings of the art were rather crude, some people scarcely count them as being the origin of rhetoric itself. Thus Cicero, in his *Brutus*, places the beginning of eloquence just after the adolescence of Athens.[22] Eloquence, he says, did not start with just anyone among the Greeks, but with the Athenians, and not when Athens was just starting out, but when it had already reached adulthood. Before Pericles and Thucydides there is no writing that has any refinement and seems the work of an orator. Then, Anaxagoras the philosopher educated Pericles, the son of Xantippe, with the result that his sweetness in speaking caused Athens to rejoice, his richness and copiousness produced admiration, and his forceful, dreadful speech provoked fear. Thus, this first age produced an almost perfect orator. With such models, eloquence began to be cultivated, and many teachers of the art suddenly made their appearance: Gorgias of Leontini, Thrasymachus of Chalcedon, Protagoras of Abdera, Prodicus of Chios, and Hippias of Elis. Isocrates, however, surpassed them all, as did Lysias, whom you might almost call the perfect orator, although you would readily say that Demosthenes was really perfect and lacked nothing at all. After him come Hyperides and Aeschines, Lycurgus and Dinarchus, and Demades, none of whose writings are extant. That age poured forth this abundance, and the sap and blood of oratory remained uncorrupted down to that time, its beauty still natural, not covered by cosmetics. These are Cicero's notions, but if you compare what he says with the evidence of Pausanias and Athenaeus, you would readily conclude that he was not indicating the origins of eloquence, but its finishing off and perfecting. If one wishes to talk about the beginnings of things, one must trace them back to their very

19. See *Iliad*, III.222.
20. Caussin is referring to the contest in which Paris judged Venus, or Aphrodite, more beautiful than Hera and Athena, and was awarded Helen as his prize, thus causing the Trojan War. There is no reference to Paris's works about Venus in Athenaeus's *The Deipnosophists*.
21. See Pausanias, *Description of Greece*, II.xxxi.3.
22. The following passage is a paraphrase of Cicero's *Brutus*, vii.26–ix.38.

cradle and not worry about whether they had any refinement then, for nothing can be both polished and, simultaneously, just born, since nature itself, the fashioner of all things, gives every one of them crude beginnings.

(The remainder of Book I is taken up with a review of the history of oratory and the major orators in Greece and Rome, ending with Cicero and a series of chapters comparing him to Demosthenes.)

Book VIII. On the Emotions

I. The Power and Excellence of the Emotions

The oracular pronouncement of the divine soothsayer is extremely well known, namely that God travels on the wings of the winds.[23] Through this saying, a remarkable image of God, as if He were driving a chariot, is placed virtually before men's eyes. Our orator, however, who has a certain portion of divinity and is an excellent image of God's wondrous sovereign power, is carried by the emotions as by the winds and is accustomed to arouse them in the minds of his auditors. Let the poets be quiet about their Aeolus who, as they say, controls "the struggling winds and noisy storms," now confining and calming them, now sending them forth like a line of soldiers armed with thunder and terror.[24] Nothing is more marvelous than the orator, who not only knows how to relax and tighten up on the reins of the emotions, as if they were winds, but seems to have been walled about and surrounded by that grand and terrifying escort, almost like lightning and thunder. Not unwisely did Lucian say this of the prince of Attic eloquence, recalling that like a truly powerful king, he had for his attendants "thunderbolts and lightning."[25] The empire of the orator's eloquence, which rules over the emotions, is the greatest, for it holds men together in society, allures their minds, impels their wills to go wherever it wishes and to come back from wherever it wishes, offers help to suppliants, lifts up those who have been struck down, offers safety to the accused, liberates men from dangers, in sum, establishes a certain gentle tyranny within the hearts of men.[26] Of it Pindar proclaims: "And it extinguishes the lightning bolt passion of Jove and moves his eagle, in its tenacious wakefulness, to sleep, and finally it tickles Jove himself, touches him in his deepest feelings, and moves him powerfully."[27]

23. See Psalms 18:10.

24. Caussin is citing (not quite accurately) Vergil's description of the god of the winds in *Aeneid*, I.53.

25. The prince of Attic eloquence is Demosthenes; the citation is from Pseudo-Lucian, *In Praise of Demosthenes*, 20.

26. Cf. Cicero, *De oratore*, I.viii.32, and Tacitus, *Dialogus*, v.4–6.

27. Pindar, *Pythian Odes*, I.5–6. In this passage Caussin first cites Pindar in Greek and then provides a rather free Latin translation; I have translated his Latin. The "it" at the start of the quotation actually refers to the lyre, the instrument of Apollo and of lyric poets.

[25]

Jean-François Le Grand

The author of the *Discours sur la Rhetorique Françoise, a Monsieur de Bary* (*A Discourse on French Rhetoric, for M. de Bary*) is identified as M. Le Grand at the end of this text, which appears at the beginning of *La Rhetorique françoise* (*The French Rhetoric*) published by René Bary (or, more typically, Barry) in 1658. The author was in actuality a certain Jean-François Le Grand, who was the Sieur du Breuil des Herminieres, a Conseiller du Roi (royal counselor) of Louis XIV, and the Substitut de M. le Procureur Général (deputy general prosecutor). Le Grand also published *Discours oratoires et dissertations critiques* (*Oratorical Discourses and Critical Essays*) in 1657 and *Dissertationes philosophicae et criticae* (*Philosophical and Critical Essays*) in 1658, in which he attacks contemporary philosophers such as Gassendi. This translation of portions of the *Discourse on French Rhetoric* is based on the text in the 1658 Paris edition of Bary's work.

FROM *A Discourse on French Rhetoric, for M. de Bary*

(The opening pages of the Discourse praise both Bary's work, which Le Grand says has placed French eloquence on a level with that of the ancient world, and Bary's own consummate eloquence, a concept Le Grand goes on to define.)

When I speak of consummate eloquence, I do not mean the kinds of declamations produced by men like Seneca [the Rhetor] and Quintilian, nor the kinds of preliminary exercises of men like Theon and Aphthonius, who often labor to make lies seem truer than truth, busy themselves giving evil the appearance of good, and employ makeup and coloring to cover up blemishes and repair faults. They have no substance or solidity at all and are nothing but surface and show. By contrast, I intend to speak of that imperious habit of speaking that reigns absolutely in the heart, exercises a legitimate power over the will, and is no less the foundation of empires than the source of triumphs. I mean that sovereign eloquence of the first order that casts its light down into the center of the soul, carries its warmth right to the bottom of the heart, has flashiness for the crowd and solidity for the wise, presides over political negotiations, decides religious controversies, and illuminates the obscurities of philosophy.

Truly, the art of speaking well, the sovereign eloquence I am speaking about, is the most important part of politics, since it is she who shows how to persuade minds and bend wills in the council rooms of princes, in the high courts, in temples, and in armies. When the spirits of the people are unruly and sicknesses of the soul agitate states, this eloquence has often brought health to sick provinces and dying republics. We know that Demosthenes and Cicero were once the supreme doctors of Athens and Rome, and that they provided a soul and a life for those political bodies that were able to extend their sway to the two poles of the earth. We know as well that the pen and the gown have often prevailed over the sword and the suit of armor, and that Caesar feared the enthymemes and apostrophes of a senator more than the axes and rods of the Roman republic.[1] Finally, we know that the arm of Ajax was of less service in the taking of Troy than was the tongue of Ulysses, and that in the Greek camp the eloquence of the one was judged more victorious than the valor of the other.[2]

It was for this reason that the preceptor of Alexander moved the heart of that great prince to make himself both a good orator and a great general, for he thought that a sovereign would gain more glory by persuading men than by subduing them, by winning them over than by vanquishing them.[3] He thought that a palm that had not germinated in blood or tears would be immortal and that it was more honorable for a conqueror to erect trophies in the minds of generals and the hearts of the people by means of oratory than to march in triumph over broken scepters and severed heads in battle. This was the very reason why men like Epaminondas and Alcibiades, Scipio and Laelius took the title of eloquent, joining it to that of noble.[4] It was why the emperor Julian felt such passion for the art of speaking that he got up every night to invoke the divinity who rules over eloquence, why he loved to give

1. The "gown" ("robe") and the "sword" ("épée") are references to the "noblesse de la robe," the nobles who obtained their titles through court service, and to the "noblesse de l'épée," the traditional nobility who had obtained theirs through military service. The phrase "axes and rods" is a periphrasis for "fasces," the device that was borne before Roman magistrates in public ceremonies. An enthymeme is a syllogism with the middle term suppressed.

2. Troy fell through the stratagem of the wooden horse, devised by Ulysses; see Vergil, *Aeneid*, II. After the death of Achilles in the Trojan War, Ajax and Ulysses both claimed his armor, but the latter prevailed through his eloquence, and in Ovid's account, Ajax committed suicide; see *Metamorphoses*, XIII.2–398.

3. Alexander's preceptor was Aristotle; for his teaching rhetoric to Alexander, see Cicero, *De oratore*, III.xxxv.141.

4. For the eloquence of Alcibiades, see Cicero, *Brutus*, vii.29; for that of Epaminondas, xiii.50, and for that of Scipio and Laelius, xxi.83–85. The Scipio here is not Scipio Africanus, but his adopted grandson Publius Scipio Aemilianus, known as Africanus Minor.

speeches as much as to fight battles, and why he did not think less of his orations than of his conquests.[5] Finally, it was for this reason that the other emperors called pleading a law case "fighting with the arms of the word," and lawyers note that they called the eloquence of the bar "the militia of the long gown."

If eloquence has contributed a great deal to sustaining the authority of princes and the grandeur of empires, it has served to resolve fully philosophical doubts and difficulties in the arts. Those wise men studying the secular world, whose principal concern was knowledge of the truth, thought that speech, the living image of the truth they conceived, could be given worthy expression if one used the most beautiful words and employed the highest kind of eloquence. They believed that a crowd of bad phrases and imperfect figures would overwhelm the force and vigor of thought, so that truth would lie buried under barbaric diction and crude elocution, that it would be a sun in eclipse and a beauty masked. Those illustrious thinkers knew with Plato that rhetoric was to the soul what medicine is to the body: the one illuminates the mind and heats the will so that truth may be known and virtue loved, while the other prescribes forms of nourishment and orders remedies to maintain health and cure illnesses.[6] This is why those extraordinary geniuses were particularly busy cultivating this important part of the study of language. They were trying to acquire the praiseworthy habit of being able to orate with grace: they wanted to become eloquent in order to avoid becoming corrupters of absolute truth and supreme goodness.

No one is ignorant of the fact that that profound thinker Democritus composed an excellent work that he rightly named the *Circular Art of Eloquence*, because it enclosed, as in a circle, grammar and logic, poetics and the art of oratory.[7] The whole world knows that the master of the peripatetics was not content with the three books of rhetoric that he had taught his disciples, but composed a fourth one as well in order to teach Alexander the Great.[8] All know that the prince of the Academy was not satisfied with the *Cratylus* or the *Gorgias*, which are two dialogues he composed about the art of discourse, but that he also continued to reveal its secrets at the end of his *Phaedrus*, which is a marvelous dialogue about the primal beauty. Epicurus, complete recluse that he was, made use of an elocution so clear and so charming that [Diogenes] Laertius assures us that his speeches were like in-

5. For Julian's praying to Hermes, the god of eloquence, see Ammianus Marcellinus, *Historia*, XVI.v.4–6.

6. Le Grand inverts the judgment Plato makes of rhetoric in the *Gorgias* in which he opposes it to medicine, and although it is identified with cooking there, that identification is not meant to be flattering; see 463a–465e.

7. I have been unable to identify any such work by Democritus.

8. The master of the peripatetics is Aristotle, whose *Rhetoric* contains three books. What Le Grand refers to as the fourth book is the *Rhetorica ad Alexandrum*, an anonymous, late antique translation of a work possibly written by Anaximenes of Lampsacus, but attributed to Aristotle. The prince of the Academy in the next sentence is Plato.

visible chains that bound the minds and hearts of his auditors, and Zeno, completely serious as he was, made a book about the properties of words, examined sayings and phrases, and wanted to unite the adornment of words to the gravity of his porch.[9]

You see then, Sir, that these great figures from antiquity had the same passion that you do, and men like Eunapius and Diogenes [Laertius], Philostratus and Hesychius have been able to show you that the philosophy of the ancients was almost always accompanied by their rhetoric and that they never offered fruit that was not adorned with flowers. But if we follow the opinion of the most subtle and critical thinkers, we will go farther and will say that rhetoric, especially French rhetoric, is the mean between dialectic and poetry, but with this difference and privilege: it can be employed in rational arguments but is free from any constraint in the use of terms; and it can make use of meter and rhythm without counting syllables. We can say even more precisely—and do so with the Stoic Posidonius—that poetry is an oration in meter and does not differ from rhetoric except in its use of regular verse forms and in the excesses permitted it by poetic license, forms and excesses that do not impair or change the substance of what is being expressed.[10] Rhetoric may thus be found not only in the rhythms of poetic and imaginative fictions, but also in the methodical use of epideictic and forensic syllogisms.

With this foundation now established, let us boldly conclude that poetry is nothing other than the most constrained and strictly observed part of the art of oratory, and thus we will remain in agreement with Cicero that great Homer was a great orator; we will admit with Hermogenes that that Homer was an excellent rhetorician; and we will confess finally with Demetrius that that same Homer was the master of eloquence.[11] Moreover, let us add that just as the first poets were the first priests and the first legislators of their nations, they also assumed the profession of interpreter of the gods. They made use of a kind of language that was more ornate and formal than that of the crowd, and with this language, which they called the language of the gods, they refined men who were stupid and savage, and made peoples civilized who wandered lost in the forests and mountains.[12] That is why Horace was correct in saying that the tigers and lions, which the voice of Orpheus made gentler and less wild, were raging, barbarous men whom the

9. See Diogenes Laertius, *Epicurus*, in *Lives of the Philosophers*, X.9. The Zeno in this sentence is Zeno the Stoic; the "porch," *stoa* in Greek, is a reference to the place where he taught his philosophy. I can find no evidence that he wrote a book on the property of words.

10. Le Grand may be thinking of a statement made about Posidonius in Diogenes Laertius, *Zeno*, in *Lives of the Philosophers*, VII.60.

11. See Cicero, *Brutus*, x.40, Hermogenes, *On Different Styles*, III.x.389, and Demetrius, *On Style*, 262.

12. Le Grand is recounting a version of the myth of the orator (or poet) as civilizer, which occurs in a number of ancient texts, including Cicero, *De inventione*, I.ii.2–3; Quintilian, *Institutio oratoria*, II.xvi.9; and Horace, *Ars poetica*, 391–401.

eloquence of his poetry had made less cruel and more sociable. He was also right in saying that that famous Amphion, who made stones and forests move at the sound of his lyre to build the walls of Thebes, was the illustrious lawgiver of that great city who engraved on the surfaces of rocks and on tablets of wood the first laws for the first people of Boeotia.

It is certain that civil laws and moral precepts, the mysteries of religion, and the secrets of nature were first revealed in the form of poetic speech so that men might understand them. The ancient masters of worldly wisdom thought that the grace and embellishments of rhythm and meter would attract the curiosity of people to learn the arts and disciplines they taught. They thought that through the embellishments of rhythmical speech they could engrave more deeply on the memory the principles of their physics, the dogmas of their theology, and the maxims of their ethics. For this reason Socrates called poetic speech popular speech, and Lucretius said in so many words that poetic speech was like honey, which he was using to sweeten the bitter wormwood the crowd would have found in the teaching of his Epicurus.[13] It was also for this reason that Xenophanes and Parmenides, Empedocles and Palaephates employed such a strictly regulated form of eloquence [i.e., verse] to teach their auditors the science of nature.

(Le Grand explains that human beings love the rhythm and regularity of poetry because such things are aspects of their spiritual natures and link them to the divine.)

You did not think, Sir, that I would take you this far, but I still want to let you see something very curious and very important. Let us finish our journey and find the primitive origin of eloquence. Let us approach that source of milk and honey and see how it first flowed from the lips of the first speakers. When men used to have nothing but caves and huts to retire to, were clothed only in the skins of dead beasts, and slept on dry leaves and straw spread out under them, they attempted, in order to amuse themselves in their leisure and solitude, to produce pleasant sounds for their crude words and to form delicate harmonies despite tongues that stuttered and voices that were incapable of articulate speech. Some time later, they got it into their heads, as Lucretius notes, to imitate the song of birds.[14] They invented reed pipes and flutes. They sang in the presence of their families and friends their first lampoons and railings. Finally, having become less savage and more sociable, they assembled together near fountains and on mountains, began to guard flocks, to seek out the shade of willows and the softness of lawns, to make bouquets and garlands for their mistresses, to put crowns and hats of leaves and flowers on their heads, and to find out, for the sake of their own pleasure, sweeter words and a less rustic pronunciation. The most

13. See Lucretius, *De rerum natura*, IV.11–25. The four figures mentioned in the next sentence were all ancient Greek natural philosophers.
14. See *De rerum natura*, V.1379–81.

ingenious among these new shepherds noted how rhythmical and sweet words could be, practiced singing them from the summits of hills and on the banks of streams, and before inventing the ideas of quantity and proportion for the syllables of words, they acquired the habit of rhythmical speech, that is, the ordering of words by means of meter. With their rhythms and meters, they composed a rough and irregular poetry that was probably nothing more than an oration accompanied by the sound of flageolets, musettes, and bagpipes. This is why the Greeks in their fables feign that the god of shepherds inspired poetry on the heights of their Parnassus and their Helicon as well as on the shores of their Aganippe and their Hippocrene.[15] But what could human industry not accomplish, given time and experience? Those savage poets, having acquired a facility with measured and rhythmical speech, ventured to sing the reflections they had in response to their first thoughts, and those reflections constituted the basic principles of their arts and sciences. They sang those poems at the games played during their festivals and at the banquets held at their marriages, in the same fashion that Vergil has Silenus and Iopas sing in his *Eclogues* and his *Aeneid.*[16]

As that form of verse without rules and art was recited at the first assemblies of men and was one of the first products of human society, the Greeks called it *political,* and insofar as during the succeeding years the most refined and accomplished spirits composed that kind of verse impromptu, without study or meditation, Aristotle called it *autoschediasmatic (improvisatory).*[17] I believe, Sir, that this adjective is not used in your circle and that it would weigh heavily on the tongues of your purists, but since people made use of it in the court of Alexander, and it is precise and belongs to the art of poetry, I am persuaded that it will not shock you completely and that in this instance, despite all your correctness, you will treat me with indulgence more than rigor. However, let me take up my discourse again and say that this kind of verse had the same origin in Italy as it did in Greece. For in those poems that were made in the Golden Age and the time of Saturn—and that a Roman author therefore calls Saturnine verse—the Latin peasants used to sing the memorable deeds of their first heroes and their *aboriginals,* that is, the first children of the earth and the elder sons of their country.[18] With the

15. The god of shepherds is Pan who also invented the reed pipe. Parnassus and Helicon are mountains in Greece sacred to Apollo, god of poetry (among other things), and the Muses. Aganippe was a fountain at the foot of Mount Helicon flowing into Mount Parnassus, and Hippocrene was a fountain on Mount Helicon; both were sacred to the Muses.

16. For Iopas's singing about the sun and moon and weather, see *Aeneid,* I.740–746; for Silenus's singing about the creation of the world, the origins of the human race, and so on, see *Eclogues,* VI.31–81.

17. "Political" in Greek means "pertaining to the polis, or city-state." For *autoschediasmatic,* see *Poetics,* III.1448a23 and III.1449a9.

18. Horace speaks of Saturnine verse (verse written in the Age of Saturn or the Age of Gold) in his *Epistulae,* II.i.158. Fescinnine verse, discussed in the next sentence, was produced in the ancient city of Fescinnia in Etruria and was famous for being sportive and jeering; it is mentioned by Horace, *Epistulae,* II.i.145; Livy, *Ab urbe condita,* VII.ii.7; and Catullus, *Carmina,* LXI.127.

same verses, which are also called *Fescennine*, Horace, Catullus, and Livy tell us that in village assemblies, the sons of the ancient Sabines and the ancient laborers of Italy would sting one another with witty repartee, and that out of such things they composed their pastoral games and rustic songs. You will note by the way that Maximus of Tyre assures us that from these pastoral games and rustic songs the Greeks and Romans derived the celebrated names of *comedy* and *tragedy*.[19] But finally, through the progress due to observations made by their first authors who used figurative language, they perfected the form of poetry; it acquired stricter rules that were more adhered to, and it was generally marked with the true character of poetical eloquence.

The free human spirit did not remain long enclosed within the limits of poetical eloquence. It was able to break its chains and free itself from its servitude and, through the teachings of rhetoric, to make free and unhindered a speech that had formerly been constrained and tied down by the rules of poetry. And without pausing for the evidence of Quintilian, who says that next after the disciples of the poets, Empedocles was the master of the oratorical art, can one doubt that the sages, who governed the peoples and made them aware through the art of eloquence of the advantages of civil society, were not the first orators whom the ancient Greeks called sophists in the best sense of the term?[20] In truth, once cities were built and people brought together, those who were eloquent became their spokesmen and published by word of mouth the ordinances of the state and the regulations of public order, and using the adornments of a freer, more drawn out speech than their poetical eloquence, they persuaded those new citizens to reform their behavior and observe discipline. Since they were employed in the noblest and most elevated functions of civic life, they received a variety of glorious appellations and titles of honor. They were not only called sophists . . . because they were wise and intelligent, but they were also called rhetoricians, as Pollux remarks, because they were prudent and politically astute.[21] And insofar as these eloquent men carried on important negotiations, calmed the passions of the people with their speeches, and by the vote of the government were made its deputies in order to arrange alliances with foreigners and conclude peace treaties with enemies, they were honored with the titles of Orators of the State, Defenders of the Nation, Masters of the People, and Fathers of the Country—so true is it that rhetoric has always been the sure foundation of political rule, the principal source of victories and triumphs, and the necessary instrument of peace and war.

But since there is nothing in the world that is permanent, things never rise except to fall, and what begins with an origin always concludes with an end, you will not be surprised, Sir, if I assure you that this eloquence, of which I

19. I can find no mention of comedy and tragedy in the *Dialexis* of Maximus of Tyre.
20. For Empedocles as poet, see Quintilian, *Institutio oratoria*, III.i.8.
21. See Pollux, *Onomasticon*, article on *rhetor*.

have just spoken to you, descended from the throne and the rostrum in order to declaim in controversies and deliver model speeches in theaters and public squares. This imperious and supreme eloquence became a servant, a slave, and the sophists who were famous because of this eloquence, which they had formerly perfected, were declared infamous because of the eloquence they corrupted after that point. And we know not only that the title itself of sophist was no longer given to anyone except charlatans, rogues, and impostors, because eloquence was sold and prostituted by those people, but also that that eloquence became hateful and despised for having unworthily accused men like Socrates, unjustly praised men like Busiris, and basely flattered those who tyrannized the people.[22] The profession became so low and mercenary that for a slender payment, eloquence boasted she could dig tombs for some and build temples for others, distribute glory and dishonor, and possessed the agreeable magic that makes the dead live and past things present. Before the Athenaeum was built at the command of the emperor Hadrian, she exhibited herself as an actress and mountebank in the spas and baths of Italy.[23] One also saw her in gardens in the country and in houses in the city looking for patrons and begging money from spectators. But finally, that shameless one withdrew from Italy and Greece, passed into Africa, and went through the whole of Asia, where she performed with effrontery and ostentation, using sentences that were half-Greek and half-Latin, making a display of her poetical prose, trafficking in makeup and coloring, and selling incense and perfumes, even poisons and their antidotes.

Having shown how the rhetoric of the Greeks and Latins owes it origin entirely to the poets, what progress it made with the sophists, and how it was perfected by the orators, it is time, Sir, that we undeceive everyone. People must know that eloquence did not originate in Italy and Greece at all, and that the Greek and Roman orators are not worthy of wearing the supreme laurel on their heads or having the caduceus in their hands. The art of oratory has not only been the glory of Italy and the adornment of Greece; it was also in the earliest times the miracle of the Chaldeans and the marvel of Palestine. Before there were men like Plato and Demosthenes, Plotius and Cicero in Athens and Rome, there had been men like Solomon in Jerusalem, who uttered three thousand proverbs and composed five thousand songs. There were men like Daniel in Babylon who confounded the magicians and enchanters, that is, the sophists and declaimers of Assyria. Even earlier, there had been men like Aaron and Moses, and the virtue of the Most High had loosened the tongue of the one and spoken through the mouth of the other. There was a long time during which the eloquence of Sinai persuaded people with more majesty and effectiveness than did that of Parnassus. And

22. Quintilian comments on how the Greek orator Polycrates composed speeches in praise of Busiris and in condemnation of Socrates; see *Institutio oratoria*, II.xvii.4.
23. The Athenaeum, built during Hadrian's reign (117–138), was a school for the study of Greek rhetoric and culture.

it is certain that when the divine lawgiver descended from the mountain to announce to the people the will of the God of terror and the God of thunder, he bore a light on his face that was completely transformed into fire in his mouth, and with that light and that fire, he opened the eyes and warmed the hearts of all the Israelites. For it is certain that that same tongue of fire that preached through the mouths of the Apostles also delivered speeches through the mouth of Moses.

(Le Grand goes on at length praising Moses and defending that praise on the basis of the authority of Longinus. He also claims that the eloquence of Greece and Rome have perished, but that that of the Christian faith, which proceeds from the Holy Spirit, will live forever.)

Since rhetoric did not originate in Italy or Greece and its fatherland is more extensive, the entire world being its home, shall we concede, Sir, to these new Latins and these modern Greeks that one cannot reach even the first degree of eloquence in France without the aid of their Aristotle and their Cicero? Will these obstinate pedants persuade us that they possess the art of oratory and that in order to speak French well it is necessary to speak Greek or Latin well? Even if the poetry of old Marot and of famous Saint-Amant, the prose of the incomparable Conrart and your own *French Rhetoric,* which I hold in my hand, were not lustrous signs and sure witnesses that there are poets and orators who are purely French and who have had no commerce with either the Greeks or the Romans, I would still maintain that French rhetoric can stand entirely on its own two feet, that she has sources in her depths and does not have to draw water from elsewhere. There is nothing borrowed about her, everything foreign disagrees with her, and ornaments and rarities from outside make her ugly.

Without doubt, minds that are full of Greek and Latin, that know everything that is of no use to their own language, and that overload their speeches with farragoes of pedantic learning and extravagant figures can never acquire the natural, pure, unaffected mode of expression that is essential and necessary to make a speech truly French. So many different grammars, so many different locutions are at war with one another in their heads; a chaos of idioms and dialects reigns there; their construction of one sentence is contradicted by the syntax of another; the Greek soils the Latin, and the Latin spoils the Greek; and the Greek and Latin, mixed together, corrupt the French. So it is indubitable, Sir, that such individuals will never achieve the brilliance and clarity of your style, or the vigor and finesse of your elocution. A host of foreign things confuses their memory; their imagination is divided; they have the habit of dead languages, not the use of a living one.

Those who are persuaded that the art of eloquence is something foreign to the French do not know that they acquired the glory of speaking and writing well by the law of nature and that from time immemorial they have enjoyed the possession of true eloquence. Those people have not heard tell of the eloquence of our Druids, or of the poetry of our bards; they have not heard tell of that Gallic Hercules who held men chained by the ears, that is, who captured their spirits by the force of his oratory; and they have not heard tell that there was once a Laelius Plotius of the Gallic nation who was the first to teach rhetoric in the city of Rome.[24]

(Le Grand goes on to discuss how eloquence was impaired during the Middle Ages and then how various poets in the sixteenth century attempted to restore it. They failed because they were seeking to make the French language into Latin and Greek. Le Grand claims that in the seventeenth century the language has finally been brought to perfection, and he thus rejects the use of ancient models, insisting that the French have plenty of their own.)

Truly there are things shared in common by all nations, but one must admit that there are also those that are peculiar to each one: rhetoric has many rules that are generally applicable in all languages and especially with regard to invention, but it has many others as well that are peculiar to each language, especially with regard to arrangement and style. Can one say that the order of a sermon or of an address to the court is similar to that of an oration by Demosthenes or Cicero? Or that the lordly, magisterial style of the Greeks and Romans has any connection with the gentleness and modesty of ours? We know that even when our kings have spoken to the assembled estates, French eloquence being seated there with a crown on its head and a scepter in its hand, their majesty was always accompanied by gentleness, their authority always surrounded by grace. The maxims of politics and the mysteries of religion change the rules of rhetoric entirely, and ancient rhetoric has no similarity to its modern counterpart. Is there not quite a difference between the Areopagus of Athens and the Parlement of Paris, between the Philippics of the first and the remonstrances of the second, between men like Demosthenes who orated and men like Bignon who petition?[25] Is there not quite a difference between Orphic mystagogy and Christian theology, between the rhapsodies of Homer and the homilies of Saint [John] Chrysostom, between the Annunciation of the Angel Gabriel and the sending of Mercury as a messenger, between the torments of the devils and the punishments of the Eumenides?[26]

(Le Grand notes a number of differences between French and the languages of Greece and Rome, and he ends his discourse by again lavishing praise on Bary for having discovered the sure rules of French eloquence.)

24. The Gallic Hercules, or Hercules Gallicus, is described in the *Herakles* of Lucian, who says he was a version of Hermes, the god of eloquence, whose picture he saw in a temple in Marseilles; Le Grand notes that the chains running from Hercules' tongue to his followers' ears symbolized the power of eloquence. Laelius Plotius is a slip for Lucius Plotius.

25. The Areopagus was a hill in Athens where the supreme tribunal of the city met; the Parlement of Paris was one of several parlements that were the supreme courts in France under the ancien régime. The *Philippics* were speeches by Demosthenes against Philip of Macedonia.

26. The Eumenides were three Greek goddesses, avenging Furies named Allecto, Megaera, and Tisiphone.

Biographical Glossary
of Historical and
Mythological Characters

Aedesius, Greek philosopher (d. ca. 355), follower of the Neoplatonic philosopher Iamblichus (ca. 250–ca. 330).

Aeschines, Greek orator (ca. 392–ca. 322 B.C.), chief opponent of Demosthenes in Athens in debates about Philip of Macedonia's expansionist policies.

Aeschylus, Greek tragedian (525–426 B.C.), founder of Greek tragedy; his principal works include the *Oresteia* and *Prometheus Bound*.

Aesop, Greek writer (7th–6th c. B.C.), supposed author of the *Fables* that go under his name.

Africanus Minor, see *Scipio Aemilianus*.

Agnes (Saint), Christian martyr (4th c.) put to death after rejecting a well-born suitor.

Agrippa, Menenius (Menenius Lanatus Agrippa), Roman politician (fl. ca. 500 B.C.), consul in 503 B.C.; he supposedly persuaded rebellious plebeians to make peace by telling them the "fable of the belly." In that fable, the body's members (the plebeians) mutiny against the belly (the patricians) because it seems to get all the food, but they discover, after having deprived the belly of food, that they are withering away and thus need what the belly provides.

Albertus Magnus (Saint), Scholastic philosopher (ca. 1193–1280), teacher of Thomas Aquinas.

Alcibiades, Athenian general (450–404 B.C.), favorite pupil of Socrates and leader of the popular party; he led Athens into a disastrous war with Sicily and was twice exiled from the city.

Alexander the Great, king of Macedonia (356–323 B.C., ruled 336–323 B.C.), son of Philip II and pupil of Aristotle; he conquered Greece and then defeated Darius II and the Persians, capturing most of the Middle East and Egypt, and even going as far as India.

Alfonso V of Aragon, Spanish king (ca. 1396–1458) who transferred his court from Spain to Naples in 1443 and studied there with the Italian humanist Lorenzo Valla.

Alfonso X of Castile, Spanish king (1221–1284), called Alfonso the Wise, who had Spanish law codified under his direction and compiled the *Alphonsian Tables*, a book of planetary tables based on Arabic sources, but updated through observations at Toledo between 1262 and 1272.

Ambrose (Saint), a father of the Church (340–397), bishop of Milan who converted Augustine to Christianity.

Amphion, musician in Greek mythology, who was the son of Zeus and the nymph Antiope and who was said to have built the walls of Thebes by using his music to make the stones move of themselves.

Anacharsis, semilegendary figure from Scythia who came to Athens around 589 B.C. and became a friend of the lawgiver Solon; he symbolized the wise barbarian for Greek writers.

Anaxagoras, Greek philosopher (ca. 500–ca. 428 B.C.), mentor of Pericles and author of *On Nature*; only fragments of his works remain.

Anaximenes of Lampsacus, Greek historian and rhetorician (ca. 380–320 B.C.).

Anselm (Saint), archbishop of Canterbury (1033–1109), one of the first Scholastic philosophers.

Antiochus, king of Syria (ca. 324–261 B.C.), a successful ruler who consolidated his realm after marrying his father's second wife, Stratonice, who, according to Hellenistic writers, made him pine for love until he was cured by the doctor Erasistratus.

Antisthenes, Greek philosopher (ca. 445–ca. 360 B.C.), a follower of Socrates.

Antoninus Pius, Marcus, Roman emperor (86–161, ruled 138–161), adopted heir of Trajan.

Antonius, Marcus, Roman orator (143–93 B.C.), member of the aristocratic party who is celebrated in Cicero's *De oratore* as one of the greatest Roman orators.

Antony, Marc (Marcus Antonius), Roman politician and orator (83–30 B.C.), ally of Julius Caesar; he formed the Second Triumvirate with Octavius Caesar (Augustus) and Lepidus, beat Brutus and Cassius at the battle of Philippi (42 B.C.), broke with Octavius, allying himself with Cleopatra of Egypt, and was defeated by Octavius at the battle of Actium (31 B.C.).

Apelles, Greek artist (4th c. B.C.) considered one of the greatest painters of antiquity.

Aphthonius of Antioch, Greek rhetorician (end of 3rd c. – start of 4th c. B.C.) who authored a collection of fables and reworked the *Progymnasmata* of Hermogenes for use in the schools.

Apollonius of Tyana, a Neopythagorean philosopher (1st c.), who was famed for his holiness.

Apuleius, Lucius, Roman satirist (b. ca. 127), author of the *Metamorphoses*, better known as *The Golden Ass*, a work that recounts the adventures of its hero Lucius after he has been transformed into an ass; its style is famously difficult and obscure.

Aquinas, Thomas (Saint), chief of the Scholastic theologians (1225–1274), author of numerous works, including the *Summa Theologica*.

Aratus, Greek poet (ca. 315–ca. 245 B.C.), author of *Phaenomena,* a long poem on astronomy.

Archidamus, Spartan king (5th c. B.C.), leader in the Peloponnesian War against Athens.

Arete of Cyrene, learned Greek woman (4th c. B.C.), the daughter of Aristippus, who founded the Cyrenaic movement; she was the teacher of her son, also named Aristippus.

Aretino, Leonard Bruni, see *Bruni, Leonardo.*

Aretino, Pietro, Italian author (1492–1556), who composed religious as well as licentious works, but was especially renowned for his satires, which earned him the nickname of *flagellum principum,* the "scourge of princes."

Aristides, Publius Aelius, Greek sophist and orator (117–165), author of *To Plato in Defense of Oratory* and *On Political Style.*

Aristippus, Greek philosopher (ca. 435–366 B.C.), disciple of Socrates and founder of the Cyrenaic school of philosophy.

Aristogeiton, Athenian orator of evil repute, taken to court for debt sometime between 338 and 324 B.C.; the speech against him that survives is falsely attributed to Demosthenes.

Ariston of Cos, Greek philosopher (2nd c. B.C.), a disciple of Critolaus, who was head of the Peripatetic school that followed Aristotle.

Aristotle, Greek philosopher (384–322 B.C.), tutor of Alexander the Great and founder of the Peripatetic school of philosophy; he wrote a large number of treatises on many subjects, including foundational works on ethics, politics, and logic, as well as the *Rhetoric.*

Ascham, Roger, English humanist (1515–1568), teacher of Greek at Cambridge, tutor to Queen Elizabeth, and author of *The Scholemaster.*

Asinius Pollio, see *Pollio, Gaius Asinius.*

Aspasia of Miletus, learned woman (late 5th c. B.C.) who was mistress to Pericles, through whom she had great influence on public affairs.

Athenaeus, Greek writer (3rd c.), author of *The Deipnosophists (The Banquet of the Sages),* a compendium of information about the classical world.

Augustine (Saint), a father of the Church (354–430), converted to Christianity by Saint Ambrose; his most important works include *The City of God, The Confessions,* and *De doctrina christiana (On Christian Teaching),* a work that deals in part with the role of rhetoric in preaching.

Augustus (Gaius Julius Caesar Octavius), Roman emperor (63 B.C.–14 A.D., ruled 31 B.C.–14 A.D.), adopted by Julius Caesar as his successor; he won the battle of Actium against Antony and brought the Roman civil wars to an end.

Aulus Gellius, see *Gellius, Aulus.*

Aurelius, Marcus, see *Marcus Aurelius.*

Averroes (Ibn Rushd), Arabic doctor and philosopher (1126–1198) whose commentaries on Aristotle were widely influential on the Scholastics.

Barbaro, Ermolao, Venetian humanist (1453/54–1493), editor of the works of the Greek philosopher Themistius, and author of commentaries on classical writers, works on celibacy and the duties of legates, and numerous letters and orations.

Bary (or *Barry*), *René,* French writer (17th c.), author of a life of Louis XIII (1649), two volumes of *Conversations* (1674), and *La Rhetorique françoise (French Rhetoric,* 1658).

Basil (Saint), a father of the Greek Church (329–379), one of the founders of monasticism, and author of a collection of *Letters*.

Bede, the Venerable (Saint), English monk (672/673–735), author of the first history of England.

Bernard (Bernard of Clairvaux) (Saint), French mystic (1090–1153), founder of the Abbey of Clairvaux.

Bignon, Jérome, French lawyer, magistrate, and writer (1589–1656) who enjoyed a great reputation for his learning and his political skills.

Boccaccio, Giovanni, Florentine writer (1309–1375), author of numerous works in Italian, including *Il Filocolo, Il Filostrato,* and the *Decameron,* and of many in Latin, including the *Genealogie deorum gentilium* (*The Genealogy of the Pagan Gods*) and *De claris mulieribus* (*Of Famous Women*).

Brocense, see *Sanchez de las Brozas, Francisco.*

Bruni, Leonardo (Leonardo Bruni Aretino), Italian humanist (ca. 1370–1444), chancellor of Florence (1427–1444) and author of an influential history of the city.

Brutus, Marcus Junius, Roman senator (ca. 85–42 B.C.) known for his eloquence and even more for having, with Cassius and other patricians, assassinated Julius Caesar; he is a principal speaker in Cicero's *Brutus,* a dialogue surveying the great orators of Greece and Rome.

Busiris, legendary pharaoh of Egypt infamous for sacrificing all the strangers who came into his realm on the altars of his gods; he was killed by Hercules.

Caesar, Julius (Gaius Julius Caesar), Roman general and politician (101–44 B.C.), conqueror of Gaul, and popular leader in Rome who was assassinated by Brutus, Cassius, and other Roman patricians; known for his eloquence in speaking, he wrote *Commentaries* on his conquest of Gaul and on the recent civil wars he fought with Pompey.

Caligula, Gaius Caesar, Roman emperor (12–41, ruled 37–41); a tyrant, he died at the hands of an assassin.

Callisthenes, Greek philosopher (360–327 B.C.), follower of Alexander, who had him put to death when he criticized Alexander's taste for oriental luxury and his pretensions to divinity.

Carafa, Cardinal (Carlo Carafa), Italian prelate (1518–1560) whose conduct scandalized Rome and led to his being tried and executed.

Carbo, Gnaeus Papirius, Roman politician and general (d. 82 B.C.), supporter of the popular leader Marius.

Carneades, Greek philosopher (214/13–129/128 B.C.), a leading representative of the skeptical, antidogmatic Middle Academy, which succeeded the Academy founded by Plato; on a diplomatic mission with Diogenes the Stoic and Critolaus the Peripatetic to Rome in 155 B.C., he displayed his skepticism by delivering a speech in praise of justice on one day and a speech in praise of injustice on the next.

Carr, Nicholas, English humanist (1524–1568), regius professor of Greek at Cambridge.

Cassius (Gaius Cassius Longinus), Roman senator (d. 42 B.C.), coconspirator with Brutus in the assassination of Julius Caesar.

Catiline (Lucius Sergius Catilina), Roman patrician (ca. 109–62 B.C.) whose plot against the Senate was denounced by Cicero in his most famous set of speeches in 63 B.C.

Cato the Censor (Marcus Porcius Cato, also called Cato the Elder), Roman statesman (234–149 B.C.), author of *De re rustica* (*On Agriculture*); known for his eloquence and his moral severity, he opposed allowing the Greek Sophists Carneades, Critolaus, and Diogenes to speak in Rome.

Cato of Utica (Marcus Porcius Cato, also known as Cato the Younger), Roman statesman (95–46 B.C.), great grandson of Cato the Censor; known for his stoicism, he was a prominent opponent of Julius Caesar.

Catullus, Quintus Valerius, Roman poet (ca. 87–ca. 54 B.C.), imitator of Greek and especially Alexandrian verse in his *Carmina (Lyric Poems).*

Celsus Africanus, opponent of Christianity (2nd c.), author of the *True Discourse,* now lost.

Charmidas (also Charmadas and Charmides), Greek philosopher (fl. ca. 100 B.C.) famous for his eloquence and the retentiveness of his memory.

Chaucer, Geoffrey, English poet (ca. 1343–1400), greatest writer of the English Middle Ages; his most famous works include *The Canterbury Tales* and *Troilus and Criseyde.*

Choerilus, Greek tragic poet (late 6th c. B.C.), beaten in poetic competition by Aeschylus and famous for the supposedly inferior quality of his verse.

Chrysippus, Greek philosopher (ca. 280–206 B.C.), one of the founders of the Stoic school, famous for his mastery of subtle dialectical arguments.

Chrysoloras, Manuel, Byzantine scholar (ca. 1353–1415) who immigrated to Italy where he pioneered the study of Greek.

Chrysostom, John (Saint), a father of the Church (347–407), patriarch of Constantinople who was celebrated for his eloquence.

Cicero, Marcus Tullius, Roman orator, philosopher, and rhetorician (106–43 B.C.), a leader of the aristocratic party; his works include *De oratore (On the Orator), Orator, Brutus, De inventione (On Invention), Paradoxa Stoicorum (The Paradoxes of the Stoics), De partitione oratoria (On the Classification of Oratory),* the *Tusculan Disputations,* as well as numerous orations, including those against Catiline and the *Philippics* (against Marc Antony), and many volumes of letters.

Cineas, Greek orator (d. ca. 277 B.C.) trained by Demosthenes; he served King Pyrrhus of Epirus and was celebrated for his rhetorical power.

Claudius (Claudius Tiberius Drusus), Roman emperor (10 B.C.–54 A.D., ruled 41–54), an able administrator, who was dominated by his wife Agrippina, who finally poisoned him.

Cleanthes, Greek philosopher (ca. 331–ca. 232 B.C.) who succeeded Zeno, the founder of Stoicism, as the head of that school.

Cleisthenes, Athenian statesman (late 6th c. B.C.), a popular leader who reformed the political system of Athens, making it more democratic.

Cleon, Greek orator and politician (d. 422 B.C.), opponent of Pericles during the Peloponnesian War; he became the leader of the Athenian democracy thanks to his eloquence.

Conrart, Valentin, French writer (1603–1675), whose house was the cradle of the Académie Française and who was its first Secrétaire Perpétuel (permanent secretary).

Corax, and his pupil *Tisias,* Greek rhetoricians (5th c. B.C.) from Syracuse who are credited with having been the first to have taught rhetoric.

Corinna, Greek lyric poet (late 6th–early 5th c. B.C.), pupil of Myrtis; she is said to have bested Pindar in at least one and possibly as many as five contests.

Crassus, Lucius Licinius, Roman orator (140–91 B.C.), tutor of Cicero, celebrated in the latter's *De oratore* as one of the greatest Roman orators.

Crassus, Marcus Licinius, Roman politician (ca. 115–53 B.C.) who formed the First Triumvirate with Julius Caesar and Pompey; he was assassinated while fighting the Parthians.

Critias, Greek politician (450–404 B.C.), the best known of the Thirty, the oligarchy that ruled Athens in the middle of the fifth century B.C.

Critolaus, Greek philosopher (fl. 2nd c. B.C.), follower of Aristotle; sent on mission to Rome with Carneades and Diogenes the Stoic in 155 B.C.

Ctesiphon, Athenian politician (4th c. B.C.) who proposed awarding a crown to Demosthenes for his patriotic opposition to Philip of Macedonia.

Cyprian (Saint), a father of the Church (ca. 210–258), bishop of Carthage who was martyred in 258.

Damon and Pythias, Peripatetic philosophers who were the protagonists of an exemplary story of friendship; they lived during the reign of Dionysius II of Syracuse. Pythias had been condemned to death and asked for a few days respite, and when Damon took his place and Pythias faithfully returned on the appointed day, Dionysius was so moved that he liberated both men.

Darius (Darius III Codommanus), Persian emperor (reigned 336/5–330 B.C.) who was defeated by Alexander the Great at the battles of Issus in 333 B.C. and Gargamela in 331, after which he was killed by one of his servants.

Demades, Greek statesman and orator (ca. 380–319 B.C.).

Demetrius (Demetrius Phalereus, or Demetrius of Phaleron), Greek orator, Peripatetic philosopher, and statesman (b. ca. 350 B.C.), ruler of Athens under the Macedonians; he is (wrongly) credited with having written *On Interpretation,* a treatise on elocution.

Democritus, Greek philosopher (470/460–380/360 B.C.) best known for his theory of atoms.

Demosthenes, Greek orator and politician (384–322 B.C.), considered the greatest Greek orator; he was an impassioned opponent of Philip of Macedonia and his son Alexander the Great, and he delivered numerous orations, including the *Philippics* and the *Olynthiacs* against Philip and his expansionist policies.

Dinarchus, the leading Greek orator (ca. 360–ca. 290 B.C.) after the death of Demosthenes.

Diogenes the Stoic, Greek philosopher (ca. 238–ca. 150 B.C.), educated in Athens by Chrysippus and head of the Stoic school there; he was sent on an embassy to Rome with Carneades and Critolaus in 155 B.C.

Diogenes Laertius, see *Laertius, Diogenes.*

Dionysius the Areopagite (Saint), a father of the Church (2nd c.), bishop of Athens where he was martyred.

Dionysius of Halicarnassus, Greek historian and teacher of rhetoric (fl. ca. 20 B.C.), author of a history of Rome, commentaries on Greek orators, and several rhetorical treatises, including *The Arrangement of Words* and *On Imitation.*

Dionysius II of Syracuse, Greek ruler of Syracuse (ca. 405–ca. 343 B.C.; ruled 367–357 and 347–343), known for his fear of the people, his unwarlike behavior, and his interest in Platonic philosophy.

Domitian (Titus Flavius Domitianus), Roman emperor (51–96, ruled 81–96).

Donatus, Aelius, Roman grammarian (4th c.), author of a commentary on Vergil.

Duns Scotus, John, Scholastic philosopher (1266–1308), Scottish theologian and opponent of Thomas Aquinas.

Biographical Glossary

Empedocles, Greek philosopher (ca. 490–430 B.C.), statesman, poet, and religious leader; he was a democrat and helped overthrow the tyrants who ruled his native Sicily; of his great poem *Nature* only fragments survive.

Epaminondas, Theban general and statesman (ca. 418–362 B.C.) who assured the dominance of Thebes by defeating the Spartans.

Epicurus, Greek philosopher (341–270 B.C.) who followed the teaching of Democritus and argued that pleasure was the highest good, although he placed spiritual and intellectual pleasures above those of the body.

Erasistratus of Iulis on Ceos, Greek doctor (ca. 315–ca. 240 B.C.) who was one of the first to practice scientific dissection and to advocate and use a mechanistic method in medicine.

Euclid, Greek mathematician (fl. ca. 300 B.C.), celebrated for his treatise on geometry, the *Elements*.

Eunapius, Greek Sophist and historian (ca. 345–ca. 414), author of *Lives of the Philosophers and Sophists*.

Euripides, Greek tragedian (480–406 B.C.), whose works include *Medea, Hecuba, Hippolytus, Electra,* and *Bacchae*.

Eustathius, Greek philosopher (d. ca. 390), pupil of the Neoplatonic philosopher Iamblichus (ca. 250–ca. 330) and follower of Aedesius.

Favorinus, Roman philosopher (ca. 85–155), a Stoic inclining toward mild skepticism, to whom is attributed a mock-oration in praise of the quartan fever (malaria).

Filelfo, Francesco, Italian humanist (1398–1481) who studied Greek in Constantinople, then taught it throughout Italy; he also composed numerous works in Latin.

Gellius, Aulus, Roman writer (2nd c.), author of *Noctes atticae* (*Attic Nights*), a compendium of information about the ancient world.

Giovanni di Conversino da Ravenna, Italian notary and humanist (1343–1408), a celebrated educator who taught Pier Paolo Vergerio.

Gorgias of Leontini (Gorgias Leontinus), Greek rhetorician (ca. 483–376 B.C.), a Syracusan who came to Athens to teach rhetoric; he left a number of speeches, including one defending Helen of Troy, and is the subject of Plato's *Gorgias*.

Gower, John, English poet (d. 1408), considered second to Chaucer in the medieval period; his best known work was the *Confessio amantis* (*The Lover's Confession*).

Gracchi, the, two brothers, Tiberius Sempronius Gracchus (162–133 B.C.) and Gaius Sempronius Gracchus (154–121 B.C.), who proposed various agrarian laws in order to curb the power of the Roman aristocracy; both were murdered.

Gregory Nazianzus (Gregory of Nazianzus), a father of the Church (ca. 329–388), bishop of Constantinople.

Gregory the Great (Saint), a father of the Church (ca. 540–604), responsible for the Gregorian calendar.

Guarino of Verona (Guarino de' Guarini), Italian humanist (1370/74–1460), one of the first teachers of Greek in Italy, editor of numerous Latin authors, and translator of many Greek ones.

Hannibal, Carthaginian general (247–183 B.C.), leader of an invasion into Italy across the Alps and winner a series of battles against the Romans; he was finally defeated by Scipio Africanus at the battle of Zama in 202 B.C.

Hegesias, Greek philosopher (fl. ca. 290 B.C.) who was called the "Death-persuader" because his emphasis on the wretchedness of the human condition was said to have encouraged people to commit suicide.

Heraclitus, Greek philosopher (ca. 535–ca. 475 B.C.) who believed that fire was the original element and whose gnomic style earned him the title of "the obscure."

Hermagoras of Temnos, Greek orator (2nd c.), author of an *Art of Rhetoric*.

Hermogenes, Greek rhetor and Sophist (b. ca. 161), author of treatises and textbooks, including *On Different Styles*, a standard stylistic manual in late antiquity.

Herodotus, Greek historian (ca. 480–ca. 425 B.C.), called "the father of history"; his *Histories*, including both legendary and historical events, places Greek civilization in opposition to the worlds of the Persians, the Medes, and the Egyptians.

Hesiod, Greek poet (8th c. B.C.), author of *Works and Days* and the *Theogony*, a work recounting stories about the Greek gods.

Hesychius of Miletus, Greek chronicler and grammarian (6th c.), author of histories, including one on the founding of Byzantium, and of the *Onomatologos*, a guide to the distinguished men of learning of antiquity.

Hilarius of Poitiers (Saint), a father of the Church (ca. 315–367), bishop of Poitiers.

Hippias of Elis, Greek Sophist (ca. 450–ca. 399 B.C.) who wrote elegies, tragedies, and treatises in prose; he appears in the two Platonic dialogues named after him as well as in Plato's *Protagoras*.

Hippocrates, Greek doctor (ca. 460–ca. 375 B.C.) whose medical theories were enormously influential from ancient times down to the end of the Renaissance.

Homer, Greek epic poet (9th c. B.C.), identified as the author of the *Iliad* and the *Odyssey*.

Horace (Quintus Horatius Flaccus), Roman poet (65–8 B.C.) whose works include the *Odes*, *Epodes*, *Epistulae* (*Epistles*), *Sermones* (*Satires*), and the *Ars poetica* (*Art of Poetry*).

Hortensius (Quintus Hortensius Hortalus), Roman orator (114–50 B.C.), the chief rival of Cicero.

Hyperides, Greek orator (389–322 B.C.) trained by Isocrates and considered second only to Demosthenes.

Hypocracia, see *Corinna*.

Ignatius (Saint), a father of the Church (798–877), bishop of Constantinople.

Isaeus, Greek orator (4th c. B.C.) who ran a school in which he taught Demosthenes.

Isidore of Seville (Saint), bishop of Seville (ca. 570–636) who organized the Spanish Church and wrote many learned works, the most influential of which was the *Etymologiae* (*Etymologies*).

Isocrates, Greek orator (436–338 B.C.) whose many speeches were considered models of Attic eloquence.

Jerome (Saint), a father of the Church (ca. 347–420), author of the Latin version of the Bible.

John Chrysostom, see *Chrysostom, John*.

John of Damascus (Johannes Damascenus) (Saint), a father of the Church (675–749) and a leading opponent of the Iconoclast Movement.

Julian the Apostate (Flavius Claudius Julianus), Roman emperor (331–363, ruled 361–363) who abandoned Christianity in about 351 and restored paganism when he succeeded Constantine on the throne; he was the author of a variety of works, including letters and a series of biographies of Roman rulers, *Caesares* (*The Caesars*).

Juvenal (Decius Junius Juvenalis), Roman satirist (ca. 65–128) whose *Saturae* (*Satires*) are known for the harshness of their denunciations of vice.

Lactantius, Lucius Caelius Firmianus, Christian apologist (ca. 250–340), author of the *Divinae institutiones* (*The Divine Institutes*) as well as other works, including poetry.

Laelius, Gaius, Roman statesman and general (ca. 190–ca. 129 B.C.) who enjoyed a considerable reputation as an orator; Cicero's treatise on friendship, *De amicitia,* also known as *Laelius,* is named after him.

Laertius, Diogenes, Greek historian (3rd c.), author of *Lives of the Philosophers,* an important source of information on the lives of many Greek and Roman philosophers.

Langland, William, English poet (ca. 1330–ca. 1400), presumed author of *Piers Plowman,* a long allegorical poem that recounts its author's dream vision.

Lentulus (Publius Cornelius Lentulus Sura), Roman politician (d. 63 B.C.) who was an undistinguished orator and a coconspirator with Catiline.

Leptines, Greek mathematician (late 4th c. B.C.) active at the court of King Seleucus I (ca. 358–280 B.C.) of Syria.

Libanius, Greek rhetorician (314–ca. 393), teacher of various fathers of the Church and an admirer of the emperor Julian the Apostate.

Linus, mythological Greek figure who is said to have been a great musician in one account and who was destroyed by Apollo when he set himself up as a rival to the god; a later tradition makes him a poet.

Livy (Titus Livius), Roman historian (ca. 59 B.C.–17 A.D.) who espoused the ideals of eloquence defined by Cicero and Demosthenes; he composed an annalistic history of Rome, *Ab urbe condita* (*From the Founding of the City*).

Longinus, Greek rhetorician (ca. 220–273), supposed author of the treatise *On the Sublime.*

Lucian of Samosate, satirical author (125–ca. 190) whose numerous works include *Herakles* (*Hercules*) and *True Histories,* a cynical parody of contemporary travel and adventure stories.

Lucretius (Titus Lucretius Carus), Latin poet (ca. 98–55 B.C.), author of *De rerum natura* (*On the Nature of Things*), a poem expounding the materialist doctrines of the Greek philosopher Epicurus.

Lucullus, Lucius Licinius, Roman general and politician (ca. 110–57/6 B.C.) who was a leading member of the aristocratic party headed by Sulla.

Luther, Martin, German religious reformer (1483–1546) who broke with the Catholic Church in 1517 over the questions of indulgences and salvation by faith, and was excommunicated in 1520; he translated the Bible into German.

Lycurgus, Athenian statesman and lawgiver (ca. 390–ca. 325 B.C.), ally of Demosthenes.

Lydgate, John, English poet (ca. 1370–ca. 1450), known for long moralistic and devotional works, among them *The Fall of Princes.*

Lysias, Greek orator (ca. 440–ca. 380 B.C.), a leading opponent of the oligarchy that ruled Athens during his life; he was known for the purity and charm of his style.

Lysippus, Greek sculptor (4th c. B.C.), famous for his slender, vivid figures.

Maevius, Latin poet sarcastically alluded to in Vergil's third *Eclogue;* his name was proverbial for bad poetry.

Marcus Aurelius (Marcus Aurelius Antoninus), Roman emperor (121–180, ruled 161–

180), best known for his *Meditations*, a collection of maxims written in Greek that express his Stoic philosophy.

Marius, Gaius, Roman general (156–86 B.C.), leader of the popular party and opponent of Sulla.

Marot, Clément, French poet (1496–1544), author of poems still largely medieval in character, but influenced by the emerging aesthetic fashions of the Renaissance.

Marsili, Luigi, Florentine cleric (1342–1394), the leader of a circle of humanist disciples who met at the convent of Santo Spirito; his writings include attacks on abuses in the Church and brief commentaries on Petrarch's poetry.

Martial (Marcus Valerius Martialis), Roman poet (ca. 40–ca. 104), celebrated for his witty and satirical collection of *Epigramata* (*Epigrams*).

Maximus, Fabius (Quintus Fabius Maximus Cunctator), Roman general (d. 203 B.C.) whose wise policy of delay ("Cunctator" means "delayer") slowed Hannibal's invading army.

Maximus of Tyre, Greek philosopher (2nd c.), a Neoplatonic thinker who has left 41 *Dialexis* (*Lectures*) primarily concerned with ethical issues.

Memnon, in Greek mythology an Ethiopian warrior who fought at Troy and was immortalized by Zeus; he was identified with two colossal statues in Egypt, one of which supposedly produced music when rays of the rising sun struck its mouth.

Menedemus, Greek philosopher (ca. 338–265 B.C.), a follower of Socrates.

Metellus, Quintus Caecilius, Roman general and politician (d. 115 B.C.) who is referred to in Cicero's *Brutus* (xxi.81) as the most eloquent man of his age.

Midas, legendary Phrygian king famous for his foolishness; asked to judge a musical contest between Apollo and Pan, he chose the latter and was given a pair of ass's ears by the former (see Ovid, *Metamorphoses*, XI.146–93).

Mithridates (Mithridates VI Eupator Dionysius), king of Pontus (120–63 B.C.), a Hellenistic ruler who was Rome's most dangerous enemy in the first century B.C.; he was defeated by Pompey and committed suicide.

Musaeus, seer and priest in Greek mythology associated with Orpheus; he is said to have produced poetry even before Homer.

Musonius (Gaius Musonius Rufus), Roman Stoic philosopher (1st c.), teacher of Pliny the Younger and the Stoic philosopher Epictetus.

Myrtis, a Greek poetess (6th c. B.C.) who taught both Corinna and Pindar

Nero (Gaius Claudius Nero), Roman emperor (37–68, ruled 54–68) renowned for his cruelty; he had his tutor, Seneca, his mother, Agrippina, and his wife, Octavia, killed, is reputed to have burned Rome, and was finally forced to commit suicide.

Nicander of Colophon, Greek poet and grammarian (2nd c. B.C.), author of didactic poems as well as works on geography.

Nicetas (Nicetas Acominatus Choniates), Byzantine Greek historian (ca. 1140–1213), author of an annalistic history of the Byzantine Empire.

Onasander, Greek Neoplatonist (1st c.), author of *The General*.

Origen, Greek theologian (185–253), famous for his allegorical exegeses of the Bible; many of his doctrines were condemned by the Church.

Orpheus, poet and musician in Greek mythology, the son of Apollo and Calliope, whose harp playing enabled him to control animals and move mountains; by its means he was able to obtain the release of his dead wife, Eurydice, from Pluto's realm, but lost her again because he could not refrain from looking back at her as they were leaving Hades.

Osorius (Jeronimo Osorio), Portuguese theologian (1506–1580), author of *De gloria* and other works in a strictly Ciceronian style.

Otho, Lucius Roscius, Roman politician (fl. ca. 60 B.C.), a tribune who proposed and had passed a very unpopular law in 67 B.C. that gave people with equestrian status special seats at the public games.

Ovid (Publius Ovidius Naso), Roman poet (43 B.C.–17 A.D.), author of the *Metamorphoses,* the *Ars amatoria* (*The Art of Love*), and collections of lyric poems.

Palaephates, Greek mythographer (late 4th c. B.C.) who composed *On Incredible Things,* a work that attempts to explain myths "rationally."

Parmenides of Elea, Greek philosopher (ca. 539–ca. 475 B.C.), founder of the Eleatic school of philosophy that believed in the unity of being; he put the tenets of his philosophy in a short poem called *Nature.*

Paulus, Lucius Aemilius, Roman general (ca. 229–160 B.C.), victorious in many battles, especially against the Macedonians; he was given the surname of "Macedonicus."

Pausanias, Greek historian and geographer (2nd c.), author of a *Description of Greece.*

Pericles, Athenian statesman (499–429 B.C.), famous for his eloquence; he led the democratic party to power in the city, oversaw the creation of an Athenian empire, and patronized the arts.

Perotto, Niccolò, Italian humanist (1429–1480), student of Guarino of Verona, apostolic secretary in Rome, and author of a Latin grammar, a treatise on letter writing, a commentary on Martial, and many translations of Greek works.

Persius (Antonius Persius Flaccus), Roman satirical poet (34–62), author of the *Saturae* (*Satires*).

Phidias, Athenian sculptor (d. ca. 431 B.C.) considered the greatest of antiquity, responsible for designing the statues on the Parthenon.

Philip of Macedonia (Philip II), king of Macedonia (382–336 B.C., ruled 356–336) and father of Alexander the Great; he pursued expansionist policies in Greece that were opposed by the Athenian orator Demosthenes.

Philo Judaeus, Hebrew philosopher (20 B.C.–54 A.D.) who wrote in Greek and whose work mixes Biblical material with Neoplatonism.

Philostratus, Flavius, Neoplatonic philosopher (ca. 172–ca. 245), author of a biography of the first-century sage Apollonius of Tyana whom he defended against the charge of being an evil magician.

Phocion, Athenian statesman and general (ca. 402–318 B.C.), pupil of Plato and opponent of the anti-Macedonian party headed by Demosthenes.

Pindar, Greek lyric poet (521–441 B.C.), author of odes and many other lyric poems.

Pisistratus, Athenian statesman (605?–528/527 B.C.), ruler of the city, thanks to his eloquence and political acumen, at various times between 561 and his death.

Plato, Greek philosopher (428–347 B.C.), author of dialogues, such as the *Phaedrus* and the *Gorgias,* in which his teacher Socrates attacks rhetoric, and of the *Republic,* in which poets are banished from the ideal state.

Pliny the Elder (Gaius Plinius Secundus), Roman writer (23–79), author of *Naturalis historia* (*Natural History*), an encyclopedic work on science.

Pliny the Younger (Gaius Plinius Caecilius), Roman orator and writer (61–ca. 113), author of letters and a panegyric on the emperor Trajan.

Plotius Gallus, Laelius, Roman rhetorician (fl. ca. 100 B.C.) who is said to have been the first person to teach rhetoric in Rome.

Plutarch, Greek biographer and philosopher (ca. 46–ca. 120), author of the *Lives of the Eminent Greeks and Romans* and the *Moralia* (*Moral Essays*).

Poliziano, Angelo, Italian poet and humanist (1454–1494), associate of Pico della Mirandola and Marsilio Ficino in the Florentine Platonic Academy, author of works in Latin as well as *La Favola di Orfeo* (*The Fable of Orpheus*) and *Le Stanze per la Giostra* (*Stanzas for the Tournament*).

Pollio, Gaius Asinius, Roman writer and orator (76 B.C.–4 A.D.), critic and opponent of Cicero, friend of Augustus, and author of a history of the civil war between Caesar and Pompey.

Pollux of Naucratis, Iulus, Greek scholar and rhetorician (2nd c.), author of *Onomasticon* (*Thesaurus*).

Pompey the Great (Gaius Pompeius), Roman general and political leader (107–48 B.C.), formed the First Triumvirate with Julius Caesar and Crassus in 60 B.C., but broke with Caesar and was defeated by him at the battle of Pharsalia in 48.

Posidonius of Apamea, Greek philosopher (ca. 135–ca. 51 B.C.), an important Stoic thinker as well as a scientist and historian.

Prodicus of Ceos, Greek Sophist (5th c. B.C.), of whose works only fragments survive; he appears as a character in Plato's *Protagoras.*

Protagoras of Abdera, Greek Sophist (485–411 B.C.) who argued that all knowledge begins in sensation; the subject of Plato's *Protagoras.*

Pylades and Orestes, characters who appear in Sophocles' *Oresteia* and who were a model of friendship in antiquity.

Pyrrhus (Pyrrhus II, king of Epirus), Greek ruler and general (ca. 318–272 B.C.) who initially fought the Romans successfully, though losing many of his troops in battle (hence, the expression "Pyrrhic victory"), but was eventually defeated by them in Argos.

Pythagoras, Greek philosopher and mathematician (ca. 530–ca. 500 B.C.), advocate of austerity and founder of the sect named Pythagoreans after him.

Pythias, see *Damon and Pythias.*

Quintilian, Marcus Fabius, Roman rhetorician (ca. 35–ca. 100), author of the *Institutio oratoria* (*Art of Oratory*), a massive compilation of material on oratory in twelve books; two collections of *Declamationes* have been attributed to him, but are probably not his.

Rufinus, Tyrannius, Christian priest (ca. 345–410/411), translator of Greek theological works into Latin; he was close to Jerome until 394 when they disagreed violently on the question of whether the views of the Greek theologian Origen were orthodox.

Saint-Amant, Marc-Antoine Girard de, French poet (1594–1661), author of vivid, picturesque verse.

Sallust (Gaius Sallustius Crispus), Roman historian (86–35 B.C.), author of the *Bellum Catilinae* (*Conspiracy of Catiline*) and the *Bellum Jugurthinum* (*War of Jugurtha*).

Sanchez de las Brozas, Francisco, Spanish humanist (1523–1601), who taught at Salamanca and wrote and edited poetry and scholarly works in both Latin and Spanish. Among his scholarly works is the *Organum dialecticum et rhetoricum* (*Organon of Dialectic and Rhetoric*).

Sapor (Shapur II, the Great), Persian king (310–379) who expanded the Persian empire to include Armenia as well as parts of the Eastern Roman Empire.

Saturninus, Lucius Appuleius, Roman politician (d. 100 B.C.), opponent of the Senate, which condemned him to death by stoning.

Scipio Aemilianus, Publius (also known as *Africanus Minor*), Roman general and politician (185/4–129 B.C.) with an interest in oratory and poetry.

Scipio Africanus, Roman general (235–183 B.C.) who opposed the Carthaginian Hannibal in Spain during the Second Punic War and defeated him at the battle of Zama in 202 B.C.

Scotus, Duns, see *Duns Scotus.*

Seneca, Lucius Annaeus, Roman Stoic philosopher (ca. 2–65), teacher of Nero by whom he was ordered to commit suicide, and author of moral essays (*Epistulae morales*) and eight tragedies based on Greek originals.

Seneca the Rhetor (Marcus Annaeus Seneca), Roman rhetorician (ca. 55 B.C.–ca. 39 A.D.), author of collections of oratorical exercises, the *Suasoriae* (*Hortatory Speeches*) and the *Controversiae* (*Disputations*).

Sinesius of Cyrene, Greek writer (ca. 370–ca. 414), bishop of Ptolemais, author of *Hymns,* works on dreams, a collection of letters, and a *Praise of Baldness.*

Socrates, Greek philosopher (470–399 B.C.), celebrated for his dialectical method of inquiry and his irony; put to death on a charge of impiety by the citizens of Athens, he left no writings behind him, his ideas being preserved in the dialogues of his pupil Plato.

Solon, Athenian lawgiver (640–558 B.C.), considered one of the Seven Sages of Greece; he wrote a liberal constitution for his city.

Statius, Publius Papinius, Roman poet (ca. 40–96), author of a lyric collection, *Silvae* (*The Forest*), and an epic, *Thebais* (*Thebaid*).

Strebaeus, Jacobus Ludovicus, French humanist (d. 1550) who taught at the University of Rheims and translated and commented on Aristotle.

Sturmius (Johann Sturm), German humanist (1507–1589), author of numerous works on rhetoric and style, including *De periodis* (*On Periodic Style*) and *De imitatione oratoria* (*On Rhetorical Imitation*).

Suetonius (Gaius Suetonius Tranquillus), Roman historian (ca. 75–ca. 160), author of a biography of the first twelve Caesars and an incomplete history of rhetoric, *De rhetoribus* (*On the Rhetors*).

Sulla, Lucius Cornelius, Roman politician (138–78 B.C.), leader of the aristocratic faction and rival of Marius; he was forced out of power in Rome by Marius in 79 B.C.

Symmachus, Quintus Aurelius, opponent of Christianity (ca. 345–402), who was the object of attacks by Ambrose.

Tacitus, Cornelius, Roman historian (ca. 55–120), known for his complex and difficult style; he is author of the *Annales* (*Annals*), *De Germania* (*On Germany*), and the *Dialogus de oratoribus* (*Dialogue on the Orators*).

Tatian, Christian apologist (2nd c.), defender of the Gnostic heresy.

Terence (Publius Terentius Afer), Roman comic dramatist (ca. 190–157 B.C.), author of six plays based on Greek New Comedy.

Thecla (Saint), virgin and martyr (1st c.), disciple of Saint Paul.

Themistius, Greek philosopher and rhetorician (ca. 317–ca. 388), author of numerous orations and of commentaries on Aristotle's works, including his *De anima* (*On the Soul*).

Themistocles, Athenian general (ca. 525–ca. 460 B.C.), victor of the battle of Salamis over the Persians; he was leader of the democratic party and opposed by Aristides, whom he had exiled.

Theon, Aelius, Greek rhetorician (3rd c. B.C.), author of *Progymnasmata* (*Preparatory Exercises*), a manual of rhetorical exercises widely used in schools in the ancient world.

Theophrastus, Greek philosopher (ca. 372–ca. 287 B.C.), successor of Aristotle as the head of his school, the Lyceum, and author of *The Characters,* a set of descriptions of character types.

Theseus, semilegendary Greek hero and king of Athens who rescued Ariadne from the labyrinth in Crete and was credited with having established the original political organization of Attica.

Thrasymachus of Chalcedon, Greek Sophist (fl. 400–425 B.C.) of whose works only fragments survive; he appears as a character in Plato's *Republic.*

Thucydides, Athenian politician (b. ca. 500 B.C.) who was the leading conservative opponent of Pericles and was exiled briefly in ca. 443 B.C.

Thucydides, Greek historian (ca. 460–ca. 395 B.C.), author of the *History of the Peloponnesian War,* celebrated for his attempt to be impartial and for his interest in historical causation.

Tiberius (Claudius Tiberius Nero), Roman emperor (42 B.C.–37 A.D., ruled 14–37 A.D.), who inherited the empire from Augustus.

Timagoras, Athenian politician (4th c. B.C.) who was sent on an embassy to Persia and was condemned to death by the Athenians for having flattered the Persian king Darius III.

Tisias, see *Corax.*

Titus (Titus Flavius Vespasianus), Roman emperor (39–81, ruled 79–81); during his reign, Vesuvius erupted, destroying Pompeii and Herculaneum.

Tully, see *Cicero.*

Varro, Marcus Teruntius, Roman writer (116–27 B.C.), author of works on agriculture and of *De lingua latina* (*On the Latin Language*).

Vergerio, Pier Paolo, Italian humanist (1370–1444), an important teacher whose treatise *De ingenuis moribus et liberalibus studiis* (*On Noble Manners and Liberal Studies*) of 1400 was widely influential on educational thinking in the Renaissance.

Volaterranus, Raphael (Raphael Maffei of Volterra), Italian humanist (1455–1522) celebrated by contemporaries for his learning and piety.

William of Occam, Scholastic philosopher (1270–1347), an English Franciscan who defended nominalism and was celebrated as the "Invincible Doctor."

Xenophanes, Greek philosopher and religious thinker (b. ca. 566 B.C.) who presented his teaching through poetry.

Xenophon, Greek historian, philosopher, and general (ca. 427–ca. 355 B.C.), pupil of Socrates and author of many works, including the *Cyropedia,* a life of the Persian king Cyrus, and the *Anabasis,* a recount of the retreat of ten thousand Greek troops stranded in Persia.

Zeno the Stoic, Greek philosopher (ca. 320–ca. 250 B.C.) considered the founder of Stoicism; none of his writings survive except in fragments.

Zoroaster, Persian religious leader (ca. 630–ca. 550 B.C.) who reformed the traditional religion of the Persians, moving it in the direction of monotheism; his thought was influential on Judaism, Greek philosophy, and Christianity.

Renaissance Rhetoric:
A Selected Bibliography

PRIMARY WORKS

For a complete bibliography listing more than a thousand primary texts concerned with rhetoric from the Renaissance, the reader is advised to consult James Murphy's *Renaissance Rhetoric* (see below under "Bibliographies").

COLLECTIONS OF PRIMARY WORKS

British and Continental Rhetoric and Elocution. Sixteen microfilm reels. Ann Arbor, Mich.: University Microfilms, 1953.

Prosatori latini del Quattrocento. Edited by Eugenio Garin. Milan: Riccardo Ricciardi, 1952.

Reden und Briefe italienischer Humanisten. Edited by Karl Müllner. Vienna, 1899. Reprint, Munich: Wilhelm Fink Verlag, 1970.

Renaissance Rhetoric: A Microfiche Collection of Key Texts, A.D. *1472–1602.* Edited by James J. Murphy. Elmsford, N.Y.: Microforms International, 1987.

Testi umanistici sulla retorica. Edited by Eugenio Garin, Paolo Rossi, and Cesare Vasoli. Rome: Fratelli Bocca, 1953.

Trattati di poetica e retorica del Cinquecento. Edited by Bernard Weinberg. 4 vols. Bari: Laterza, 1970.

Modern Editions and Reprints of Primary Works in English

Bacon, Francis. *Selected Writings.* Introduction by Hugh G. Dick. New York: Random House, 1955.

———. *A Critical Edition of the Major Works.* Edited by Brian Vickers. Oxford: Oxford University Press, 1996.

Blount, Thomas. *The Academie of Eloquence.* Edited by R. C. Alston. London: 1654. Reprint, Menston, England: Scolar Press, 1971.

Bulwer, John. *Chirologia: or the Natural Language of the Hand* and *Chironomia: or the Art of Manual Rhetoric.* Edited by James W. Cleary. Carbondale: Southern Illinois University Press, 1974.

Coxe, Leonard. *The Arte or Craft of Rhethoryke.* London, 1524. Reprint, Amsterdam: Walter J. Johnson, 1977.

Day, Angel. *The English Secretary.* Introduction by Robert O. Evans. Gainesville, Fla.: Scholars' Facsimiles and Reprints, 1967.

Fenner, Dudley. *The Artes of Logike and Rhetorike.* In *Four Tudor Books on Education,* edited by Robert D. Peer, 151–80. Gainesville, Fla.: Scholars' Facsimiles and Reprints, 1966.

Fraunce, Abraham. *The Arcadian Rhetorike.* Edited by Ethel Seaton. Oxford: Basil Blackwell, 1950.

Hobbes, Thomas. *The Whole Art of Rhetoric, The Art of Rhetoric, plainly set forth with pertinent examples for the more easy understanding of the same,* and *The Art of Sophistry.* In *English Works,* edited by Sir William Molesworth, 419–536. London, 1840. Reprint, Aalen: Scientia Verlag, 1966.

Hoskins, John. *Directions for Speech and Style.* Edited by Hoyt H. Hudson. Princeton, N.J.: Princeton University Press, 1935.

Peacham, Henry. *The Garden of Eloquence (1593).* Introduction by William G. Crane. Gainesville, Fla.: Scholars' Facsimiles and Reprints, 1954.

Puttenham, George. *The Arte of English Poesie.* Introduction by Baxter Hathaway. Kent, Ohio: Kent State University Press, 1970.

Rainolde, Richard. *The Foundacion of Rhetorike.* London, 1563. Reprint, Amsterdam: Da Capo, 1969.

Sherry, Richard. *A Treatise of Schemes and Tropes (1550) and His Translation of "The Education of Children" by Desiderius Erasmus.* Introduction by Herbert W. Hildebrandt. Gainesville, Fla.: Scholars' Facsimiles and Reprints, 1961.

Sidney, Sir Philip. *An Apology for Poetry.* Edited by Forrest G. Robinson. Indianapolis: Bobbs-Merrill, 1970.

Smith, John. *The Mysterie of Rhetorique Unvail'd.* Edited by R. C. Alston. Menston, England: Scolar Press, 1969.

Wilson, Thomas. *The Arte of Rhetorique (1560).* Edited by G. H. Mair. Oxford: The Clarendon Press, 1909.

———. *The Arte of Rhetoric (1560).* Edited by Peter E. Medine. University Park: Pennsylvania State University Press, 1994.

Modern English Translations of Primary Works

Breen, Quirinus. "Giovanni Pico della Mirandola on the Conflict of Philosophy and Rhetoric." *Journal of the History of Ideas* 13 (1952): 384–412. (This is a translation of the letter from Pico to Ermolao Barbaro that is included in this anthology.)

Erasmus, Desiderius. *Ciceronianus.* Edited by A. H. T. Levi. Vol. 6 of *Collected Works: Literary and Educational Writings.* Toronto: University of Toronto Press, 1986.

Bibliography

Harvey, Gabriel. *Ciceronianus*. Edited by Harold S. Wilson. Translated by Clarence A. Forbes. Lincoln: University of Nebraska Press, 1945.

Hudson, Hoyt H. "Jewel's Oration against Rhetoric: A Translation." *Quarterly Journal of Speech* 14 (1928): 374–92.

McNally, J. R. "Rudolph Agricola's *De inventione dialectica libri tres:* A Translation of Selected Chapters." *Speech Monographs* 34 (1967): 393–422.

Montaigne, Michel de. *The Complete Works*. Translated by Donald M. Frame. Stanford, Calif.: Stanford University Press, 1967.

Petrarca, Francesco. *Letters on Familiar Matters: Books I–VIII*. Translated by Aldo Bernardo. Albany: State University of New York Press, 1975.

Ramus, Peter (Pierre de la Ramée). *Arguments in Rhetoric against Quintilian (1549)*. Translated by Carole Newlands and James J. Murphy. DeKalb: University of Northern Illinois University Press, 1983.

———. *Peter Ramus's Attack on Cicero: Text and Translation of Ramus's "Brutinae Quaestiones."* Edited by James J. Murphy. Translated by Carole Newlands. Davis, Calif.: Hermagoras Press, 1992.

Rainolds, John. *Oratio in laudem artis poeticae*. Edited by William Ringler and Walter Allen, Jr. Princeton, N.J.: Princeton University Press, 1940.

———. *Oxford Lectures on Aristotle's "Rhetoric."* Edited and translated by Lawrence D. Green. Newark: University of Delaware Press, 1986.

BIBLIOGRAPHIES

Abbott, Don Paul. "The Renaissance." In *The Present State of Scholarship in Historical and Contemporary Rhetoric*, edited by Winifred Bryan Horner, rev. ed., 84–113. Columbia: University of Missouri Press, 1990.

Murphy, James J., with Kevin Roddy. *Renaissance Rhetoric: A Short-Title Catalogue of the Works on Rhetorical Theory from the Beginning of Printing to* A.D. *1700, with Special Reference to the Holdings of the Bodleian Library, Oxford. With a Special Basic Bibliography of Secondary Works on Renaissance Rhetoric*. New York: Garland, 1981.

Stanford, Charles L. "The Renaissance." In *Historical Rhetoric: An Annotated Bibliography of Selected Sources in English*, edited by Winifred Bryan Horner, 111–84. Boston: G. K. Hall, 1980.

SECONDARY WORKS

Altman, Joel. *The Tudor Play of Mind: Rhetorical Inquiry and the Development of Elizabethan Drama*. Berkeley: University of California Press, 1978.

Biester, James. *Lyric Wonder: Rhetoric and Wit in Renaissance English Poetry*. Ithaca, N.Y.: Cornell University Press, 1997.

Bushnell, Rebecca. *A Culture of Teaching: Early Modern Humanism in Theory and Practice*. Ithaca, N.Y.: Cornell University Press, 1996.

Cahn, Michael. "The Eloquent Names of Rhetoric: The Gardens of Eloquence." In *Anglistentag 1990 Marburg, Proceedings*, edited by Claus Uhlig and Rüdiger Zimmermann, 129–38. Tübingen: Max Niemeyer Verlag, 1991.

Cantimori, Delio. "Rhetoric and Politics in Italian Humanism." *Journal of the Warburg and Courtauld Institutes* 1 (1937): 83–102.

Cave, Terence. *The Cornucopian Text: Problems of Writing in the French Renaissance*. Oxford: Oxford University Press, 1979.

Cheyfitz, Eric. *The Poetics of Imperialism: Translation and Colonialization from "The Tempest" to "Tarzan."* New York: Oxford University Press, 1991.

Conley, Thomas. *Rhetoric in the European Tradition.* New York: Longman, 1990.

Cossutta, Fabio. *Gli umanisti e la retorica.* Rome: Ateneo, 1984.

Doglio, Maria Luisa. "Retorica e politica nel secondo cinquecento." In *Retorica e politica,* edited by D. Goldin, Atti del II Congresso Italo-tedesco, 55–77. Padua: Liviana, 1977.

Florescu, Vasile. *La retorica nel suo sviluppo storico.* Bologna: Il Mulino, 1971.

Fumaroli, Marc. *L'Age de l'éloquence: Rhétorique et "res literaria" de la Renaissance au seuil de l'époque classique.* Geneva: Droz, 1980.

——. "Réflexions sur quelques frontispices gravés d'ouvrages de rhétorique et d'éloquence (1594–1641)." *Bulletin de la Société de l'Histoire et de l'Art Français* 101 (1975): 19–34.

——. *Héros et orateurs: Rhétorique et dramaturgie cornéliennes.* Geneva: Droz, 1990.

Garin, Eugenio. *Medioevo e Rinascimento: Studi e ricerche.* 2d ed. Bari: Laterza, 1961.

——. *L'umanesimo italiano: Filosofia e vita civile nel Rinascimento.* 2d ed. Bari: Laterza, 1965.

Grafton, Anthony, and Lisa Jardine. *From Humanism to the Humanities: Education and the Liberal Arts in Fifteenth- and Sixteenth-Century Europe.* Cambridge: Harvard University Press, 1986.

Graham, Kenneth. *The Performance of Conviction: Plainness and Rhetoric in the Early English Renaissance.* Ithaca, N.Y.: Cornell University Press, 1994.

Grassi, Ernesto. *Rhetoric as Philosophy: The Humanist Tradition.* University Park: Pennsylvania State University Press, 1980.

Gray, Hanna H. "Renaissance Humanism: The Pursuit of Eloquence." *Journal of the History of Ideas* 24 (1963): 497–514.

Grendler, Paul F. *Schooling in Renaissance Italy.* Baltimore: Johns Hopkins University Press, 1989.

Hallowell, Robert G. "L'Hercule gallique: Expression et image politique." In *Lumières de la Pléiade,* 243–53. Paris: Vrin, 1966.

Howell, Wilbur S. *Logic and Rhetoric in England, 1500–1700.* Princeton, N.J.: Princeton University Press, 1956.

Jardine, Lisa. *Francis Bacon: Discovery and the Art of Discourse.* Cambridge: Cambridge University Press, 1974.

——. "Lorenzo Valla and the Intellectual Origins of Humanist Dialectic." *Journal of the History of Philosophy* 15 (1977): 143–64.

Joseph, Sister Miriam. *Shakespeare's Use of the Arts of Language.* New York: Columbia University Press, 1947.

Jung, Marc-René. *Hercule dans la littérature française du XVIe siècle.* Geneva: Droz, 1966.

Kahn, Victoria. *Machiavellian Rhetoric: From the Counter-Reformation to Milton.* Princeton, N.J.: Princeton University Press, 1994.

——. *Rhetoric, Prudence, and Skepticism in the Renaissance.* Ithaca, N.Y.: Cornell University Press, 1985.

Kallendorf, Craig. *In Praise of Aeneas: Virgil and Epideictic Rhetoric in the Early Italian Renaissance.* Hanover, N.H.: University Press of New England, 1989.

Kennedy, George A. *Classical Rhetoric and Its Christian and Secular Tradition from Ancient to Modern Times.* Chapel Hill: University of North Carolina Press, 1980.

Kennedy, William J. *Rhetorical Norms in Renaissance Literature.* New Haven, Conn.: Yale University Press, 1978.

Kibédi-Varga, A. *Rhétorique et littérature: Études de structures classiques.* Paris: Didier, 1970.

Kinney, Arthur F. *Continental Humanist Poetics: Studies in Erasmus, Castiglione, Marguerite de Navarre, Rabelais, and Cervantes.* Amherst: University of Massachusetts Press, 1989.

Kinney, Daniel. "More's Letter to Dorp: Remapping the Trivium." *Renaissance Quarterly* 34 (1981): 179–207.

Kristeller, Paul Oskar. "The Humanist Movement." In *Renaissance Thought: The Classic, Scholastic, and Humanist Strains,* 3–23. New York: Harper and Row, 1961.

———. "Philosophy and Rhetoric from Antiquity to the Renaissance." In *Renaissance Thought and Its Sources,* edited by Michael Mooney, 211–59. New York: Columbia University Press, 1979.

Lanham, Richard. *The Motives of Eloquence: Literary Rhetoric in the Renaissance.* New Haven, Conn.: Yale University Press, 1976.

Martí, Antonio. *La preceptiva retórica española en el siglo de oro.* Madrid: Editorial Gredos, 1972.

Mazzacurati, Giancarlo. *La crisi della retorica umanistica nel cinquecento (Antonio Riccobono).* Naples: Libreria Scientifica, 1961.

McNally, James R. "*Rector et Dux Populi:* Italian Humanists and the Relationship Between Rhetoric and Logic." *Modern Philology* 67 (1969): 168–76.

Meerhoff, Kees. *Rhétorique et poétique au XVIe siècle en France: Du Bellay, Ramus, et les autres.* Leiden: E. J. Brill, 1986.

Monfasani, John. "Episodes of Anti-Quintilianism in the Italian Renaissance: Quarrels on the Orator as a *Vir Bonus* and Rhetoric as the *Scientia Bene Dicendi.*" *Rhetorica* 10 (1992): 119–38.

———. *George of Trebizond: A Biography and a Study of His Rhetoric and Logic.* Leiden: E. J. Brill, 1976.

———. "Humanism and Rhetoric." In *Renaissance Humanism: Foundations, Forms, and Legacy,* vol. 3, *Humanism and the Disciplines,* edited by Albert Rabil, Jr., 171–235. Philadelphia: University of Pennsylvania Press, 1988.

Murphy, James J., ed. *Renaissance Eloquence: Studies in the Theory and Practice of Renaissance Rhetoric.* Berkeley: University of California Press, 1983.

O'Malley, John W. *Praise and Blame in Renaissance Rome: Rhetoric, Doctrine, and Reform in the Sacred Orators of the Papal Court, c. 1450–1521.* Durham: Duke University Press, 1979.

Ong, Walter J., S.J. *Ramus: Method and the Decay of Dialogue.* Cambridge: Harvard University Press, 1958.

Parker, Patricia. *Literary Fat Ladies: Rhetoric, Gender, Property.* London: Methuen, 1987.

———. "On the Tongue: Cross Gendering, Effeminacy, and the Art of Words." *Style* 23 (1989): 445–65.

Patterson, Annabel M. *Hermogenes and the Renaissance: Seven Ideas of Style.* Princeton, N.J.: Princeton University Press, 1970.

Plett, Heinrich F. *Rhetorik der Affekte: Englische Wirkungsästhetik im Zeitalter der Renaissance.* Tübingen: Max Niemeyer Verlag, 1975.

Rebhorn, Wayne A. "Baldesar Castiglione, Thomas Wilson, and the Courtly Body of Renaissance Rhetoric." *Rhetorica* 11 (1993): 241–74.

———. *The Emperor of Men's Minds: Literature and the Renaissance Discourse of Rhetoric.* Ithaca, N.Y.: Cornell University Press, 1995.

———. "Petruchio's 'Rope Tricks': *The Taming of the Shrew* and the Renaissance Discourse of Rhetoric." *Modern Philology* 92 (1995): 294–327.

Rhodes, Neil. *The Power of Eloquence and English Renaissance Literature.* New York: St. Martin's, 1992.

Seigel, Jerrold E. *Rhetoric and Philosophy in Renaissance Humanism: The Union of Eloquence and Wisdom, Petrarch to Valla.* Princeton, N.J.: Princeton University Press, 1968.

Shuger, Debora K. *Sacred Rhetoric: The Christian Grand Style in the English Renaissance.* Princeton, N.J.: Princeton University Press, 1988.

Skinner, Quentin. *The Foundations of Modern Political Thought.* 2 vols. Cambridge: Cambridge University Press, 1978.

Sloane, Thomas O. *Donne, Milton, and the End of Humanist Rhetoric.* Berkeley: University of California Press, 1985.

Struever, Nancy. *The Language of History in the Renaissance.* Princeton, N.J.: Princeton University Press, 1970.

Trousdale, Marion. *Shakespeare and the Rhetoricians.* Chapel Hill: University of North Carolina Press, 1982.

Vasoli, Cesare. *La dialettica e la retorica dell'Umanesimo: "Invenzione" e "metodo" nella cultura del XV e XVI secolo.* Milan: Feltrinelli, 1968.

Vickers, Brian. *Classical Rhetoric in English Poetry.* London: Macmillan, 1970.

——. *In Defence of Rhetoric.* Oxford: The Clarendon Press, 1988.

Wallace, Karl R. *Francis Bacon on Communication and Rhetoric, or: The Art of Applying Reason to Imagination for the Better Moving of the Will.* Chapel Hill: University of North Carolina Press, 1943.

Index

Index

Gorgias of Leontini, 77, 84, 193, 200, 242, 282
Gower, John, 211
Gracchi, the (Tiberius Sempronius Gracchus
    and Gaius Sempronius Gracchus), 79,
    144, 149, 169
Gracchus, Gaius Sempronius, 281
Grammar. See Rhetoric: and grammar
Gregory Nazianzus, 25, 276
    Oratio IX, 275
Gregory the Great (saint), 25, 39
Guarino of Verona, 91
Guzman, Juan de, 233
    The First Part of Rhetoric, 233–43

Hadrian, 291n
Hannibal, 25
Hegesias, 132, 210
Heliodorus: Aethiopica, 128
Henry II, king of France, 128, 152
Henry III, king of France, 4, 128, 135n
Henry IV, king of France, 218, 244
Henry VIII, king of England, 82, 161
Heraclitus, 63, 102, 263
Hercules, 58, 282
Hercules Gallicus, 80n–81n, 131, 176, 210, 293
Hercules Ogmios, 277
Hermagoras, 167
Hermogenes, 27, 167, 267
    On Different Styles, 287
Herodotus, 35
Hesiod, 204
    Theogony, 237–38, 271n
    Works and Days, 98
Hesychius of Miletus, 287
Hilarius of Poitiers (saint), 25, 39
Hippias of Elis, 242, 282
Hippocrates, 155
Homer, 24, 35, 66, 103–4, 111, 163, 243, 287,
    293
    Iliad, 62n, 103n, 156n, 162, 252, 281–82
    Odyssey, 102–3n, 162, 164n, 236, 248n, 254
Homeric Hymns, 271n
Horace
    Ars poetica, 16n–17n, 22, 26, 72, 150n, 158,
        175n, 204n, 225, 242n, 248n, 275n,
        287–88
    Epistulae, 289–90
    Odes, 281
    Sermones, 51, 151
Hortensius, 246
Humanities. See Liberal arts
Hyperides, 239, 282
Hypocracia, 240

Iarchas, 277
Ignatius (saint), 25
Invention, 28, 33, 42–46, 152–53. See also
    Places, the
Isaeus, 246
Isaiah, 275

Isidore of Seville (saint): Etymologies, 234, 238
Isocrates, 162, 239, 242, 282

Jacob, 229–30
James I, 7, 208n, 261
Jerome (saint), 25, 36–39, 239
Jewel, John, 161
    Oration Against Rhetoric, 162–72
John of Damascus, 25
John the Evangelist, 25
Julian the Apostate, 81, 285
    The Caesars, 276n
    Letters, 279
Julius Caesar, 5, 79, 117, 130, 167, 220, 239,
    285
Juvenal, 51–52
    Saturae, 16, 221

Lactantius, 39
    Divine Institutes, 63
Laelius, Gaius, 285
Laertius, Diogenes, 12, 287
    Lives of the Philosophers, 30n, 144n, 170n,
        262n, 286–87
La Fayette, Mlle. Louise de, 273
Lais, 69
Langland, William, 211
Le Grand, Jean–François, 284
    A Discourse on French Rhetoric, 2, 284–93
Lentulus, Publius Cornelius, 220
Leptines, 239
Libanius, 81
Liberal arts, 1, 33, 44, 140, 142, 255–56, 279
Linus, 204, 206
Livy, 24–25, 35, 148
    Ab urbe condita, 148n, 220n, 289n–90
Logic. See Dialectic
Longinus, 183, 197
    On the Sublime, 184, 245n, 252n, 275
Longus: Daphnis and Chloe, 128
Louis XI, 134
Louis XIII, 273
Louis XIV, 5, 284
Louise of Savoy, 76
Lucian, 55
    Herakles, 80n–81n, 131, 210, 277n, 293n
Lucian (Pseudo-Lucian): In Praise of Demos-
    thenes, 283
Lucretius, 66
    De rerum natura, 63, 288
Lucullus, Lucius Licinius, 220
Luther, Martin, 68, 81, 97, 266
Lycurgus, 153, 282
Lydgate, John, 211
Lysias, 77, 144, 149, 239, 246, 282
Lysippus, 69

Machiavelli, Niccolò, 9
Macrobius, 12
    Saturnalia, 25n, 134n

Index

Index